World Scriptures

II

While journal writings are multi-dimensional and may include dialogues, dreams, comparisons, associations, disagreements, and new insights, I will focus here upon the possibility of writing or rewriting sacred texts.

In 1827 Joseph Smith found a stone box in a New York hillside in which was an ancient record engraved on gold plates. They were a record of the Nephi people and the Lamanites, a remnant of the house of Israel, who lived in North America from ancient times. By God's power Joseph Smith translated what is today called the Book of Mormon and which is accepted along with the Bible as holy scripture by The Church of Jesus Christ of the Latter-day Saints. Seven years later (1834) in Iran, Mizra Ali Muhammad, the Bab-ud-Din (Gate of Faith), and his follower Baha'u'llah declared their writings equal to the holy Qur'an. From this declaration, the Baha'i faith arose whose sacred Book of Certitude teaches the unity of all faiths.

Psychologist Ira Progoff, creator of the "Intensive Journal," remarks that experiences like these suggest that it is possible to "draw new spiritual scriptures from the same great source out of which the old ones come."[2] After studying the journals of creative artists, and having been inspired by the work of Carl Jung, Progoff concluded that the scriptures of humankind remain stored as images and symbols in the collective unconscious. In dreams, while influenced by certain drugs, in visions, trances, and in meditative, twilight awareness, we have access to what Progoff calls "the Bible within." Following Jung's notion of individuation in which the psyche is elevated to become the creator of what is known, and in which psychic wholeness and creativity coincide with God's image, Progoff indicates that journal explorations of peak and depth experiences can be viewed as biblical.

Further, Progoff believes that renewing Bibles may become necessary to the extent that ancient sacred texts "no longer speak with their original power" for "they have been atrophying spiritually from within."[3] We have become so accustomed to associating hypocrisy with the use of certain terms that they have lost their significance. The ecstatic Vedic hymns and Mahayana sutras, the simple wisdom of Confucius and the spontaneous verses of the Ch'an masters, the salvation history of the Bible and the recitation of the Qur'an, all need to be rephrased and restoried.

My difficulty with his approach is simple, and I suspect it reveals the western faith of this author. How can a "twilight image" or other psychic experience, which originates in my own inner-subjective consciousness, replace the God of Judaism, Christianity and Islam (to say nothing of the Buddhist and Taoist Void), who is wholly other, wholly beyond?

If we for a moment shift our attention to comparative understanding of the classical sacred scriptures of the world, we discover each to be characterized by at least two realities, both of which are incompatible with writing one's own scripture—event and group. First, sacred scriptures are not comprised just of visions, dreams and inner-awareness, but of objective historic events—of prophets and prophecy, of sages and avatars, of wars and imprisonments, of solitary searchers and corporate rituals—events which cannot be reduced to the human unconscious. And, second, sacred texts are ethically practiced and liturgically ritualized in groups or faith communities. Just as sacred rituals were classically practiced and celebrated only within a community structure, for a text to be sacred it must be initiated, shared, written and canonized through the collaborative efforts of that community.

While uneasy with Progoff's suggestion that we can create Bibles anew, I am convinced on the other hand that writing scripture-styled passages is a valuable way to study classical texts. In addition to stimulating student writing, itself a badly needed enterprise, creating scripture-like passages demonstrates the relationship between writing (to produce meaning) and rewriting (to communicate meaning), the relationship between something old (traditional teachings) and something new (rephrased teachings). In this way educational dialogues between reader and text, and within the reader, are facilitated.

To stimulate a deeper appreciation for, and understanding of, the sacred texts studied, I encourage students to create their own scripture-like passages. These can be written in several ways: by imitating the style and genre of existing texts (e.g., parable, maxim, drama, myth, philosophical discourse, or ko'an), by recreating the message of a past master in a contemporary language, by imagining what a past master teacher would say today about a contemporary issue (e.g., abortion, taxation, nuclear arms, or capital punishment), and, most significantly, by creating a dialogue between yourself and a sacred teacher or teaching.

Since not all will want to keep a journal as they read this text (nor is it necessary to do so) readers may wish instead to ruminate upon and discuss some of the exercises which are placed at the conclusion of each chapter. In some cases, the suggested questions would make provocative writing topics. The main point is to reflect upon the images and symbols within the scriptures, and to understand and appreciate the idiosyncratic practices and universal teachings of each sacred tradition.

NOTES

1. Interestingly, I find that when I explain the difference between primary source materials and secondary sources in my classes, students overwhelmingly prefer the former, especially since the religious east stresses the study of one's own direct experience of truth, not the study of words about the truth.

2. Ira Progoff, *The Practice of Process Meditation* (New York: Dialogue House Library, 1980), 10. In *At A Journal Workshop* (New York: Dialogue House, 1975), Ira Progoff describes the structure of the Intensive Journal. While I have learned a great deal from this text, from attending Progoff's workshops, and especially from his book, *The Practice of Process Meditation* (New York: Dialogue House, 1980), my use of the journal is thematic, is functionally limited to the study of religious stories and sacred texts, and encourages imaginative writings. The creative exercises are neither objective rehearsals of data nor subjective confessions, but an integral dialogue with the texts.

3. *Ibid.*, 13, 14.

Chapter 1 SACRED TRADITIONS AND TEXTS

BEING RELIGIOUS

On the Christian sabbath, a thirteen year old Philadelphia girl stands with the minister of the Alpha Baptist Church in the baptismal pool before the entire congregation. After she has spent months of studying the Christian scriptures and prayerfully searching her conscience, and with her family and friends in the congregation, the minister looks at her and says: "Do you take Jesus to be your Lord and Savior?" When she answers "I do!" he lowers her into the pool with the words: "I now baptize you in the name of the Father, the Son and the Holy Spirit." Her entire body is immersed (symbolizing a death of the old self) and is then lifted up out of the water (symbolizing her purification and new birth into Christian life). She is now born into the Body of Christ through baptism, an outward sign of an inward grace, and is initiated into the wider Christian community.

The day before, in another part of the city, a thirteen year old Jewish boy becomes *Bar Mitzvah*, a "son of the commandment," a "man of duty." To prepare properly, he must know the essentials of Judaism. He is taught not only to revere and respect the Torah scroll upon which the language of his ancestors is written, but also to become aware of its teachings. In modern practice, this ritual is marked by a public reading from the Torah in synagogue on the morning of the sabbath nearest his thirteenth birthday. He is then counted as one of the *minyan*, one who is responsible for his own acts and for all the religious rules and duties befitting a man.

On the same day, halfway around the world in a Southeast Asian Buddhist village, at an hour which is determined to be astrologically correct, a young boy of thirteen is ritually cleansed, his hair shaved, and his clothes exchanged by his family for a saffron robe. The boy has prepared for this event by studying and learning to read from Buddhist Sutras, and by taking a vow of obedience to his monastic superior. A golden thread is placed around his neck and the ceremony begins with a chanting of the prayer of the Twice-Born and with a recitation of his monastic vows.

In common with Baptism and *Bar Mitzvah*, whose initiation rituals re-enact historic events of a transhistoric source, the Buddhist *Shin Byu* re-enacts the "Going Forth" of Siddhartha Gautama who became the Buddha. This reanimation of the "Great Renunciation" commemorates Buddha's departure from the world of material pleasures, and his entry into unknown spiritual deserts. How long the boy remains in a monastery varies—some leave after a few weeks, others never.

Reflecting upon these stories of individual and communal initiation, we find that each ritual becomes transparent to and expresses a sacred dimension of reality.[1] And, significantly, each "coming of age" ceremony, whether sacramental (Baptism) or non-sacramental (*Bar Mitzvah* and *Shin Byu*), not only marks an adolescent passage rite, but provides a sacred context for the whole of one's life. The sacred is characterized by occasions of personal transformation and, at the same time, identification with a holy tradition.[2] In what follows we will discuss what it means to be religious and how religious meaning can best be studied through sacred texts. In the core of the book (Chapters 2–10), we will examine major eastern and western sacred texts, and we will conclude by interfacing several texts.

The Religious Impulse

According to our oldest written records, religious images and symbols are largely associated with sacred actions and sacred stories which depict human origins, purpose and destiny. As early as seventeen thousand years ago, prehistoric cave dwellers, who were largely nomadic hunter-gatherers, left cave-paintings which depict the practice of sacred rituals. These earliest symbols have led anthropologists to identify ritual and myth as early human attempts to express sacredness.

No one is born into a society where the sacred is not pervasive, even in "secular" societies. At the same time in all ages, the religious impulse begins with one's need for transformation. If there is no question whose answer is beyond questioner (e.g., where does life originate?), no sought-for ultimate answer worth more than conventional wisdoms (e.g., what happens at death?), and no practical understanding of mysteries (e.g., what is life's purpose?), then the sacred remains of little consequence.

This is nowhere more poignantly stated than in Samuel Beckett's tragicomedy *Waiting for Godot* in which Vladimir (Didi) and Estragon (Gogo) wait by a tree on a country road for the coming of Godot. While waiting, the afflicted outcasts, who are bound to each other out of fear, and who are repulsed by each other's mistrust, are interrupted by a dictatorial master, Pozzo, and his pitiful slave, Lucky. In one of the most revealing speeches of the play, Lucky mechanically describes a God who is impotent, outside of time, and who loves humans albeit speechlessly and apathetically.

When forced to speak, Lucky says: "Given the existence as uttered forth in the public works of Puncher and Wattmann of a personal God quaquaquaqua with white beard quaquaquaqua outside time without extension who from the heights of divine apathia divine athambia divine aphasia loves us dearly with some exceptions for reasons unknown . . ."[3]

Vladimir and Estragon, each in his own way, realize that they are enslaved by everything they are, do, say, and by their monotonously deadening habits. Each is tied down to waiting helplessly amidst the dead voices, wanting to leave, wanting to help Pozzo and Lucky, wanting to support each other caringly—but failing. It is in this hellish context, in what could be called the long, slow process of dying, that religious questions arise: What is to be done in the midst of suffering? Of what should we repent? To whom are we tied? Who cares? Does God see us? Will Godot ever come? If Godot comes, will we be saved?

Questions such as those asked by Vladimir and Estragon are asked by all humans in all cultures. Without questions larger than any answer that we can find, without existential and ontological impasses, without the self-restricting limitations of language and thought, humans would have little interest in religious answers. The religious impulse takes form when one responds to life's limitations in an authentically sacred way.

So that we will be better equipped to respond intelligently to what we read, the remainder of this chapter will introduce some vital terms and tools for the journey.

STUDYING RELIGIONS

When we approach the sacred scriptures of the historic religions (called "Developed" to distinguish them from the less developed archaic religions, and called "Living" to distinguish them from religions no longer practiced), we discover that they originate in two main geographic areas. The so-called eastern faiths originate in the far east (India and China) and the so-called western faiths in the near east (the Mediterranean). We should recognize that what has been characterized as the religious east (i.e., monistic, non-dualistic, self-actualizing and meditative) and the religious west (i.e., monotheistic, dualistic, revelatory and prayerful) would be better understood as points of view (faith-attitudes) rather than geographical distinctions. Historically, we see only a continuum of developments in which each sacred tradition was preceded by a host of complex events, and in which each tradition significantly overlaps the others.

Since the word "religion" is often used to designate these sacred traditions, we should at the outset of our study consider its meaning. Etymologically, "religion" is rooted in the Latin *religio* (response of awe/fear to a power outside the self) and *relegere* (to bind together, to yoke). Thus—as used to describe western faiths—it originally referred to both an objective supra-natural reality on the one hand, and to an inner-subjective response on the other. However, we must expand this understanding, as we shall see, in the light of eastern traditions. Globally speaking, religions or sacred traditions involve both personal and communal experiences of sacred mystery, and expressions of ultimate meaning, value and truth (a sacred transformation of consciousness).[4]

Given a more wholistic understanding of the field, teachers often use a scientific approach to the study of religions (*religionwissenschaft*). This has been called "phenomenology of religions," "comparative religions," or the "history of religion." Each term suggests that this sort of study of religions is to be carried on outside the aegis of a confessional faith stance (in which one speaks apologetically in behalf of one religion over another). One studies religions scientifically primarily to *understand*, not to become more religious oneself. This process is characterized by attitudes which are necessary if our study is not to be dogmatic or narrow-minded: objective and equal treatment of the data, an inter-disciplinary approach, a search for the intention behind the surface appearance of the data, a temporary suspension of belief (or disbelief), and attention to both history and comparative typology.[5]

That our study of religions will be scientific rather than religious in aim means that we seek understanding rather than specifically religious goals such as virtue, devotion, and the conversion of others. This does not imply that we must give up these goals or our religion itself or our belief in certain dogmas. Pursuing the end of understanding implies that our end is neither the enhancement nor the destruction of whatever religiosity or lack thereof we may possess. The understanding we seek is compatible with our retaining all of these. However, the scientific study of religion does require a temporary suspension of some of our religious attitudes and beliefs. The reason for this is one of expedience: it is a means to the end of understanding the data studied. If this is not done, the result will probably be a kind of narrowness or blindness or superficiality or lack of authenticity which will infect the quality of the understanding we may obtain. And since religion is one realm in which feelings of commitment and beliefs about important matters run deep, it is particularly important to be clear about the distinctions that we have just made, and to be clear about the consequences they imply for the proper way to approach our study here.

Each culture tells stories of the highest and deepest truths known to humankind in its scriptures, what it means to be sacredly human. Comparing sacred traditions, we see that they share a similar development from sacred events to sacred stories to sacred texts which then serve as conduits for sacred teachings. Since scriptures are the fundamental source of authority for a believer's religious self-understanding, they become the primary-source-materials of faith. In this text, scriptures will be presented as paradigms for understanding what it means to be religious in each sacred tradition.

CHARACTERIZING SACRED TEXTS

As one of the early collectors and editors of sacred writings, Max Müller wrote: "I wish that I could read you extracts I have collected from the sacred books of the ancient world, grains of truth more precious to me than grains of gold . . ."[6] There are at least four ways in which it is helpful to understand these sacred books: etymologically, generically, comparatively, and self-reflectively.

Since scriptures are the primary sources for sacred stories, we should note at the outset that the word scripture comes from the Latin (*Scriptura*), which etymologically refers to the act of writing, to one who writes (*scribere*), and to the end product (the canonized script). Peoples of a Holy Book (whether of the Torah, New Testament or Qur'an), tend to think of scriptures as the inspired word of God communicated through holy prophets. As W.C. Smith has remarked, western culture conceives of scripture "as something sent down, maybe verbatim, from another world, and imagines that if a given text is not divinely revealed then it is not scripture."[7]

This understanding has two obvious limitations: it does not cover writings which claim inspiration of a non-divine nature (e.g., the Buddhist Sutras or the Taoist stories). Nor does it adequately describe what have been called "non-literary scriptures," sacred words and stories which are memorized and transmitted orally from generation to generation. The Bible and the Qur'an for instance were recited and sung before they were written down. For centuries Hindus refused to commit the Vedas to writing and Chinese sages, as late as the fifth century CE remark on their reluctance to write sutras. As is often assumed, scriptures are not just the script, the actual handwritten words. They include as well the life or spirit of the letters. For this reason scriptures are often sung, chanted, recited, and dramatized. In the

Islamic tradition for instance, hearing the Qur'an is as important if not more important than reading it. Hearing the sacred Qur'an as it is being recited by a professionally and religiously trained cantor increases one's appreciation for its literary quality, rhythms, and nuances of meaning which are not as fully grasped through a reading of the script.

Given these limitations within the etymological definition of *scriptura,* we need to formulate generic and comparative understandings which enlarge our definitional horizon.

Scriptures contain the primary source materials of faith both doctrinally and ritually, and serve therefore as a paradigm for understanding sacred traditions. Generically speaking, sacred texts record the vicissitudes of human religious experience in literary forms which include: sacred words and holy sounds (mantras); wisdom teachings (aphorisms, parables, ko'ans, stories); prescribed standards of behavior (commandments, principles, analects); images and symbols of ultimacy (Brahman, Tao, YHWH); and liturgical formulations (prayers, chants, sacrifice, pilgrimage, sacraments).

Comparatively speaking, it is important from the start to recognize that the word "scripture" has a normative use, for those whose aim is religious, and a descriptive use, for those whose aims are scientific. For example, we can imagine a person on the religious path asking: "Given all the texts that qualify scientifically as scriptures, which are *genuine* revelations of the Way?" Whatever the answer to this normative question (e.g. divine revelation, mystical inspiration, liturgical use, moral teachings), we will focus upon scriptures descriptively. Each of the readings in the next chapters are texts which have been traditionally accepted, from *within* a particular tradition, as scripture in the normative sense of the word.

It is also important to note that, comparatively speaking, scriptures have an exoteric and an esoteric meaning. Exoterically, scripture refers to: 1) sacred or inspired texts (writings) which 2) teach orthodox standards and practices, and which 3) are accepted by a community of believers. Esoterically, on the other hand, scripture refers to an inner meaning, or essence, to what might be called alphabets of mystery. Jewish mystics for example often referred to the white spaces on the scroll left by the printed words as YHWH's true communication.

Here the word "scripture" will refer to each tradition's sacred canon. The word canon, derived from the Greek word *kanon* (rule, norm, measuring rod), refers to a community's officially accepted corpus of sacred literature. Scriptures are a sacred tradition's most authoritative writings, whether that authority has been established by a holy person (Qur'an), by its use in ritual (Vedas), by its revealed covenant (Torah), by the spiritual potency of the words (Upanishads), or by a combination of factors. The significance of scriptures for the student of *religionwissenschaft* stems from its source or original composition, and in part from its acceptance as the final authority in secular and sacred affairs for a believing community.

There are two footnotes to this discussion which must be kept in mind as we read the sacred scriptures. First, while canons of sacred texts exist in eastern faiths, they are defined with less rigidity than in the west, and usually include several texts for each tradition. Also often a tradition's officially canonized writings are not necessarily the most widely read, or the best understood writings. Popularly speaking for instance, the Bhagavad Gita, an epic poem about the avatar Lord Krishna, is far better known in India than the official sacred canons (the Vedas and Upanishads).

The World's Scriptures

A final, and perhaps most significant way of understanding scriptures is to view images of their self-reflective consciousness. The major scriptures from which we will read—the Vedas (Uncreated Wisdom), the Upanishads (Sitting Devotedly by the Foot of a Guru), the Bhagavad Gita (Song of the Lord), the Dhammapada (Path of the Dhamma or Teaching), the Analects of Confucius (Selected Sayings of the Master Teacher), the Tao Te Ching (The Way and Its Power), the Diamond and the Platform Sutra (the true Teaching), the Torah (Divine Teaching), the Gospel (Good News), and the Qur'an (Recital)—each characterize themselves imagistically and symbolically.[8]

In the Upanishads, sacred texts are said to be a great bow of the sacred word (*Vac*), with the arrow of Self (*Atman*) aimed at the center of a target (*Brahman*).[9] In the Bhagavad Gita Lord Krishna pictures scripture as an upside down Cosmic Tree whose everlasting roots are in heaven and whose branches and leaves bloom on earth as sacred songs and texts.[10] In the Dhammapada Buddha compares implicitly the sacred text to a raft which the disciple takes to reach the other shore of *nirvana,* and also to the most exquisite flower whose virtuous perfume travels against the wind to reach the ends of the earth.[11] For Confucius the classics provide a traditional mandate which he transmits and reanimates, while for Lao Tzu sacred lyrics are like the valley spirit, the virgin block, and the bamboo—all hollow at the center. Of course the Zen Master might say, "If you find a sutra—burn it!"

In the Semitic faiths of the mid-east, the Torah and the Qur'an are pictured as God's Word, as a heavenly tablet of stone written by the finger of the Lord. For the Jew, Hebrew scriptures are God's holy and sacred words which are to be read, studied and prayed liturgically. For the Muslim the Holy Qur'an is unrepeatable, untranslatable, unfathomable and irreplacable. For the Christian, the New Testament depicts itself as a double-edged sword, inspired by God, and used for teaching holiness. The author of the letter to the Hebrews writes that scripture is alive and active, cuts both ways like a two edged sword but more finely, judges secret emotions and thoughts and, crucially, slips through the space where one's soul and the Spirit meet.[12] In each of the above mentioned cases, scripture is set apart as sacred and holy, and is approached with reverence and awe.

UNDERSTANDING SACRED TEXTS

Acknowledging that sacred texts are a special genre and therefore fundamentally different from any other form of literature, two questions arise: how are we to read scriptures and how are we to interpret them?

For most of human history, sacred stories were spoken and heard, not read. Reading texts aloud, and therefore more slowly, catches deeper meanings, and allows the reader to hear the rhythms of the text. It also allows the reader the chance to add her or his own accentuations, pauses and pitches, and therefore to reanimate the text. Sacred writings should be read aloud, not of course as we would read a stock report, but as we would read a poem, or a prayer, with a sense of awe, respect and anticipation.

At the same time reading silently, even meditatively, interiorizes sacred language, and allows the text to suggest how it should be understood. Classically, monastic traditions have articulated methods of reading meditatively. *Lectio divina* for instance, is the Christian monastic practice of interiorly chanting the psalms, of mediatively "chewing" upon a sacred text in order to transcend the limitations of language and to cross over into the fabric of the story. This type of reading requires a quiet atmosphere, a withdrawal from distractions and a reader's attentive focus on the text.

In a similar vein, Nichiren (1222–1282), a believer in the absolute correctness of the Lotus Sutra, wrote in a letter to a favorite disciple in prison:

> When some people read the Lotus Sutra, they mouth the words but don't read with the mind. And if they read with the mind, they don't read with the body. To read with body and mind is the most exalted.[13]

For Nichiren it was not enough only to read words with one's mind; it was also necessary to experience the rhythms of their meaning with one's body mind.

Participatory Reading

Lectio divina and "body-reading" are metaphors for what is called here a participatory reading. The reader becomes a participant in the story, becomes more willing to listen for meanings behind words, within sentences and between lines, than to impose a structure upon the text from the outside. There are four elements in this way of approaching the texts: suspending temporarily (as far as possible) *a priori* beliefs or disbeliefs, in order to "cross over" from the reader's initial position into the fabric of the text; approaching the text with questions about its content and method, about its sacred images; reading aloud and mediatively to hear the sound meaning makes; and then stepping back from the text, to interpret critically and comparatively what has been read. We will return to this last point in the final chapter.

It is necessary to keep in mind, when reading sacred scriptures, that they are an integral part of a larger sacred story. By sacred story I mean here the coalescence of three inter-connected aspects: the conceptual story (the teachings and practices of a sacred tradition as a whole); the foundational story (the origins of a sacred tradition whether through a person or process); and the individual stories which scripture tells (be they didactic, dramatic or narrative). These three aspects cannot be separated, for the deepest meaning of each sacred faith is manifested in its inner dynamism. In the next nine chapters we will view the scriptures through each of them.

Interpretive Dialogue

For the student of sacred texts, the crucial transition is from reading texts to interpreting them, for without interpretation understanding is incomplete. However one interprets the text (literally, allegorically, morally, anagogically, structurally or typologically), the common denominator is always the same—a dialogue between the reader and the sacred words. This dialogue is really triadic, for between the reader and the text lies meaning which both clarifies the story and draws the reader back into its narrative. This triadic dialogue is the depth dimension of one's study of scriptures and includes critical and self-critical reflection, self-reflective comparison and self-developmental integration. This hermeneutical process can be visualized in the form of a pyramid viewed from the top (see page 15).

Interpreting a particular passage is a process which includes a coalescence of reader, text and understanding, one that is neither statically fixed nor reducible to any single meaning. As a result of this journey we will be able not only to enter into dialogues with the scriptures of the world, but also to facilitate dialogues between the texts and contemporary worldviews. Our intention will be to allow each scripture to speak with its own voice, crisply, subtly and as directly as an arrow penetrates the heart of a target.

NOTES

1. Mircea Eliade in *The Sacred and The Profane* (New York: Harcourt, Brace & World, 1957) proposes that historically religions begin when humans become aware of the sacred, for according to Eliade, there are two modes of being—the sacred and the profane. The sacred dimension of life points to a center of meaning and value beyond itself, and subordinates all non-sacred elements to itself. The profane points only to itself, or to other non-self-transcending events. For Eliade, the sacred is disclosed in space and time. Sacred space (temples, churches, shrines, mountains) and sacred time (festivals, rituals, stories, holidays) are the fabric or context of what he calls a *hierophany,* the revealed manifestation of an absolute reality.

One needs to be careful not to absolutise this sacred/profane dichotomy since, ultimately, as the mystics of the world's religions remind us, the sacred is identified with the profane, and vice-versa. Since we have no records of the first religions, the *historical* beginning is pure speculation.

2. In *The Meaning and End of Religion* (New York: Mentor Books, 1962), Wilfred Cantwell Smith suggests that the word "religion" be replaced by the more operative terms "faith" and "cumulative tradition." By holy or sacred tradition I include what Smith means by each of these: "faith," or ritual and ethical behavior, and "cumulative tradition," the entire mass of a community's religio-historical data.

3. Samuel Beckett, *Waiting for Godot,* (New York: Grove Press, 1954), 28a.

4. Joachim Wach in *The Comparative Study of Religions* (New York: Columbia University Press, 1958), writes that religious are said to have four leading features: a response to what is considered the ultimate, unconditional mystery; a total, synergetic response of

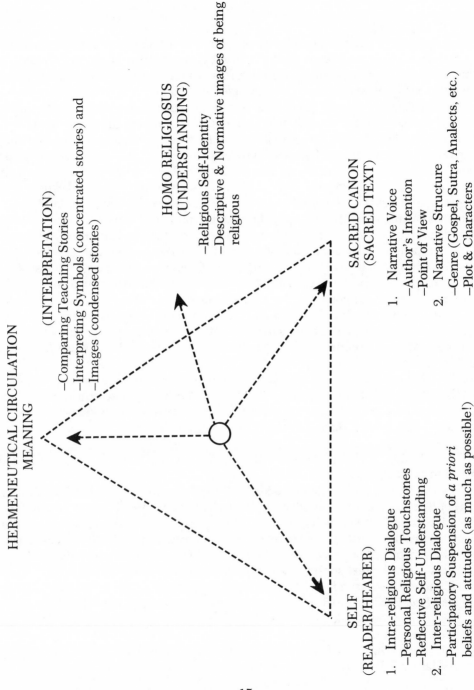

HERMENEUTICAL CIRCULATION
MEANING

(INTERPRETATION)
–Comparing Teaching Stories
–Interpreting Symbols (concentrated stories) and
–Images (condensed stories)

HOMO RELIGIOSUS
(UNDERSTANDING)

–Religious Self-Identity
–Descriptive & Normative images of being
    religious

SACRED CANON
(SACRED TEXT)

1. Narrative Voice
    –Author's Intention
    –Point of View
2. Narrative Structure
    –Genre (Gospel, Sutra, Analects, etc.)
    –Plot & Characters

SELF
(READER/HEARER)

1. Intra-religious Dialogue
    –Personal Religious Touchstones
    –Reflective Self-Understanding
2. Inter-religious Dialogue
    –Participatory Suspension of *a priori*
    beliefs and attitudes (as much as possible!)

one's whole person; a blissful, peaceful response of certainty; and a life-transforming response. Religious experience leads naturally to religious expression which is collected: in thought (doctrines, theologies, ethics, scriptures), in action (worship, prayer, meditation, ritual), and in groups (institutions and collective identity actions).

5. Minimally, this means: (1) that no one particular faith is viewed as superior to or inferior to any other; (2) that to study religions properly is to study the data cross-culturally and trans-historically; (3) that one cannot reduce the study of religions to the study of any one religion, or to any particular form which religions take (e.g., the ecclesiastical) or to any particular expression (e.g., "I believe in God the Father Almighty . . ."); (4) that one cannot be limited to the data uncovered, but must always ask about the *meaning behind* the data (e.g., what is the *intention* of any religious activity and how does that intention fit into the total religious picture); (5) that to study the material fairly one must temporarily suspend beliefs or disbeliefs, judgments and critical evaluations so that one can first *understand* the data before responding to it from a position of previous belief or disbelief; (6) that the best way to study religions is with the help of other disciplines (e.g., Psychology, Philosophy, Sociology, Theology, Anthropology) each of which offers a valuable perspective on the problem of what it means to be religious; and (7) that the scientific study of religion combines two concerns—the need for study to be firmly founded in concrete historical data (the descriptive factuality of events), and the use of typologies by which those events are organized (the normative classification of structures). The opening three episodes in this chapter, for example, represent types of initiation rituals.

6. Max Müller, quoted in *The Bible: Its Origin, Growth and Character* by Jabez Sunderland (New York: G.P. Putnams Sons, 1903), 22. As Max Müller notes, these ancient books have become "sacred heirlooms, sacred because they came from an unknown source, from a distant age." Max Müller, *Sacred Books of the East: The Upanishads* (New Delhi: Motilal Banarsidas), XIII.

7. W.C. Smith, "The True Meaning of Scripture" in the *International Journal of Middle East Studies,* 1980, 489.

8. Lynda Sexson has eloquently addressed this in an abstract of her 1983 American Academy of Religion presentation titled "Alphabets of Secrets: Metaphors of Text in Popular and Esoteric Stories", a title which inspired a similar phrase used in this chapter—"alphabets of mystery." She writes that "sacred texts seem to be characterized by their 'self-consciousness', by their talking about themselves." She calls this process "the metaphors of texting itself," that is when the text speaks as a text to the reader.

9. *Mundaka Upanishad,* 11.11.3.

10. *The Bhagavad Gita,* 15, 1.

11. *The Dhammapada,* 4, 44.

12. Hebrews 4:12.

13. Nichiren, "Dungeon Letter" quoted by William Johnston, *The Mirror Mind* (San Francisco: Harper & Row, 1981), 92.

JOURNAL SECTION

1. List your goals. What do you wish to gain by the end of this study? Are there specific questions you want answered, specific terms you do not understand?
2. Define the "sacred" in your own words and then recreate a "sacred experience" that you have had, that you have read about, or encountered in a film. If you are not religiously oriented, describe a "Peak Experience" (Maslow) or a time when you experienced something more than yourself.
   a. Tell your own story about that experience:
      What led up to it?
      What happened during it?
      What happened after it?
   b. Describe your feelings associated with that experience. How did it feel at the time of the event and how does it feel now as you look back to the event?
3. List about a dozen major pivotal events, persons, symbols, dates, activities, or insights from birth till now, which outline your religious (or irreligious) self-identity. List events that are the crucial turning points in your life, when your attitudes and feelings were turned around, reorganized, given new priorities.
4. In all cultures the meaning of being religious (*Homo Religiosus*) combines two elements: the descriptive (real) and the normative (ideal). Draw a line down the center of a page and list on one side of the line who *I am now* (physically, emotionally, vocationally, relationally, etc.), and on the other side of the line *who I should be* (physically, ethically and spiritually). How do these two dimensions relate? In what ways are you both? Write about a time in your life when the "real" and the "ideal" merged, when you did act the way you feel you should act.
5. First, imagine that you have everything you want. Visualize it! When you have done that, then ask yourself (and answer) the following question: Having everything, what do I still lack?
   Then imagine that a fire burns down your house and you lose everything. Visualize it! Then ask yourself (and answer) this question: After losing everything (and everyone!) what do I still have?
6. "To know only one religion and only one sacred text is to know none!" What do you think of this statement? Does it contain some truth for you, and, if so, in what way?

17

Chapter 2 THE HINDU TRUE SELF

Pilgrimage to India

As mental travelers on a pilgrimage through the sacred stories of the world, we begin our adventure in an ancient land of diverse and complex spiritual heritages—India. Whether we arrive to the incandescent beauty of the Taj Mahal in Agra, or to the unforgettable smell of cremated bodies in Banares, whether to a south Indian village without electricity, phones and running water, or to a man dying in the streets of Calcutta, we arrive as pilgrims.

India has been and is still today an international center for pilgrims of all faiths. Not only do orthodox Hindus journey once a year to honor their local *guru*, they also during the year visit temples, shrines, ashrams, special rivers, mountains, and holy birthplaces such as Vrindaban where Lord Krishna was born. Vrindaban is a remarkable sight to the visitor, for it seems as if every third building is a temple dedicated to one of many gods, from Krishna to

Namaste

the monkey-god Hanuman, from Shiva to Kali. And Vrindaban is not atypical because India seems to breathe an eternal spirit.

No wonder the traveler is likely to be greeted with *"Namaste":* I bow down to the True Self *(Atman)* in you. What a greeting—True Self honors True Self! We begin our journey then as contemporary westerners about to enter the variety of uncanny, sacred stories and texts of the holy motherland, India.

> So Krishna, as when he admonished Arjuna
> On the Field of battle.
>   Not fare well,
> But fare forward voyagers.[1]

The genius of the Hindu sacred story is that what makes a person religious is not belief, not whether there is a God or not, but how one lives. Anyone can be a Hindu, whether Christian or Muslim, whether Buddhist or Taoist, anyone who lives righteously (according to the highest teachings), who loves and serves others and who works toward unity and peace in the world. There are no necessary ethnic or philosophic pre-conditions. One can believe in *Brahman* (the Absolute), in a particular *deva* (god), or not believe at all. What Hindus call *Sanatana Dharma* (Universal Teaching) is not limited to Indian expressions of ultimacy alone. Hindus follow the teachings of Buddha and of Christ as readily as they worship Ram, Lord Shiva or Lord Krishna, for Truth is manifest whenever one lives righteously. As a modern Hindu writes:

> After all, what counts is not creed but conduct. By their fruits ye shall know them and not by their beliefs. Religion is not correct belief but righteous living. The truly religious never worry about other people's beliefs. Look at the great saying of Jesus: "Other sheep I have which are not of this fold." Jesus was born a Jew and died a Jew. He did not tell the Jewish people among whom he found himself, "It is wicked to be Jews. Become Christians." He did his best to rid the Jewish religion of its impurities. He would have done the same with Hinduism had he been born a Hindu. The true reformer purifies and enlarges the heritage of mankind and does not belittle, still less deny it.[2]

An exclusive attitude toward other sacred traditions would be a needless restriction in a tradition which has neither creed nor dogma, where cults exist side-by-side and where the only tolerable denial is the denial of denials. Yet in spite of the immense range of customs, attitudes, theologies, practices, and spiritual paths, there is a flowing unity within the Hindu tradition, a unity with as much diversity as exists in a family. It is this unity, found in the variety of ways in which the Hindu sacred story is expressed, that we will now examine.

The Early Hindu Story

The historical story of Hindu culture begins with the arrival of the light-skinned, Indo-European Aryan peoples across the Himalayan mountain range and into the Indus River Valley (around 2000 BCE). The non-Aryan, darker-skinned Harappan culture, often referred to as "Dravidians" (people of Southern India), practiced asceticism, developed yoga techniques and private *puja* (worship), and, more significantly, devalued the meaning of the external world.

After the Aryans arrived, a progressive fusion of the indigenous culture and the incoming tradition occurred. The term "Hindu," a Muslim misproununciation of the "Indus," refers to the teachings and spiritual practices which originated in the cross-fertilization of Indo-European Aryan cultures and Indus River Valley cultures. To the agricultural Dravidians, the Aryans brought a collection of hymns (the Vedas), sacrificial rituals and a cosmic house of thirty-three Devas (gods and goddesses) such as *Agni* (Fire), *Indra* (Sky), *Soma* (Moon Juice), and *Vac* (Word). As importantly, the Aryans crossed the Himalayas with the primitive roots of what became, in its developed form, the sacred language of Sanskrit.[3] Sanskrit became an ideal tongue for sacred texts because of its triple level of meanings: the primary force of the utterance (usage and derivation), a secondary or extended sense in which a reader goes beyond primary meanings (metaphoric, symbolic, mystical), and the suggested meaning (context and resonance).

The Original Story

How did everything begin? The Hindu cosmological story is told in various ways. One of the most arresting versions is the myth of the cosmic person (the primal being) who emanated into every thing through his self-sacrifical dismemberment. Interestingly, while a similar dismemberment of a cosmic person appears in Mesopotamian and Greek mythology, there it is the result of a battle, not, as in India, the result of a self-sacrifical action.

Of the various stories of creation—from the cosmic egg, to the dream of *Brahman*—one of the most profound is the Hymn of Creation. It begins before the beginning; before the distinction of being and non-being:

> Non-being then existed not nor being:
> There was no air, nor sky that is beyond it.
> What was concealed? Wherein? In whose protection?
> And was there deep unfathomable water?
> Death then existed not nor life immortal;
> Of neither night nor day was any token.
> By its inherent force the One breathed breathless:
> No other thing than that beyond existed.
> Darkness there was at first by darkness hidden;
> Without distinctive marks, this all was water.
> That which, becoming, by the void was covered.
> That One by force of heat came into being.
> Desire entered the One in the beginning:
> It was the earliest seed, of thought the product.

The sages searching in their hearts with wisdom.
Found out the bond of being in non-being.[4]

Before the beginning begins, the non-differentiated Unity (that One), who paradoxically neither is nor is not, breathes breathlessly, and comes into being by force of its own heat (*tapas*). Through trans-human desire, that One emanates into all that is. But how, when and why the sages ponder?

Who knows truly? Who can here declare it?
Whence it was born, whence is this emanation.
By the emanation of this the gods
Only later [came to be].
Who then knows whence it has arisen?
Whence this emanation hath arisen,
Whether [God] disposed it, or whether he did not,
Only he who is its overseer in highest heaven knows.
[He only knows,] or perhaps he does not know.[5]

Readers should notice the impact of the last two stanzas, for each poses penetratingly honest questions. Who can know when this human emanation occurred? Only the highest One (*Tad Ekam*) can possibly know or perhaps even the One does not know. The Hindu story truly begins with a not-knowing knowing.

At this point we should note a key difference between western and eastern stories of origination. In the Judaeo-Christian and Islamic traditions, God creates either *ex nihilo* (out of nothing) or out of chaos. For Hindus on the other hand, in the beginningless beginning that One *emanates* existence. While in western faiths humans are created of different form and substance from the creator, in India humans are of different form but of the same emanation as the creator. Thus as a Hindu, I bow down to the True Self that is within the other because I acknowledge all others as emanations of that True Self which has neither beginning nor end.

The power of this small hymn is in the way it takes the reader not only back to creation ("in the beginning"), but behind creation, to a beginningless beginning. As Ramundo Panikkar writes: "The Vedic seers make the staggering claim of entering into that enclosure where God is not yet God, where God is thus unknown to himself, and, not being creator, is 'nothing.' Without this perspective we may fail to grasp the Vedic message regarding the absolute Prelude to everything. . . ."[6]

Stories of Sacrifice

When the Indo-Aryans arrived in the Indus Valley, they brought a ritual system which focused on two central religious personalities—the rishi and the priest. The rishi was a visionary, ascetic, poet, who wrote hymns of his direct experience of ultimate mystery and power. The priests (Brahmins) conducted the sacrificial cult and served its irreplacable god *Agni*, through whom all sacrifices and offerings were transformed and carried to the gods. The purpose of these early sacrifices was to empower the celestial and terrestial gods and thereby to be empowered by the reanimation of the original sacrifice. The universe, and all that was created, as various stories tell us in the Vedas, was created through the self-sacrifice of the Absolute One.

At this point let us visualize the story of an ancient sacrifical rite as it was performed in about 900 BCE. The sacrificer, in this case a farmer from northern India, wished to strengthen his relationship with the gods, to keep away evil forces and in turn to receive the boon of a good harvest. He and his family invited the local priests to their home to perform the appropriate ceremony. A site was prepared, a fire pit dug, an altar of earth made ready, and a thatched roof constructed under which the participants would sit.

At dusk, the farmer began a period of purification, seclusion and fasting. His hair and nails were cut; he bathed and then put on new clothing. This created a suitable atmosphere for relating to the gods. The next day, a priest started the fire, poured into the pit a libation of melted butter (*ghee*), and invoked *Agni*:

> Now get dressed in your robes, lord of powers and master of the sacrificial food, and offer this sacrifice for us.
>
> Young Agni, take your place as our favourite priest with inspirations and shining speech. The father sacrifices for his son, the comrade for his comrade, the favourite friend for his friend.[7]

As the sacrifical tradition developed, the Vedic priests accorded *Agni* the central role in all ritual. Since *Agni* was said to extend the sacrifice to heaven, *Agni* was invited to every sacrifice:

> I pray to Agni, the household priest who is the god of the sacrifice, the one who chants and invokes and brings most treasure. Agni earned the prayers of the ancient sages, and of those of the present, too; he will bring the gods here.[8]

Agni, who dwells both on earth and in heaven, is believed to carry the libations of barley meal and sacrificial animals to the appropriate gods in their heavenly abodes. The sacrificers praised the gods whose favor they were seeking to influence, and the priests pronounced short prose formulas to propitiate them.

The other *deva* linked to the sacrificial rituals was *Soma*, an inebriating juice which was drunk ceremoniously to allow the practitioner to feel immortal, to experience the silent sound of Atman's breath and to unite the sacrificer to the one receiving the sacrifice. Many of the early Vedas described a ritual in which rishis used the vision-producing plant (*Soma*) which R. Gordon Wasson in *Soma: Divine Mushroom of Immortality* linked with hallucinogenic mushrooms. Whether this is the case or not, drinking *Soma* transported the rishis into a sacred realm of the divine inspiration.

You speak of the sacred, as your brightness is sacred; you speak the truth, as your deeds are true. You speak of faith, King Soma, as you are carefully prepared by the sacrificial priest. O drop of Soma, flow for Indra.[9]

The *Soma* plant was pounded with stones on a board until its juices were extracted, strained then mixed with water. Part of the drink was poured into the fire and the rest was drunk by the sacrificers who then felt possessed by extra-ordinary insights:

Inflame me like a fire kindled by friction; make us see far; make us richer, better. For when I am intoxicated with you, Soma, I think myself rich. Draw near and make us thrive. We would enjoy you, pressed with a fervent heart, like riches from a father. King Soma, stretch out our life-spans as the sun stretches the spring days.[10]

When every part of the sacrificial animal had been consumed, either by the fire or by those present, and after the gods had been praised and reminded of the sacrificer's needs, the farmer bathed and put on his customary clothing. He then paid the priests, usually in the form of livestock, and the sacrifice was complete.

The one who made the sacrifice and the gods to whom the sacrifice was made were now regenerated along with nature herself. As we will see, the external sacrifices of the Vedas developed into an interior sacrifice in the Upanishads, one accompanied by a knowledge of the Self within the sacrificer. In each case, whether that which is sacrificed is an animal or grain offering, or the false self, the sacrificer reanimates the primordial emanation of the world.

Hindu Scriptures

To properly understand the Hindu sacred experience it is necessary now to introduce the basic sacred texts from which we will draw our understanding of the Hindu Path. While there is a great variety of Indian sacred literature, there are two main sources of the Hindu story: *shruti* (what is heard) and *smriti* (what is remembered).

Shruti is the eternal word (*Vac*) revealed by Brahman, heard by sages, chanted, told as stories and studied as divinely revealed truth. As such it has canonical status. *Shruti,* which includes the Vedas and the Upanishads, is revered by all Hindus as part of its classically authoritative scriptures. *Smriti,* on the other hand, refers to the popular sacred traditions and stories which, while not as authoritative as *shruti,* are revered by all Hindus. The limited availability of the Vedic material and its intellectual difficulties created the need for a secondary authority among Hindus which would pertain to matters not covered in the Vedas. This authority, called *smriti* (recollection), came to signify a "tradition" which, unlike *sruti* (beginningless revelation), had an earthly author. This shift from *sruti* to *smirti* (cf. Chapter 3) was accompanied by a shift in philosophical outlook from the immutable, unthinkable, impersonal monism of the Upanishads to an emphasis on the supremely personal God who created us, inspired us to devotion and sacrifice and entered into a personal relation with us through yogic discipline. These texts are usually better known and understood by a majority of Hindus. The following outline illustrates this relationship:

SHRUTI	SMIRTI
(What is "heard")	(What is "recollected")
Text of a Divine origin.	Text of a Human origin.

1) VEDAS (1500–500 BCE)
"Uncreated Knowledge" Brought to India by the Indo-European Aryan invaders, it became the infallible, eternal authority in all matters of teaching and practice. The Vedas are living words which were chanted, recited, memorized and later written in Sanskrit in Four Collections:

A. RIG-VEDA (*Mantras* & Hymns) 1,028 lyric hymns & prayers to one of 33 Gods and Goddesses (*Devas*); each verse is called a *Rig;*

B. SAMA-VEDA (Songs and Hymns) used in sacred ritual;

C. YAJUR-VEDA Sacrifical Rituals, liturgical formulas and prayers;

D. ATHARVA-VEDA Collected poetry of the atharvan priests along with magic spells and popular medicinal rituals.

2) BRAMANAS Books concerned with ritual and prosaic commentaries on Vedas.

3) UPANISHAD (800–500 BCE)
"Sitting near the Foot of the Guru Devotedly." The secret or esoteric teaching of Transcendental knowledge in speculative and philosophic treatises, also referred to as Vedanta (Concluding Sections of each of the four Vedas), which are preserved in 108 philosophical books.

1. SUTRAS (guides);

2. SHASTRAS or textbooks—e.g., Manu (Legal Codes);

3. PURANAS or old stories myths & history of royal families;

4. NATIONAL EPICS

1. Ramayana

The epic of *Vishnu* as incarnate in *Rama* who battles the demon King Ravana and defeats Ravana with the aid of *Hanuman* (the Monkey God);

2. Mahabharta

The Epic battle of the Bharata families in which relatives dispute for political control over Northern India.

Bhagavad Gita (500–200 BCE)

Celestial "Song of God" which is book six in the Mahabharata; arranged in 700 2-line stanzas in 18 chapters; written by the poet Vyasa (the compiler of the Vedas) through Ganapati, in the form of a teaching-dialogue between Lord Krishna and Arjuna, as overheard by Sanjaya.

Upanishadic Stories

The word Upanishad means sitting devotedly near the teacher. It is written in Hindu sacred texts that one needs a teacher (guru) in order to understand its sublime and secret treasures.[11] The Upanishads occur at the end of each of the Vedas (*Vedanta*), and are written in a prose style, some in the form of dialogues and metaphysical speculations. They dissolve the gods of the early Vedic hymns into a monistic affirmation that *Brahman* is the breath of true selfhood. This shift from external to interior sacrifice coincided with a Upanishadic stress on the urgent need for realization of one's true inner nature (*Moksha*).

Whereas the Vedas of the formative period (1500–800 BCE) are concerned with the potency of rituals, with correct procedures and ecstatic responses, the Upanishads (800–500 BCE) present the interior quest for spiritual awareness taught by sages in forest hermitages. And whereas the Vedas reflect a plurality of gods, the Upanishads reflect only one, *Brahman*.

By the beginning of the sixth century, at a time when ritual interest had shifted from external Vedic sacrifices to interior forms of meditation, numerous teachers appeared with new theories and new spiritual practices. Such teachers often were homeless ascetics who, in small groups, searched for the truth behind appearances. Called by various names such as *shamanas* (ascetics) or *bhikshus* (almsmen), their interest was less in ascetical practices than in actual attainment of Ultimate Reality. It was during this period that a Hindu ascetic named Siddhartha Gautama became the Buddha.

The Brahman-Atman Identity

The fundamental theme of these reclusive teachers was the actualization of *Brahman*. In the early Vedic period, Brahman referred to the words recited at Vedic rituals, and to the power present in the chanting of the canonical hymns. These forest-dwelling reformers taught that *Brahman* was not just the hidden power of sacrifice, but also the hidden source of all creation, not only one *deva,* but the highest and holiest reality, not only an external truth, but one to be realized within. Thus, when asked about the many names of the Absolute, the sages said: though there are many names, there is but one reality. *Brahman* is one throughout the universe, the ultimate ground behind all forms which holds all forms together. In fact, there are two dimensions of expanded view of *Brahman:* behind the multiplicity of forms is the one (*Tad Ekam*) eternal reality; and this Self (*Atman*) is the inner identity of all individual selves.[12]

If the *Atman* is each person's deepest truth, why is this truth not recognized by everyone?

Traditionally, four interrelated causes are described which perpetuate a false perspective and foster suffering and selfishness: *karma* (action), *samsara* (the repeated cycles of birth and death), *maya* (playful illusion), and *avidya* (ignorance). *Avidya* (literally not knowing) refers to a beginningless ignorance of, and subsequent confusion about, the identity of the self (*Atman*). *Maya* is a confusion about the nature and objective reality of the world and refers to the collective hallucination of thinking that our ordinary waking consciousness is real when, from the Hindu standpoint, it is a dream. For example: a rope in the garden is seen as a snake. Taken in the most universal sense, *karma* is all the actions, movements, events that influence our experience in the world regardless of time, place or persons involved. *Samsara,* called reincarnation or transmigration of souls, is the Hindu belief that at death the psychic sub-stratum (soul) of each human person (depending upon elements of his or her *karma*) is reborn into another form—either human, animal, vegetable or inorganic.

While these unliberating realities keep humans imprisoned in a false perspective, as India's long history of gurus, saints and holy persons attest, liberation is possible. Called *moksha,* liberation from the stream of *avidya* and *karma* comes with the realization of one's true self. *Moksha,* the final freedom, is gained through various paths (*marga*) also called *yogas* in which one proceeds from hearing the truth, thinking and meditating upon it, to internally realizing it. The guru is one who attains full, unbounded liberation while yet in this life.

Early in the twentieth century, Sri Aurobindo Ghose was imprisoned by the British for his revolutionary activities. While in the Alipore Jail he wrote: "I had the Gita and the Upanishads with me, practiced the Yoga of the Gita and meditated with the help of the Upanishads; these were the only books from which I found guidance."[13] As a result, he realized the Divine in all beings, and was so transformed by the experience of cosmic consciousness that his jailer voluntarily released him.

In a related story, the twentieth century saint Ramana Maharshi reports that it was the fear of death which drove him into his true self. He reports that one day he was suddenly overtaken with a violent fear of death. Rather than consulting a physician, he decided to dramatize the occurrence of death. He lay on the floor imitating a corpse and held his breath. With an equal suddenness, he perceived in a flash that his true self was a deathless spirit. "All this was not dull thought," he reports. "It flashed through me vividly as living truth which I perceived directly, almost without thought-process."[14] From that moment on, Ramana Maharshi lost all fear of dying and became absorbed in the power of the imborn, undying *Atman*.

The identity of *Brahman* and *Atman* answers two fundamental religious questions— where did I come from, and what happens at death—because upon discovering and actualizing Atman, each question disappears:

> A certain wise man, while seeking immortality,
> Introspectively beheld the Soul (Atman) face to face.
> The childish go after outward pleasures;
> They walk into the net of widespread death.
> But the wise, knowing immortality,
> Seek not the stable among things which are unstable here.[15]

In the shortest of all the Upanishads, the Isa, the transcendent, yet immanent, impersonal, yet personal "One," takes the form of Isa (the Lord), unmoving, yet swifter than the fastest mind. As the Eternal Witness:

It moves. It moves not.
It is far, and It is near.
It is within all this,
And It is outside of all this
Now, he who on all beings
Looks as just in the Self (Atman),
And on the Self as in all beings—
He does not shrink away from
Him.

The unrealized fail to recognize it because:

With a golden vessel (disc)
The Real's face is covered o'er.
That do thou, O Pushan, uncover
For one whose law is the Real to see.
O Nourisher, the sole Self, O Controller,
O Sun, offspring of Prajapati, spread forth thy rays!
Gather thy brilliance! What is the fairest form—that of thee I see.
He who is yonder, yonder Person—I myself am he![16]

Even though the onlooker cannot see the real, since it is hidden behind the blinding light of the sun's blaze, or name it, he or she can experience union with it. Here the identity of the *rishi* with "The Real" is announced.

The great search in the Upanishads is for the identity of that True Self. In the Mudaka Upanishad, it is said that there are two kinds of knowledge, represented as two birds in a tree: the lower knowledge and the higher. The higher knowledge is:

That which is invisible, ungraspable, without family, without caste—
Without sight or hearing is, It, without hand or foot,
Eternal, all-pervading, omnipresent, exceedingly subtle;
That is the Imperishable, which the wise perceive as the source of beings.
As a spider emits and draws in [its thread],
As herbs arise on the earth,
As the hairs of the head and body from a living person,
So from the Imperishable arises everything here.[17]

In the Mandukya Upanishad, the Imperishable is said to be the nameless, soundless, sound "AUM . . ." Aum is depicted in four dimensions: the letter "A" which corresponds to waking consciousness, the letter "U" which corresponds to dreaming consciousness, and the letter "M" which corresponds to dreamless-sleep consciousness. In each progressively deeper stage, it is still the lesser self who is awake, dreaming or dreamless. The fourth dimension,

Aum

signified by the three dots, corresponds to supreme consciousness, where there is neither inner nor outer, neither known nor knowable. Here *Atman* is realized.

Svetaketu and Nachiketas

There are two stories which especially reflect the inner philosophical subtleties of *Atman*—the story of Svetaketu and that of Nachiketas.

Svetaketu in the Chandogya Upanishad (6.10:1–3) is a young man of the priestly caste who, according to caste expectations, between the ages of twelve and twenty-four attends a school of Vedic studies. Since classical Hindu pedagogy practiced memorization, Svetaketu spends twelve years memorizing all the words and instructions in the Vedic hymns and ritual-texts. When he returns home, no doubt feeling immense satisfaction and pride, he is greeted by his father who immediately asks what he has learned. Naturally Svetaketu talks about the One with many names, and about the *Atman*. When he was finished his father asks: "Well, then, who are you? Who is the one who has studied the *Atman*?"

For twelve years he has studied *Atman* without having realized who the student is. Svetaketu is nonplussed and honestly admits that he does not know. He knows how to discuss what the texts say about True Self, and he can theorize about it, but Svetaketu does not know the knower. His father says: "See that tree! Bring me the fruit of that tree." So Svetaketu picks the fruit of the Nyagrodha (Banyan) tree. His father says: "Break it open. What do you find there?" "Some seeds, Sir, exceedingly small." "Take one and break it open; what do you find there?" "Some seeds, Sir, exceedingly small." "Take one and break it open; what do you find there?" "Nothing at all, Sir." *"That,"* says his father, "That subtle essence, That Nothingness is your True Self. That, Svetaketu, That Thou Art *(Tat Tvam Asi).*"

Likewise, in the Katha Upanishad (1.1–6.18) we read about Nachiketas and his father Vajashravasa who, in order to gain divine favor, performs a Vedic sacrifice. Instead of sacrificing his best, deceitfully he brings diseased and worthless animals from his flocks to sacrifice. His young son Nachiketas, who has already studied the sacred texts, sees through this ruse and approaches his father: "I am your best; whom will you give me to!" When his father does not answer, again and again Nachiketas pesters him until his father turns and says: "Go to Hell! I give you to death!"

Determined to keep his father's words, Nachiketas travels straight to the underworld. As his *karma* would have it, Lord Yama (King of Death) was not there.[18] For three days Nachiketas waits. When the Yama returns, he is impressed with the Brahmin's courage and patience, and awards Nachiketas three boons.

First, Nachiketas asks that his father will not be worried about him, that his anger will be appeased and that he will be welcomed to return home. His wish is immediately granted.

Second, he asks to know the secret of the fire sacrifice itself. Impressed with Nachiketas' persistence and with the profundity of his question, Yama, after revealing the inner workings of the ritual to him, names the sacrifice after Nachiketas—henceforth the fire-sacrifice was to be called the "Nachiketas Fire Sacrifice."

Third, Nachiketas requests to know the truth of death. Yama tries to dissuade him by offering other boons. He argues that even the gods don't know the answer to that question, but Nachiketas will not be turned away. So Yama tells Nachiketas about the goal of the Vedas—*Aum*—the breath of *Brahman,* the highest symbol, the True Self of each person, unborn, imperishable and undying. The secret of death, Death tells him, is to realize *Atman* for:

> If the slayer thinks he slays
> If the slain thinks he's slain
> Neither knows the truth.
> The Self slays not, is not slain.[19]

In both of these stories, what is required of the aspirant is not knowledge (that *Atman* is True Self and that *avidya* keeps one ignorant of *Atman*), but the actualization which transforms one from a searcher to one who has been found. Nachiketas discovers that when he dies his True Self will continue to exist.

The following passages from Hindu texts will be understood best if we temporarily set aside our prior worldviews. It will be helpful for the reader to look for a key image in each of the texts and to allow the suggestive power of that image to carry the text's meaning. For example in the Upanishads we could note the golden disc (Isa), the eye of the eye (Kena), the chariot and upside down tree (Katha), the great bow and arrow (Mundaka), *aum* (Mandukya), the mirror of gold (Svetasvatara), and *Tat Tvam Asi* (Chandogya). Each is like a diamond located at the intersecting streams of light in Indra's heavenly net. Each diamond-image transmits its own light, its own meaning, and also reflects the other diamonds. Together they form the sages' attempt to picture the unpicturable truth of *Brahman-Atman*.

NOTES

1. T.S. Eliot, *The Four Quartets* (New York: Harcourt Brace Jovanovich, 1943), 40–41.

2. S. Radhakrishan, *The Hindu View of Life* (New York: The Macmillan Company, 1968), 37.

3. The first result of this cross-cultural encounter was what we call the Vedas, that is, the entire body of Vedic literature. It is chanted, spoken, and written in the old Indo-Aryan language known as Vedic, which is ancestral to the literary Sanskrit (formalized around the middle of the first millennium BCE). Vedic writings are regarded as revelation (*shruti*—that which is heard). R. Panikkar, *The Vedic Experience* (Berkeley: University of California Press, 1977), 30–31.

4. R.C. Zaehner, Translator, *Hindu Scripture* (New York: E.P. Dutton, 1966), 11–12.

5. *Ibid.*

6. Panikkar, *op. cit.*, 50.

7. (Rig Veda 1.26:1–), translated by Wendy O'Flaherty in *The Rig Veda* (New York: Penguin Books, 1981); 100. All further references to the *Vedas* are from this text.

8. Rig Veda 1.1: 1–9; 99.

9. Rig Veda 9.113: 4–6; 133.

10. Rig Veda 8.48: 6–7; 135.

11. Among the early Upanishads, the oldest thirteen are called the principal Upanishads and have no rival in the formation of Hindu thought. These principal Upanishads are: Brihad-Aranyaka Upanishad; Chandogya Upanishad; Taittiriya Upanishad; Aitareya Upanishad; Kaushitaki Upanishad; Kena Upanishad; Katha Upanishad; Isa Upanishad; Mundaka Upanishad; Prasna Upanishad; Mandukya Upanishad; Svetasvatara Upanishad; Maitri Upanishad.

12. According to traditional attitudes toward the human person, the self is in fact comprised of various layers, sheaths or bodies: gross, subtle, causal, and essential. At death, the outermost shell falls away and the next inward subtle psychic substratum is reborn in another body according to the aggregate *karma* of the next inward layer of causal body. The causal body ensheathes the innermost, essential self, or *Atman*. The final liberation of *moksha* occurs when human attachment to these three bodies dissolves, so that *Atman*, as consciousness alone, as sacred breath, and as *Brahman*, is liberated within.

13. Sri Aurobindo, *The Mind of Light* (New York: E.P. Dutton & Co., 1971), 10, 11.

14. Quoted from *The Teachings of Ramana Maharshi,* edited by Arthur Osborne (London: Rider & Company, 1962), 10.

15. *Katha Upanishad* 4:1–2, translated by Robert Hume in *The Thirteen Principal Upanishads* (London: Oxford University Press, 1931), 353. All further references to the Upanishads are from this text.

16. *Isa Upanishad* 5–6, 15–16; 363–364.

17. *Mundaka Upanishad* 1:6–7; 367.

18. Yama, originally a solar deity, was the first immortal to choose a mortal fate. Yama surrenders immortality in order to conquer death.

19. *Katha Upanishad* 2.19.

Selections

Selections from the Creation Hymns, and Hymns to Agni, Soma and Yama from the Rig Vedas translated by Wendy O'Flaherty.

Selections from the Isa, Kena, Katha, Mundaka, Mandukya, and Chandogya Upanishads translated by R.E. Hume.

10.129 Creation Hymn (Nāsadīya)

1 There was neither non-existence nor existence then; there was neither the realm of space nor the sky which is beyond. What stirred? Where? In whose protection? Was there water, bottomlessly deep?

2 There was neither death nor immortality then. There was no distinguishing sign of night nor of day. That one breathed, windless, by its own impulse. Other than that there was nothing beyond.

3 Darkness was hidden by darkness in the beginning; with no distinguishing sign, all this was water. The life force that was covered with emptiness, that one arose through the power of heat.

4 Desire came upon that one in the beginning; that was the first seed of mind. Poets seeking in their heart with wisdom found the bond of existence in non-existence.

5 Their cord was extended across. Was there below? Was there above? There were seed-placers; there were powers. There was impulse beneath; there was giving-forth above.

6 Who really knows? Who will here proclaim it? Whence was it produced? Whence is this creation? The gods came afterwards, with the creation of this universe. Who then knows whence it has arisen?

7 Whence this creation has arisen—perhaps it formed itself, or perhaps it did not—the one who looks down on it, in the highest heaven, only he knows—or perhaps he does not know.

10.121 The Unknown God, the Golden Embryo

1 In the beginning the Golden Embryo arose. Once he was born, he was the one lord of creation. He held in place the earth and this sky. Who is the god whom we should worship with the oblation?

2 He who gives life, who gives strength, whose command all the gods, his own, obey; his shadow is immortality—and death. Who is the god whom we should worship with the oblation?

3 He who by his greatness became the one king of the world that breathes and blinks, who rules over his two-footed and four-footed creatures—who is the god whom we should worship with the oblation?

4 He who through his power owns these snowy mountains, and the ocean together with the river Rasā, they say; who has the quarters of the sky as his two arms—who is the god whom we should worship with the oblation?

5 He by whom the awesome sky and the earth were made firm, by whom the dome of the sky was propped up, and the sun, who measured out the middle realm of space—who is the god whom we should worship with the oblation?

6 He to whom the two opposed masses looked with trembling in their hearts, supported by his help, on whom the rising sun shines down—who is the god whom we should worship with the oblation?

7 When the high waters came, pregnant with the embryo that is everything, bringing forth fire, he arose from that as the one life's breath of the gods. Who is the god whom we should worship with the oblation?

8 He who in his greatness looked over the waters, which were pregnant with Daksa, bringing forth the sacrifice, he who was the one god among all the gods—who is the god whom we should worship with the oblation?

9 Let him not harm us, he who fathered the earth and created the sky, whose laws are true, who created the high, shining waters. Who is the god whom we should worship with the oblation?

10 O Prajāpati, lord of progeny, no one but you

embraces all these creatures. Grant us the desires for which we offer you oblation. Let us be lords of riches.

10.90 *Purusa-Sūkta, or The Hymn of Man*

1 The Man has a thousand heads, a thousand eyes, a thousand feet. He pervaded the earth on all sides and extended beyond it as far as ten fingers.

2 It is the Man who is all this, whatever has been and whatever is to be. He is the ruler of immortality, when he grows beyond everything through food.

3 Such is his greatness, and the Man is yet more than this. All creatures are a quarter of him; three quarters are what is immortal in heaven.

4 With three quarters the Man rose upwards, and one quarter of him still remains here. From this he spread out in all directions, into that which eats and that which does not eat.

5 From him Virāj was born, and from Virāj came the Man. When he was born, he ranged beyond the earth behind and before.

6 When the gods spread the sacrifice with the Man as the offering, spring was the clarified butter, summer the fuel, autumn the oblation.

7 They anointed the Man, the sacrifice born at the beginning, upon the sacred grass. With him the gods, Sādhyas, and sages sacrificed.

8 From that sacrifice in which everything was offered, the melted fat was collected, and he made it into those beasts who live in the air, in the forest, and in villages.

9 From that sacrifice in which everything was offered, the verses and chants were born, the metres were born from it, and from it the formulas were born.

10 Horses were born from it, and those other animals that have two rows of teeth; cows were born from it, and from it goats and sheep were born.

11 When they divided the Man, into how many parts did they apportion him? What do they call his mouth, his two arms and thighs and feet?

12 His mouth became the Brahmin; his arms were made into the Warrior, his thighs the People, and from his feet the Servants were born.

13 The moon was born from his mind; from his eye the sun was born. Indra and Agni came from his mouth, and from his vital breath the Wind was born.

14 From his navel the middle realm of space arose; from his head the sky evolved. From his two feet came the earth, and the quarters of the sky from his ear. Thus they set the worlds in order.

15 There were seven enclosing-sticks for him, and thrice seven fuel-sticks, when the gods, spreading the sacrifice, bound the Man as the sacrificial beast.

16 With the sacrifice the gods sacrificed to the sacrifice. These were the first ritual laws. These very powers reached the dome of the sky where dwell the Sādhyas, the ancient gods.

10.14 *Yama and the Fathers*

1 The one who has passed beyond along the great, steep straits, spying out the path for many, the son of Vivasvan, the gatherer of men, King Yama—honour him with the oblation.

2 Yama was the first to find the way for us, this pasture that shall not be taken away. Where our ancient fathers passed beyond, there everyone who is born follows, each on his own path.

3 Mātalī made strong by the Kavyas, and Yama by the Angirases, and Brhaspati by the Rkvans—both those whom the gods made strong and those who strengthen the gods: some rejoice in the sacrificial call, others in the sacrificial drink.

4 Sit upon this strewn grass, O Yama, together with the Angirases, the fathers. Let the

verses chanted by the poets carry you here. O King, rejoice in this oblation.

5 Come, Yama, with the Angirases worthy of sacrifice: rejoice here with the Vairūpas, sitting on the sacred grass at this sacrifice. I will invoke Vivasvan, who is your father.

6 Our fathers, the Angirases, and the Navagvas, Atharvans, and Bṛhgus, all worthy of Soma—let us remain in favour with them, as they are worthy of sacrifice, and let them be helpful and kind.

7 [To the dead man:] Go forth, go forth on those ancient paths on which our ancient fathers passed beyond. There you shall see the two kings, Yama and Varuna, rejoicing in the sacrificial drink.

8 Unite with the fathers, with Yama, with the rewards of your sacrifices and good deeds, in the highest heaven. Leaving behind all imperfections, go back home again; merge with a glorious body.

9 [To demons:] Go away, get away, crawl away from here. The fathers have prepared this place for *him*. Yama gives him a resting-place adorned by days, and waters, and nights.

10 [To the dead man:] Run on the right path, past the two brindled, four-eyed dogs, the sons of Saramā, and then approach the fathers, who are easy to reach and who rejoice at the same feast as Yama.

11 Yama, give him over to your two guardian dogs, the four-eyed keepers of the path, who watch over men. O king, grant him happiness and health.

12 The two dark messengers of Yama with flaring nostrils wander among men, thirsting for the breath of life. Let them give back to us a life of happiness here and today, so that we may see the sun.

13 For Yama press the Soma; to Yama offer the oblation; to Yama goes the well-prepared sacrifice, with Agni as its messenger.

14 Offer to Yama the oblation rich in butter, and go forth. So may he intercede for us among the gods, so that we may live out a long life-span.

15 Offer to Yama, to the king, the oblation most rich in honey. We bow down before the sages born in the ancient times, the ancient path-makers.

16 All through the three Soma days, he flies to the six broad spaces and the one great one. Tristubh, Gāyatrī, the metres—all these are placed in Yama.

10.18 Burial Hymn

1 Go away, death, by another path that is your own, different from the road of the gods. I say to you who have eyes, who have ears: do not injure our children or our men.

2 When you have gone, wiping away the footprint of death, stretching farther your own lengthening span of life, become pure and clean and worthy of sacrifice, swollen with offspring and wealth.

3 These who are alive have now parted from those who are dead. Our invitation to the gods has become auspicious today. We have gone forward to dance and laugh, stretching farther our own lengthening span of life.

4 I set up this wall for the living, so that no one else among them will reach this point. Let them live a hundred full autumns and bury death in this hill.

5 As days follow days in regular succession, as seasons come after seasons in proper order, in the same way order their life-spans, O Arranger, so that the young do not abandon the old.

6 Climb on to old age, choosing a long life-span, and follow in regular succession, as many as you are. May Tvastr who presides over good births be persuaded to give you a long life-span to live.

7 These women who are not widows, who have good husbands—let them take their places, using butter to anoint their eyes. Without

tears, without sickness, well dressed let them first climb into the marriage bed.

8 Rise up, woman, into the world of the living. Come here; you are lying beside a man whose life's breath has gone. You were the wife of this man who took your hand and desired to have you.

9 I take the bow from the hand of the dead man, to be our supremacy and glory and power, and I say, 'You are there; we are here. Let us as great heroes conquer all envious attacks.'

10 Creep away to this broad, vast earth, the mother that is kind and gentle. She is a young girl, soft as wool to anyone who makes offerings, let her guard you from the lap of Destruction.

11 Open up, earth; do not crush him. Be easy for him to enter and to burrow in. Earth, wrap him up as a mother wraps a son in the edge of her skirt.

12 Let the earth as she opens up stay firm, for a thousand pillars must be set up. Let them be houses dripping with butter for him, and let them be a refuge for him here for all his days.

13 I shore up the earth all around you; let me not injure you as I lay down this clod of earth. Let the fathers hold up this pillar for you; let Yama build a house for you here.

14 On a day that will come, they will lay me in the earth, like the feather of an arrow. I hold back speech that goes against the grain, as one would restrain a horse with a bridle.

I.1 I Pray to Agni

1 I pray to Agni, the household priest who is the god of the sacrifice, the one who chants and invokes and brings most treasure.

2 Agni earned the prayers of the ancient sages, and of those of the present, too; he will bring the gods here.

3 Through Agni one may win wealth, and growth from day to day, glorious and most abounding in heroic sons.

4 Agni, the sacrificial ritual that you encompass on all sides—only that one goes to the gods.

5 Agni, the priest with the sharp sight of a poet, the true and most brilliant, the god will come with the gods.

6 Whatever good you wish to do for the one who worships you, Agni, through you, O Angiras, that comes true.

7 To you, Agni, who shine upon darkness, we come day after day, bringing our thoughts and homage

8 to you, the king over sacrifices, the shining guardian of the Order, growing in your own house.

9 Be easy for us to reach, like a father to his son. Abide with us, Agni, for our happiness.

8.79 This Restless Soma

1 This restless Soma—you try to grab him but he breaks away and overpowers everything. He is a sage and a seer inspired by poetry.

2 He covers the naked and heals all who are sick. The blind man sees; the lame man steps forth.

3 Soma, you are a broad defence against those who hate us, both enemies we have made ourselves and those made by others.

4 Through your knowledge and skills, rushing forward you drive out of the sky and the earth the evil deed of the enemy.

5 Let those who seek find what they seek: let them receive the treasure given by the generous and stop the greedy from getting what they want.

6 Let him find what was lost before; let him push forward the man of truth. Let him stretch out the life-span that has not yet crossed its span.

7 Be kind and merciful to us, Soma; be good to our heart, without confusing our powers in your whirlwind.

8 King Soma, do not enrage us; do not terrify

us; do not wound our heart with dazzling light.

9 Give help, when you see the evil plans of the gods in your own house. Generous king, keep away hatreds, keep away failures.

*   *   *

1. Īśā Upaniṣad

1. By the Lord (Īśa) enveloped must this all be—
Whatever moving thing there is in the moving world.
With this renounced, thou mayest enjoy.
Covet not the wealth of anyone at all.
2. Even while doing deeds here,
One may desire to live a hundred years.
Thus on thee—not otherwise than this is it—
The deed adheres not on the man.
3. Devilish are those worlds called,
With blind darkness covered o'er.
Unto them, on descending, go
Whatever folk are slayers of the Self.
4. Unmoving, the One is swifter than the mind.
The sense-powers reached not It, speeding on before.
Past others running, This goes standing.
In It Mātariśvan places action.
5. It moves. It moves not.
It is far, and It is near.
It is within all this,
And It is outside of all this.
6. Now, he who on all beings
Looks as just in the Self (Ātman),
And on the Self as in all beings—
He does not shrink away from Him.
7. In whom all beings
Have become just the Self of the discerner—
Then what delusion, what sorrow is there,
Of him who perceives the unity!
8. He has environed. The bright, the bodiless,

the scatheless,
The sinewless, the pure, unpierced by evil!
Wise, intelligent, encompassing, self-existent,
Appropriately he distributed objects through the eternal years.
9. Into blind darkness enter they
That worship ignorance;
Into darkness greater than that, as it were, they
That delight in knowledge.
10. Other, indeed, they say, than knowledge!
Other, they say, than non-knowledge!
—Thus we have heard from the wise
Who to us have explained It.
11. Knowledge and non-knowledge—
He who this pair conjointly knows,
With non-knowledge passing over death,
With knowledge wins the immortal.
12. Into blind darkness enter they
Who worship non-becoming;
Into darkness greater than that, as it were, they
Who delight in becoming.
13. Other, indeed—they say—than origin!
Other—they say—than non-origin!
—Thus have we heard from the wise
Who to us have explained It.
14. Becoming and destruction—
He who this pair conjointly knows,
With destruction passing over death,
With becoming wins the immortal.
15. With a golden vessel
The Real's face is covered o'er.
That do thou, O Pūsan, uncover
For one whose law is the Real to see.
16. O Nourisher, the sole Seer, O Controller, O Sun, offspring of
Prajāpati, spread forth thy rays! Gather thy brilliance! What
is thy fairest form—that of thee I see. He who is yonder,
yonder Person—I myself am he!
17. [My] breath to the immortal wind! This body then ends in
ashes! *Om!*

O Purpose, remember! The deed remember!
O Purpose, remember! The deed remember!
18. O Agni, by a goodly path to prosperity lead
us,
Thou god who knowest all the ways!
Keep far from us crooked-going sin!
Most ample expression of adoration to thee
would we render.

2. *Kena Upaniṣad*

[Question:] *The real agent in the individual?*

1. By whom impelled soars forth the mind projected?
By whom enjoined goes forth the earliest
breathing?
By whom impelled this speech do people utter?
The eye, the ear—what god, pray, them en-
joineth?

[Answer:] *The all-conditioning, yet inscrutable
agent, Brahman*

2. That which is the hearing of the ear, the
thought of the mind,
The voice of speech, as also the breathing of
the breath,
And the sight of the eye! Past these escap-
ing, the wise,
On departing from this world, become im-
mortal.
There the eyes go not;
Speech goes not, nor the mind.
We know not, we understand not
How one would teach It.
Other, indeed, is It than the known,
And moreover above the unknown.
—Thus have we heard of the ancients
Who to us have explained It.   (I.1–3)

THE PARADOX OF ITS INSCRUTABILITY

3. [Teacher:]
It is conceived of by him by whom It is not

conceived of.
He by whom It is conceived of, knows It not.
It is not understood by those who [say they]
understand It.
It is understood by those who [say they] understand It not.
  4. When known by an awakening, It is
conceived of; . . .   (II.3–4)

3. *Kaṭha Upaniṣad*

THE STORY OF NACIKETAS: KNOWLEDGE PREFER-
ABLE TO THE GREATEST EARTHLY PLEASURES

1. Now verily, with zeal did Vājaśravasa give
his whole possession
[as a religious gift].
He had a son, Naciketas by name.
2. Into him, boy as he was, while the sacrificial
gifts were being
led up, faith entered. . . .
4. Then he said to his father: "Papa, to whom
will you give me?"—
a second time—a third time.
To him then he said: "To Death I give you!"

[Here follows a conversation between Death
(Yama) and Naciketas. Death, just returned
from a three days' absence and finding that Naciketas has not received the hospitality which is
due a *Brāhmin,* says, "Therefore in return
choose three boons!" His first wish is that he
might return to his father on earth; his second is
for an understanding of the Naciketas sacrificial
fire that leads to heaven. These are granted. The
account of the third and most important wish follows in part:]

[Naciketas:]
20. This doubt that there is in regard to a man
deceased:
"He exists," say some; "He exists not," say
others—
This would I know, instructed by thee!
Of the boons this is boon the third.

[Death:]

21. Even the gods had doubt as to this of yore!
    For truly, it is not easily to be understood.
    Subtile is this
    matter.
    Another boon, O Naciketas, choose!
    Press me not! Give up this one for me!

[Naciketas:]

22. Even the gods had doubt, indeed, as to this,
    And thou, O Death, sayest that it is not easily
    to be understood.
    And another declarer of it the like of thee is
    not to be obtained.
    No other boon the equal of it is there at all.

[Death:]

23. Choose centenarian sons and grandsons,
    Many cattle, elephants, gold, and horses.
    Choose a great abode of earth.
    And thyself live as many autumns as thou
    desirest.

24. This, if thou thinkest as equal boon,
    Choose—wealth and long life!
    A great one on earth, O Naciketas, be thou.
    The enjoyer of thy desires I make thee.

25. Whate'er desires are hard to get in the mor-
    tal world—
    For all desires at pleasure make request.
    These lovely maidens with chariots, with
    lyres—
    Such [maidens], indeed, are not obtainable
    by men—
    By these, from me bestowed, be waited on!
    O Naciketas, question me not regarding
    dying!

[Naciketas:]

26. Ephemeral things! That which is a mortal's,
    O End-maker,
    Even the vigor of all the powers, they wear
    away.
    Even a whole life is slight indeed.
    Thine be the vehicles! Thine be the dance
    and song!

27. Not with wealth is a man to be satisfied.

Shall we take wealth, if we have seen thee?
Shall we live so long as thou shalt rule?
—This, in truth, is the boon to be chosen by
me.

28. When one has come into the presence of un-
    decaying immortals
    What decaying mortal, here below, that un-
    derstands,
    That meditates upon the pleasures of beauty
    and delight,
    Would delight in a life over-long?

29. This thing whereon they doubt, O Death:
    What there is in the great passing-on—tell
    us that!
    This boon, that has entered into the hid-
    den—
    No other than that does Naciketas choose.
                        (I.1–2, 4, 20–29)

THE FAILURE OF PLEASURE AND OF IGNORANCE;
  THE WISDOM OF THE BETTER KNOWLEDGE

[Death:]

1. The better (śreyas) is one thing, and the
   pleasanter (preyas) quite another.
   Both these, of different aim, bind a person.
   Of these two, well it is for him who takes the
   better;
   He fails of his aim who chooses the pleasanter.

2. Both the better and the pleasanter come to
   a man.
   Going all around the two, the wise man dis-
   criminates.
   The wise man chooses the better, indeed,
   rather than the pleasanter.
   The stupid man, from getting-and-keeping,
   chooses the pleasanter.

3. Thou indeed, upon the pleasant and pleas-
   antly appearing desires
   Meditating, hast let them go, O Naciketas.
   Thou art not one who has taken that garland
   of wealth
   In which many men sink down.

4. Widely opposite and asunder are these two:
   Ignorance and what is known as "knowledge."

I think Naciketas desirous of obtaining knowledge!
Many desires rend thee not.

9. As the one fire has entered the world
And becomes corresponding in form to every form,
So the one Inner Self (*antarātman*) of all things
Is corresponding in form to every form, and yet is outside.

10. As the one wind has entered the world
And becomes corresponding in form to every form,
So the one Inner Self of all things
Is corresponding in form to every form, and yet is outside.

11. As the sun, the eye of the whole world,
Is not sullied by the external faults of the eyes,
So the one Inner Self of all things
Is not sullied by the evil in the world, being external to it.

12. The Inner Self of all things, the One Controller,
Who makes his one form manifold—
The wise who perceive Him as standing in oneself,
They, and no others, have eternal happiness!   (V.8–12)

THE WORLD-TREE ROOTED IN BRAHMAN; [WAYS TO BRAHMAN]

1. Its root is above, it branches below—
This eternal fig-tree!
That (root) indeed is the Pure. That is *Brahman*.
That indeed is called the Immortal.
On it all the worlds do rest,
And no one soever goes beyond it.
This, verily, is That!

2. This whole world, whatever there is,
Was created from and moves in Life.
The great fear, the upraised thunderbolt—
They who know That, become immortal.

3. From fear of Him fire doth burn.

From fear the sun gives forth heat.
From fear both Indra and Wind,
And Death as fifth, do speed along. . . .

6. The separate nature of the senses,
And that their arising and setting
Is of things that come into being apart [from himself],
The wise man recognizes, and sorrows not.

9. His form is not to be beheld.
No one soever sees Him with the eye.
He is framed by the heart, by the thought, by the mind.
They who know That become immortal.

10. When cease the five
[Sense-] knowledges, together with the mind,
And the intellect (*buddhi*) stirs not—
That, they say, is the highest course.

11. This they consider as *yoga*—
The firm holding back of the senses.
Then one becomes undistracted.
Yoga, truly, is the origin and the end.

12. Not by speech, not by mind,
Not by sight can He be apprehended . . .
How can He be comprehended
Otherwise than by one's saying "He is"? . . .

13. He can indeed be comprehended by the thought "He is"
And by [admitting] the real nature of both [his comprehensibility and his incomprehensibility].
When he has been comprehended by the thought "He is"
His real nature manifests itself.

14. When are liberated all
The desires that lodge in one's heart,
Then a mortal becomes immortal!
Therein he reaches *Brahman*!

15. When are cut all
The knots of the heart here on earth,
Then a mortal becomes immortal!
(VI.1–15)

THE DOCTRINE OF BRAHMAN-ĀTMAN

1. This is the truth:—

As, from a well-blazing fire, sparks
By the thousand issue forth of like form,
So from the Imperishable, my friend, beings
manifold
Are produced, and thither also go.

2. Heavenly, formless is the Person.
   He is without and within, unborn,
   Breathless, mindless, pure,
   Higher than the high Imperishable.

3. From him is produced breath,
   Mind, and all the senses,
   Space, wind, light, water,
   And earth, the supporter of all.

4. Fire is His head; His eyes, the moon and
   sun;
   The regions of space, His ears; His voice,
   the revealed Vedas;
   Wind, His breath; His heart, the whole
   world. Out of His
   feet, The earth. Truly, He is the Inner Self
   (Ātman) of all.

5. Those abiding in the midst of ignorance,
   Self-wise, thinking themselves learned,
   Running hither and thither, go around de-
   luded,
   Like blind men led by one who is himself
   blind.   (II.1–5)

THE ETERNAL INDESTRUCTIBLE SELF

18. The wise one [i.e., the Ātman, the Self] is
    not born, nor dies.
    This one has not come from anywhere, has
    not become anyone.
    Unborn, constant, eternal, primeval, this
    one
    Is not slain when the body is slain.

19. If the slayer think to slay,
    If the slain think himself slain,
    Both these understand not.
    This one slays not, nor is slain.

20. More minute than the minute, greater than
    the great,
    Is the Self that is set in the heart of a crea-
    ture here.

1. One who is without the active will beholds
   Him, and becomes
   freed from sorrow—
   When through the grace of the Creator he
   beholds the greatness
   of the Self.

2. Him who is the bodiless among bodies,
   Stable among the unstable,
   The great, all-pervading Self—
   On recognizing Him, the wise man sorrows
   not.

3. This Self is not to be obtained by instruction,
   Nor by intellect, nor by much learning.
   He is to be obtained only by the one whom
   he chooses;
   To such a one that Self reveals his own per-
   son.

4. Not he who has not ceased from bad con-
   duct,
   Not he who is not tranquil, not he who is not
   composed,
   Not he who is not of peaceful mind
   Can obtain Him by intelligence (prajñā).

5. He for whom the priesthood and the nobility
   Both are as food,
   And death is as a sauce—
   Who really knows where He is?   (II.18–20,
                                        22–5)

THE UNIVERSAL AND THE INDIVIDUAL SELF

6. Know thou the self (ātman) as riding in a
   chariot,
   The body as the chariot.
   Know thou the intellect (buddhi) as the
   chariot-driver,
   And the mind as the reins.

7. The senses, they say, are the horses;
   The objects of sense, what they range over.
   The self combined with senses and mind
   Wise men call "the enjoyer."

8. He, however, who has not understanding,
   Who is unmindful and ever impure,
   Reaches not the goal,
   But goes on to transmigration [rebirth].

9. He, however, who has understanding,

Who is mindful and ever pure,
Reaches the goal
From which he is born no more. . . .

10. Higher than the senses are the objects of
sense.
Higher than the objects of sense is the
mind;
And higher than the mind is the intellect
(*buddhi*).
Higher than the intellect is the Great Self
(*Ātman*).

11. Higher than the Great is the Unmanifest
(*avyakta*).
Higher than the Unmanifest is the Person.
Higher than the Person there is nothing at
all.
That is the goal. That is the highest course.

12. Though He is hidden in all things,
That Self shines not forth.
But He is seen by subtle seers
With superior, subtle intellect.

13. An intelligent man should suppress his
speech and his mind.
The latter he should suppress in the Under-
standing-Self (*jñāna ātman*).
The understanding he should suppress in
the Great Self.
That he should suppress in the Tranquil
Self. . . .

14. Arise ye! Awake ye!
Obtain your boons and understand them!
A sharpened edge of a razor, hard to trav-
erse,
A difficult path is this—poets declare!

15. What is soundless, touchless, formless, imperishable,
Likewise tasteless, constant, odorless,
Without beginning, without end, higher
than the great, stable—
By discerning That, one is liberated from the
mouth of death.   (III.3–4, 7–8, 10–15)

THE IMMORTAL SELF NOT TO BE SOUGHT BY OUT-
WARD KNOWLEDGE

1. The Self-existent pierced the openings [of

the senses] outward;
Therefore one looks outward, not within
himself.
A certain wise man, while seeking immor-
tality,
Introspectively beheld the Self face to face.

2. The childish go after outward pleasures;
They walk into the net of widespread death.
But the wise, knowing immortality,
Seek not the stable among things which are
unstable here.

3. That by which [one discerns] form, taste,
smell,
Sound, and mutual touches—
It is with That indeed that one discerns.
What is there left over here!
This, verily, is That!

4. By recognizing as the great pervading Self
That whereby one perceives both
The sleeping state and the waking state,
The wise man sorrows not.

10. Whatever is here, that is there.
What is there, that again is here.
He obtains death after death
Who seems to see a difference here.

11. By the mind, indeed, is this [realization] to
be attained:—
There is no difference here at all!
He goes from death to death
Who seems to see a difference here.   (IV.1–
4, 10–11)

ONE'S REAL PERSON (SELF), THE SAME AS THE
WORLD-GROUND

8. He who is awake in those that sleep,
The Person who fashions desire after de-
sire—
That indeed is the Pure. That is *Brahman*.
That indeed is called the Immortal.
On it all the worlds do rest;
And no one soever goes beyond it.
This, verily, is That!
The male pours seed in the female.

Many creatures are produced from the Person.

9. From Him, too, gods are manifoldly produced,
The celestials, men, cattle, birds,
The in-breath and the out-breath, rice and barley, austerity,
Faith, truth, chastity, and the law.

10. The Person himself is everything here;
Work and austerity and *Brahman,* beyond death.
He who knows That, set in the secret place [of the heart]—
He here on earth, my friend, rends asunder the knot of ignorance. (II.i.1–5, 7, 10)

THE ALL-INCLUSIVE BRAHMAN

1. Manifest, [yet] hidden; called "Moving-in-secret";
The great abode! Therein is placed that
Which moves and breathes and winks.
What that is, know as Being and Non-being,
As the object of desire, higher than understanding,
As what is the best of creatures!

2. That which is flaming, which is subtler than the subtle,
On which the worlds are set, and their inhabitants
That is the imperishable *Brahman.*
It is life, and It is speech and mind.
That is the real. It is immortal.
It is [a mark] to be penetrated. Penetrate It, my friend!

3. Taking as a bow the great weapon of the Upaniṣad,
One should put upon it an arrow sharpened by meditation.
Stretching it with a thought directed to the essence of That,
Penetrate that Imperishable as the mark, my friend.

4. The mystic syllable *Om* is the bow. The arrow is the Self (*Ātman*).
Brahman is said to be the mark.

By the undistracted man is It to be penetrated.
One should come to be in It, as the arrow [in the mark].

9. In the highest golden sheath
Is *Brahman,* without stain, without parts.
Brilliant is It, the light of lights—
That which knowers of the Self (*Ātman*) do know! (II.ii.1–4, 9)

THE WAY TO BRAHMAN

1. Two birds, fast bound companions,
Clasp close the self-same tree.
Of these two, the one eats sweet fruit;
The other looks on without eating.

2. On the self-same tree a person, sunken,
Grieves for his impotence, deluded;
When he sees the other, the Lord (*Īśa*), contented,
And his greatness, he becomes freed from sorrow.

3. When a seer sees the brilliant
Maker, Lord, Person, the *Brahman*-source,
Then, being a knower, shaking off good and evil,
Stainless, he attains supreme identity [with Him].

5. This Self (*Ātman*) is obtainable by truth, by austerity,
By proper knowledge, by the student's life of chastity constantly [practiced].
Within the body, consisting of light, pure is He
Whom the ascetics, with imperfections done away, behold.

8. Not by sight is It grasped, not even by speech,
Not by any other sense-organs, austerity, or work.
By the peace of knowledge, one's nature purified—
In that way, however, by meditating, one does behold Him who is without parts.
(III.i.1–3, 5, 8)

1. . . . They who, being without desire, worship the Person
   And are wise, pass beyond the seed [of rebirth] here.
2. He who in fancy forms desires,
   Because of his desires is born [again] here and there.
   But of him whose desire is satisfied, who is a perfected self,
   All desires even here on earth vanish away.
3. This Self (*Ātman*) is not to be obtained by instruction,
   Nor by intellect, nor by much learning.
   He is to be obtained only by the one whom He chooses;
   To such a one that Self reveals His own person.
4. This Self is not to be obtained by one destitute of fortitude,
   Nor through heedlessness, nor through a false notion of austerity.
   But he who strives by these means, provided he knows—
   Into his *Brahman*-abode this Self enters.
   (III.ii.1–5)

6. *Māṇḍūkya Upaniṣad*

THE MYSTIC SYMBOLISM OF THE SYLLABLE "OM"
DEPICTING THE FOUR STATES OF CONSCIOUSNESS

1. *Om!*—This syllable is this whole world.
   Its further explanation is:—
   The past, the present, the future—everything is just the word *Om*.
   And whatever else that transcends threefold time—that, too, is just the word *Om*.
2. For truly, everything here is *Brahman;* this self is *Brahman*. This same self has four fourths.
3. The waking state, outwardly cognitive, having seven limbs, having nineteen mouths, enjoying the gross, the Common-to-all-men, is the first fourth.
4. The dreaming state, inwardly cognitive, having seven limbs, having nineteen mouths, enjoying the exquisite, the Brilliant, is the second fourth.
5. If one asleep desires no desire whatsoever, sees no dream whatsoever, that is deep sleep.
   The deep-sleep state, unified, just a cognition-mass, consisting of bliss, enjoying bliss, whose mouth is thought, the cognitional, is the third fourth.
6. This is the lord of all. This is the all-knowing. This is the inner controller. This is the source of all, for this is the origin and the end of beings.
7. Not inwardly cognitive, not outwardly cognitive, not both-wise cognitive, not a cognition-mass, not cognitive, not non-cognitive, unseen, with which there can be no dealing, ungraspable, having no distinctive mark, non-thinkable, that cannot be designated, the essence of the assurance of which is the state of being one with the Self, the cessation of development, tranquil, benign, without a second (*a-dvaita*)—[such] they think is the fourth. He is the Self. He should be discerned.
8. This is the Self with regard to the word *Om*, with regard to its elements. The elements are the fourths; the fourths, the elements: the letter *a*, the letter *u*, the letter *m*.
9. The waking state, the Common-to-all-men, is the letter *a*, the first element, from *āpti* (obtaining) or from *ādimatva* (being first).
   He obtains, verily, indeed, all desires, he becomes first—he who knows this.
10. The sleeping state, the brilliant, is the letter *u* the second element, from *utkarsa* (exaltation) or from *ubhayatvā* (intermediateness).
    He exalts, verily, indeed, the continuity of knowledge; and he becomes equal; no one ignorant of *Brahman* is born in the family of him who knows this.
11. The deep-sleep state, the cognitional, is the letter *m*, the third element, from *miti* ("erecting") or from *apiti* ("immerging").
    He, verily, indeed, erects (*minoti*) this

whole world, and he becomes its immerging—he who knows this.

12. The fourth is without an element, with which there can be no dealing, the cessation of development, benign, without a second. Thus *Om* is the Self (*Ātman*) indeed.
He who knows this, with his self enters the Self—yea, he who knows this!

9. *Chāndogya Upaniṣad*

IN SLEEP ONE REACHES BEING

1. Then Uddālaka Āruṇi said to Svetaketu, his son: . . . "When person here sleeps, as it is called, then, my dear, he has reached Being, he has gone to his own. . . ."   (VI.viii. 1)

1. "Now, when one is sound asleep; composed, serene, and knows no dream—that is the Self (*Ātman*)," said he. "That is the immortal, the fearless. That is *Brahman*. . . ."
(VIII.xi. 1)

THE UNITARY WORLD-SELF, THE IMMANENT
REALITY OF ALL THINGS AND OF MAN

1. "As the bees, my dear, prepare honey by collecting the essences of different trees and reducing the essence to a unity, [2] as they are not able to discriminate 'I am the essence of this tree,' 'I am the essence of that tree'—even so, indeed, my dear, all creatures here, though they reach Being, know not 'We have reached Being.'

3. "Whatever they are in this world, whether tiger, or lion, or wolf, or boar, or worm, or fly, or gnat, or mosquito, that they become.

4. "That which is the finest essence—this whole world has that as its self. That is Reality. That is *Ātman*. That art thou [*Tat tvam asi*], Śvetaketu. . . ."   (VI.ix.1–4)

1. "These rivers, my dear, flow, the eastern toward the east, the western toward the west. They go just from the ocean to the

ocean. They become the ocean itself. As there they know not 'I am this one,' 'I am that one'—[2] even so, indeed, my dear, all creatures here, though they have come forth from Being, know not 'We have come forth from Being.' Whatever they are in this world, whether tiger, or lion, or wolf, or boar, or worm, or fly, or gnat, or mosquito, that they become.

3. "That which is the finest essence—this whole world has that as its self. That is Reality. That is *Ātman*. That art thou, Śvetaketu. . . ."   (VI.x.1–3)

1. "Bring hither a fig from there."
"Here it is, sir."
"Divide it."
"It is divided, Sir."
"What do you see there?"
"These rather fine seeds, Sir."
"Of these, please, divide one."
"It is divided, Sir."
"What do you see there?"
"Nothing at all, Sir."

2. Then he said to him: "Verily, my dear, that finest essence which you do not perceive—verily, my dear, from that finest essence this great Nyagrodha (sacred fig) tree thus arises.

3. "Believe me, my dear," said he, "that which is the finest essence—this whole world has that as its self. That is Reality. That is *Ātman*. That art thou, Śvetaketu. . . ."
(VI.xii.1–3)

1. "Place this salt in the water. In the morning come unto me." Then he did so.
Then he said to him: "That salt you placed in the water last evening—please bring it hither."
Then he grasped for it, but did not find it, as it was completely dissolved.

2. "Please take a sip of it from this end," said he. "How is it?"
"Salt."

"Take a sip from the middle," said he. "How is it?"

"Salt."

"Take a sip from that end," said he. "How is it?"

"Salt."

"Set it aside. Then come unto me."

He did so, saying, "It is always the same."

Then he said to him: "Verily, indeed, my dear, you do not perceive Being here. Verily, indeed, it is here.

3. That which is the finest essence—this whole world has that as its self. That is Reality. That is *Ātman*. That art thou, Śvetaketu."   (VI.xiii.1–3)

HINDU JOURNAL EXERCISES

1. Imagine yourself in India—either classical or current India—and imagine that you have the surprise opportunity to meet a holy person, a guru, whom you have been told by devotees is God incarnate! Construct the dialogue that you would most likely have with the guru. What are your most significant questions, and how does the guru reply? First you speak, then the guru, then you, etc.

2. After reading the Vedic hymns of creation, write your own creation myth. How did life really begin? An easy way to do this is to imitate the style of the Vedic authors, to recast your understanding and intuition of creation in the Vedic form. Tell the whole tale as imagistically as possible. Then reread the Vedic hymns of creation and compare them with the one you have written. What are the most significant points of comparison, of agreement and of disagreement? What did you gain from this exercise?

3. Imagine that you have graduated from your school with a major in journalism and a minor in religious studies. The editor of the paper you are writing for asks you to provide a background article on a Hindu speaker. He asks you to select a favorite Vedic or Upanishadic text and edit it into a five-line, prose statement. Then, after you have completed that, pick the one image, idea, concept, or word which you feel best expresses the meaning of the text, and indicate why. What makes your choice central to the whole text?

4. A student once wrote in her journal:

   "To fully understand the scriptures it is imperative to relate them to the present experience of humankind."

   Select something from the Upanishads which either clearly does apply or clearly does not apply to your life-experience and discuss why. Is it possible to understand a Hindu without being Hindu? Is it possible to apply classical "Eastern" spiritual insights to contemporary, "Western" secular life?

5. Imagine, in a dream, that you are taken to the heart of the earth like Nachiketas. Feel your body not being subject to its usual limitations. You can see, breathe and walk as if you are in a familiar above-ground environment. Imagine that the King of the Underworld speaks to you:

   "Since you defy mortality I grant you any three boons you wish!"

   What three wishes would you ask for? List them! Then after you list yours, compare your wishes with those of Nachiketas. What does the similarity/difference show you about yourself?

6. What story best captures the essence of the Hindu image of being religious? What images most clearly describe that story's movement? How does it compare with your image of yourself?

7. What is the deepest insight you have discovered in your reading of the Hindu texts?

Chapter 3   THE DIVINE LORD KRISHNA

As early as 500 BCE in northern India, devotional cults, which were to be the forerunners of the *bhakti* movement, were beginning to develop and spread. Brahmanical studies centering on the Vedas had dominated early Indian religious life until the time of Siddhartha Gautama, the Buddha (563–483 BCE), but when Buddhists rejected a thousand years of Vedic study and sacrifice, the door was opened for yet more change. By the last century before Christ there existed a variety of devotional sects which stressed the value of worship rather than sacrifice, the heart rather than the mind, service rather than performance, spontaneity rather than ritual precision.

One of the central deities of popular Hindu faith and the focus of numerous devotional cults is Lord Shiva (the auspicious one). Not being one of the thirty-three gods brought by the conquering Aryans, Shiva was the deity of the common people, and was glorified by Shavites (Shiva-devotees) in 108 names or aspects. Shiva symbolized destruction—the destruction necessary for regeneration—and is often therefore visualized dancing on top of *Durga* (the evil dwarf), within a surrounding ring of flames. In other depictions, the headwater of the Ganges flows forth from Shiva's crown *chakra* while he is meditating in the Himalayas. Devotees practice surrendering their wills to Lord Shiva who becomes the sole object of the followers devotion. But it is to the story of another divine being, Lord Krishna, that we now turn.

Whether as a response to static Vedic sacrificial liturgies, or as a further reformation, by the third century BCE two of India's greatest epic poems—the Mahabharata and the Ramayana—were written. While our concern here is with the Bhagavad Gita (the sixth book of the Mahabharata), we will first briefly familiarize ourselves with the two main epics of India—the Ramayana and the Mahabharata. From earliest times these epics permeated the cultural consciousness, both uneducated and educated alike. Children were, and are today, taken by their mothers in the quiet of the evening to hear trained storytellers recite events from the lives of Ram and Krishna. These works are accepted as what might be called "auxiliary scriptures," that is, texts which expand and illustrate the Vedas.[1]

The Life of Ram was written by India's first poet, Valmiki. Briefly, as the story unfolds, the lotus-eyed Ram is offered King Janaka's daughter Sita in marriage. Only Ram, of all the noblemen, could bend the king's mighty bow. When he was thereupon installed as prince regent of his country, the Queen's jealous maid aroused her mistress to have Bharata, the Queen's son, placed on the throne, and to have Ram exiled for fourteen years.

Taking Sita and his faithful brother Laksman, they journey into the forest and build

Shiva

little cottages for shelter. One day Sita is abducted by Ravana, the evil King of Ceylon, disguised as a beggar. Relying on the monkey god Hanuman and his army, Ram wages war on Ravana and defeats him. Bowing to his people's requests, Ram allows Sita's loyalty to be tested. When the gods finally exonerate her, she disappears into the bosom of the earth. Realizing his true nature, Ram departs from his earthly body and joins Sita in a celestial abode.

The other auxiliary scripture is the Mahabharata. Comprising one book of the world's longest epic poem, the Mahabharata (ascribed to the poet Vyasa), modern scholars attribute the text to a composite authorship most likely between the third and second century BCE. Unlike the philosophically abstract Upanishadic discourses, its Gita is epic poetry, like the *Odyssey* or the *Iliad* in the West. The Bhagavad Gita is often called India's New Testament, and is India's most often read, most deeply revered sacred text. In fact, the first and the eighteenth chapters end by referring to themselves the Bhagavad-Gita-Upanishad.

The Mahabharata is the story of the descendants of King Bharta after King Kuru and King Pandu had died, and while Pandu's blind brother Dhritarashtra lived. Though Dhritarashtra had a hundred sons of his own (sons of Kuru), the eldest being Duryodhana; he gave his throne to his nephew Yudhishthira (Arjuna's brother), one of King Pandu's five sons (Pandavas). Duryodhana conspired to gain the kingdom and arranged a crooked game of dice. Yudhishthira lost badly, and in the final game, attempting to win everything back, lost the entire kingdom. He and his brothers (and their common wife Draupadi) were forced to spend twelve years in exile and a thirteenth year undetected in their home village. Dhritarashtra promised the Pandavas that if they successfully fulfilled this requirement they could return to reclaim their kingdom. When this was successfully accomplished, however, Duryodhana refused to surrender his power. After all attempts at reconciliation and negotiation failed, each side appealed to friends and to political allies for support. The battle lines are thus drawn for a conflict that involved the whole of India. In what follows Krishna gives Arjuna the immortal teachings of the Bhagavad Gita.

The Gita's Story (500–100 BCE)

There are three contexts in which the story of the Bhagavad Gita ("Song of the Lord") must be viewed—that of the Mahabharata as a whole, as already described, that of Sanjaya's point of view, and that of dramatic dialogue itself.

Aside from its historic context, the reader should notice that the Bhagavad Gita is narrated by Sanjaya who retells what he overhears on the battlefield to the blind King Dhirtarashtra. This is made possible by a gift of telesonic hearing granted through the grace of the poet Vyasa. Dhirtarashtra, who originally inherited the kingdom from King Bharata through King Kuru, and who ruled along with his brother Pandu until Pandu died, has asked his charioteer, Sanjaya, to provide a running observation on the fratricidal war between his sons and his nephews. Sanjaya hears the entire conversation and sees, as Arjuna does, the infinite divinity of Krishna facing all sides in the light of a thousand suns. It is Sanjaya who has the final words:

> Wherever Krishna, the Lord of Yoga, is,
> Wherever Arjuna, Prithā's son,
> There is good fortune, victory, success,
> Sound policy assured. This do I believe.[2]

In some ways Sanjaya represents the readers more than Arjuna because he is the one who, as we are, is allowed, to see and hear everything that transpires.

The third context is the dialogue itself between Arjuna, the warrior, and Krishna. Basically, there are three discernible movements in the Gita's story: (1) the opening scene (chapter 1), the context, point of view, and Arjuna's despondency; (2) Krishna's response to Arjuna's despondency (chapters 2–17)—2–4, why fight, 5–6, 8, the yoga of action, 7, 9–11, Krishna's self-revelations, and 12–17, Krishna's teachings; (3) Arjuna's final surrender (chapter 18), the yoga of devotion.

Lord Krishna

Indian paintings of Krishna usually picture him dressed as a prince, with blue skin, onyx-black hair, a flute, and more beautiful than handsome. The word "Krishna" actually means "black" because it is said that he was born at midnight, black as a thundercloud, and because he emanated from the black hair of Lord Vishnu. His blue skin is the blue of sky and ocean, Vishnu's original and mythic associations, and is also the color of Vishnu's incarnation as Ram in the Ramayama.

In an appendix to the Mahabharata, we learn the details of Krishna's childhood and adolescence. Born in the state of Mathura to Vasudeva and Devaki, as a child he miraculously escaped from Kainsa, an evil uncle, was adopted by foster parents, Nanda and Yasoda, and lived in the cowherd village of *Vrndavana* (Vrindabon). As an eternally youthful child, Krishna's activities were graceful and completely spontaneous, if a bit devilish. He became the embodiment of *lila* (the unconditional play of the divine) whether by stealing butter from the kitchen, by defeating a threatening demon or by playing his flute.

Krishna's flute, as scholars have noted, is an extension of his divinity into the physical world, and it compels all who hear him, especially the gopis (cowherdesses), to sport with him in the Vrindabon woods. It is said that once, as a young man, he stole upon a group of gopis bathing in the Ganges. Promptly he collected their sarees, climbed a nearby tree and then sang to the bathers to come for their clothes. Delightedly, the divine lover witnessed their dilemma. On another occasion, on a full-moon night:

> Krsna stood at the edge of a forest near the settlements of the cowherds. With a mischievous smile he put his flute to his lips. The flute's enchanting notes carried afar until they reached the houses of the cowherds where the dutiful wives of the herdsmen were preparing food and attending to the needs of their families. But when they heard the bewitching notes, they were helpless. Beside themselves, they dropped their wifely tasks and hurried into the dusk. At the forest's edge they came upon Krsna. . . . Then he begins the magnificent Maharasha, the rasa dance in its most splendid form. Moving into the great circle of the dance, Krsna multiplies his own form until there is a Krsna at every gopi's side. As the partners whirl on, romantic feeling rises to a crescendo with the place of the music. Every gopi's longing for Krsna is satisfied by his special presence beside her.[3]

The Bhagavata Purana describes the romance of India's ideal couple Krishna and his favorite milkmaid Radha. Her passion for Lord Krishna symbolizes, according to Hindu interpreters, the human soul's intense desire for union with God. As we have already noted, *kama* (pleasure) is one of the four goals of life, one which was to be developed in the Tantric traditions of sexual yoga.

In the Gita Govinda (The Song of the Cowherd), a twelfth century Bengali poem, we read of Radha's bitter rejection of Krishna because of his amorous adventures with the other cowmaids, and of their subsequent, inevitably rapturous reunion:

Krishna and Radha

Radha yields and as the night passes they achieve height upon height of sexual bliss.

Their love play grown great was very delightful, the love play where thrills were a hindrance to firm embraces,

Where their helpless closing of eyes was a hindrance to longing looks at each other, and their secret talk to their drinking of each the other's nectar of lips, and where *the skill of their love was hindered by boundless delight.*[4]

In the Mahabharata, and in the Bhagavad Gita in particular, we find another image, namely Krishna the charioteer who reveals himself as an *avatar*. While the Chandogya Upanishad speaks of Krishna as the son of Devaki, "so far as the teaching of the Bhagavad Gita is concerned, it is immaterial whether Krishna, the teacher, is a historical individual or not."[5] The role assumed by Krishna oscillates between heroic and divine, between Krishna as Arjuna's charioteer and Krishna as the one who says in the Bhagavad Gita:

> I make my dwelling in the hearts of all:
> From Me stem memory, wisdom, refuting [doubt].

Through all the Vedas it is I that should be known,
For the Maker of the Veda's end am I, and I the Vedas know.[6]

The Gita's stress, therefore, is less upon the person of Krishna and more upon the transcendental, cosmic aspect of the great "I am" who manifests his universal form to inspire devotion.

As *avatara* Krishna is distinguished from gurus, masters, holy persons and saints in that from the beginning he is *karma*-free. As the historic Jesus was born without sin and was like humans in all ways except in sin, similarly the legendary Krishna is a direct descendant of God without *karmic* accumulations from past lives. In the Gita Krishna says:

अजोऽपि सन्नव्ययात्मा भूतानामीश्वरोऽपि सन् ।
प्रकृतिं स्वामधिष्ठाय संभवाम्यात्ममायया ॥६॥

यदा यदा हि धर्मस्य ग्लानिर्भवति भारत ।
अभ्युत्थानमधर्मस्य तदात्मानं सृजाम्यहम् ॥७॥

परित्राणाय साधूनां विनाशाय च दुष्कृताम् ।
धर्मसंस्थापनार्थाय संभवामि युगे युगे ॥८॥

Unborn am I, changeless is my Self;
Of [all] contingent beings I am the Lord!
Yet by my creative energy I consort
With Nature—which is mine—and come to be [in time].

For whenever the law of righteousness
Withers away, and lawlessness
   Raises its head
Then do I generate Myself [on earth].

For the protection of the good,
For the destruction of evildoers,
For the setting up of righteousness,
I come into being, age after age.[7]

The purpose of the *avatar's* entry into the human world is to overcome the *adharma* and to inspire humans to become transcendingly actual. In the Gita, for example, when Lord Krishna externally manifests his avataric form, he invites Arjuna to realize that form internally.

Arjuna

The other major character in the story is Arjuna, the warrior, the expert bowsman who heroically guided his brothers through twelve years of forest adventures with his cunning, courage and prowess. As a member of the warrior caste, he had been trained in military tactics, and at the beginning of the Gita is pictured in his chariot, dressed for battle. We recognize a deeper dimension to this image when we recall the chariot-Atman image in the Katha Upanishad:

> Know thou the soul (*atman*) as riding in a chariot,
> The body as the chariot.
> Know thou the intellect (*buddhi*) as the chariot-driver,
> And the mind (*manas*) as the reins.
> The senses, they say, are the horses;
> The objects of sense, what they range over.
> The self combined with senses and mind
> Wise men call 'the enjoyer.'[8]

Traditionally, the chariot represented the house or context of a warrior's military talents, for it was both an offensive and a defensive weapon. In it Arjuna had become one of India's finest bowsmen; in fact, in the early portions of the Mahabharata we read how he dramatically and skillfully defeated a variety of enemies.

But the champion archer and warrior-strategist is also a person of advanced spiritual awareness, for when offered the choice of Krishna or Krishna's army, he selects Krishna as his charioteer.

The story of the intimate conversation between Krishna and Arjuna opens with the despondency of Arjuna who, as S. Radhakrishnan remarks, "typifies the representative human soul seeking to reach perfection and peace. . . ."[9] The ensuing conversation encompasses the difficulties and complexities of Arjuna's questions and Krishna's answers—(2:54, 3:2, 3:36, 4:4, 5:1, 6:33, 6:37, 8:1, 10:12, 11:1, 11:31, 11:46, 12:1, 14:21, 17:1, 18:1). But the last question is Krishna's to Arjuna (18:72): "Have you seen the Light?" Krishna asks, and Arjuna replies: "There is no more doubt!" In this sense the Gita is the story of Arjuna's transformation from doubt, uncertainty and darkness, to assurance, certainty, and light, from a despondent warrior to a confident devotee of Lord Krishna.

Why Fight?

As J.A.B. van Buitenen indicates in his bilingual edition, the beginning of Bhagavad Gita must be read in context of the announcement of Bhisma's death in battle. Bhisma, the supreme commander of Duryodhana's army, was the first casualty. Bhisma was thought to be invincible, and though he opposed Arjuna, he was nonetheless a distant family member. No wonder, when Arjuna looks out over the battlefield, he drops his bow and asks: "Is it worth it? Even if I win, I lose, for victory will be followed by a destruction of the family rituals."

Krishna, in response to Arjuna's seeming conscientious rejection of war, tells Arjuna's that his reluctance to fight should not override his warrior's courage:

> Play not the eunuch, son of Prithā,
>   For this ill beseems thee:
> Give up this vile faint-heartedness,
>   Arise, O scorcher of the foe.[10]

Neither should his faintheartedness affect his awareness that the True Self never dies. Recalling the Upanishads Krishna continues:

> Who thinks that he can be a slayer,
> Who thinks that he is slain,
> Both these have no [right] knowledge:
> He slays not, is not slain.[11]

Nor should Arjuna forget his military and caste duties:

> Likewise consider thine own (caste-)duty
> Then too hast thou no cause to quail;
> For better than a fight prescribed by duty
> Is nothing for a man of the princely class.[12]

But most paramountly, Krishna teaches Arjuna the way of *Karma* yoga:

> Stand fast in Yoga, surrendering attachment;
> In success and failure be the same,
> And then get busy with thy works.
> Yoga means 'sameness' and 'indifference.'[13]

Implicit in these remarks is the realization that fighting, as one's *dharma* prescribes, must be a yogic activity which is therefore performed, not to gather rewards, but to serve God.

When one's heart is set upon action (work) but never on the results of the action (rewards), when action is consecrated and free from attachments to its fruits, when inaction is at the center of all actions, and when actions are done in the name of and for the glory of Lord Krishna, then one's dharmic duty will be done perfectly.

There is no choice between action and inaction, Krishna continues, for even inaction is an activity. The real choice is between acting as a true yogin in harmony with the soul's lamp, or acting selfishly with the mind fixed on rewards, results, evaluations and remunerations. Here the ritual sacrifice of the Vedas, and the self-sacrifice of the Upanishads, become one's everyday work done as a holy sacrifice. "He who performs his work as a sacrifice," Lord Krishna says, "for him the bondage of action is completely dissolved" (4:23).

Krishna's answer to Arjuna's question is profoundly simple: it is not the action itself which binds the actor to *samsara*, but rather the actor's attitude and intention. Actions performed in compliance with one's dharmic duty and without desiring certain outcomes, Krishna says, become instruments of human liberation.

Although Krishna accepts the way of knowledge, and the way of action as viable paths to enlightenment, it is the way of *bhakti,* the yoga of full surrender and loving devotion, that is finally favored. The central teaching of the Gita is that one reaches the Self through selfless, devotional love to the Supreme Lord. "Worship me with unswerving mind" (9:13), Krishna says. "Honor me with devotion" (9:14). "Adore me with pure oneness of soul" (9:22). "Give mind and heart to me in sacrifice and adoration" (18:65).

Krishna's Full Glory

At the core of the drama in chapters seven through eleven, Arjuna, Sanjaya, the old King and the reader are shown Krishna's full glory—His visible forms and invisible spirit; His beginningless and endless "I am":

> I am the rite, the sacrifice . . .

> I am the father of this world,
> Mother, ordainer, grandsire, [all] that need be known;
> Vessel of purity [am I, the sacred syllable] Om;
> And the three Vedas am I too.[14]

It is to this "I am" that Krishna bids Arjuna surrender:

> In all contingent beings the same am I;
> None do I hate and none do I fondly love;
> But those who commune with me in love's devotion
> [Abide] in Me, and I in them.[15]

In the beginning of chapter eleven, Arjuna asks for a vision of the Divine Reality. Since no mortal can behold God, Krishna first grants Arjuna divine sight with which to perceive his divine splendor. Then he appears to Arjuna in his supreme form:

> [A form] with many a mouth and eye
> And countless marvellous aspects;
> Many [indeed] were its divine adornments,
> Many the celestial weapons raised on high.

> Garlands and robes celestial He wore,
> Fragrance divine was his anointing:
> [Behold] this God whose every [mark] spells wonder,
> The infinite, facing every way![16]

Arjuna, struck with amazement, then addresses Lord Krishna:

> Thou art the Imperishable, [thou] wisdom's highest goal,
> Thou, of this universe the last prop and resting-place,
> Thou the changeless, [thou] the guardian of eternal law,
> Thou art the eternal Person; [at last] I understand![17]

Here we have one of the supreme revelations of the divine in all of Hindu sacred literature—the appearance of Krishna's Universal Form. Arjuna, Sanjaya, and the reader/hearer are shown the resplendent, boundless face of Krishna everywhere alive in the whole universe, the light of a thousand suns.

In the final chapter Arjuna asks Krishna the central question—how do I surrender? In response Krishna calls for the sacrifice of mind and heart for Krishna:

> Let him then do all manner of works,
>   Putting his trust in Me;
> For by my grace he will attain
> To an eternal, changeless state.
>
> Give up in thought to Me all that thou dost;
>   Make Me thy goal:
> Relying on the Yoga of the soul,
>   Think on Me constantly.
>
> Thinking on Me thou shalt surmount
>   All dangers by my grace,
> But if through selfishness thou wilt not listen,
>   Then wilt thou [surely] perish.[18]

Arjuna's final remarks indicate that he has been transformed by receiving the transmission of truth from his divine master, for he has seen Krishna's True Self. Arjuna says:

> Destroyed is the confusion; and through thy grace
> I have regained a proper way of thinking
>   With doubts dispelled I stand
>   Ready to do thy bidding.[19]

But it is Sanjaya who has the last words. He testifies that whenever he remembers the holy words and recalls the sacred vision of Krishna, he is filled with joy and faith.

What then of Arjuna's original question? It is important to note that the Gita presents a twofold standard for moral actions: universal (beyond local caste duties) and specific (relative to caste and station in life). If there is a conflict, Krishna instructs Arjuna to perform the specific duty yogically. Thus while Arjuna probably felt that not fighting is the higher principle, Krishna advises him to follow his highest awareness (the undying Atman) and his caste duties.

Since the central idea in the Gita is the truth of Arjuna's relationship to Krishna, it will be helpful as you read through the Gita to follow its development. Note specifically Arjuna's questions and Krishna's answers. As we turn to the text itself we hear again Krishna's words:

> Therefore let Scripture be thy norm,
> Determining what is right and wrong.
> Once thou dost know what the ordinance of Scripture bids thee do,
> Then shouldst thou here perform the works [therein prescribed].[20]

NOTES

1. The phrase "auxiliary scriptures" is used by Swami Prabhavananda in *The Scriptural Heritage of India* (Hollywood, CA.: Vedanta Press, 1963), 79–94.

2. 18:78 in "The Bhagavad-Gita," translated by R.C. Zaehnor in *Hindu Scriptures* (London: J.M. Dent & Sons, 1966). All further references to the Bhagavad Gita are from this text.

3. Quoted in *Religions of Asia* by John Fenton, *et al.* (New York: St. Martin's Press, 1983), 135. There are eighteen major Puranas which appeared from 300–1200 CE though some of its material originated in pre-Vedic times and are noted by the Vedas. Like the Vedas, the Puranas were originally passed on orally from teachers to disciples and were read or chanted in temples to the accompaniment of music. As well, since their theology is told against a backdrop of political, social and sexual events, the Puranas are often dramatized, especially two of the greatest Puranas—the Ramayana and the Mahabharata.

4. Quoted by W.G. Archer in *Loves of Krishna* (New York: Grove Press, n.d.), 82, 83.

5. S. Radhakrishan, translator, *The Bhagavadgita* (New York: Harper & Row, 1948), 28. Unlike a guru or saint, an avatar is a direct manifestation of Vishnu. Krishna is eighth incarnation of Vishnu (Fish, Tortoise, Boar, Man-Lion, Dwarf, Rama with the Axe, and Prince Rama of the Ramayana). It is said that when the *dharma* was overcome by *adharma* (forces which work against the *dharma* as a result of *avidya* and karma), Vishnu took the form of Lord Krishna.

6. 15:15.

7. 4:6–8.

8. Katha Upanishad, 3:3–4.

9. S. Radhakrishnan, *op. cit.*, 51.

10. 2:3.

11. 2:19.

12. 2:31.

13. 2:48.

14. 9:16–17.

15. 9:29.

16. 11:10–11.

17. 11:18.

18. 18:56–58.

19. 18:73.

20. 16:24.

BHAGAVAD GITA JOURNAL EXERCISES

1. To you, what are the essential differences between the Gita and the Upanishads? Do differences in style and genre (philosophical teachings versus epic poetry) have anything to do with differences in meaning? To which do you relate to best and why?
2. Instigate an inner dialogue with Lord Krishna in which you do any or all of the following:
    *   ask about material you do not understand,
    *   ask for further self-revelation as Arjuna did,
    *   challenge, disagree and question Krishna's teachings, and
    *   apply Krishna's teachings to a current issue of topic.
3. Rewrite the beginning and/or the end of the Bhagavad Gita. If you could rewrite either scene how would you recreate it? Would Arjuna still agree with Krishna? Would Krishna use different demonstrations of his truth? Imagine you were writing a screen play for a television special on the Bhagavad Gita. How would you recreate the scene you choose?
4. What are the elements of pure devotion? Are you or have you ever been devoted to anyone or anything? How does this compare with Krishna's teaching—"Be devoted to me." What is your response to Krishna's request for total devotion?
5. The Gita presents three slightly different views of Lord Krishna—Sanjaya's view (the story teller), Arjuna's view (the foil), and Krishna's self-revelation (the hero-avatar). Characterize Krishna from each of these perspectives. Then comment on the differences—are they crucial in any way to the reader's full understanding of the story? Or you may wish to have a direct debate between yourself and Lord Krishna over whether one should fight. Respond specifically to Krishna's reasons for fighting.
6. In chapter four, Krishna gives practical instructions for the practice of yoga—a clean place, a solid seat, concentration, self-purification, mind absorbed in Krishna. "Whoever sits with thoughts absorbed, in Krishna," Krishna says, "rests in me" and "attains me"! What does Krishna mean by this? Is it possible? Could you imagine yourself absorbed in Krishna? What would that be like?
7. Of the Bhagavad Gita Mohandas Gandhi has remarked: "The book struck me as one of priceless worth. This impression has ever since been growing on me with the result that I regard it today as the book *par excellence* for the knowledge of Truth." How do you respond to this statement?

Selections

Selections from the Bhagavad Gita are from chapters 1, 2, 3, 4, 8, 9, 10, 11, 12, 15, 16, and 18 translated by R.C. Zaehner.

I

Dhritarsāshtra said:

§ 1. On the field of justice, the Kuru-field,
My men and the sons of Pāndu too
Stand massed together, intent on war.
What, Sanjaya, did they do?

Sanjaya said:

§ 2. Then did Duryodhana, the king,
Surveying the host of Pāndu's sons
Drawn up in ranks, approach
His teacher (Drona) saying:

§ 3. 'Teacher, behold this mighty host
Of Pāndu's sons
Drawn up by the son of Drupada,
Thine own disciple, wise and skilled.

§ 4. Here are men, brave and mighty archers,
Equals of Bhīma and Arjuna in [the art of] war,—

§ 20. Then (Arjuna,) whose banner is an ape,
(Hanuman),
Gazed upon the serried ranks
Of Dhritarāshtra's sons. The clash of arms
Began. He lifted up his bow.

§ 21. To Krishna then
These words he spake:
'Halt thou my chariot [here]
Between the armies twain,

§ 22. That I may see these men drawn up,
Spoiling for the fight,
[That I may see] with whom I must do battle
In this enterprise of war.

§ 23. I see them [now], intent on strife,
Assembled here;
All eager they to please by waging war
[Old] Dhritarāshtra's baleful son.'

§ 24. Thus Arjuna: and Krishna,
Hearkening to his words,
Brought that splendid chariot to a halt
Between the armies twain.

§ 25. And there in front of them Bhīshma and
Drona stood
And all the [assembled] kings;
And Krishna said: 'Arjuna, behold
These Kurus gathered [here].'

§ 26. And Arjuna beheld
Fathers, grandsires,
Venerable teachers, uncles, brothers, sons,
Grandsons and comrades,

§ 27. Fathers-in-law and friends
Standing there in either host.
And the son of Kuntī, seeing them,
All his kinsmen thus arrayed,

§ 28. Was filled with deep compassion
And, desponding, spake these words:
'Krishna, when these mine own folk I see
Standing [before me], spoiling for the fight,

§ 29. My limbs give way [beneath me],
My mouth dries up, and trembling
Takes hold upon my frame;
My body's hairs stand up [in dread].

§ 30. [My bow,] Gāndīva, slips from my hand,
My very skin is all ablaze;
I cannot stand, my mind
Seems to wander [all distraught].

§ 31. And portents too I see
Boding naught but ill.
Should I strike down in battle mine own folk,
No good therein see I.

§ 32. Krishna, I hanker not for victory,
Nor for the kingdom, nor yet for things of plea-
sure.
What use to us a kingdom, friend,
What use enjoyment or life [itself]?

§ 33. Those for whose sake we covet
Kingdom, delights and things of pleasure,
Here stand they, arrayed for battle,
Surrendering both wealth and life.

§ 34. They are our venerable teachers, fathers,
sons,
They too our grandsires, uncles,
Fathers-in-law, grandsons,
Brothers-in-law, kinsmen all;

§ 35. These would I nowise slay
Though they slay [me], my friend,
Not for dominion over the three [wide] worlds,
How much less for [this paltry] earth.

§ 36. And should we slaughter Dhritarāshtra's
    sons,
Krishna, what sweetness then is ours?
Evil, and only evil, would come to dwell with us,
Should we slay them, hate us as they may.

§ 37. Therefore have we no right to kill
The sons of Dhritarāshtra, our own kinsmen [as
    they are].
Should we lay low our own folk, Krishna,
How could we find any joy?

§ 38. And even if, bereft of sense by greed,
    They cannot see
That to ruin a family is wickedness (*doṣa*)
And to break one's word a crime,

§ 39. How should we not be wise enough
To turn aside from this evil thing?
For the annihilation of a family
We know full well is wickedness.

§ 40. Annihilate a family, and with it
Collapse the eternal laws that rule the family.
Once law's destroyed, then lawlessness
Overwhelms all [we know as] family.

§ 46. O let the sons of Dhritarāshtra, arms in
    hand,
Slay me in battle, though I,
Unarmed myself, will offer no defence;
Therein were greater happiness for me!'

§ 47. So saying Arjuna sat down
Upon the chariot-seat [though] battle [had be-
    gun],
Let slip his bow and arrows,
His mind distraught with grief.

II

Sanjaya said:
§ 1. To him thus in compassion plunged,
His eyes distraught and filled with tears,
[To him] desponding Krishna spake
    These words.

The Blessed Lord said:
§ 2. Whence comes this faintness on thee?
[Now] at this crisis-hour?
This ill beseems a noble, wins none a heavenly
    state,
But brings dishonour, Arjuna.

§ 3. Play not the eunuch, son of Prithā,
    For this ill beseems thee:
Give up this vile faint-heartedness,
Arise, O scorcher of the foe.

Arjuna said:
§ 4. Krishna, how can I in battle
With Bhīshma and Drona fight,
Raining on them my arrows?
For they are worthy of respect.

§ 5. For better were it here on earth to eat a beg-
    gar's food
Than to slay preceptors of great dignity.
Were I to slay here my preceptors, ambitious
    though they may be,
Then should I be partaking of blood-sullied food.

§ 6. Besides we do not know which is the better
    part,
Whether that we should win the victory or that
    they should conquer us.
There facing us stand Dhritarāshtra's sons:
Should we kill them, ourselves would scarce de-
    sire to live.

§ 7. My very being (*svabhāva*) is assailed by
    compassion's harmful taint.
With mind perplexed concerning right and
    wrong (*dharma*) [I turn] to thee and ask:
Which is the better course? Tell me, and [let thy
    words be] definite and clear;
For I am thy disciple: teach me, for all my trust's
    in thee.

§ 8. I cannot see what could dispel
My grief, [this] parching of the senses,—
Not though on earth I were to win an empire,—
Unrivalled, prosperous,—or lordship over the
    gods themselves.

Sanjaya said:
§ 9. So speaking Arjuna, scorcher of the foe,
    To Krishna said:

'I will not fight':
And having spoken held his peace.

§ 10. And Krishna faintly smiled
Between the armies twain,
And spake these words to Arjuna
In his [deep] despondency.

The Blessed Lord said:
§ 11. Thou sorrowest for men who do not need
    thy sorrow,
And speakest words that [in part] are wise.
    Wise men know no sorrow
    For the living or the dead.

§ 12. Never was there a time when I was not,
Nor thou, nor yet these lords of men;
Nor will there be a time when we shall cease to
    be,—
    All of us hereafter.

§ 13. Just as in this body the embodied soul
Must pass through childhood, youth and age,
So too [at death] will he take another body up:
In this a thoughtful man is not perplexed.

§ 14. But contacts with the world outside
Give rise to heat and cold, pleasure and pain:
They come and go, impermanent;
Arjuna, put up with them!

§ 15. For wise men there are,
The same in pleasure as in pain
Whom these [contacts] leave undaunted:
Such are conformed to immortality.

§ 16. Of what *is* not there is no becoming;
Of what is there is no ceasing to be:
For the boundary-line between the two
Is seen by men who see things as they really are.

§ 17. Indestructible [alone] is That,—know
    this,—
By Which this whole [universe] was spun.
No one at all can bring destruction
On This which passes not away.

§ 18. Finite, they say, are these [our] bodies
[Indwelt] by an eternal embodied soul,—
[A soul] indestructible, incommensurable.
    Fight then, O scion of Bharata!

§ 19. Who thinks that he can be a slayer,
Who thinks that he is slain,
Both these have no [right] knowledge:
    He slays not, is not slain.

§ 20. Never is he born nor dies;
Never did he come to be, nor will he ever come
    to be again:
Unborn, eternal, everlasting he—primeval:
He is not slain when the body is slain.

§ 21. If a man knows him as indestructible,
Eternal, unborn, never to pass away,
How and whom can he cause to be slain
    Or slay?

§ 22. As a man casts off his worn-out clothes
And takes on other new ones [in their place],
So does the embodied soul cast off his worn-out
    bodies
    And enters others new.

§ 23. He cannot be cut by sword,
    Nor burnt by fire;
The waters cannot wet him,
Nor the wind dry him up.

§ 24. Uncuttable, unburnable,
    Unwettable, undryable
Is he,—eternal, roving everywhere,
Firm-set, unmoving, everlasting.

§ 25. Unmanifest, unthinkable,
Unchanging is he called:
So realize that he is thus
And put away thy useless grief.

§ 26. And even if thou thinkst that he
Is constantly [re-]born and constantly [re-]dies,
Even so, [my] strong-armed [friend],
Thou lamentest him in vain.

§ 27. For sure is the death of all that comes to
    birth,
Sure the birth of all that dies.
So in a matter that no one can prevent
Thou hast no cause to grieve.

§ 28. Unmanifest are the beginnings of contin-
    gent beings,
    Manifest their middle course,
Unmanifest again their ends:
What cause for mourning here?

§ 29. By a rare privilege may someone behold
     him,
And by a rare privilege indeed may another tell
     of him,
And by a rare privilege may such another hear
     him,
Yet even having heard there's none that knows
     him.

§ 30. Never can this embodied soul be slain
In the body of anyone [at all].
And so for no contingent being
Hast thou any cause for sorrow.

§ 31. Likewise consider thine own (caste-)duty
     (*dharma*),
Then too hast thou no cause to quail;
For better than a fight prescribed by duty
Is nothing for a man of the princely class.

§ 32. Happy the warriors indeed
Who become involved in war,—
[A war] like this presented by pure chance
And opening the gates of paradise!

§ 33. But if thou wilt not wage this war
     Prescribed by thy (caste-)duty,
Then, by casting off both honour and (caste-)
     duty,
Thou wilt bring evil on thyself.

§ 34. Yes, this thy dishonour will become a by-
     word
In the mouths of men in ages yet to come;
And dishonour in a man well-trained to honour
[Is an ill] surpassing death.

§ 35. 'From fear he fled the battlefield,'—
So will they think, the mighty charioteers.
Greatly esteemed by them before,
Thou wilt bring upon thyself contempt.

§ 36. Many a word that is better left unsaid
Will such men say as wish thee ill,
     Disputing thy competence.
What could cause thee greater pain than this?

§ 37. If thou art slain, thou winnest paradise;
And if thou gain the victory, thine the earth to
     enjoy.
     Arise, then, son of Kuntī,
     Resolved to fight the fight.

§ 38. [First learn to] treat pleasure and pain as
     things equivalent,
Then profit and loss, victory and defeat;
     Then gird thyself for battle.
Thus wilt thou bring no evil on thyself.

§ 39. This wisdom (*buddhi*) has been revealed
     to thee in theory (*sākhya*);
Listen now to how it should be practised (*yoga*):
If by this wisdom thou art exercised (*yukta*),
Thou wilt put off the bondage inherent in [all]
     works (*karma*).

§ 47. Work alone is thy proper business,
Never the fruits [it may produce];
Let not your motive be the fruit of work,
Nor your attachment to [mere] worklessness
     (*akarma*).

§ 48. Stand fast in Yoga, surrendering attach-
     ment;
In success and failure be the same,
And then get busy with thy works.
Yoga means 'sameness' and 'indifference' (*sa-
matva*).

§ 49. For lower far is the [path of] active work
     [for its own sake]
     Than the Yoga of the soul (*buddhi*).
     Seek refuge in the soul!
[How] pitiful are they whose motive is the fruit
     [of works]!

§ 50. Whoso is integrated by [the Yoga of] the
     soul
Discards both good and evil works:
Brace thyself (*yuj-*) then for [this] Yoga!
Yoga is skill in [performing] works.

§ 51. For those wise men who are integrated by
     [the Yoga of] the soul,
Who have renounced the fruit that's born of
     works,
These will be freed from the bondage of [re-
     birth]
And fare on to that region that knows no ill.

§ 52. When thy soul shall pass beyond
Delusion's turbid quicksands,
Then wilt thou learn disgust

For what has been heard (The Vedas)
And for what may yet be heard.

§ 53. When once thy soul, by Scripture (*śruti*)
  once bewildered,
  Stands motionless and still,
  Immovable in ecstasy,
Then shalt thou win [the prize which is] Yoga,
  [integration].

IV

The Blessed Lord said:
§ 1. This changeless way of life (*yoga*) did I
To Vivasvat [once] proclaim;
To Manu Vivasvat told it,
And Manu to Ikshvāku passed it on.

§ 2. Thus was the tradition from one to another
  handed on,
The Royal Seers came to know it;
[But] in the long course of time
  The way of life (*yoga*) on earth was lost.

§ 3. This is the same primeval way of life (*yoga*)
  That I preach to thee today;
For thou art loyal, devoted (*bhakta*), and my
  comrade,
  And this is the highest mystery.

Arjuna said:
§ 4. Later thy birth,
  Earlier Vivasvat's:
How should I understand thy words,
That in the beginning thou didst proclaim it?

The Blessed Lord said:
§ 5. Many a birth have I passed through,
And [many a birth] hast thou:
  I know them all,
  Thou knowest not.

§ 6. Unborn am I, changeless is my Self;
Of [all] contingent beings I am the Lord!
Yet by my creative energy (*māyā*) I consort
With Nature—which is mine—and come to be
  [in time].

§ 7. For whenever the law of righteousness
  (*dharma*)
Withers away, and lawlessness (*adharma*)

Raises its head
Then do I generate Myself [on earth].

§ 8. For the protection of the good,
For the destruction of evildoers,
For the setting up of righteousness,
I come into being, age after age.

§ 9. Who knows my godly birth and mode of op-
  eration (*karma*)
  Thus as they really are,
He, his body left behind, is never born again:
  He comes to Me.

§ 10. Many are they who, passion, fear and an-
  ger spent,
Inhere in Me, making Me their sanctuary:
Made pure by wisdom and hard penances
They come [to share in] the manner of my being.

§ 11. In whatsoever way [devoted] men ap-
  proach Me,
In that same way do I return their love (*bhaj-*).
Whatever their occupation and wherever they
  may be,
  Men follow the path I trace.

§ 12. Desiring success in their (ritual) acts
  (*karma*),
  Men worship here the gods;
For swiftly in the world of men
Comes success, engendered by the act [itself].

§ 13. The four-caste system did I generate
With categories of 'constituents' and works;
Of this I am the doer, know thou this:—
And yet I am the Changeless One
Who does not do [or act].

§ 14. Works can never affect Me.
I have no yearning for their fruits.
Whoso should know that this is how I am
Escapes the bondage [forged] by works.

§ 15. This knowing, the ancients too did work,
Though seeking [all the while] release [from
  temporal life]:
  So do thou work [and act]
As the ancients did in the days of old.

§ 16. What is work? What worklessness?
Herein even sages are perplexed.

So shall I preach to thee concerning work;
And once thou hast understood my words,
From ill thou'lt win release.

§ 17. For a man must understand
[The nature] of work, of work ill-done,
   And worklessness, [all three]:
Profound, [hard to unravel,] are the ways of
   work!

§ 18. The man who sees worklessness in work
   [itself],
   And work in worklessness,
   Is wise among his fellows,
Integrated (*yukta*), performing every work.

§ 19. When all a man's emprises
Have neither motive nor desire [for fruit],—
His works burnt up in wisdom's fire,—
Then wise men call him learned.

§ 20. When he's cast off [all] attachment to the
   fruit of works,
   Ever content, on none dependent,
Though he embark on work [himself],
In fact he does no work at all.

§ 21. Nothing hoping, his thought and mind
   (*ātman*) restrained,
   Giving up all possessions,
He only does such work
As is needed for the body's maintenance,
   And so avoids defilement.

§ 22. Content to take whatever chance may
   bring his way,
Surmounting all dualities (*dvandva*), knowing
   no envy,
The same in failure and success,
Though working [still], he is not bound.

§ 23. Attachments gone, deliverance won,
His thoughts are fixed on wisdom:
He works for sacrifice [alone],
And all the work [he ever did]
Entirely melts away.

§ 24. The offering is Brahman, Brahman the
   sacrificial ghee
Offered by Brahman in Brahman's fire:
Who fixes all his thought (*samādhi*) on this sacrificial rite (*karma*)

[Indwelt by] Brahman, to Brahman must he go.

§ 25. Some Yogins offer sacrifice
To the gods as their sole object,
In the fire of Brahman others
Offer sacrifice as sacrifice
[Which has merit in itself].

§ 26. Yet others offer the senses,—hearing and
   the rest,—
   In the fires of self-restraint;
Others the senses' proper objects,—sounds and
   the like,—
   In the fires of the senses.

§ 27. And others offer up all works of sense,
All works of vital breath,
In the fire of the practice (*yoga*) of self-control
   By wisdom kindled.

§ 28. Some offer up their wealth, some their
   hard penances,
Some spiritual exercise (*yoga*), and some again
Make study and knowledge [of Scripture] their
   sacrifice,—
Religious men whose vows are strict.

§ 29. Some offer the inward breath in the out-
   ward,
Likewise the outward in the inward,
   Checking the flow of both,
   On breath control intent.

§ 30. Others restrict their food
And offer up breaths in breaths.
All these know the [meaning of] sacrifice,
For by sacrifice all their defilements are made
   away.

§ 31. Eating the leavings of the sacrifice,
The food of immortality,
   They come to eternal Brahman.
This world is not for him who performs no sac-
   rifice,—
   Much less another [world].

§ 32. So, many and various are the sacrifices
Spread out athwart the mouth of Brahman.
They spring from work, all of them; be sure of
   this,
[For] once thou knowest this, thy deliverance is
   sure.

VIII

Arjuna said:

§ 1. What is That Brahman? What that which
    appertains to self?
[And] what, O best of men, are works (*karma*)?
What is that called which appertains to contin-
    gent beings?
What that which appertains to the divine?

§ 2. Who and in what manner is he
Who appertains to the sacrifice here in this
    body?
And how, at the time of passing on,
Mayst thou be known by men of self-restraint?

The Blessed Lord said:

§ 3. The Imperishable is Brahman, the All-
    Highest,
Nature (*svabhāva*), they say, is what appertains
    to self:
Creative force (*visarga*) is known as 'works'
    (*karma*),
For it gives rise to the [separate] natures of con-
    tingent beings.

§ 4. To contingent beings a perishable nature
    appertains,
    To the divine [pure] spirit (*puruṣa*);
But it is I myself who appertain to the sacrifice
Here in this body, O best of men who bodies
    bear.

§ 5. Whoso at the hour of death,
Abandoning his mortal frame,
Bears Me in mind and passes on,
Accedes to my Divinity (*mad-bhāva*): have no
    doubt of that.

§ 6. Whatever state (*bhāva*) a man may bear in
    mind
When the time comes at last to cast the mortal
    frame aside,
    Even to that state does he accede,
For ever does that state of being make him grow
    into itself (*tad-bhāva-bhāvita*).

§ 7. Then muse upon Me always,
    And go to war;
For if thou fixest mind and soul (*buddhi*) on Me,
    To Me shalt thou most surely come.

IX

The Blessed Lord said:

§ 1. But most secret and mysterious
Is the teaching I will [now] reveal,—
[A teaching] based on Holy Writ, consonant with
    experience:
To thee [will I proclaim it,] for in thee there is no
    envy;
And knowing it, thou shalt be freed from ill.

§ 2. Science of kings, mystery of kings
Is this,—distilling the purest essence,
To the understanding evident, with righteous-
    ness enhanced,
How easy to carry out! [Yet] it abides forever.

§ 3. Men who put no faith
In this law of righteousness (*dharma*),
Fail to reach Me and must return
To the road of recurring death.

§ 4. By Me, Unmanifest in form,
This whole universe was spun:
In Me subsist all beings,
I do not subsist in them.

§ 5. And [yet] contingent beings do not subsist
    in Me,—
Behold my sovereign power (*yoga*)!
My Self sustains [all] beings, it does not subsist
    in them;
    It causes them to be.

§ 6. As in [wide] space subsists the mighty
    wind,
    Blowing [at will] ever and everywhere,
So too do all contingent beings
Subsist in Me: so must thou understand.

§ 7. All contingent beings pass
Into material Nature which is Mine
When an aeon comes to an end; and then again
When another aeon starts, I emanate them forth.

§ 8. Firm-fixed in my material Nature
    Ever again I emanate
This whole mighty host of beings,
Powerless themselves,—from Nature comes the
    power.

§ 9. These works of mine

Bind Me not limit Me:
As one indifferent I sit
Among these works, detached.

§ 16. I am the rite, the sacrifice,
The offering for the dead, the healing herb;
I am the sacred formula, the sacred butter am I,
I am the fire, and I the oblation [offered in the
fire].

§ 17. I am the father of this world,
Mother, ordainer, grandsire, [all] that need be
known;
Vessel of purity [am I, the sacred syllable] Om;
And the three Vedas am I too.

§ 18. [I am] the Way, sustainer, Lord and wit-
ness,
[True] home and refuge, friend,—
Origin and dissolution and the stable state be-
tween,—
A treasure-house, the seed that passes not away.

§ 19. It is I who pour out heat, hold back
The rain and send it forth;
Death am I and deathlessness,
What is not and that which is.

§ 34. On Me thy mind, for Me thy loving service
(*bhakta*),
For Me thy sacrifice, and to Me be thy prostra-
tions:
Let [thine own] self be integrated, and then
Shalt thou come to Me, thy striving bent on Me.

XI

Arjuna said:
§ 1. Out of thy gracious favour to me Thou
Hast uttered the all-highest mystery
Called 'what appertains to Self',
And by that word [of thine] banished is my per-
plexity.

§ 2. For I have heard of the coming-to-be
And passing away of contingent beings;
[This hast Thou told me] in detail full,
As well as the majesty of [thine own] Self which
passes not away.

§ 3. Even as Thou hast described [thy] Self to
be,
So must it be, O Lord Most High;
[But] fain would I *see* the [bodily] form
Of Thee as Lord, All-Highest Person.

§ 4. If, Lord, Thou thinkest that I can
Thus see Thee, then show Thou forth,
Lord of creative power (*yoga*),
[This] Self that passes not away.

The Blessed Lord said:
§ 5. Son of Prithā, behold my forms
In their hundreds and their thousands;
How various are they, how divine,
How many-hued and multiform!

§ 6. Ādityas, Rudras, Vasus, the Aśvins twain,
The Maruts too—behold them!
Marvels never seen before,—how many!
Arjuna, behold them!

§ 7. Do thou today this whole universe behold
Centred here in One, with all that it contains
Of moving and unmoving things;
[Behold] it in my body,
And whatsoever else thou fain wouldst see.

§ 8. But never canst thou see Me
With this thy [natural] eye.
A celestial eye I'll give thee:
Behold my creative power (*yoga*) as Lord!

Sanjaya said:
§ 9. So saying Hari,
The great Lord of Yogic power,
Revealed to the son of Prithā
His all-highest sovereign form,—

§ 10. [A form] with many a mouth and eye
And countless marvellous aspects;
Many [indeed] were its divine adornments,
Many the celestial weapons raised on high.

§ 11. Garlands and robes celestial He wore,
Fragrance divine was his anointing:
[Behold] this God whose every [mark] spells
wonder,
The infinite, facing every way!

§ 12. If in [bright] heaven together should arise
The shining brilliance of a thousand suns,

Then would that [perhaps] resemble
The brilliance of that God so great of Self.

§ 13. Then did the son of Pāndu see
The whole [wide] universe in One converged,
There in the body of the God of gods,
Yet divided out in multiplicity.

§ 14. Then filled with amazement Arjuna,
His hair on end, hands joined in reverent greet-
     ing,
Bowing his head before the God,
     [These words] spake out:

     Arjuna said:
§ 15. O God, the gods in thy body I behold,
And all the hosts of every kind of being;
Brahmā, the Lord [I see], throned on the lotus-
     seat,
Celestial serpents and all the [ancient] seers.

§ 16. Arms, bellies, mouths and eyes all mani-
     fold—
So do I see Thee wherever I may look,—infinite
     thy form.
End, middle or beginning in Thee I cannot see,
O Monarch Universal, [manifest] in every form.

§ 17. Thine the crown, the mace, the discus,—
A mass of glory shining on all sides,
So do I see Thee,—yet how hard art Thou to
     see,—for on every side,
There's brilliant light of blazing fire and sun. O,
     who should comprehend it?

§ 18. Thou art the Imperishable, [thou] wis-
     dom's highest goal,
Thou, of this universe the last prop and resting-
     place,
Thou the changeless, [thou] the guardian of
     eternal law (dharma),
Thou art the eternal Person; [at last] I under-
     stand!

§ 19. Beginning, middle, end Thou knowest
     not,—how infinite thy strength!
How numberless thine arms,—thine eyes the
     sun and moon!
So do I see Thee,—thy mouth a flaming fire
Burning up this whole [universe] with its blaz-
     ing glory.

     Arjuna said:
§ 51. Now that I see [again] thy human form,
     Friendly and kind,
I have returned to my senses
And regained my normal state.

     The Blessed Lord said:
§ 52. Right hard to see is this my form
     Which thou has seen:
This is the form the gods themselves
     Forever crave to see.

§ 53. Not by the Vedas or grim ascetic practice,
Not by the giving of alms or sacrifice
Can I be seen in such a form
     As thou didst see Me.

§ 54. But by worship of love (bhakti) addressed
     to Me alone
Can I be known and seen
In such a form and as I really am:
[So can my lovers] enter into Me.

§ 55. Do works for Me, make Me thy highest
     goal,
Be loyal in love (bhakta) to Me,
Cast off [all other] attachments,
Have no hatred for any being at all:
For all who do thus shall come to Me.

XV

     The Blessed Lord said:
§ 1. With roots above and boughs beneath,
They say, the undying fig tree [stands]:
Its leaves are the [Vedic] hymns:
     Who knows it, knows the Veda.

§ 2. Below, above, its branches straggle out,
Well nourished by the constituents; sense-ob-
     jects are its twigs.
Below, its roots proliferate
Inseparably linked with works in the world of
     men.

§ 3. No form of it can here be comprehended,
No end and no beginning, no sure abiding-place:
This fig tree with its roots so fatly nourished—
[Take] the stout axe of detachment and cut it
     down!

§ 4. And then search out that [high] estate
To which, when once men go, they come not
　　back again.
I fly for succour to that Primeval Person
'From whom flowed forth primordial creativity
　　(*pravṛtti*).'

§ 5. Not proud, not fooled, [all] taint of attach-
　　ment crushed,
Ever abiding in what concerns the self, desire
　　suppressed,
Released from [all] dualities made known in
　　pleasure as in pain,
The undeluded march ahead to that state which
　　knows no change.

§ 6. That [state] is not illuminated
　　By sun or moon or fire:
Once men go thither, they come not back again,
For that is my all-highest home (*dhāma*).

XVIII

Arjuna said:
§ 1. Krishna, fain would I hear the truth
　　Concerning renunciation,
　　And apart from this
[The truth] of self-surrender.

The Blessed Lord said:
§ 2. To give up works dictated by desire,
Wise men allow this to be renunciation;
Surrender of all the fruits [that accrue] to works
Discerning men call self-surrender.

§ 3. '[All] works must be surrendered, [for works
　　themselves are] tainted with defect':
　　So say some of the wise;
But others say that works of sacrifice, the gift of
　　alms
And works of penance are not to be surrendered.

§ 4. Hear then mine own decision
In [this matter of] surrender:
Threefold is [the act of] self-surrender;
　　So has it been declared.

§ 5. Works of sacrifice, the gift of alms and
　　works of penance
Are not to be surrendered; these must most cer-
　　tainly be done;

It is sacrifice, alms-giving and ascetic practice
　　That purify the wise.

§ 6. But even those works should be done [in a
　　spirit of self-surrender],
For [all] attachment to what you do and [all] the
　　fruits [of what you do]
　　Must be surrendered.
This is my last decisive word.

§ 55. By love and loyalty he comes to know Me
　　as I really am,
　　How great I am and who;
And once he knows Me as I am,
　　He enters [Me] forthwith.

§ 56. Let him then do all manner of works,
　　Putting his trust in Me;
For by my grace he will attain
To an eternal, changeless state (*pada*).

§ 57. Give up in thought to Me all that thou dost;
　　Make Me thy goal:
Relying on the Yoga of the soul (*buddhi*),
　　Think on Me constantly.

§ 58. Thinking on Me thou shalt surmount
　　All dangers by my grace,
But if through selfishness thou wilt not listen,
　　Then wilt thou [surely] perish.

§ 59. [But] if thou shouldst think, relying on
　　thine ego,
　　'I will not fight,'
Vain is thy resolution,
[For] Nature will constrain thee.

§ 64. And now again give ear to this my all-high-
　　est Word,
　　Of all the most mysterious:
　　'I love thee well.'
Therefore will I tell thee thy salvation (*hita*).

§ 65. Bear Me in mind, love Me and worship Me
　　(*bhakta*),
Sacrifice, prostrate thyself to Me:
So shalt thou come to Me, I promise thee
Truly, for thou art dear to Me.

§ 66. Give up all things of law (*dharma*),
Turn to Me, thine only refuge,
[For] I will deliver thee

From all evils; have no care.

§ 67. Never must thou tell this [Word] to one
Whose life is not austere, to one devoid of love
    and loyalty (*bhakta*),
To one who refuses to obey,
Or one who envies Me.

§ 68. [But] whoever shall proclaim this all-high-
    est mystery
    To my loving devotees (*bhakta*),
Showing the while the highest love and loyalty
    (*bhakti*) to Me,
    Shall come to Me in very truth.

§ 69. No one among men can render Me
More pleasing service than a man like this;
Nor shall any other man on earth
Be more beloved of Me than he.

§ 70. And whoso shall read this dialogue
Which I and thou have held concerning what is
    right (*dharmya*),
It will be as if he had offered Me a sacrifice
Of wisdom: so do I believe.

§ 71. And the man of faith, not cavilling,
Who listens [to this my Word],—
He too shall win deliverance, and attain
To the goodly worlds of those whose works are
    pure.

§ 72. Hast thou listened, Arjuna, [to these my
    words]
With mind on them alone intent?
And has the confusion [of thy mind]
That stemmed from ignorance, been dispelled?

    Arjuna said:
§ 73. Destroyed is the confusion; and through
    thy grace
I have regained a proper way of thinking (*smrti*):
    With doubts dispelled I stand
    Ready to do thy bidding.

    Sanjaya said:
§ 74. So did I hear this wondrous dialogue
    Of [Krishna,] Vasudeva's son
    And the high-souled Arjuna,
[And as I listened,] I shuddered with delight.

§ 75. By Vyāsa's favour have I heard

This highest mystery,
This Yoga from [great] Krishna, Yoga's Lord
    himself,
    As he in person told it.

§ 76. O king, as oft as I recall
This marvellous, holy dialogue
    Of Arjuna and Krishna
I thrill with joy, and thrill with joy again!

§ 77. And as often as I recall that form of
    Vishnu—
    Utterly marvellous—
    How great is my amazement!
I thrill with joy, and thrill with joy again!

§ 78. Wherever Krishna, the Lord of Yoga, is,
    Wherever Arjuna, Pritha's son,
There is good fortune, victory, success,
Sound policy assured. This do I believe.

Chapter 4   THE TRACELESS BUDDHA

By the early sixth century BCE during Buddha's lifetime, India was in the process of rapid cultural developments: from tribal governments to political empires, from village economies to commercial cities, from simple caste definitions of social roles to the emergence of new social classes based on wealth, and from an unquestioned acceptance of Vedic and early Upanishadic sacrifical rites to a latter Upanishadic emphasis on the power of meditational thinking.

Independent groups of homeless, celibate wanderers, who begged for food and lived in the forests, formed small, *ad hoc* communities around inspired teachers who emerged equal in importance with the Vedic priests and the Upanishadic sages. Called *shamanas* (ascetics) or *bhikshus* (almsmen), they were teachers who abandoned family life and wandered from village to village, not worshiping local deities, but accumulating spiritual merit and practicing spiritual virtues. Old *karma*, it was believed, could be eliminated through austerity and the intensification of spiritual practices in this life. One such homeless "striver" was Siddhartha.

Buddha's Life Story (563–483 BCE)

Siddhartha (surname) Gautama (family name) was born into the Sakya Tribe, raised a prince in the northern Indian Himalayan foothills (now Nepal), and became known as *Buddha* (the awakened), *Tathagata* (the Traceless one) and Sakyamuni (sage of the Sakya clan).[1] The extant sources of Buddha's life were composed hundreds of years after his death and therefore provide a legendary history which weaves myth and dramatic imagination together with remembered historic facts.

Buddha's life had no beginning. Eons ago, according to the legends, Buddha, who lived then in another form, took a vow to attain Buddhahood. The *Jataka Tales* (birth-stories) tell of some of Buddha's former lives (as bird, animal and man). They include for instance the story of Buddha's compassionate self-sacrifice to a lion and its cub who were too weak to catch their own food. When he saw that they were also too weak to consume him, he pierced his own throat with a sharp piece of bamboo to arouse them with the scent of his blood.

According to Buddhist tradition, Buddha's earthly mother, Maya, King Shuddhodhana's first wife, dreamed that she was carried away to the Himalayas where "a beautiful white elephant (symbol of perfect wisdom), bearing in his trunk a white lotus flower, approached from the North, and seemed to touch her right side and to enter her womb."[2] When she gave birth, the newborn child named Siddhartha (He who has achieved his goal) stood, surveyed the four quarters, and spoke these words:

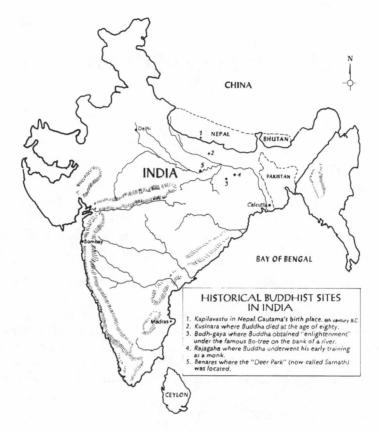

For enlightenment I was born, for the good of all that lives. This is the last time that I have been born into this world of becoming.[3]

After his birth in the Lumbini Grove near India's northern border of Nepal, Siddhartha was taken to his parents' palace. His horoscope determined that he was to be a "universal monarch," and that he would leave his family in the process. In order to protect the young heir, his father provided him with three palaces (one for each of the three seasons—hot, cold, rainy) and four pleasure parks. All his needs and desires were attended to and he was married at a young age to Yasadhara by whom he had a son Rahula. Biographical accounts elaborate upon the comfort and luxury of his princely existence; suffice it to say that here Siddhartha had everything he wanted.

The Great Renunciation

The legend continues that, despite the protective screening constructed around him, Siddhartha experienced, while with his charioteer Channa, what are called the "four passing sights"—old age, sickness, death, and a wandering ascetic.

One day while riding in his chariot, he saw a toothless, arthritic, wrinkled old person, too feeble to care about life; one day he saw a feverish, vomiting, diseased person, most likely a leper, whose skin was a continuous open wound; one day he saw a dead body being carried on a platform to be burned. Seeing sickness, old age and death for the first time raised questions in his mind which the teachings of his family did not answer to his satisfaction.

When he saw the procession to a funeral pyre, he turned to his charioteer, as he had in the past, and asked about the ritual. "That is death, Sire!" the charioteer said. "Do all humans face death?" Siddhartha replied. "All of us die, sire!" At this moment, and in later moments of reflection, Siddhartha for the first time faced the certainty of his own mortality. Realizing this led him to a logical question—if I am going to die, what does that say about the purpose of my life and about how I should live?

A fourth time with his charioteer, Siddhartha saw a wandering ascetic and asked: "Who is that man of calm temper?" "He is a Bhikkhu (a religious beggar who has abandoned all longings and who lives without passion or envy)," his charioteer answers. At that moment, Siddhartha realized that if he could not avoid old age, sickness and death, he could at least strive to overcome another rebirth.

Ready then to pursue the homeless life, he arose one night and announced to his charioteer that he was resolved to renounce his homelife and to seek truth. After taking one last look at his wife and sleeping son, he gave his clothing to his servant, put on mendicant robes, cut off his long hair and beard and departed into the woods. Like Stephen Daedelus in James Joyce's *Portrait of the Artist as a Young Man,* who left family, home, country and religion, Siddhartha at the age of twenty-nine began searching for a truth that would free him from all doubts and anxieties.

The Six-Year Search

The story continues that Siddhartha first sought teachers and practitioners of meditation throughout northeastern India. Various yogins taught him successive stages of ecstatic meditation leading to the attainment of the state called "nothing at all." While Gautauma soon mastered this yoga, it gave him no resolution to the questions of old age, sickness and death. Then he took to heart wholeheartedly the wisdom of "neither conception nor non-conception" which involved contemplation upon colored shapes (*rupa*) until they became transparent. Siddhartha was thereby able to escape the limits of his body, and to abide in an ecstasy which was neither attainment nor non-attainment. But this too left him unsatisfied.

Next he tried austerities—fasting, breath-control, self-induced trances—but these left him too weak to walk (like the lion in the *Jataka Tales*). Finally, a *gopi* (milk maiden), seeing Siddhartha so thin that his belly almost touched his spine, so emaciated that his remaining hair fell out and his skin turned yellow, nourished him back to strength. "What good are all my austerities," Siddhartha realized, "if I die before resolving the questions which led me to search in the first place?" Upon regaining his health, he gathered strands of Kusha grass, sat under a *Bodhi* (Banyan) Tree and resolved not to leave his seat until he attained enlightenment.

The Supreme Enlightenment

That night, continues the legend, Mara (the Tempter), the Evil One, along with all Mara's hosts attacked the Prince. Like Jesus in the desert after his baptism, Siddhartha experienced three temptations, or what might be called neurotic upheavals—an army of frightening demons, Mara's own magical power, and lastly the seductive advance of Mara's three daughters. Able to brush aside each attack, Siddhartha turned Mara's missiles into a rain of heavenly flowers and called upon the earth to witness a superior merit. To the sexual temptation Siddhartha answered:

> Pleasure is brief as a flash of lightning
> Or like an Autumn shower, only for a moment. . . .
> I seek the highest praise, hard to attain by men—
> The true and constant wisdom of the wise.[4]

That same evening, under a calm, full moon, Siddhartha passed through four meditative stages: detachment from objects and desires, non-reasoning concentration, dispassionate mindfulness (concentrated consciousness), and peaceful awareness. According to traditional accounts, his victory was achieved in four watches of a full-moon night in which he achieved knowledge of former existences, of his own previous lives just as they had been in the first watch (early evening), the Omniscient Eye in which all the universal diseases and rebirths were mirrored to him in the second watch (midnight), knowledge of the chain of causation and the Four Holy Truths in the third watch (early morning), and, in the fourth, when the sun first appeared, the imperishable state.

As the new day broke with light flooding the moon-filled darkness, Siddhartha awoke to Buddha, saw Buddha, realized Buddha, became Buddha! A spontaneous hymn of victory arose in him:

> Looking for the maker of this tabernacle, I shall have to run through a course of many births, so long as I do not find (him); and painful is birth again and again. But now, maker of the tabernacle, thou hast been seen; thou shalt not make up this tabernacle again. All thy rafters are broken, thy ridge-pole is sundered; the mind, approaching the Eternal (nirvâna), has attained to the extinction of all desires.[5]

According to the traditional story the whole universe was illumined, rain and blossoms fell from the heavens, and even the sages in heaven, recognizing the supremacy of his enlightenment, bowed to him.

Dying to his desires, he died to himself dying to himself, Siddhartha was reborn Buddha. He realized that the builder of his house is none other than himself, and that he alone therefore determines the effects of his *karma*. He realized that there is no God, no *Brahman*, no Self (*Atman*), nothing outside himself and at the same time that he is empty (*anatta*) of all

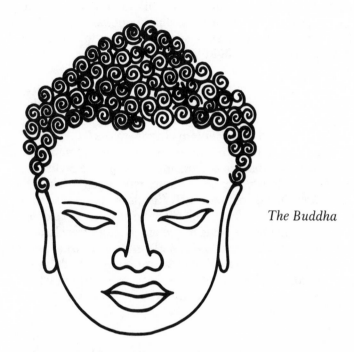

The Buddha

sense of self. It was as if when he awoke he saw things as they are without any egocentric interpretation standing between the seer and reality and thus gained the highest peace.

Gautama Buddha remained at the spot of his awakening for the next forty-nine days realizing the bliss of *nirvana* and meditating upon whether to teach or to remain silent. His initial silence indicates that Buddha was aware that (1) there's nothing to teach, (2) there's no teacher, and (3) there's no one to teach. Compassionately, he realized that whether he spoke or not he would still be communicating the truth of his awakening. Thus to spur his followers to find their own truth, Sakyamuni decided to actively promulgate the *dharma*.

The Awakened Teacher

The best way to begin to answer the question "Who is the real Buddha?" is to reflect upon his awakening experience and to examine his teachings. Focus for a minute on the illustrated face of Buddha. His eyes are half closed, awake and gazing without focus. His mouth is loosely closed and there is the faintest trace of a smile on his lips. The meditative control of his face expresses the alert stillness of his whole body. He speaks without words. Herman Hesse describes this aspect of the Buddha poetically:

He seemed to be smiling gently inwardly. With a secret smile, not unlike that of a healthy child, he walked along, peacefully, quietly. He wore his gown and walked along exactly like the other monks, but his face and his step, his peaceful downward glance, his peaceful downward-handling hand, and every finger of his hand spoke of peace, spoke of completeness, sought nothing, imitated nothing, reflected a continual quiet, an unfading light, an invulnerable peace.[6]

As we have mentioned, Siddhartha is called *Tathagata,* the traceless one, the one who teaches merely by the way he comes and the way he goes. It would be difficult to understand fully the significance of *Tathagata* without realizing that Buddha is simultaneously three bodies: the historic Siddhartha Gautama born into the Sakya republic in northern India, the ultimate Buddha-nature prior to Siddhartha, hidden and manifested within all beings, and the one who is both the historic person and the supreme reality.

Tathagata is Buddha's incarnate nature who, upon awakening, becomes peaceful, undetermined by *karma* and spontaneously traceless. As we read in the Buddhist sacred texts, the Tathagata's path cannot be traced since he soars in the sky of liberation; this path is as difficult to trace as that of the birds in the air. Though traceless, Buddha described himself as a teacher (or one could say as a teacherless teacher) who has conquered all, and who is free within all conditions of life. "Having learnt myself," Buddha says, "to whom shall I point as teacher?"[7] Buddha is the one who has discovered himself what to teach, who *is* what he teaches and who is one with what is taught.

The Middle Way

After his awakening under the Bodhi Tree in Bod-Gaya, Buddha traveled to what is now called Sarnath, north of Benares, 130 miles west of Bod-Gaya, where he gave his first sermon at Deer Park. Here Buddha addressed five monks, among others, who had at one time studied with him.

> There are two extremes which he who has gone forth ought not to follow—habitual *devotion* on the one hand to the *passions,* to the pleasures of sensual things, a low and pagan way of seeking satisfaction, ignoble, unprofitable, fit only for the worldly-minded; and habitual devotion, on the other hand, to *self-mortification,* which is painful, ignoble, unprofitable. There is a *Middle Path* discovered by the Tathagatha—a path which opens the eyes, and bestows understanding, which leads to peace, to insight, to the higher wisdom, to Nirvana.[8]

While this may be interpreted as controlled moderation (as if rolling a bowling ball down the center of the alley), there is a more radical way to understand it, namely that the path of self-annihilation *is* at the same time the path of self-indulgence, each of which is to be transcended. In this view there are no extremes.

The deepest unlocking of the Middle Way is to recall the awakening experience which reveals that all ways are empty, including the Middle Way itself. Buddha's Middle Way teaches that no matter what way one practices, it itself is empty of wayness. The Middle Way then is any way which is at the same time wayless, without the karmic stain of past events, thoughts, actions, attitudes, and without pre-conceived notions about what the traceless way might be.

The Middle Way is characterized by the "Four Noble Truths" and the "Noble Eightfold Path" which can be outlined as follows:

The Four Noble Truths:

1. *Dukkha* - all life is suffering and pain
2. *Tanha* - this suffering is rooted in desire
3. *Dukkha* and *Tanha* can be extinguished by
4. The Eightfold Path:
   - Right Understanding, Right Resolve
   - Right Speech, Right Acts, Right Livelihood
   - Right Effort, Right Mindfulness, Right Concentration

Dukkha means that all life is filled with pain and suffering, whether it be physical or psychological. This insight came directly from his first three passing sights, and from Buddha's observation of human anxieties. We are born through a painful process, we suffer throughout our lives, and we often die painfully. The comparative study of religion reminds us that suffering for Buddhists, like ignorance for the Hindu, and sin for the Jew, Christian and Muslim, is the fundamental condition from which humans seek liberation.

Tanha (desire) is the root cause of this physical psychic and spiritual suffering. Once Buddha addressed his monks with the following unforgettable image:

Everything, brethren, is on fire. How, brethren, is everything on fire? The eye, brethren, is on fire, visible objects are on fire, the faculty of the eye is on fire, the sense of the eye is on fire, and also the sensation, whether pleasant or unpleasant or both, which arises from the sense of sight, is on fire. With what is it on fire? With the fire of passion, of hate, of illusion is it on fire, with birth, old age, death, grief, lamentation, suffering sorrow, and despair.[9]

The fire of one's passionate attachment to desires consumes all senses and keeps disciples from the cool extinction of karmic fires in *nirvana*. Not that humans can be free from desires, but rather, as Buddha teaches, one is to be free from attachment to desires. Desires simply produce more desires, which are never satisfied even if they are attained, for attainment only produces more desires.

The way out, says Buddha, is to become unattached to desire, to cut it at its origin within the self, to transcend the limitations of what he calls the five aggregates of ego-attachment (Matter, Sensations, Perceptions, Mental Formations, and Consciousness). This is achieved through what Buddha calls the Noble Eightfold Path—Right Understanding, Right Resolve, Right Speech, Right Acts, Right Livelihood, Right Effort, Right Mindfulness and Right Concentration.

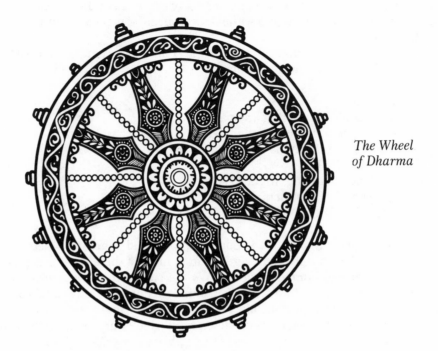

*The Wheel
of Dharma*

Unlike the eight-limbs of *Raja Yoga* which are sequential, the actualization of any one of these eight paths is the full realization of Nirvana. The common denominator, of course, is the word "right" (complete). What is the right way to do anything? If we recall what was said about the Middle Way, then we know that "right" here does not mean the opposite of wrong. The right-way, like the middle-way, is the way empty of wayness, empty of self. In other words the right way to do anything is to be so fully identified with what is being done that what is being done is doing the doing. As R.D. Laing writes:

> I am doing it
> the it I am doing is
> the I that is doing it
> the I that is doing it is
> the it I am doing
> it is doing the I that am doing it
> I am being done by the it I am doing
> it is doing it.[10]

In the accompanying illustration we see that each of the eight spokes (representing the eightfold path) are equidistant from center to circumference. In fact, as the wheel of Buddha's *dharma* turns, the individuality of each spoke disappears, for they are not finally different from one another. Each one arises from and returns to the center of the wheel which is empty. Each of the eight—whether Wisdom-oriented (Understanding and Resolve), Ethically-oriented (Speech, Acts, Livelihood) or Meditationally-oriented (Effort, Mindfulness, Concentration)—originates in, arises from and returns to the Emptiness of egolessness.

Siddhartha, it will be remembered, during his six-year quest for awakening, practiced many yogic forms of concentration, some of which led him to elevated spheres of "Nothingness." Considering these to be only moments of happy, peaceful living, he recognized and practiced the transformational power of *vipassana* ("insight" into the nature of reality). The key to this meditation is to become mindful and fully aware in the present moment of the really real reality.

The initial goal of Vipassana Meditation is to reactivate awareness of *anicca* (change) within oneself and to reach inner and outer *samadhi* (awakened mindfulness). Practically speaking, *vipassana* meditation focuses upon one's breathing, upon each inhalation and each exhalation. The practitioner is instructed, as in the practice of *raja yoga,* to sit with erect back, here with eyes opened and focused, and to be solely aware of each breathing-in, of each breathing-out. Without effort or struggle, the meditator gradually loses himself or herself into a complete mindfulness of breathing. With this process develops a deeply intuitive knowledge of the *tathagata's* teachings.

Until his death in 483 BCE, Buddha taught that all life was filled with suffering, was marked by change and was egoless. Then, according to traditional accounts, after unknowingly eating rancid pork or poisoned mushrooms (according to which interpretation one accepts), he immediately became sick. When he was laid on his right side in a hammock stretched between trees, nature paid her last respects, and the local village people, at his invitation, visited the *Tathagata* for the last time. In response to the mourning followers, Buddha said: "Anything born contains within itself the inherent necessity of dissolution!" Therefore he dishonored his own remains and asked his followers to work out their own awakening with diligence.

At this moment Subhadda, a wandering seeker who wished to speak with Buddha, approached but was detained by the disciple Ananda's concern for Buddha's condition. But Buddha interceded and Subhadda was given access to the Exalted One who taught, as he had in his first sermon, the spiritual necessity of the Eightfold Path. Any teaching which does not contain the truth of the Eightfold Path, Buddha re-emphasized, has no saintliness in it. Subhadda was at once awakened and became the last disciple whom Buddha converted.

Seeing Ananda his close friend and disciple weeping, Buddha repeated an earlier teaching:

"Therefore, O Ananda, be you lamps unto yourselves. Rely on yourselves, and not on any external help. Hold fast to the truth as a lamp. Seek salvation alone in the truth. Look not for assistance to any beside yourselves. Such, Ananda, among all my bhikkus shall reach the topmost height. . . ." His voice trailed away, and then he aroused himself to repeat, "Decay is inherent in all component substances. Work out your salvation with diligence."[11]

Thus he entered *parinirvana* in 483 BCE in the third watch, in a serene, full-moon evening. Just as he was conceived miraculously, so too he died, for at his funeral rite, the elements on the pyre spontaneously combusted to cremate his body.

The Story of Early Buddhism

In the *Mahaparinibbana Sutra* (Sermon of the Great Decease) we read that the Buddha did not transmit his teaching authority to any specific disciple, but instead encouraged monastic life and communal polity. He encouraged monks, nuns and laity alike to cultivate "mindfulness" and to take the *dharma* of his teachings and the rules of the order (*sangha*) as their teacher. During the following several hundred years, the *dharma* was elaborated and expanded, and collections of sacred texts were written and gathered by monastic communities.

During the last century before Christ, a shift occurred within the Buddhist community when a group of liberal reformers—the Mahayanans (greater vehicle)—emphasized the potential liberation of all beings as over and against the Theravadins (the elders) who emphasized personal emancipation. Of course there is no exact time and no unique event which triggered the first Buddhist reform, and, as scholars have noted, Theravadin and Mahayanan monks often lived together. Nevertheless by the time of Christ there were in India two distinct interpretations of the *dharma*.

While the Theravadins (the conservative Southeast Asian wing of Indian Buddhism) stressed becoming personally enlightened (*arhat*), the reform Mahayanans of China, Korea and later Japan stressed the Bodhisattva vow ("I will not enter *nirvana* until all sentient beings enter *nirvana*!"). For Theravadins, *nirvana* meant an individual's delivery from the *samsara* (hell) of this world's sufferings into the *nirvana* of the "other shore." It is as if one comes to a river (the edge of knowledge), builds a raft (*yana*) of the teachings of Buddha, and then, using the raft (Buddha's *dhamma* body), crosses the river to the "other shore."

Mahayanans utilize the same image, only halfway across the stream, after recognizing that a *nirvana* without "all sentient beings" is a hollow victory, an incomplete fulfillment, the Mahayanan *bodhisattva* returns to the shore of *samsara,* and refuses to enter *nirvana* until all sentient beings (including humans, animals, plants, organic and inorganic forms) can enter as well.[12] For Theravadins, *nirvana* is not equal to *samsara;* rather it transcends passions, desires and suffering, and is accompanied by self-perfection, supreme peace, immortality, emptiness of name and form and freedom. For Mahayanans, *samsara* is *nirvana*, for the other shore is no different from this one.

THE TWO SCHOOLS

THERAVADA (HINAYANA)—Elders	MAHAYANA—Reformers
• goal: individual liberation from the world	• goal: communal awakening and deliverance into the world
• ideal human: the Arhat ("worthy one")	• ideal human: the Bodhisattva ("enlightenment being")
• stress on wisdom (Prajna)	• stress on compassion (karuna)
• practice: Vipassana (insight) meditation	• practice: zazen & koan; sutra recitation
• canon: Pali; Sanskrit	• canon: Pali, Sanskrit, Chinese, Tibetan, Japanese, Vietnamese
• authority: Sermons & Discourses of the Buddha	• authority: not dependent on scripture
• geography: Southeast Asia, Ceylon	• geography: China, Korea, Japan, Vietnam
• nirvana: individual & personal	• nirvana: collective & cosmic
• ultimacy: Buddha-nature	• ultimacy: sunyata (emptiness)
• teaching: Buddha's literal word	• teaching: Buddha's awakening example
• teacher: emphasized the historic person—Siddhartha Gautama	• teacher: accepted Siddhartha as one of many appearances of Buddha

Buddhist Sutras

For our purposes, an important consequence of this distinction is a canonical one. Theravadan Buddhists limit their canon to just that material which Buddha himself spoke or which he was heard to speak, whereas Mahayanans include teachings of many Buddhas.

The Theravadin canon is fixed. It includes only those texts written in Pali (the language of Buddha) or in Sanskrit. The Tripitaka (Three Baskets) is the name given to the Theravadan sacred canon. It contains monastic rules, five collections of discourses and dialogues by Buddha, and doctrinal analysis. The three *Pitaka* include:

1. *Vinaya-Pitaka* (Discipline Basket) which contains monastic rules for the members of the *Sangha*;
2. *Sutta-Pitaka* (Sermon Basket) or *sutra* in Sanskrit which means a "weave" or "thread" and which refers to five collections of discourses and dialogues supposed to have been spoken by Buddha, and which includes the *Jataka* (stories of previous births of Buddha) and the *Dhammapada* (Path of the Teaching), comprised of 423 verse-aphorisms;
3. *Abhidhamma-Pitaka* (Metaphysical Basket) which contains doctrinal analysis and refinements of a specific and technical nature.

Early Buddhist chronicles tell the story of the first council, held at Rajagraha, on the slope of a great mountain during the monsoons. Ananda (the sage closest to the Buddha) repeated sermons that had just been recited by the best of the speakers, sermons originally spoken by Buddha. Each one he began with: "Thus I have Heard." In this way the sacred texts were established in conjunction with the *dhamma* of the Great Sage and which are still today authoritative for Theravadin Buddhists.

The Mahayanan canon on the other hand is open and includes not only the Theravadin texts, but also Tibetan and Chinese writings which came into being as Buddhist teaching spread. They are called the *Prajna-Paramitra Sutras* (Sutras of Perfect Wisdom), two of which we will study in Chapter 7.

Buddha's Dhammapada

We will draw our focus now to the most fundamentl Theravadin text, the Dhammapada. *Dhamma* (Sanskrit: dharma) comes from the root "Dhr" (to support, to remain) and thus means the eternal Law; *Pada* means foot or step and thus refers to a path. Dhammapada equals the path of the Supreme Truth. The Dhammapada contains the words of Buddha transmitted orally for hundreds of years before being compiled in treatises or Sutras arranged in a manual of inspiration, support and guidance, and accepted as such by King Asoka in 240 BCE. The 423 aphorisms originally written in Pali verse form, perhaps in the third century before Christ, are said to be from Buddha's sermons.

The Dhammapada contains no systematic structure of teachings, but rather is a collection of sermons on being watchful, clear-minded, self-pressured and calmly self-controlled. It stresses the invisible path of deep contemplation, of forsaking anger and transient pleasures and of persistent endurance. Each sermon is a snapshot of a single reality, that of emptiness. Empty the boat of your life, says the Buddha, for when it is empty it will sail swiftly. Only a fool thinks that "it was I" who did the work. The wise person follows the path of the dhamma, free from passionate attachments and anxious fears. The wise person therefore does not afflict another with words or deeds, but practices the four noble truths. Only they soar in the traceless sky of *nirvana*.

At the heart of Buddha's teaching is *anatta* (no self), Buddha's unconditional "no" to all of existence. Realizing that there is no *atman* (*anatman* = *anatta*) liberated Siddhartha from his former questions about old age, sickness and death. Buddha insisted that just as there is no permanent consciousness, neither is there anyone who is reborn into the next life. Since the self is forever changing, the true self is formless, empty of ego, of role, of title, of form, of opposites, and of emptiness itself.

One's *karma* (*kamma* in Pali) determines the locus of one's birth (in various heavens, hells, or on earth), but since in Buddhism there is no self to begin with, rebirth takes place without any transmigration. Described as eternal joy, nothingness, and the other shore, the indescribable state of *nirvana* (*nibbana* in Pali) eliminates suffering, desire, and new *karma* from imprisoning the self within itself.

According to Buddha all existence can be characterized as having three marks:

'All created things perish,' he who knows and sees this becomes passive in pain; this is the way to purity.

'All created things are grief and pain,' he who knows and sees this becomes passive in pain; this is the way that leads to purity.

'All forms are unreal,' he who knows and sees this becomes passive in pain; this is the way that leads to purity.

He who does not rouse himself when it is time to rise, who, though young and strong, is full of sloth, whose will and thought are weak, that lazy and idle man will never find the way to knowledge.[13]

Everything perishes, changes, becomes new so that the only thing in life which is constant is change itself. It was partly because of this doctrine of *anicca* (impermanence) that Buddhist teachings, as we shall see in Chapter 7, took root in China. Just as all conditioned elements in the universe are impermanent, so too is the so-called self an impermanent combination of the five aggregates of ego-attachment: matter, sensations, aggregates perceptions, impulses, consciousness. Therefore while one is forced to speak with pronouns, as if there are selves, in fact the self is merely a social convention.

One day a disciple questioned Buddha:

"Are you a Deva?" (god)
And Buddha said "No!"
"Are you a Gandharva?" (Vedic cloud spirit)
And Buddha said "No!"
"Are you a Yaksha?" (Vedic tree spirit)
And Buddha said "No!"
"Are you a man?"
And Buddha said "No!"
And Buddha said:
"Know O Disciple that I have completely annihilated individualism.
"Know O Disciple that I am Buddha! I am the Perfect One! I have obtained Nirvana!"[14]

The *telos* of Buddha's teaching is *nirvana,* the extinction (*nir*) of cravings and desires (*vana*), the snuffing out of the flames of passion and desire. Described as eternal joy, nothingness, the other shore, in this indescribable *nirvana,* suffering, desire, and *karma* no longer imprison one. Since *nirvana* is ultimately empty and absolutely traceless, it has no existence, cannot be achieved, cannot be understood, and cannot be described. *Nirvana* is deathless (free from impermanence), peaceful (free from suffering and desire), and secure (free from anxieties about life and fears of dying). As Buddha teaches:

A wise man should leave the dark state (of ordinary life), and follow the bright state (of the Bhikshu). After going from his home to a homeless state, he should in his retirement look for enjoyment where there seemed to be no enjoyment. Leaving all pleasures behind, and calling nothing his own, the wise man should purge himself from all the troubles of the mind.[15]

NOTES

1. The names of the Buddha include:
   Siddhartha—"He who has achieved his goal";
   Gautama—His given family name;
   Sakyamuni—Born into the warrior caste, in the Sakya clan in northern India ("Sage of the Sakyas");
   Buddha—The "Awakened One" (self-declared title);
   Tathagata—The "Traceless One" (a title for Buddha and for all succeeding Buddhas), the one who follows in the footsteps the ancestors.

2. Ananda Coomaraswarmy, *Buddha and the Gospel of Buddhism* (New York: Harper & Row, 1964), 13.

3. Edward Conze, translator, *Buddhist Scriptures* (New York: Penguin Books, 1959), 36.

4. Coomaraswarmy, 34.

5. The "Dhammapada," 11:153, 154 translated by F. Max Müller in *The Sacred Books of the East,* Vol. X, (India: Motilal Banarsidas, 1965). All quotations from the *Dhammapada* are from this translation unless otherwise noted.

6. Herman Hesse, *Siddhartha* (New York: New Directions Books, 1951), 30.

7. Dhammapada 7:97, & 24:353.

8. Coomaraswarmy, 39.

9. Quoted in *Buddhism,* ed. by Clarence Hamilton (New York: Bobbs-Merrill Co., 1952), 49.

10. R.D. Laing, *Knots* (New York: Pantheon Books, 1970), 84.

11. Quoted by George Marshall, *Buddha: The Quest for Serenity* (Boston Beacon Press, 1978), 215.

12. "I take upon myself the burden of all suffering, I am resolved to do so, I will endure it. I do not turn or run away, do not tremble, am not terrified, nor afraid, do not turn back or

despond." Quoted from the Vajradhvaja Sutra, translated by Edward Conze in *Buddhist Texts Through the Ages* (New York: Harper & Row, 1964), 131–32.

13. *Dhammapada* 20:277–280.

14. Paraphrased from *The Buddhist Bible,* ed. by Dwight Godard (Boston: Beacon Press, 1938), 5.

15. *Dhammapada* 6:87–88.

Selections

Selections from the Dhammapada from chapters 1, 2, 5, 6, 7, 8, 12, 13, 14, 18, 19, 20, 24, 25, and 26 translated by F. Max Müller.

Chapter I.
The Twin-Verses.

1. All that we are is the result of what we have thought: it is founded on our thoughts, it is made up of our thoughts. If a man speaks or acts with an evil thought, pain follows him, as the wheel follows the foot of the ox that draws the carriage.
2. All that we are is the result of what we have thought: it is founded on our thoughts, it is made up of our thoughts. If a man speaks or acts with a pure thought, happiness follows him, like a shadow that never leaves him.
3. 'He abused me, he beat me, he defeated me, he robbed me,'—in those who harbour such thoughts hatred will never cease.
4. 'He abused me, he beat me, he defeated me, he robbed me,'—in those who do not harbour such thoughts hatred will cease.
5. For hatred does not cease by hatred at any time: hatred ceases by love, this is an old rule.
6. The world does not know that we must all come to an end here;—but those who know it, their quarrels cease at once.
7. He who lives looking for pleasures only, his senses uncontrolled, immoderate in his food, idle, and weak, Mâra (the tempter) will certainly overthrow him, as the wind throws down a weak tree.
8. He who lives without looking for pleasures, his senses well controlled, moderate in his food, faithful and strong, him Mâra will certainly not overthrow, any more than the wind throws down a rocky mountain.
19. The thoughtless man, even if he can recite a large portion (of the law), but is not a doer of it, has no share in the priesthood, but is like a cowherd counting the cows of others.
20. The follower of the law, even if he can recite only a small portion (of the law), but, having forsaken passion and hatred and foolishness, possesses true knowledge and serenity of mind, he, caring for nothing in this world or that to come, has indeed a share in the priesthood.

Chapter II.
On Earnestness.

21. Earnestness is the path of immortality (Nirvâna), thoughtlessness the path of death. Those who are in earnest do not die, those who are thoughtless are as if dead already.
22. Those who are advanced in earnestness, having understood this clearly, delight in earnestness, and rejoice in the knowledge of the Ariyas (the elect).
23. These wise people, meditative, steady, always possessed of strong powers, attain to Nirvâna, the highest happiness.

Chapter IV.
Flowers.

44. Who shall overcome this earth, and the world of Yama (the lord of the departed), and the world of the gods? Who shall find out the plainly shown path of virtue, as a clever man finds out the (right) flower?
45. The disciple will overcome the earth, and the world of Yama, and the world of the gods. The disciple will find out the plainly shown path of virtue, as a clever man finds out the (right) flower.
46. He who knows that this body is like froth, and has learnt that it is as unsubstantial as a mirage, will break the flower-pointed arrow of Mâra, and never see the king of death.
47. Death carries off a man who is gathering flowers and whose mind is distracted, as a flood carries off a sleeping village.

48. Death subdues a man who is gathering flowers, and whose mind is distracted, before he is satiated in his pleasures.

58, 59. As on a heap of rubbish cast upon the highway the lily will grow full of sweet perfume and delight, thus the disciple of the truly enlightened Buddha shines forth by his knowledge among those who are like rubbish, among the people that walk in darkness.

Chapter VI.
The Wise Man.

85. Few are there among men who arrive at the other shore (become Arhats); the other people here run up and down the shore.

86. But those who, when the law has been well preached to them, follow the law, will pass across the dominion of death, however difficult to overcome.

87, 88. A wise man should leave the dark state (of ordinary life), and follow the bright state (of the Bhikshu). After going from his home to a homeless state, he should in his retirement look for enjoyment where there seemed to be no enjoyment. Leaving all pleasures behind, and calling nothing his own, the wise man should purge himself from all the troubles of the mind.

Chapter VII.
The Venerable (Arhat).

90. There is no suffering for him who has finished his journey, and abandoned grief, who has freed himself on all sides, and thrown off all fetters.

91. They depart with their thoughts well-collected, they are not happy in their abode; like swans who have left their lake, they leave their house and home.

92. Men who have no riches, who live on recognised food, who have perceived void and unconditioned freedom (Nirvâna),

their path is difficult to understand, like that of birds in the air.

93. He whose appetites are stilled, who is not absorbed in enjoyment, who has perceived void and unconditioned freedom (Nirvâna), his path is difficult to understand, like that of birds in the air.

94. The gods even envy him whose senses, like horses well broken in by the driver, have been subdued, who is free from pride, and free from appetites.

95. Such a one who does his duty is tolerant like the earth, like Indra's bolt; he is like a lake without mud; no new births are in store for him.

Chapter X.
Punishment.

129. All men tremble at punishment, all men fear death; remember that you are like unto them, and do not kill, nor cause slaughter.

130. All men tremble at punishment, all men love life; remember that thou art like unto them, and do not kill, nor cause slaughter.

131. He who seeking his own happiness punishes or kills beings who also long for happiness, will not find happiness after death.

132. He who seeking his own happiness does not punish or kill beings who also long for happiness, will find happiness after death.

133. Do not speak harshly to anybody; those who are spoken to will answer thee in the same way. Angry speech is painful, blows for blows will touch thee.

134. If, like a shattered metal plate (gong), thou utter not, then thou hast reached Nirvâna; contention is not known to thee.

Chapter XI.
Old Age.

146. How is there laughter, how is there joy, as this world is always burning? Why do you

not seek a light, ye who are surrounded by darkness?

147. Look at this dressed-up lump, covered with wounds, joined together, sickly, full of many thoughts, which has no strength, no hold!

148. This body is wasted, full of sickness, and frail; this heap of corruption breaks to pieces, life indeed ends in death.

149. Those white bones, like gourds thrown away in the autumn, what pleasure is there in looking at them?

150. After a stronghold has been made of the bones, it is covered with flesh and blood, and there dwell in it old age and death, pride and deceit.

151. The brilliant chariots of kings are destroyed, the body also approaches destruction, but the virtue of good people never approaches destruction,—thus do the good say to the good.

152. A man who has learnt little, grows old like an ox; his flesh grows, but his knowledge does not grow.

153, 154. Looking for the maker of this tabernacle, I shall have to run through a course of many births, so long as I do not find (him); and painful is birth again and again. But now, maker of the tabernacle, thou hast been seen; thou shalt not make up this tabernacle again. All thy rafters are broken, thy ridge-pole is sundered; the mind, approaching the Eternal (visaṅkhâra, nirvâna), has attained to the extinction of all desires.

155. Men who have not observed proper discipline, and have not gained treasure in their youth, perish like old herons in a lake without fish.

156. Men who have not observed proper discipline, and have not gained treasure in their youth, lie, like broken bows, sighing after the past.

Chapter XII.
Self.

157. If a man hold himself dear, let him watch himself carefully; during one at least out of the three watches a wise man should be watchful.

158. Let each man direct himself first to what is proper, then let him teach others; thus a wise man will not suffer.

159. If a man make himself as he teaches others to be, then, being himself well subdued, he may subdue (others); one's own self is indeed difficult to subdue.

160. Self is the lord of self, who else could be the lord? With self well subdued, a man finds a lord such as few can find.

Chapter XIII.
The World.

167. Do not follow the evil law! Do not live on in thoughtlessness! Do not follow false doctrine! Be not a friend of the world.

168. Rouse thyself! do not be idle! Follow the law of virtue! The virtuous rests in bliss in this world and in the next.

169. Follow the law of virtue; do not follow that of sin. The virtuous rests in bliss in this world and in the next.

170. Look upon the world as a bubble, look upon it as a mirage: the king of death does not see him who thus looks down upon the world.

171. Come, look at this glittering world, like unto a royal chariot; the foolish are immersed in it, but the wise do not touch it.

Chapter XIV.
The Buddha (The Awakened).

179. He whose conquest is not conquered again, into whose conquest no one in this world enters, by what track can you lead him, the Awakened, the Omniscient, the trackless?

180. He whom no desire with its snares and poisons can lead astray, by what track can you lead him, the Awakened, the Omniscient, the trackless?

181. Even the gods envy those who are awakened and not forgetful, who are given to meditation, who are wise, and who delight in the repose of retirement (from the world).

182. Difficult (to obtain) is the conception of men, difficult is the life of mortals, difficult is the hearing of the True Law, difficult is the birth of the Awakened (the attainment of Buddhahood).

183. Not to commit any sin, to do good, and to purify one's mind, that is the teaching of (all) the Awakened.

184. The Awakened call patience the highest penance, long-suffering the highest Nirvâna; for he is not an anchorite (pravra*g*ita) who strikes others, he is not an ascetic (srama*n*a) who insults others.

185. Not to blame, not to strike, to live restrained under the law, to be moderate in eating, to sleep and sit alone, and to dwell on the highest thoughts,—this is the teaching of the Awakened.

186. There is no satisfying lusts, even by a shower of gold pieces; he who knows that lusts have a short taste and cause pain, he is wise;

187. Even in heavenly pleasures he finds no satisfaction, the disciple who is fully awakened delights only in the destruction of all desires.

188. Men, driven by fear, go to many a refuge, to mountains and forests, to groves and sacred trees.

189. But that is not a safe refuge, that is not the best refuge; a man is not delivered from all pains after having gone to that refuge.

190. He who takes refuge with Buddha, the Law (Dhamma), and the Church (Sangha); he who, with clear understanding, sees the four holy truths:—

191. Viz. pain, the origin of pain, the destruction of pain, and the eightfold holy way that leads to the quieting of pain;—

192. That is the safe refuge, that is the best refuge; having gone to that refuge, a man is delivered from all pain.

193. A supernatural person (a Buddha) is not easily found, he is not born everywhere. Wherever such a sage is born, that race prospers.

Chapter XX.
The Way.

273. The best of ways is the eightfold; the best of truths the four words; the best of virtues passionlessness; the best of men he who has eyes to see.

274. This is the way, there is no other that leads to the purifying of intelligence. Go on this way! Everything else is the deceit of Mâra (the tempter).

275. If you go on this way, you will make an end of pain! The way was preached by me, when I had understood the removal of the thorns (in the flesh).

276. You yourself must make an effort. The Tathâgatas (Buddhas) are only preachers. The thoughtful who enter the way are freed from the bondage of Mâra.

277. 'All created things perish,' he who knows and sees this becomes passive in pain; this is the way to purity.

278. 'All created things are grief and pain,' he who knows and sees this becomes passive in pain; this is the way that leads to purity.

279. 'All forms are unreal,' he who knows and sees this becomes passive in pain; this is the way that leads to purity.

Chapter XXIV.
Thirst.

334. The thirst of a thoughtless man grows like a creeper; he runs from life to life, like a monkey seeking fruit in the forest.

348. Give up what is before, give up what is be-

hind, give up what is in the middle, when thou goest to the other shore of existence; if thy mind is altogether free, thou wilt not again enter into birth and decay.

351. He who has reached the consummation, who does not tremble, who is without thirst and without sin, he has broken all the thorns of life: this will be his last body.

352. He who is without thirst and without affection, who understands the words and their interpretation, who knows the order of letters (those which are before and which are after), he has received his last body, he is called the great sage, the great man.

353. 'I have conquered all, I know all, in all conditions of life I am free from taint; I have left all, and through the destruction of thirst I am free; having learnt myself, whom shall I teach?'

369. O Bhikshu, empty this boat! if emptied, it will go quickly; having cut off passion and hatred, thou wilt go to Nirvâna.

370. Cut off the five (senses), leave the five, rise above the five. A Bhikshu, who has escaped from the five fetters, he is called Oghatinna, 'saved from the flood.'

371. Meditate, O Bhikshu, and be not heedless! Do not direct thy thought to what gives pleasure, that thou mayest not for thy heedlessness have to swallow the iron ball (in hell), and that thou mayest not cry out when burning, 'This is pain.'

Chapter XXVI.
The Brâhmana (Arhat).

383. Stop the stream valiantly, drive away the desires, O Brâhmana! When you have understood the destruction of all that was made, you will understand that which was not made.

384. If the Brâhmana has reached the other shore in both laws (in restraint and contemplation), all bonds vanish from him who has obtained knowledge.

385. He for whom there is neither this nor that shore, nor both, him, the fearless and unshackled, I call indeed a Brâhmana.

414. Him I call indeed a Brâhmana who has traversed this miry road, the impassable world and its vanity, who has gone through, and reached the other shore, is thoughtful, guileless, free from doubts, free from attachment, and content.

415. Him I call indeed a Brâhmana who in this world, leaving all desires, travels about without a home, and in whom all concupiscence is extinct.

416. Him I call indeed a Brâhmana who, leaving all longings, travels about without a home, and in whom all covetousness is extinct.

420. Him I call indeed a Brâhmana whose path the gods do not know, nor spirits (Gandharvas), nor men, whose passions are extinct, and who is an Arhat (venerable).

421. Him I call indeed a Brâhmana who calls nothing his own, whether it be before, behind, or between, who is poor, and free from the love of the world.

422. Him I call indeed a Brâhmana, the manly, the noble, the hero, the great sage, the conqueror, the impassible, the accomplished, the awakened.

423. Him I call indeed a Brâhmana who knows his former abodes, who sees heaven and hell, has reached the end of births, is perfect in knowledge, a sage, and whose perfections are all perfect.

BUDDHIST JOURNAL EXERCISES

1. Who is the real Buddha? From your reading about Buddha and from reading his teachings, who do you think he really was/is? Can you imagine Buddha alive today? Whom do you know at this time who is most like Buddha?
2. Create a dialogue with Buddha in which you ask him for further explanation of his teachings and/or in which you challenge him on his principles!
3. Look at a picture of Buddha's face (or any other Buddha-icon that you have). Look especially at his eyes and at his lips. Are his eyes open or closed? Is his mouth smiling or stern? Is his expression focused or unfocused? What does Buddha see in deep meditation? See with what the Buddhists call the "Third eye," the eye beyond the dualistic vision of our ordinary eyes! Imagine that you are the Buddha of the image you are looking at. What do you see with your own "Third eye"?
4. After reading the Dhammapada write your own verse in the style in the Dhammapada discourses. Imitate the complete form as a beginning painter imitates a master work. Pick a contemporary issue (e.g., nuclear arms, abortion, capital punishment, taxation, feminism, etc.) and write a Buddhistic couplet about it, as if you were Buddha! A variation is to rewrite an existing couplet in today's vernacular (e.g., 1:1–2, 11:8–9, 14:1–2, 26:32–3).
5. At Buddha's death, his last words were reportedly: "Be ye a lamp unto your own feet!" How do you understand and interpret this direction? Why did Buddha use the image of light and feet? What would your "last words" be? Could you see yourself dying as peacefully as Buddha did?
6. Look at and contemplate the accompanying contrasting images of the human form— Rodin's "The Thinker" and a statue of the Buddha. Draw a line down the center of your journal page and list the differences between the two. In what ways is Buddha's countenance reflective of a person who is beyond the questions that obviously trouble the thinker? How do their bodies reflect their inner condition? Whom do you feel more drawn to and why?
7. Comment upon the following Dhammapada:

> There is no fire like passion,
> no capturer like hatred;
> There is no net (snare) like delusion,
> no torrent like craving.　　　(18:17)

Does this address the relationship between sexuality and spirituality? Why are monks and priests mostly celibate? Do you agree with this teaching? If so, how do you see it apply in your life? If not, provide your response to the quote.

Chapter 5 THE CONFUCIAN WAY

Crossing the Himalayas from India, traveling through what was once known as Tibet where *Vajrayana* Buddhism (the Lightening Bolt School) flourished, we arrive in the vast world of China. As Fung Yu-Lan writes, there are two expressions for world in the Chinese language: "One is 'all beneath the sky' and the other is 'all within the Four Seas.' "[1] Each indicates an immense, naturalistic universe, within which humans play a harmonious role.

The Yin-Yang Circle

When we shift our focus from India to China, we notice that her stories of ultimacy shift from the metaphysically abstract to the naturalistic and practical. The monism of the Upanishads and the theism of the Bhagavad Gita are replaced by a complementary harmony of Confucius' active, "cultivated" self, and Lao Tzu's contemplative, "natural" self. But most significantly, philosophical Sanskrit is replaced by ideographic calligraphy.

In Chinese language, words as pictures originated by imitating nature as closely as possible. For instance, the word-picture for "sun" looks like a sun, and the word-picture for a human being looks like a stick figure of a person. It is this intense focus upon natural phenomena which molds Chinese language and thought, and which also inspired its creation story:

> In the beginning there was the unity of *Yang-Yin* (light-darkness, heat-cold, dry-moist). When the subtle went upward, and the gross downward, when heavens formed from the subtle, and earth from the gross, then there was and is now *Yang* and *Yin* (active and receptive, male and female). From the harmonious interaction of *Yang* and *Yin* come the seasons and all of earth's products. *Yang* produced fire whose subtlest parts formed the sun; *Yin* produced water whose subtlest parts formed the moon. The sun's interaction with the moon produced the stars which fill heaven, just as rivers and dust fill earth. When *Yang* combines with *Yin*, all creatures are produced. In these two is the All (*Tai Chi*).[2]

The ancient sages viewed nature as a bi-polar reality in which each dimension contains its opposite, and in which each dimension is constantly transforming into its opposite. Thus there is no female without male, no day without night, no evil without good, no Yin without Yang and vice versa. As you see in the accompanying drawing, the Yin/Yang symbol represents a complementary or harmonious dualism in which the following opposites always interpenetrate, interest and replace each other.

YANG (Sun)	YIN (Moon)
1. Positive charge	1. Negative charge
2. Heaven (aspiration)	2. Earth (matter, mother)
3. Day	3. Night
4. Male	4. Female
5. Active, aggressive	5. Receptive, yielding
6. Hard (the river bank)	6. Soft (the river)
7. Hot (dry)	7. Cold (moist)
8. Transcendence	8. Immediacy
9. Discipline, order	9. Spontaneity, flowing
10. Confucian Maxims	10. Taoist stories

In China's theory of natural evolution, Yin is always in the process of changing to Yang and Yang to Yin, for the nature of nature is never fixed. Like Buddha's teaching of *annica* (the impermanence of all phenomena), the Chinese understood, integrated and applied the implications of natural changes. Yin was seen as mother earth, night, female, receptive, soft, flowing and spontaneous, whereas Yang was viewed as heaven, day, male, active, hard, ordered, and disciplined. The point is that while each seems to have a separate existence, at the same time each harmoniously interfuses the other.

We can perhaps understand this mutual interpenetration of Yin and Yang better if we take brief note of the Chinese view of death. To the ancient sages, life was already in death, and death already in life. Just as light is in darkness, male in female, and vice versa, so with life and death. To separate one from the other would be to render each incomplete. Life (Yang) is seen as the foreground of death and death (Yin) as the backdrop to life. The process of death then was the natural and necessary transition from a conscious state to an unconscious one, from a life-body to a death-body.

A story is told of a Chinese sage who once appeared before an emperor dressed in a Buddhist cap, Confucianist robes and Taoist slippers. The story is told not because of anything said, but rather to illustrate the harmony among Chinese sacred traditions, a harmony which existed between its three religious ways and also between heaven, earth and humanity. Confucianism and Taoism can be introduced as complementary halves of China's native Great Tradition, both of which later interacted with Buddhism. In fact the central sacred symbol of Yin/Yang can be said to be comprised of Confucianism (*Yang*) and Taoism (*Yin*), within the circumference of the circle of Buddhism (*Tai Chi* or the Great Ultimate).

Three indigenous religions and three advanced religions characterized classical China. Indigenously, early primitive animism (in which it was believed that the world of observable events really have causes, and which guarded against two kinds of spirits associated, respectively, with Yang and Yin—Shen and Kwei) developed into a naturalism (which later became Taoism) and ancestor worship (which became the ethical humanism of Confucius). Still later, various schools of Buddhism arrived from India and provided the third major religious imprint on China along with Confucius and Lao Tzu.

The interplay of these three advanced religions characterizes classical China—Confu-

Confucius

cius' ethical humanism, Lao Tzu's spontaneous mysticism and, later, Indian Buddhism's emptiness. In this and the next two chapters we will examine each separately.

The Story of Confucius (551–479 BCE)

Confucius, known in China as K'ung Tzu or Master K'ung (family name), was born in 551 BCE as K'ung Ch'iu, in the principality of Lu in Northeastern China into an impoverished family (though his ancestors may have descended from the royal house of Shang). Chinese tradition gives us this portrait of Confucius:

> Confucius was tall, though his legs were rather short, if credence on the latter point is to be given to his school's Taoist adversary, Chuang-tse. He had the "five projections": protuberant eyes, a prominent nose with large nostrils, a pronounced Adam's apple, flat ears, and teeth that protruded slightly beyond his lips so that they were not quite closed . . . his face was broad, with marks like those that are to be seen "on a ripe melon." His hands were strong, resembling a tiger's paws; his beard was luxuriant, his mouth was wide. His walk was rapid. His complexion was dark. It is difficult to determine whether his portrait is accurate.

His manner was gentle, calm, and austere; he inspired respect without arousing fear; he was sober and serene. At court or in the temple he expressed himself clearly but with respectful attention and a noble gravity. With simple people he too was simple, though speaking little.[3]

Of the several depictions of Confucius in the Analects, two especially correspond with this portrait and provide us with an insight into his sage character. It is said that while from afar he looked severe, when approached he was found to be mild and incisive, and that his manner was affable yet firm, commanding yet easy.[4] How unlike the un-self-conscious tracelessness of Buddha.

What we know of Confucius is largely gained from the forty-seventh chapter of the *Shih Chi* (Historical Records), in which we learn that as a youth he was poor, that he married at eighteen or nineteen, had a son and at least one daughter, and that he managed to acquire an education in the classics. In a time of great socio-political civil strife and cultural turmoil, Confucius became convinced, as H.G. Creel says, "that it was his mission to save the world, and he undertook to do so in the only way that appeared possible, by trying to win a commanding place in the administration."[5]

Few details about the childhood of Confucius are known except that he was raised in a poor family, that his father died when he was three, and that Confucius took great pleasure from handling sacrificial objects. At this time he was appointed to several minor governmental posts, an experience which stimulated his appetite for public office. Confucius was as much a political theorist as he was an ethical humanist.

In 530 BCE Confucius, according to a traditional though uncritical account, began teaching in Lu. Two years later, when his mother died, Confucius exhumed his father's body, which had been buried for several years, in order to bury them side by side. Confucius then entered a three-year period of mourning for his mother. When a disciple suggested that one year was long enough, Confucius said:

Would you then (after a year) feel at ease in eating good rice and wearing silk brocades? Tsai Yu said, Quite at ease. (The Master said) If you would really feel at ease, then do so. But when a true gentleman is in mourning, if he eats dainties, he does not relish them, if he hears music, it does not please him, if he sits in his ordinary seat, he is not comfortable. That is why he abstains from these things. But if you would really feel at ease, there is no need for you to abstain.[6]

When a political crisis in Lu erupted between northern and southern factions, Confucius, along with the exiled prince, left Lu and began to attract disciples and to formulate and teach the politics of speaking the truth. When Confucius did in fact reach an influential post in Lu, he was forced to resign as the result of his uncompromising policies.

Then, at the age of 56, he left for what was to become a thirteen-year teaching pilgrimage, a period from which many of the Analects are drawn. This period ended in 483 BCE when a former disciple Jen K'yu achieved great military fame. When he credited Confucius as his teacher, Confucius was summoned back to Lu to finish his life in honor, even if unemployed. Just before Confucius died in 478 BCE at the age of 73, he rose early, walked to his door and recounted a dream of his own death. He sang:

> See how Tai shan crumbles;
> How the great tree will be destroyed;
> And the wise man vanishes like a withered plant!

> Under the Hias, the coffin was placed at the head of the eastern stairway; under the Chus, at the head of the western stairway; under the Yins [Shang Dynasty], between the two pillars. Last night I dreamed that I was sitting between the two pillars, facing the sacrifices that are made to the dead. No doubt this is because I am descended from the Yins [Kings of Chang].[7]

In these last words, Confucius reiterates his central teaching concern—the necessity of cultivating ritualized behavior.

The Master Teacher

Like the story of Socrates, the life story of Confucius is of a master teacher who undertook to teach four subjects: "culture, conduct of affairs, loyalty to superiors and the keeping of promises."[8] All these virtues of a *chün tzu* (the perfectly cultivated self) are the goal of a methodology, not explained by doctrines. With the collapse of the Chou Dynasty and the ensuing civil-strife of his time, Confucius proposed neither force nor utopian ideals, but instead operated according to the tradition's antiquity. He collected, internalized and retaught China's humanistic attitudes, and in the process, developed the pedagogy of reanimation. For Confucius:

> To learn and at due times to repeat what one has learnt, is that not after all a pleasure?[9]

But it was not just by rote repetition that Confucius taught the virtues of cultivated behavior, for the student had to learn how to reactivate the traditional truths.

> He who by reanimating the Old can gain knowledge of the New is fit to be a teacher. . . .[10]

Confucius' genius was to selectively preserve the classics, to transmit them with reanimated meaning and thereby to restore an ancient harmony between the teacher, the taught and the teaching. His aim was to repair the then present disharmonies by applying ancient wisdoms to help humanity rebalance itself.

There are three concepts which key his venerable teachings—*chün tzu* (lit.: "ruler's son"), a gentleman in both a social and (especially for Confucius) a moral sense, *jen* (human-heartedness), and *li* (ritualistic and behavioral propriety).

Prior to Confucius, *chün tzu* referred to the ruler, or the son of aristocratic, feudal ruling family, to educated, mannered behavior. For Confucius it came to mean a moral superiority of conduct and character. The birth and background of a person were less important, for anyone could cultivate and refine one's humanity through personal effort and training.

Confucius tells us that a person of *chün tzu* is not a specialist, practices what he preaches, is above narrowed-minded egoism, and is without bias. When asked by his disciple Tzu Lu about the "perfect man," Confucius said that if one possessed the wisdom, uncovetousness, valor, and dexterity of the scholarly and artistic ancestors, "and had graced these virtues by cultivation of ritual and music, then indeed I think we might call him a perfect man!"[11]

The question arises: Was Confucius himself a *chün tzu*? After saying that the ways of a *chün tzu* are three—human hearted, wise and brave—Confucius says that he "has met with success in none of them." Immediately his disciple Tzu Kung, as if making an aside to the audience, says: "That, Master, is your own way!"[12]

Confucius based his picture of the *chün tzu* on sages and emperors from remote antiquity like Yao and Shun and the Duke of Chou, each mentioned in the Analects. To Confucius these men possessed virtue, classical learning and insight that transcended ordinary human expectations. Each inspired proper conduct, scholarship and humility. The *chün tzu* does not worry about how others view him, does not judge others narrow-mindedly, and above all is a person of profound humanity.

A harmonious combination of two further concepts describes the reality of *chün tzu*—*jen* (pronounced "wren" with a rolled "r") or individual humanity, and *li,* propriety or social customs. In each case Confucius reanimates the traditional meaning by adding his own interpretation. *Jen* referred to the "freeman" of the ruling party as opposed to the commoners, to the uneducated slaves. Confucius redefined the term to indicate one who cultivates virtuous, humane, loving qualities of inner goodness or altruism for which the homonym *jen* was used. The character for *jen* is the equivalent of the figure for man ($\wedge$) and the figure for two ($=$). Jen then equals true-humaness, heart-to-heart goodness, true ethical behavior. And traditionally *li* referred to the use of sacrificial vessels in observing rituals for ancestors and spirits.

Along with reverence for nature, another major component in the classical Chinese sacred story was ancestor worship, or reverence for the human, what Joseph Kitagawa calls "family-ism."[13] The dead, it was thought, benefit the living with next-worldly wisdom, whereas the living benefit the dead with reverential remembrances through prayers, sacrifices, and commemorations. Just as there was a synchronistic relationship between humans and natural processes, so too there was a synchronistic connection between the living and the dead. To revere the aged as wise and the dead as most wise was to participate in the sacredness of life through funeral rites, mourning observances and continual sacrifices. Such rituals were not merely confined to one's blood-family, but included kings, queens, even the heavenly king of all kings (*Shang Ti*), the ancestor of ancestors, the Supremely Wise.

Confucius expanded the concept to emphasize the ritual correctness of every activity.

He was less concerned with correct performance of rituals than with the appropriate attitude (reverence, respect and constraint) in each of what later became the "five great relationships": between ruler and subject, father and son, elder brother and younger brother, husband and wife, and elder friend and junior friend. Common to each of these, as well as to other relationships, is filial piety—honoring not only one's living superiors but one's ancestors as well.

Sacred or Not?

The central question with regard to the story of Confucius and the Analects is whether or not it is in any way sacred. The teachings of Confucius, some have argued, are not religious, for they contain no belief in god, no religious rituals, no miracles, no creeds, no metaphysics or theology, and make no pronouncements about supernatural beings or an afterlife. The Master said, "Till you know about the living, how are you to know about the dead?"[14] At the same time, it will be maintained here that certain sayings of Confucius reanimate the sacred in the midst of the secular. There are at least two such sacred reanimations in his teachings.

If the sacred is defined, as we have earlier defined it—as a transformation of human consciousness by that which is ultimately beyond or within us—then some of his teachings are sacred by virtue of his teachings of *jen* and *li*.

As we have seen, *jen* is true human-heartedness, empathetic concern, or altruistic-intentionality. *Jen* is an inner quality without which a person can neither long endure adversity, nor long enjoy prosperity, and with which a person will dislike no one.[15] For Confucius *jen* has a definite socio-political reality which is clearly illustrated in his teaching of the rectification of names. In the Analects we read:

> Tzu-lu said, If the prince of Wei were waiting for you to come and administer his country for him, what would be your first measure? The Master said, It would certainly be to correct language. Tzu-lu said, Can I have heard you aright? Surely what you say has nothing to do with the matter. Why should language be corrected? The Master said, Yu! How boorish you are! A gentleman, when things he does not understand are mentioned, should maintain an attitude of reserve. If language is incorrect, then what is said does not concord with what was meant, what is to be done cannot be effected. If what is to be done cannot be effected, then rites and music will not flourish. If rites and music do not flourish, then mutilations and lesser punishments will go astray. And if mutilations and lesser punishments go astray, then the people have nowhere to put hand or foot.
>
> Therefore the gentleman uses only such language as is proper for speech, and only speaks of what it would be proper to carry into effect. The gentleman, in what he says, leaves nothing to mere chance.[16]

This story represents a supreme moment in the life of Confucius. When asked the ultimate political question—if elected, what will you do first?—Confucius replies: Correct language! Correct language, Tzu Lu queries—what are you saying? What a stupid question, Confucius retorts; a *chün tzu* never speaks when he is in ignorance. If language is inaccurate then hypocrisy abounds; if hypocrisy abounds then nothing is completed; if nothing is completed then ritual dies; if ritual dies then law is unjust; and if the law is unjust then the people have no one to trust. Therefore, he concludes, the life of a *chün tzu* leaves nothing to mere chance. To constantly speak the truth is a sacred task for one who seeks to manifest true human-heartedness.

The other, and the most persuasive, sacred dimension is what Herbert Fingarette calls the secular as sacred, or what might be called the holiness of ceremony. *Li* as we recall means both inner and external propriety. For Confucius, one experiences a sacred transformation of the secular (any secular) in and through communal ritualization. Through collective reverence and respect for ancestors, and in the practice of refined social manners, one participates in a whole experience greater than the sum of its parts. Like the sacrificial vase, a person is sacred (or morally self-realized) by virtue of participation in ceremony. As Herbert Fingarette notes, for Confucius virtue does not exist in isolation; there must be neighbors, for one is "transformed by participation with others in ceremony which is communal."[17] Until such transformation, one is only potentially authentic.

There is a ritually correct way to do everything: to rise, to wash, to dress, to eat, to speak, not to speak, to work, to socialize, to study and to sleep, (cf. Analects, Book X). Each gesture, each request, each birth, each marriage, each funeral is given meaning by personal presence fused with ceremonial actions. For example, I greet my former teachers with a probing reserve, with a respectful deference which is spontaneous, and which is acknowledged without words.

The Analects

The sacred literature of ancient China is normally divided between the five classics and the four books and is indicated in the following descriptive outline:

In the Analects (Selected Sayings) Confucius teaches in fragmentary, often puzzling, aphorisms, maxims, proverbs, biographical and philosophical observations, and short, short stories.[18] His teachings on ceremonies, education, ritual, government, heaven, human nature, the rectification of names, the superior person, the sage, the silver rule, virtue and the Way are unsystematic and sometimes repetitive.

There is little doubt that the Analects were probably compiled more than a century after Confucius' death. Indeed, the Analects contain anti-Confucian stories and traditional ritual maxims which pre-date his teaching. We must remember however that Confucius depicted himself as a reanimator, not as an originator, and that the proverbial teachings are stamped not only with his insights but also with his style. Even if none of the Analects are directly attributable to Confucius, and were the compilation of later disciples who gathered written memorials and oral statements, they are nonetheless a genuine testament to the master's pragmatic, ethical spirit.

We have noted that Confucius was a reanimating teacher of aristocratic morals and principles who transmitted and applied China's wisdom to his own day. While the Analects reanimate conversations, dialogues, aphorisms and short, short stories, this series of pragmatic sayings characterize one figure—the sage. Whereas in India, *homo religiosus* was pictured as a guru, an avatar, a holy man, or the Buddha-nature, in China virtue was depicted as an ideal human achievement of the sage.

For Confucius, the sage studied, meditated upon and taught wisdom (e.g., the wisdom of acting as wisely as one speaks and of speaking as wisely as one understands). Though Confucius was certainly a powerful intellectual thinker, the Analects are more often the product of his penchant for wise discernments. Like King Solomon in the Hebrew Scriptures, Confucius did not seek his own gain ahead of the pursuit of wisdom, for the sage's truest pleasure is the transmission of that wisdom.

The opening saying—"To learn and at due times to repeat what one has learned, is that not after all a pleasure?"—casts the Analects within the point of view of one who loves wisdom, loves teaching and loves learning. Indeed the word "to learn" in Chinese means to be awakened, to be self-realizing, to witness to a moral or spiritual self-understanding. The sage is one who teaches not simply by repeating a given teaching without change, but one who creatively represents it in a new situation. Reflecting upon this wisdom Confucius remarks:

> Do I regard myself as a possessor of wisdom? Far from it. But if even a simple peasant comes in all sincerity and asks me a question, I am ready to thrash the matter out, with all its pros and cons, to the very end.[19]

As we have seen, as far as Confucius was concerned, the key to the sagely life was self-cultivation, the process of self-refinement through the arts and through rituals. Yet it was not enough for the sage to be wise, if that wisdom was not clothed in humility. When asked for an explanation of the Ancestral Sacrifice, Confucius once said:

> I do not know. Anyone who knew the explanation could deal with all things under Heaven as easily as I lay this here; and he laid his finger upon the palm of his hand.[20]

As simple as his teachings were, they were often misunderstood by his disciples. One day Tzu Lu asked the master sage why he gave different answers to the same question asked by two different novices. Confucius said: "Ch'iu is backward; so I urged him on. Yu is fanatical about Goodness; so I held him back" (XI, 21). The sage's teachings are always situational yet reflect the universal of perfect humanity.

The same Tzu Lu on another occasion asked Confucius what was meant by the "perfect man"? Confucius answered that the perfect man combined the ethical virtues of wisdom, uncovetousness, valor and the dexterity of traditional heroes with a cultivation of ritual and music. The perfect human cultivates diligence and the capacity to ease the life of society, and most importantly embraces both the first step and the last. The authentic person in sum holds

THE FIVE CHING (CLASSICS) (Truths of the Highest Subject Matter, which were written by early sages)	THE FOUR SHU (BOOKS) (Writings by either disciples of Confucius or by later Sages which were of a Confucian style and which are accepted as authoritative)
1. *Shu Ching* (Book of Historical Documents) Important ordinances and decrees of wise rulers	1. *Analects* (*Lun Yü*) Digested Conversations, Sayings Discourses and Dialogues between the master teacher and the disciples of the Way, assembled in the Han period from several collections compiled by disciples and disciples' disciples
2. *Shi Ching* (Book of Songs) 305 songs & poems in 4 sections: folk-songs; small songs; great songs; hymns of ancient times	2. *The Great Learning* (*Ta Hsueh*) Instructions on how to perform rituals, usually considered the essence of early Confucian social-political theory
3. *Li Ching* (Books of Manners or Rites) Rules and regulations on morals and manners, one of the classics on ritual	3. *The Doctrine of the Mean* (*Chung Yung*) Mystical and metaphysical stress on "the central Way"
4. *I Ching* (Book of Changes) 64 Hexigrams which provide oracular insight into human behavior	4. *The Book of Mencius* (372–289 BCE) One of the best interpretations of Confucius; a conversation in which Mencius states that 'righteousness' is more important than life-itself
5. *Ch'un Ch'iu* (Book of Spring & Autumn) Only book possibly dictated by Confucius himself; a history of his home state from 722–481 BCE	

to the one thread upon which all wisdom is strung: "Never do to others what you would not like them to do to you."[21]

NOTES

1. Fung Yu-Lan, *A Short History of Chinese Philosophy* (New York: The Free Press, 1948), 16.

2. Composed from varying sources. This view of creation is not as old as early "picture writing" in China; it is in spirit. In this actual form, it's no earlier than Han dynasty commentaries on the *Yi-ching*.

3. Pierre Do-Dinh, *Confucius and Chinese Humanism,* (New York: Funk & Wagnalls, 1969), 89.

4. *The Analects of Confucius,* translated by Arthur Waley (New York: Vintage Books, 1938), XIX, 9 and VII, 37. All references to the Analects will be from this edition.

5. H.G. Creel, *Confucius and Chinese Way* (New York: Harper Torchbooks, 1949), 53.

6. *Analects,* XVII, 21.

7. Do-Dinh, 87.

8. *Analects,* VII, 24.

9. *Analects,* I, 1.

10. *Analects,* II, 11.

11. *Analects,* XIV, 13.

12. *Analects,* XIV, 30.

13. The term "family-ism" is used by Joseph Kitagawa in *Religions of the East* (Philadelphia: The Westminster Press, 1976), 43 as an indication of the Kinship system which bound Chinese culture together and which was based on Confucius' teaching of filial piety.

14. *Analects,* XI, 11.

15. *Analects,* IV, 2–4.

16. *Analects,* XII, 3.

17. Herbert Fingarette, Confucius—*The Secular as Sacred* (New York: Harper Torchbooks, 1972), 77.

18. From 1313 to 1905 the *Analects,* along with *The Great Learning,* the *Doctrine of the Mean* and *The Book of Mencius,* provided the basic material a person in China had to study to pass the civil service examination.

19. *Analects,* IX, 7.

20. *Analects,* III, 11.

21. *Analects,* XV, 23.

Selections

Selections from the Analects of Confucius from Books 1, 2, 4, 7, 9, 10, 11, 13, 14, 15, 19 and 20 translated by Arthur Waley.

The Analects
(Lun-yü)

BOOK I

1. The Master said, To learn and at due times to repeat what one has learnt, is that not after all, a pleasure? That friends should come to one from afar, is this not after all delightful? To remain unsoured even though one's merits are unrecognized by others, is that not after all what is expected of a gentleman?

2. Master Yu said, Those who in private life behave well towards their parents and elder brothers, in public life seldom show a disposition to resist the authority of their superiors. And as for such men starting a revolution, no instance of it has ever occurred. It is upon the trunk that a gentleman works. When that is firmly set up, the Way grows. And surely proper behaviour towards parents and elder brothers is the trunk of Goodness?

3. The Master said, 'Clever talk and a pretentious manner' are seldom found in the Good.

4. Master Tsêng said, Every day I examine myself on these three points: in acting on behalf of others, have I always been loyal to their interests? In intercourse with my friends, have I always been true to my word? Have I failed to repeat the precepts that have been handed down to me?

5. The Master said, A country of a thousand war-chariots cannot be administered unless the ruler attends strictly to business, punctually observes his promises, is economical in expenditure, shows affection towards his subjects in general, and uses the labour of the peasantry only at the proper times of year.

6. The Master said, A young man's duty is to behave well to his parents at home and to his elders abroad, to be cautious in giving promises and punctual in keeping them, to have kindly feelings towards everyone, but seek the intimacy of the Good. If, when all that is done, he has any energy to spare, then let him study the polite arts.

7. Tzu-hsia said, A man who

Treats his betters as betters,
Wears an air of respect,
Who into serving father and mother
Knows how to put his whole strength,
Who in the service of his prince will lay down his life,
Who in intercourse with friends is true to his word—

others may say of him that he still lacks education, but I for my part should certainly call him an educated man.

8. The Master said, If a gentleman is frivolous, he will lose the respect of his inferiors and lack firm ground upon which to build up his education. First and foremost he must learn to be faithful to his superiors, to keep promises, to refuse the friendship of all who are not like him. And if he finds he has made a mistake, then he must not be afraid of admitting the fact and amending his ways.

9. Master Tsêng said, When proper respect towards the dead is shown at the End and continued after they are far away the moral force (*té*) of a people has reached its highest point.

10. Tzu-Ch'in said to Tzu-kung, When our Master arrives in a fresh country he always manages to find out about its policy. Does he do this by asking questions, or do people tell him of their own accord? Tzu-kung said, Our Master gets things by being cordial, frank, courteous, temperate, deferential. That is our Master's way of enquiring—a very different matter, certainly, from the way in which enquiries are generally made.

11. The Master said, While a man's father is alive, you can only see his intentions; it is when his father dies that you discover whether or not he is capable of carrying them out. If for the whole three years of mourning he manages to carry on the household exactly as in his father's day, then he is a good son indeed.

12. Master Yu said, In the usages of ritual it is harmony that is prized; the Way of the Former Kings from this got its beauty. Both small matters and great depend upon it. If things go amiss, he who knows the harmony will be able to attune them. But if harmony itself is not modulated by ritual, things will still go amiss.

16. The Master said, (the good man) does not grieve that other people do not recognize his merits. His only anxiety is lest he should fail to recognize theirs.

BOOK II

1. The Master said, He who rules by moral force (*té*) is like the pole-star, which remains in its place while all the lesser stars do homage to it.

2. The Master said, If out of the three hundred *Songs* I had to take one phrase to cover all my teaching, I would say 'Let there be no evil in your thoughts.'

3. The Master said, Govern the people by regulations, keep order among them by chastisements, and they will flee from you, and lose all self-respect. Govern them by moral force, keep order among them by ritual and they will keep their self-respect and come to you of their own accord.

4. The Master said, At fifteen I set my heart upon learning. At thirty, I had planted my feet firm upon the ground. At forty, I no longer suffered from perplexities. At fifty, I knew what were the biddings of Heaven. At sixty, I heard them with docile ear. At seventy, I could follow the dictates of my own heart; for what I desired no longer overstepped the boundaries of right.

8. Tzu-hsia asked about the treatment of parents. The Master said, It is the demeanour that is difficult. Filial piety does not consist merely in young people undertaking the hard work, when anything has to be done, or serving their elders first with wine and food. It is something much more than that.

9. The Master said, I can talk to Yen Hui a whole day without his ever differing from me. One would think he was stupid. But if I enquire into his private conduct when he is not with me I find that it fully demonstrates what I have taught him. No, Hui is by no means stupid.

10. The Master said, Look closely into his aims, observe the means by which he pursues them, discover what brings him content— and can the man's real worth remain hidden from you, can it remain hidden from you?

11. The Master said, He who by reanimating the Old can gain knowledge of the New is fit to be a teacher.

12. The Master said, A gentleman is not an implement.

13. Tzu-kung asked about the true gentleman. The Master said, He does not preach what he practises till he has practised what he preaches.

14. The Master said, A gentleman can see a question from all sides without bias. The small man is biased and can see a question only from one side.

BOOK IV

1. The Master said, It is Goodness that gives to a neighbourhood its beauty. One who is free to choose, yet does not prefer to dwell among the Good—how can he be accorded the name of wise?

2. The Master said, Without Goodness a man

Cannot for long endure adversity,
Cannot for long enjoy prosperity.

The Good Man rests content with Goodness; he that is merely wise pursues Goodness in the belief that it pays to do so.

3, 4. Of the adage 'Only a Good Man knows how to like people, knows how to dislike them,' the Master said, He whose heart is in the smallest degree set upon Goodness will dislike no one.

15. The Master said, Shên! My Way has one (thread) that runs right through it. Master Tsêng said, Yes. When the Master had gone out, the disciples asked, saying What did he mean? Master Tsêng said, Our Master's Way is simply this: Loyalty, consideration.

16. The Master said, A gentleman takes as much trouble to discover what is right as lesser men take to discover what will pay.

17. The Master said, In the presence of a good man, think all the time how you may learn to equal him. In the presence of a bad man, turn your gaze within!

BOOK VII

1, 2, 3. The Master said, I have 'transmitted what was taught to me without making up anything of my own.' I have been faithful to and loved the Ancients. In these respects, I make bold to think, not even our old P'êng can have excelled me. The Master said, I have listened in silence and noted what was said, I have never grown tired of learning nor wearied of teaching others what I have learnt. These at least are merits which I can confidently claim. The Master said, The thought that 'I have left my moral power (*té*) untended, my learning unperfected, that I have heard of righteous men, but been unable to go to them; have heard of evil men, but been unable to reform them'—it is these thoughts that disquiet me.

4. In his leisure hours the Master's manner was very free-and-easy, and his expression alert and cheerful.

5. The Master said, How utterly have things gone to the bad with me! It is long now in-deed since I dreamed that I saw the Duke of Chou.

6. The Master said, Set your heart upon the Way, support yourself by its power, lean upon Goodness, seek distraction in the arts.

7. The Master said, From the very poorest up-wards—beginning even with the man who could bring no better present than a bundle of dried flesh—none has ever come to me without receiving instruction.

8. The Master said, Only one who bursts with eagerness do I instruct; only one who bub-bles with excitement, do I enlighten. If I hold up one corner and a man cannot come back to me with the other three, I do not continue the lesson.

9. If at a meal the Master found himself seated next to someone who was in mourning, he did not eat his fill. When he had wailed at a funeral, during the rest of the day he did not sing.

19. The Master said, I for my part am not one of those who have innate knowledge. I am sim-ply one who loves the past and who is dili-gent in investigating it.

20. The Master never talked of prodigies, feats of strength, disorders or spirits.

21. The Master said, Even when walking in a party of no more than three I can always be certain of learning from those I am with. There will be good qualities that I can select for imitation and bad ones that will teach me what requires correction in myself.

22. The Master said, Heaven begat the power (*té*) that is in me. What have I to fear from such a one as Huan T'ui?

23. The Master said, My friends, I know you think that there is something I am keeping from you. There is nothing at all that I keep from you. I take no steps about which I do not consult you, my friends. Were it other-wise, I should not be Ch'iu.

24. The Master took four subjects for his teach-ing: culture, conduct of affairs, loyalty to su-periors and the keeping of promises.

25. The Master said, A Divine Sage I cannot

hope ever to meet; the most I can hope for is to meet a true gentleman. The Master said, A faultless man I cannot hope ever to meet; the most I can hope for is to meet a man of fixed principles. Yet where all around I see Nothing pretending to be Something, Emptiness pretending to be Fullness, Penury pretending to be Affluence, even a man of fixed principles will be none too easy to find.

BOOK IX

4. There were four things that the Master wholly eschewed: he took nothing for granted, he was never over-positive, never obstinate, never egotistic.

7. The Master said, Do I regard myself as a possessor of wisdom? Far from it. But if even a simple peasant comes in all sincerity and asks me a question, I am ready to thrash the matter out, with all its pros and cons, to the very end.

BOOK XI

11. Tzu-lu asked how one should serve ghosts and spirits. The Master said, Till you have learnt to serve men, how can you serve ghosts? Tzu-lu then ventured upon a question about the dead. The Master said, Till you know about the living, how are you to know about the dead?

21. Tzu-lu asked, When one hears a maxim, should one at once seek occasion to put it into practice? The Master said, Your father and elder brother are alive. How can you whenever you hear a maxim at once put it into practice? Jan Ch'iu asked, When one hears a maxim, should one at once seek occasion to put it into practice? The Master said, When one hears it, one should at once put it into practice.

    Kung-hsi Hua said, When Yu asked, 'When one hears a maxim, should one at once put it into practice?' you said, 'You have a father and elder brother alive.' But when Ch'iu asked, 'When one hears a maxim, should one at once put it into practice,' you said, 'When you hear it, put it into practice.' I am perplexed, and would venture to ask how this was. The Master said, Ch'iu is backward; so I urged him on. Yu is fanatical about Goodness; so I held him back.

BOOK XIII

1. Tzu-lu asked about government. The Master said, Lead them; encourage them! Tzu-lu asked for a further maxim. The Master said, Untiringly.

2. Jan Yung, having become steward of the Chi Family, asked about government. The Master said, Get as much as possible done first by your subordinates. Pardon small offences. Promote men of superior capacity. Jan Yung said, How does one know a man of superior capacity, in order to promote him? The Master said, Promote those you know, and those whom you do not know other people will certainly not neglect.

3. Tzu-lu said, If the prince of Wei were waiting for you to come and administer his country for him, what would be your first measure? The Master said, It would certainly be to correct language. Tzu-lu said, Can I have heard you aright? Surely what you say has nothing to do with the matter. Why should language be corrected? The Master said, Yu! How boorish you are! A gentleman, when things he does not understand are mentioned, should maintain an attitude of reserve. If language is incorrect, then what is said does not concord with what was meant; and if what is said does not concord with what was meant, what is to be done cannot be effected. If what is to be done cannot be effected, then rites and music will not flourish. If rites and music do not flourish, then mutilations and lesser punishments will go astray. And if mutilations

and lesser punishments go astray, then the people have nowhere to put hand or foot.

Therefore the gentleman uses only such language as is proper for speech, and only speaks of what it would be proper to carry into effect. The gentleman, in what he says, leaves nothing to mere chance.

BOOK XIV

30. The Master said, The Ways of the true gentleman are three. I myself have met with success in none of them. For he that is really Good is never unhappy, he that is really wise is never perplexed, he that is really brave is never afraid. Tzu-kung said, That, Master, is your own Way!

31. Tzu-kung was always criticizing other people. The Master said, It is fortunate for Ssu that he is so perfect himself as to have time to spare for this. I myself have none.

32. The Master said, (A gentleman) does not grieve that people do not recognize his merits; he grieves at his own incapacities.

18. The Master said, A gentleman is distressed by his own lack of capacity; he is never distressed at the failure of others to recognize his merits.

19. The Master said, A gentleman has reason to be distressed if he ends his days without making a reputation for himself.

20. The Master said, 'The demands that a gentleman makes are upon himself; those that a small man makes are upon others.'

21. The Master said, A gentleman is proud, but not quarrelsome, allies himself with individuals, but not with parties.

22. The Master said, A gentleman does not

Accept men because of what they say,
Nor reject sayings, because the speaker is what he is.

23. Tzu-kung asked saying, Is there any single saying that one can act upon all day and every day? The Master said, Perhaps the saying about consideration: 'Never do to others what you would not like them to do to you.'

The Master said, A man can enlarge his Way; but there is no Way that can enlarge a man.

29. The Master said, To have faults and to be making no effort to amend them is to have faults indeed!

30. The Master said, I once spent a whole day without food and a whole night without sleep, in order to meditate. It was no use. It is better to learn.

CONFUCIAN JOURNAL EXERCISES

1. In the Analects, Confucius says:

   at 15, I eagerly sought knowledge;
   at 30, I had both feet on the ground;
   at 40, I had no more doubts;
   at 50, I knew of the will of heaven;
   at 60, I had peace inside;
   at 70, ethics became spontaneous. (II,4)

   This is a spiritual x-ray of a sage who is profoundly wise, one could even say transcendingly wise, and yet, at the same time, totally human in every way. Think of at least four major shifts in your own life direction, times when new, life-changing insights took hold for you. Write them out in a style that imitates this Analect. For instance:
   at 7, I . . .
   at 13, I . . .
   at 21, I . . .
   at 32, I . . .
2. Imagine that you are Confucius alive today. What do you think of the world political situation? What would you do and have others do to rectify the situation? What part does, or should, religious ritual play in government? Attempt a Confucianistic analysis of today's world political situation along with what you imagine his proposals to be. Do you agree with his approach?
3. Study the picture of Confucius on page 116 and then create a dialogue with him. Imagine that you (in your own time-space continuum) and Confucius (in his own time-space continuum) are able to enter into a dialogue. Either you travel backward in history or bring Confucius forward in history, and in your imagination construct a dialogue in which you discuss the assertion that the Analects is a religious text. You may wish to define terms that Confucius could not understand since you have lived on the planet longer.
4. Either as a separate exercise, or as a portion of the previous one, compare your image of the religious person (of the *homo religiosus*) with that image found in Confucius. Discuss the implications for your life of the similarity and/or disparity. Is there any aspect of your image that has been influenced or in any way shaped by what Confucius says?
5. Write your own Analect. Style it after one that Confucius has written. Address it to a contemporary socio-political issue (e.g., nuclear arms, pollution, starvation) and/or to a punishment (euthanasia). Before writing, reread several of the Analects so that his style, wording and imagery are fresh, and then write your own Analect as if you were Confucius.
6. Because of a new F.C.C. regulation which grants equal television time to all candidates,

Confucius

you find yourself, as an announced candidate for the presidency of the United States, waiting to give a campaign interview. You are nervous, of course, and want to make the correct presentation. After the initial introductions, the red light on the camera facing you lights and the moderator of the 60-minute program turns to you and asks: "What would be the first thing you would do if elected to the Presidency?" Write the first thing that comes to your mind! Don't think about it or try to be clever. Just write down whatever the first insight is, the first image that came to you. What is the first thing that you would do if elected President of the U.S.?

Take about five minutes to write whatever comes spontaneously. Then reread how Confucius answered a similar question.

Tzu Lu said, "If the prince of Wei were waiting for you to come and administer his country for him, what would be your first measure?" The Master said, "It would certainly be to correct language . . ."

Return then to your journal, draw a line under what you have already written and compare what you said to what Confucius said. Did you learn anything through the comparison? Did you change your opinion in any way after rehearing the way Confucius answered the question? Is Confucius' answer still applicable in our situation today?

7. Imagine what would have happened if Buddha and Confucius would have met. What would Buddha have thought of the sayings of Confucius and vice versa? Select what you

consider to be their key teachings and place them in dialogue with one another. You may wish to have them speaking to one another or to record your own thoughts as you ruminate upon their key teachings. Is there anything in Confucius' teachings that lends itself to Buddhism?

Chapter 6   THE TAOIST WAY

There once was an old man and his son who owned a horse which provided their only source of income. One night the horse ran away. The next day, all the villagers trotted out to the old farmer's and said: "Oh no! This is the worst thing that could have happened to you."

The old farmer quietly answered, "It's too early to tell."

Soon thereafter the horse returned with five others. The next morning all the villagers trotted out to the farmer and said, "Congratulations! This is the best thing that could ever happen to you."

But the old farmer quietly said, "It's too soon to tell."

Shortly thereafter, his son tried to ride one of the new horses. The horse was wild, and threw him into the corral fence. He was left him with a permanent limp. The next morning the villagers came again and said, "This is the worst tragedy that could ever happen to you."

But the old farmer said quietly, "It's too soon to tell."

A year later, the army came through the village to take all the healthy young men off to war. The old farmer's son was of no use to them and was left behind. None of the other young men ever returned. The farmer's constant response reflects the nature of the Tao.

As taught by Lao Tzu (604–?) and later by Chuang Tzu (369–286 BCE), the root-source of human and natural life is the Tao: the mysterious, eternal, nameless, spontaneous inactivity at the center of all actions. In the remainder of this chapter we will focus upon the verse of Lao Tzu and the short stories of Chuang Tzu which depict the sublime nuances of the Taoist way.

The Story of Lao Tzu

Around 100 BCE Ssu-ma Ch'ien, in the first comprehensive history of China, the *Records of the Historian* (historical memoirs), presented a brief biography of Lao Tzu, but one that is uncertain and sometimes puzzling. From this account we learn that "Lao Tzu" is an honorary title, and that the sage's real name was Li Erh (surname and given name) or Li Tan (surname and public name). "Lao" means old or venerable and was a title applied to the legendary sages of ancient China, whereas "Tzu" (a term of respect used by disciples) was used like a social prefix such as "Master" or "Sir." The title Lao Tzu then means the grand old master, the venerable philosopher.

Though his life-story cannot be verified, and although there is widespread disagreement about his dates (including a reputed meeting with Confucius in 518 BCE), Chinese tradition affirms the historical veracity of a school of mystical hermits who followed the teachings attributed to the ancient philosopher. According to this tradition, Lao Tzu was a native of Ch'u

Lao Tzu

Jen born to the Li family, spent years as a petty civil servant and curator of the imperial archives, and later became a hermit during which time he met Confucius. As Da Liu indicates, Taoist hermits "had no interest whatever in anything ordinarily regarded as characteristic of organized religion."[1]

No doubt Lao Tzu lived much like another rebel, mystic Chinese sage of the Ch'an School, Han Shan (Cold Mountain) who lived in a barren mountainous seclusion, in the heart of the Void (or Tao). A poor, eccentric, idiot-like hermit, Han Shan is pictured walking with a frog in a bird's nest on his head. He, like Lao Tzu, left conventional society, and lived independent of worldly considerations. At home anywhere, Han Shan, who depicted himself as a "naked insect," and who carried with him a copy of the Tao Te Ching (pronounced Dao Deuh Jing), describes his homeless life in the following two lyrics:

In my house there is a cave,
And in the cave is nothing at all—
Pure and wonderfully empty,
Resplendent, with a light like the sun . . .

If you're looking for a place to rest, Cold Mountain is good for a long stay. The breeze blowing through the dark pines sounds better the closer you come. And under the trees a white-haired man mumbles over his Taoist texts. Ten years now he hasn't gone home; he's even forgotten the road he came by.[2]

Like Han Shan, the early Taoists often lived solitary lives in remote sections of China, choosing personal freedom and intimacy with nature over socially determined interactions. This state of homelessness was the epitome of creative insecurity which stimulated an exploration into the nature of things as they really are.

While we know virtually nothing of the life of Lao Tzu, Chinese tradition contains two accounts of a meeting between Confucius and Lao Tzu in about 518 BCE. In each version, Confucius is reportedly anxious to query Lao Tzu about ritual and rites, but when Confucius asks about ancestor-worship, Lao Tzu replies:

> The bones of all of those of whom you speak have crumbled into dust; only their words remain. When the wise man finds work to occupy him, he travels in a chariot; otherwise he walks, carrying his pulpit himself. I have heard it said that a good merchant carefully conceals his goods and acts as if he had nothing, and that a perfect sage makes himself appear a fool. Put aside your arrogant manner and your insatiable desire, your affected demeanor and your excessive ambitions. None of that is of any use to you.[3]

After the meeting Confucius, at first unable to speak, confides to Nan Kung and Ching Shu on his return home:

> I know that the bird flies, that the fish swims, that animals walk; but animals can be taken with the net, fish with the line, birds with an arrow attached to a cord. As for the dragon, I know nothing, except perhaps that he ascends to heaven carried by the clouds and the wind. Today I saw Lao-tse. He is like the dragon.[4]

Lao Tzu, like his disciple Chuang Tzu, was far more skeptical about the accomplishments of human action and humanistic education than was Confucius. He took a more passive though not inactive approach toward the human condition and urged individuals to be quiet and spontaneous, and to be trained by the vicissitudes of nature rather than by the structures of a classical education.

Comparing the story of Lao Tzu and the story of Confucius is like comparing Yin to Yang. A Taoist stresses unlearning while a Confucianist stresses learning; a Taoist returns to original simplicity or *p'u* while a Confucianist cultivates virtuous behavior; a Taoist practices actionless action or *wu wei* while a Confucianist refines ritual action; and the Taoist returns to natural spontaneity while a Confucianist develops disciplined protocol. While each teaches the Tao and esteem for individual and social harmony, Confucius emphasizes communal moral perfection through social rituals, whereas Lao Tzu emphasizes the individual, mystical realization of the unnamable Tao.

	CONFUCIUS	LAO TZU
Goal	Cultivated Dignity (Learning)	Spontaneous Simplicity (Unlearning)
Method	Reanimation of Classical Values	Reversal/Letting Go Return to Original Nature
Result	Moral Perfection	Mystical Individuality
Politics	Moral Charisma[5]	Laissez-Faire

Like the Amerindians, when Lao Tzu sensed that death was near, he took leave of familiar circumstances and traveled west. When he reached the border of his village a customs official, recognizing him as a sage, asked him to write a summary of his teaching and experience of the Tao. Lao Tzu compliantly retired into the official's hut, and when he departed, he left the border guard a five thousand-character document which came to be called the Tao Te Ching. These mystical lyrics teach inactive action, quietude, reversal, emptiness, humility, and the Tao, which is ". . . natural, eternal, spontaneous, nameless, and indescribable. It is at once the beginning of all things and the way in which all things pursue their course."[6]

Tao Te Ching

For the size of its impact and influence upon Chinese culture, the Tao Te Ching, pronounced Dow De Jing (The Way and Its Virtue), is a remarkably small classic of eighty-one brief lyrics. It combines poetry, philosophical speculation, and mystical reflection. The eighty-one lyrics comprised of 5,250 characters are organized in two parts—from 1–37 (on the nature of the Tao) and from 38–81 (on the nature of Te).

The Tao Te Ching begins with the cryptic, paradoxical line—the Tao that can be tao-ed (named, described, spoken of) is not the eternal Tao. There are as many translations of these significant lines as there are translators:

> The Tao that can be told of is not the Absolute Tao (Lin Yutang).
> The Way that can be told of is not an Unvarying Way (Waley).
> The Tao that is the subject of discussion is not the true Tao (Old).
> The Way that may truly be regarded as the Way is other than a permanent way (Duyvendak).
> The Flow that can be followed is not the eternal Flow (auct.).
> The course that can be discoursed is not the eternal Course (auct.).
> The Force that is forced isn't true Force (auct.).
> The Tao that can be tao-ed is not the invariable Tao (Fung Yu-lan [Bodde]).[7]

As in the Hindu story where *Brahman* is both *nirguna* and *saguna*, the Tao is both name-

Tao

less and named. Tao is ultimately nameless, the Tao beyond Tao which (when named) is called: the "mother of All," the "Mystery," the "Doorway" (#1); a "wordless teaching" (#2); the "empty vessel" (#4); a "substanceless image," the "Mysterious Feminine" (#4); a "Bellows" (#5); like waters (#8); elusive, rarefied, infinitesimal (#14); an infant (#20); a great formless form with nothing to see or hear (#35); and the mother of all (#25, #52).

To understand the seeming internal reversals of the opening line, it is important to see that line in its immediate context:

1. A Tao that can be told of [tao] is not the Permanent Tao.
2. A name that can be named is not the Permanent Name.
3. The nameless (wu-ming) is the origin of Heaven and Earth.
4. The named (yu-ming) is the Mother of the Ten Thousand Creatures.
5. Hence, in the permanent state of undesire, we see its mysteries;
6. In the permanent state of desire, we see its boundaries [or: its surface].
7. These two [modes] have the same principle but different names.
8. Together, I call them the Obscure;
9. The most obscure in this obscurity is the Gate to all Mysteries.[8]

These nine lines contain a completed cycle, beginning with the Tao and ending at the "Gate to all Mysteries" which is also the Tao. The first two lines present an intentional ambiguity in terms of two oppositions—one concerning the nature of the Tao and the other concerning the name of the Tao. Since neither is permanent, the reader is alerted that the Tao is a word like a finger which points beyond itself. Therefore, as Lao Tzu later remarks: "Those who know do not speak; those who speak do not know" (#41).

Lines three and four present a further opposition, one between the Tao's two fundamental modes: the nameless (*wu-ming*) and the named (*yu-ming*). *Wu*, often translated as non-being, means "not to have," and *yu*, generally translated as being, means "to have." Just as the Hindu Hymn of Creation begins prior to being and non-being, and just as the Hindu speaks of Brahman as both *nirguna* (without attributes) and *saguna* (with characteristics), so too the Tao is depicted both without and with characteristics. The point is that *wu* and *yu* produce each other, complement each other, offset each other and harmonize each other (#2).

The unseen Tao (wu-ming, or "nameless") is pictured as the void at the center of a wheel and as the emptiness at the center of a cup without which neither could function. On the other hand the seen Tao (yu-ming, "named") is depicted as the feminine which gives birth to the myriad creatures, and as water which flows effortlessly beyond any obstacle.

Lines five and six join these two modes of the Tao through two states of human perception. To fully apprehend what is paradoxically beyond apprehension one must both rid oneself of desires, to perceive the *wu-ming* aspect, and allow oneself desires, to perceive the *yu-ming* aspect. This is necessary since, as line seven states, these two aspects are the same and diverge in name only.

Together *wu* and *yu* are called mysteries—mystery upon mystery—which line eight refers to as the Obscure, and line nine as the Gate to all Mysteries. Just as the Hymn of Creation concludes with the provocative question—Who can truly say how the one arose?—Lao Tzu concludes with an equally provocative image. The Tao is finally ineffable, a mystery with no end in which *wu* and *yu* are one, yet not one, a paradoxical, enigmatic image which can be known only by being entered.

Tao occurs seventy-six times in the Tao Te Ching, each time with different connotations. According to a more spiritual than linguistic etymology, the Chinese character for Tao is composed of three pictures: the head of a sage (one anciently wise), the body of the man walking in a motionless manner, and the character as a whole, which means a road, path or way. While Tao is the ultimate reality and ground of being and non-being, it is not to be equated with a personal, transcendent God. Rather Tao is the maternal, flowing, spontaneous, *sui generis* (self-generating) organic course of the universe. In other words, as Chuang Tzu remarked in one of his most often remembered characterizations of the Tao, there is nowhere that it does not exist.

Te means variously virtue or power, the power or force of the Way, of acting in accord with the process of the Way.

The appearance of great virtue follows only the Tao.[9]

Etymologically *Te* too consists of three characters: going, toward, and heart, or going straight to the heart. While *Te*, or "virtuality," is the actualization and communication of Tao in everyday living, the wisdom of *Te* is not a function of knowledge or intelligence, for, according to Lao Tzu, when "intelligence and knowledge appeared . . . the great artifice began" (#18). *Te* cannot be faked, imitated, or copied in any way. Instead *Te* is the virtue of acting without striving (*wei wu wei*). Literally *wei wu wei* (often reduced to *wu wei*) means to do, not, to do, or doing without doing. It has been variously translated as inaction, passivity, quietude, non-aggressive action, spontaneous naturalness, non-interference and spontaneous inaction. Therefore the sage produces actionless actions and wordless teachings. Lao Tzu writes that:

> The softest thing in the world can command the hardest thing in the world.
> Nothingness can penetrate where there is no space
> That is why I know the advantage of non-action.
> The teaching without words,
> The advantage of non-action,
> Very few in the world can attain them.[10]

While difficult to achieve, the attitude of *wu wei* confers strength, agility and endurance upon one who spontaneously actualizes it, for, as Lao Tzu says, the soft and the weak overcome the hard and the strong. Thus Lao Tzu uses water as a symbol of Tao's non-resistance, of letting be and following the flow of reality:

> The highest good is like water.
> Water is good in benefitting all things and does not compete.
> It puts itself in a place which everybody detests.
> Therefore it is approaching Tao.[11]

Examples of *wu wei* abound in athletics and in the arts. I remember the effortless grace of an Esther Williams who swam as if the water was swimming her, of a Roberto Clemente who glided under fly balls others would not reach as if the ball drew him to itself, and of a Van Cliburn who plays the piano as if the music were playing him, as if another music (the Tao's) played through his fingers and accommodated itself to the piano concerto being performed. In each case personal effort joined the calm dynamic inherent in all movement; in each case the movement was spontaneously uninhibited and childlike.

For Lao Tzu there are three stages in human growth—the infant, the adult, and the sage. We could refer to these as *original nature* (the natural pre-self-reflective innocence of infancy), *human nature* (the conditioned self-reflective experience of mature consciousness) and *Tao-nature* (the un-self-reflective emptiness of spontaneous awareness). The True Sage actualizes a process of mystical reversal, and returns to the original nature or *p'u* (the uncarved block). This reversal is characterized as "reversion" in which the action of the Tao comes through weakness, through appearing to fall backward. As Lao Tzu says:

> Returning is the movement of Tao;
> Weakness is the use of Tao.
> All things in the world come from being.
> Being comes from non-being.[12]

Lao Tzu often returned to the image of *p'u* (uncarved block) to give expression to the paradoxical reversal of the Tao's courseway. *P'u* is original nature, one's childlike innocence, before civilization, culture and education shape the natural mind. To this end one must "banish wisdom and discard knowledge" (#19) to return to the simplicity of the primal, undifferentiated unity with Tao. To become whole, one must first become fragmented, or twisted, "for true wholeness can only be achieved by return" (#22). Lao Tzu stressed the necessity of passing on and going far away in order to return to what was true at the beginning, to the what-is-so-of-itself nature of the Tao. We might even say, based on this discussion, that if Confucius reanimated tradition, that Lao Tzu reversed it.

> In learning, (the desire to know) increases day by day;
> In practicing Tao, (it) decreases day by day.
> Decreasing and decreasing until one reaches non-action.
> Non-acting and yet nothing is undone.
> The world should be ruled by non-interference.
> If he rules by interference,
> He is not worthy to rule the world.[13]

The question which arises is how—How does one practice this reversal, this "return to the state of infancy" (#27)?

The rishis of India and the Taoist mystics of China after Lao Tzu agreed that there exists, within the human body, an invisible network of energy centers, sometimes called *chakras,* a psychophysiological power related to breath, blood, and the circulatory systems, but not limited to them, centers which are activated through meditation and motion.

To stimulate the unlearning process, Taoist spiritual practices began by activating *ch'i* (life-breath or vital energy stored in the solar plexus) through breath-control, visualizations, and patterned, slow-motion movements. Called *Ch'i Kung* and *Tai Ch'i,* these movements are repeated to attune the practitioner to the rhythm of his or her own nature. To subtract day by day, to let go, to forget the self, to surrender one's own desires until one has reached true inactivity is to practice the Tao—for where there is stillness in movement the Tao appears.

Unfortunately, Lao Tzu provides only one mention of *ch'i*-activation or breath control, a technique which Taoists practiced for prolonging life and for returning subtleness to the body. In chapter ten Lao Tzu asks his hearers to "concentrate your vital force (breath) and achieve the highest degree of weakness like an infant" in order to be able to "penetrate all without taking any action."

The Story of Chuang Tzu

A final consequence of this reversal is that true Taoists "have no 'deathspot' in them" (#50) because they have already died to name, to form, and to cultural definitions. To aim at life is to achieve death, Lao Tzu wrote, whereas to act without striving, without fearing death, is to reach the immortality of one's original nature. The action of inaction is clearly the pathway to this end, the pure inaction of heaven and the peaceful inaction of earth. This inactive-activity allows one to overcome the fear and anxiety associated with dying.

In Chuang Tzu's "Supreme Happiness" we read that after his wife died, he sat with his legs sprawled out, pounding on a tub and singing. Hui Tzu said:

> "It should be enough simply not to weep at her death. But pounding on a tub and singing—this is going too far, isn't it?"
>
> Chuang Tzu said, "You're wrong. When she first died, do you think I didn't grieve like anyone else? But I looked back to her beginning and the time before she was born. Not only the time before she was born, but the time before she had a body. Not only the time before she had a body, but the time before she had a spirit. In the midst of the jumble of wonder and mystery a change took place and she had a spirit. Another change and she had a body. Another change and she was born. Now there's been another change and she's dead. It's just like the progression of the four seasons, spring, summer, fall, winter.
>
> "Now she's going to lie down peacefully in a vast room. If I were to follow after her bawling and sobbing, it would show that I don't understand anything about fate. So I stopped."[14]

For the Taoist, life and death are transmutations into different forms, like the metamorphosis of silkworms into moths. Chuang Tzu himself, as he approached his own death, had to deter his disciples who wished to provide him with an elaborate funeral. He said:

> The heavens and the earth will serve me as a coffin and a coffin shell. The sun and moon and stars will decorate my bier. All creation will be at hand to witness the event. What more need I than these?[15]

Little is known about Chuang Chou, the author of the *Chuang Tzu*. For some time he served as a petty official at the Lacquer Garden in Meng or what is now known as Honan. Whoever Chuang Chou was, he had a uniquely defiant wit and no use for commercial or political customs. Ssu-ma Ch'ien (145–89 BCE) provides a revealing biographical detail illustrative of Chuang Tzu's spontaneous, often humorous independence:

> King Wen of Ch'u, hearing of Chuang Tzu's talents, sent a messenger to him, bearing costly gifts, and inviting him to come to court as his minister. Chuang Tzu laughed and told the messenger from Ch'u: "A thousand pounds of gold make a

handsome sum indeed; ministerhood is indeed very honorable. But have you ever seen the ox being led to the sacrifice? After being fattened up for several years, it is decked out in embroidered trappings and led into the great temple. At this moment it would undoubtedly prefer to be an uncared-for piglet, but it is too late, isn't it? Go away! Do not defile me! I would rather frolic joyously in the mire than be haltered by the ruler of a state. I will never take office. Thus I will remain free to live as I see fit."[16]

This story is the sole biographical detail that we have of Chuang Tzu and points to the central theme of the *Chuang Tzu*—freedom. For Chuang Tzu, since all human problems are world-initiated and world-dependent, the solution was to free oneself from the world.

But how? Like Lao Tzu's lyrics before him, Chuang Tzu's short stories are studded with paradoxical anecdotes and idiotic *non sequiturs* which depict the sage as one who has mystically realized Tao. Such a person needs no system of logic, no ordered set of ethical principles nor theological doctrines by which to live. And like his predecessor Lao Tzu who denounced culture's perversion of the natural mind, Chuang Tzu's mystical preoccupation was *wu wei*, and how to teach what cannot be taught. Therefore one of his favorite themes is the wisdom of uselessness.

Chuang Tzu tells of an old tree that stood by the side of a road so full of knots, its branches so twisted, that no carpenter would ever look at it. It produced no fruit, had too few leaves to offer anyone shade, and even the birds stayed away from its uninviting limbs. There it stood, big and useless. One day, in response to a friend's disgust at the tree's uselessness, Chuang Tzu remarked: "But it will die a natural death. No axe blade will ever cut it down. You should be so useless, for if there's no use for it, how can it come to grief?"

The Pivot of Tao

Echoing Lao Tzu's realization of stillness in motion, the not-I in the I, Chuang Tzu was grasped by the limitless possibilities of "Yes" and "No," of life and death (seeing that opposites constantly become each other). He realized that pleasure and displeasure are not opposites to be chosen among or avoided, but that they condition human responses to ever-changing situations.

The key to Chuang Tzu's stories is the complementarity of opposites, for the pivot of Tao passes through the center of reality where yes and no, life and death, pleasure and displeasure converge. To be able to realize intuitively the rightness of each action, whether yes or no, is to perform the one action prior to all action, the actionless action. Just as the truth of the Tao comes from the lowliest teacher, to be free from the world necessitates a path of reversal. As Chuang Tzu tells, one day, after watching his cook cut up an ox like a gentle wind with sacred rhythm and timing, Prince Wen Hui exclaimed: "Good work! Your method is perfect!" "Method?" the cook replied. "I follow the Tao beyond all methods!" The cook then explained that whereas most cooks need a new chopper at least once a year, his had cut a thousand oxen in nineteen years. When he cut, he said:

I see nothing
With the eye. My whole being
Apprehends.
My senses are idle. The spirit
Free to work without plan
Follows its own instinct
Guided by natural line,
By the secret opening, the hidden space,
My cleaver finds its own way.
I cut through no joint, chop no bone.[17]

Of course from the Taoist standpoint, it would be dangerous to think that this story taught anything permanent, for as Chuang Tzu reminds his hearers:

The fish trap exists because of the fish; once you've gotten the fish, you can forget the trap. The rabbit snare exists because of the rabbit; once you've gotten the rabbit, you can forget the snare. Words exist because of meaning; once you've gotten the meaning, you can forget the words. Where can I find a man who has forgotten words so I can have a word with him?[18]

NOTES

1. Da Liu, *The Tao and Chinese Culture* (New York: Schocken Books, 1979), 21.

2. *Cold Mountain,* translated by Burton Watson (New York: Grove Press, n.d.), 68.

3. Pierre Do-Dinh, *Confucius and Chinese Humanism,* (New York: Frank & Wagnalls, 1969), 43–44.

4. *Ibid.*

5. This term is discussed in Christian Jochim's *Chinese Religions: A Cultural Perspective* (Englewood Cliffs, N.J.: Prentice-Hall, Inc., 1986), 125–126.

6. Wing-Tsit Chan, *A Sourcebook in Chinese Philosophy* (Princeton: Princeton U. Press, 1963), 136.

7. Alan Watts, *Tao: The Watercourse Way* (New York: Pantheon Books, 1975), 39.

8. Max Kaltenmark, *Lao Tzu and Taoism,* trans. by Roger Greaves (Stanford, Cal.: Stanford U. Press, 1965), 30.

9. *Tao Te Ching,* translated by Ching-yi Dougherty (unpublished), #21. All selections from the *Tao Te Ching* will be from this translation.

10. *Tao Te Ching,* 43.

11. *Tao Te Ching,* 8.

12. *Tao Te Ching,* #40.

13. *Tao Te Ching,* #48.

14. *Chuang Tzu: Basic Writings,* translated by Burton Watson (New York: Columbia University Press, 1964), 113.

15. *The Wheel of Death*, edited by Philip Kapleau (New York: Harper Torchbooks, 1971), 70–71.

16. Kaltenmark, 71.

17. Thomas Merton, *The Way of Chuang Tzu* (New York: New Directions, 1965), 46.

18. Watson, 140.

Selections

Selections from the Tao Te Ching translated by Ching-yi Dougherty and from the Writings of Chuang Tzu translated by Burton Watson.

Tao Te Ching

1

The Tao that can be spoken of is not the eternal Tao.

The name that can be named is not the eternal name.

Non-being is the name of the beginning of heaven and earth.

Being is the name of the mother of all things.

Therefore (one) is constantly non-being,

In order to see its wonders.

Constantly being in order to see its limits.

These two come from the same origin but differ in names.

Both are called mysteries.

The mystery of the mystery is the gate to all wonders.

2

The world knows beauty as being beautiful,

Just because there is ugliness.

The world knows good as being good,

Just because there is bad.

Therefore being and non-being produce each other,

Difficult and easy complement each other,

Long and short form each other,

High and low incline to each other,

Sound and noise harmonize with each other,

Front and back follow each other.

Therefore the sage engages in non-action,

And teaches without words.

All things are done,

But he did not initiate them.

Creating but not possessing,

Doing but not depending,

He achieves but does not dwell on the achievement.

Just by not dwelling on it,

He never loses it.

3

Not esteeming the talented prevents people from competing.

Not treasuring hard-to-get things prevents people from robbing

Not seeing the desirable prevents people from confusion.

Therefore the rule of the sage is to empty people's mind,

Fill their stomachs,

Weaken their will,

And strengthen their bones,

Constantly cause them to be ignorant and desire-less,

And cause the wise ones not to dare to do.

By non-action, there is no misrule.

4

Tao is empty,

But it never exhausts itself through use.

Fathomless, it seems to be the genesis of all things.

It dulls its sharpness,

Unties its tangles,

Dims its luster,

And mixes with the dust.

Hidden as it is exists.

I do not know whose son it is.

It seems to have existed before the emperor of heaven.

6

Vacuous, divine and everlasting,

It is called the mysterious female.

The gate to the mysterious female is the root of heaven and earth.

It is continuous as if it exists.

Being used, it is inexhaustible.

7

The heaven and earth last forever.

The reason that heaven and earth last forever is that they do not live for themselves.

That is why they live so long.

Therefore the sage places himself last,

He is in the front.

He disregards himself and yet exists.

It is not because he is selfless and thus he becomes himself?

8

The highest good is like water.
Water is good in benefitting all things and does not compete.
It puts itself in a place which everybody detests.
Therefore it is approaching Tao.
In living (the man of highest good) is good in remaining low.
In thought he is good in being profound.
In dealings he is good in compassion.
In speech he is good in fulfilling his promises.
In administration he is good in orderly rule.
In work he is good in being effective.
In action he is good in choosing the right moment.
Because he does not compete,
He makes no enemy.

9

Holding and filling (the cup) is not as good as ceasing.
Tempering and sharpening (the sword) it will be dull before long.
The house is filled with gold and jade,
And none can guard it.
Wealthy, titled and arrogant,
A man will be followed by disaster.
When achievement is accomplished,
One retires.
This is the Tao of heaven.

10

Can you harness your spirit and soul and hold to the One, not departing from it?
Can you concentrate your breath to attain the suppleness of the infant?
Can you clean your inner vision, so it is without blemish?
Can you love your state and rule the people by non-action?
Can you be receptive when the heavenly gate opens and closes?
Can you be without cunning while you know everything?
Produce everything.

Nurture everything.
Producing but not possessing,
Doing but not depending,
Leading but not dominating is called the mysterious virtue.

14

To look at it, but not see,
It is called formless.
To listen to it, but not hear,
It is called soundless.
To reach it but not catch it,
It is called intangible.
These three cannot be thoroughly investigated,
Therefore they merge into one.
Above it, it is not bright.
Below it, it is not dark.
Boundless, it cannot be named.
It returns again to non-substance.
It is called the formless form,
Substance-less image.
It is called elusive.
Meeting it, one cannot see its head.
Following it, one cannot see its tail.
Grasp the Tao of the ancient time to master what we have now.
To be able to know what has been since the beginning in ancient time is
Called the discipline of Tao.

16

Attain the utmost void.
Maintain the utmost quietude.
All things come to being.
Then I see they return (to non-being).
Of millions of things,
Each returns to its root again.
Returning to its root is called quietude.
It means returning to nature.
Returning to nature is called constant.
Knowing the constant is called enlightenment.
Not knowing the constant blindly creates disaster
He who knows the constant is all embracing.
Then he is impartial.
Then he is universal.
Then he is in accord with nature.

Then he is in accord with Tao.
Then he is everlasting.
He is free from danger throughout his life.

19

Discard knowledge and abandon wisdom,
People are benefitted a hundredfold.
Discard humaneness and abandon righteous-
ness,
People will again be filial and loving.
Discard cleverness and abandon profit,
Robbers and thieves will disappear.
These three are mere ornaments,
And not sufficient (in themselves).
Therefore people should follow other (virtues).
They should appear unadorned,
Embrace simplicity,
Less selfishness,
Fewer desires.

20

Discard learning,
There will be no worry.
What difference is there between "Yes, sir." and
"Mm"?
What difference is there between good and evil?
What people fear must be feared.
How vast and endless it is!
The people are happy as enjoying a feast or hik-
ing in the spring.
I alone am calm without feeling,
As the infant who cannot yet smile.
Inertly, as though I have no place to go.
All the people seem to have plenty.
I alone seem to be wanting.
I have the mind of a fool, so ignorant.
The common people are very bright.
I alone am unclear.
The *common people are discriminating.*
I alone do not see the distinction,
Calm as the sea,
And free as the unceasing wind.
Everybody is capable.
I alone am stupid and crude.
I alone am different from others,
And value drawing nourishment from Mother.

21

The appearance of great virtue follows only the
Tao.
The thing, Tao, is elusive.
Elusive and yet there is image in it.
Elusive and yet there is substance in it.
Deep and dark, there is essence in it.
Its essence is very true.
There is truth in it.
Since ancient times till now,
Its name remains,
And thus we see the beginning of things.
How do we know the beginning of things was
like this?
Because of Tao.

22

The yielding will be preserved.
The bent will be straightened.
The hollow will be filled.
The old will be renewed.
Having little, he will get more.
Having much, he will be confused.
Therefore the sage holds to the One and be-
comes the model of the world.
He who does not show himself will be illustrious.
He who does not assert himself will be famous.
He who does not boast will be meritorious.
He who is not conceited will be lasting.
What the ancients say "The yielding will be pre-
served" is not empty words.
The yielding is truly preserved and followed.

25

There was a thing formed out of chaos.
It existed before heaven and earth.
Soundless, formless, independent, unchanging,
All pervading and unceasing,
It may be the mother of the world.
I do not know its name,
And name it Tao.
I am forced to call it great.
Great means moving.
Moving means far.
Far means returning.
Therefore Tao is great,

Heaven is great, earth is great,
People are also great.
There are four greats in the universe.
People are only one of them.
People follows the laws of the earth.
Earth follows the laws of heaven.
Heaven follows the laws of Tao.
Tao follows the laws of nature.

27

A good traveler leaves no trace.
A good speech has no flaw.
A good calculator needs no counting tools.
A good gate needs no lock and cannot be opened.
A good knot needs no rope and cannot be untied.
Therefore the sage is always good in saving people,
And none is rejected;
Is always good in saving things,
And nothing is discarded.
This is called the inherent understanding.
Therefore the "good" people are the teachers of the "bad" people;
The "bad" people are the lessons of the "good" people.
The person who does not honor the teacher and love the lessons,
Though he were wise,
He is confused.
This is called the essential mystery.

28

Knowing masculinity, but holding to femininity,
He is the ravine of the world.
Being the ravine of the world,
He does not stray from the constant virtue,
And again returns to the state of being an infant.
Knowing the white [but keeping to the black,
He is the model of the world.
Being the model of the world,
The constant virtue will not change,
And again returns to infinity.
Knowing the glory,] but keeping to the disgrace,
He is the valley of the world.
Being the valley of the world,
The constant virtue will suffice,

And again returns to the natural state.
The uncarved wood is chisled to make into a vessel.
The sage uses the natural state,
And becomes the chief of ministers.
Therefore the greatest rule does not cut.

37

Tao never acts, and nothing is undone.
If the dukes and princes can hold it,
All people will develop by themselves.
Having developed they may desire to act.
Then I will restrain them with the nameless "simplicity",
They will have no desire.
Without desire they will be quiet.
Then the world will be peaceful by itself.

38

The man of superior virtue is not conscious of his virtue,
Therefore he has virtue.
The man of inferior virtue always abides with virtue,
Therefore he is without virtue.
The man of superior virtue practices non-action without a purpose;
The man of inferior virtue practices non-action with a purpose.
The man of superior humaneness acts without a purpose;
The man of superior righteousness acts with a purpose.
The man of superior propriety acts,
If none responds to him,
He will raise his arm to enforce it.
Therefore when Tao is lost there appears virtue,
When virtue is lost there appears humaneness,
When humaneness is lost there appears righteousness,
When righteousness is lost there appears propriety.
Propriety shows the lack of loyalty and trust,
And it is the beginning of disorder.
Those who can predict are the flowers of Tao,
And are the beginning of folly.

Therefore the man of Tao places himself on substance,
And does not rest on superficiality.
He stays with the fruit and not with the flowers.
He rejects that and takes this.

40
Returning is the movement of Tao;
Weakness is the use of Tao.
All things in the world come from being.
Being comes from non-being.

41
When the superior man hears Tao,
He practices it diligently.
When the average man hears Tao,
He is not sure whether it exists.
When the inferior man hears Tao,
He laughs at it.
If he had not laughed at it,
It is not qualified to be Tao.
Therefore the proverb has it:
"Bright Tao appears dark;
Advancing Tao appears retreating;
Level Tao appears tortuous;
Superior virtue appears void;
Great purity appears stained;
Vast virtue appears insufficient;
Solid virtue appears lax;
True virtue appears unreal;
Great square has no corners;
Great vessel is never finished;
Great tones are not audible;
Great image has not shape."
Tao is hidden and nameless,
Only Tao is good in providing and completing.

42
Tao produces one;
One produces two;
Two produces three;
Three produces all things.
All things carry the Ying on their backs and hold the Yang.
The two vital forces are blended into harmony.
What people detest is to be orphans, widowers and poor,

And yet kings use them for "I".
Therefore things are either decreased in order to increase,
Or are increased in order to decrease.
What people teach,
I also teach:
"Men of violence will be killed."
I will use it as a principle of teaching.

50
People are born and people die.
One third of them live long.
One third of them die young.
One third of them live but reach death (by their own doing).
Why is this so?
Because they live too lavishly.
I heard that those who are good in preserving themselves
Will not meet wild buffalo and tigers while travelling on land,
Will not be hurt by weapons in war.
There is no place for the buffalo to plunge its horns;
There is no place for the tiger to dig in its claws;
There is no place for the weapons to sink its blade.
Why is this so?
Because he provides no place for death.

56
He who knows does not not speak.
He who speaks does not know.
(He) blocks the senses,
Closes the doors,
Blunts the sharpness,
Unties the tangles,
Dims the glare,
Mixes with the dust.
This is called the mysterious identification.
Therefore it is impossible to be close to him,
And it is impossible to be indifferent to him.
It is impossible to benefit him,
And it is impossible to harm him.
It is impossible to honor him,
And it is impossible to disgrace him.

That is why he is regarded the best in the world.

76

When people are born, they are soft and weak;
When they are dead, they are stiff and hard.

When the plants are born,
They are supple and crisp.
When they are dead,
They are dry and brittle.
Therefore hard and strong are the followers of
  death,
Soft and weak are the followers of life.
That is why when the army is strong,
It will not be victorious.
When the tree is strong,
It will be cut.

Strong and big are inferior,
Soft and weak are superior.

81

Truthful words are not beautiful,
Beautiful words are not truthful.
Good people are not eloquent.
The eloquent people are not good.
He who is wise does not know everything,
He who knows everything is not wise.
The sage does not accumulate;
The more he does for people,
The more he saves;
The more he gives to people,
The more he has.
The Tao of heaven benefits and does not harm;
The Tao of sage does but does not compete.

Chuang Tzu:

SECTION 3. THE SECRET OF CARING FOR LIFE

Your life has a limit but knowledge has none. If you use what is limited to pursue what has no limit, you will be in danger. If you understand this and still strive for knowledge, you will be in danger for certain! If you do good, stay away from fame. If you do evil, stay away from punishments. Follow the middle; go by what is constant, and you can stay in one piece, keep yourself alive, look after your parents, and live out your years.

Cook Ting was cutting up an ox for Lord Wen-hui. At every touch of his hand, every heave of his shoulder, every move of his feet, every thrust of his knee—zip! zoop! He slithered the knife along with a zing, and all was in perfect rhythm, as though he were performing the dance of the Mulberry Grove or keeping time to the Ching-shou music.

"Ah, this is marvelous!" said Lord Wen-hui. "Imagine skill reaching such heights!"

Cook Ting laid down his knife and replied, "What I care about is the Way, which goes beyond skill. When I first began cutting up oxen, all I could see was the ox itself. After three years I no longer saw the whole ox. And now—now I go at it by spirit and don't look with my eyes. Perception and understanding have come to a stop and spirit moves where it wants. I go along with the natural makeup, strike in the big hollows, guide the knife through the big openings, and follow things as they are. So I never touch the smallest ligament or tendon, much less a main joint.

"A good cook changes his knife once a year—because he cuts. A mediocre cook changes his knife once a month—because he

hacks. I've had this knife of mine for nineteen years and I've cut up thousands of oxen with it, and yet the blade is as good as though it had just come from the grindstone. There are spaces between the joints, and the blade of the knife has really no thickness. If you insert what has no thickness into such spaces, then there's plenty of room—more than enough for the blade to play about in. That's why after nineteen years the blade of my knife is still as good as when it first came from the grindstone.

"However, whenever I come to a complicated place, I size up the difficulties, tell myself to watch out and be careful, keep my eyes on what I'm doing, work very slowly, and move the knife with the greatest subtlety, until—flop! the whole thing comes apart like a clod of earth crumbling to the ground. I stand there holding the knife and look all around me, completely satisfied and reluctant to move on, and then I wipe off the knife and put it away."

"Excellent!" said Lord Wen-hui. "I have heard the words of Cook Ting and learned how to care for life!"

When Lao Tan died, Ch'in Shih went to mourn for him; but after giving three cries, he left the room.

"Weren't you a friend of the Master?" asked Lao Tzu's disciples.

"Yes."

"And you think it's all right to mourn him this way?"

"Yes," said Ch'in Shih. "At first I took him for a real man, but now I know he wasn't. A little while ago, when I went in to mourn, I found old men weeping for him as though they were weeping for a son, and young men weeping for him as though they were weeping for a mother. To have gathered a group like *that*, he must have done something to make them talk about him, though he didn't ask them to weep. This is to hide from Heaven, turn your back on the true state of affairs, and forget what you were born with. In the old days, this was called the crime of hiding from

Heaven. Your master happened to come because it was his time, and he happened to leave because things follow along. If you are content with the time and willing to follow along, then grief and joy have no way to enter in. In the old days, this was called being freed from the bonds of God.

"Though the grease burns out of the torch, the fire passes on, and no one knows where it ends."

Chuang Tzu's wife died. When Hui Tzu went to convey his condolences, he found Chuang Tzu sitting with his legs sprawled out, pounding on a tub and singing. "You lived with her, she brought up your children and grew old," said Hui Tzu. "It should be enough simply not to weep at her death. But pounding on a tub and singing—this is going too far, isn't it?"

Chuang Tzu said, "You're wrong. When she first died, do you think I didn't grieve like anyone else? But I looked back to her beginning and the time before she was born. Not only the time before she was born, but the time before she had a body. Not only the time before she had a body, but the time before she had a spirit. In the midst of the jumble of wonder and mystery a change took place and she had a spirit. Another change and she had a body. Another change and she was born. Now there's been another change and she's dead. It's just like the progression of the four seasons, spring, summer, fall, winter.

"Now she's going to lie down peacefully in a vast room. If I were to follow after her bawling and sobbing, it would show that I don't understand anything about fate. So I stopped."

TAOIST JOURNAL EXERCISES

1. According to Chinese tradition, Lao Tzu was reportedly a historian in charge of the Chou archives. When Confucius visited Lao Tzu to ask about the correct practice of rituals, Lao Tzu said:

> "What you are talking about concerns merely the words left by people who have rotted along with their bones. Rid yourself of your arrogance and your lustfulness, your ingratiating manners and your excessive ambition. These are all detrimental to your person." On leaving, Confucius told his disciples, "I know a bird can fly, a fish can swim, and an animal can run. For that which runs a net can be made; for that which swims a line can be made; for that which flies a corded arrow can be made. But the dragon's ascent into heaven on the wind and the clouds is something which is beyond my knowledge. Today I have seen Lao Tzu who is like a dragon."

Why did Confucius react the way he did? After thinking about the legendary meeting, imagine the two figures meeting again in today's North American cultural context. What would they have to say to each other? How would their disagreements in the classical story be manifest in today's context? Whose side do they tend to accept and why?

Lao Tzu

2. Imagine that you were the gatekeeper and the last person to see Lao Tzu as he is about to leave the town, an old man, never to return again. Imagine you are the one who asks him to leave some of his teachings and that at the same time you have the opportunity to dialogue with him. What would you ask him about his teachings and practices and/or about what to do in your own life? What would Lao Tzu's advice be in your present circumstances?

3. Review all of the images used in the Tao Te Ching to depict the actionless action of the Tao. It is helpful to list them (e.g., void, water, bamboo, valley spirit, mysterious feminine). Find a contemporary image or symbol which in your understanding depicts the Tao. You may wish to draw a fresh realistic abstract, human to natural image of the Tao or to depict it in poetic, dramatic or prosaic words.

4. As in a beginning painting class or writing class, where students deliberately imitate the subject-matter and form of a great master painter or writer, select one of the Lao Tzu's verses and rewrite it—as closely resembling the original as possible and yet with an additive, a nuance, a subtle-as-the-Tao shift in perspective or in content. For example, rewrite #40:

> In Tao there is an inescapable emptiness
> It never increases, it never decreases.
> By it are all things as they are.
> Without it nothing holds true to itself!

Rewrite this as if you are Lao Tzu today. What images would you select to make Lao Tzu's voice contemporary?

5. In Arthur Waley's translation of the Tao Te Ching we read:

> The Valley Spirit never dies.
> It is named the Mysterious Female.
> And the Doorway of the Mysterious Female
> Is the base from which Heaven and Earth
>   sprang.
> It is there within us all the while,
> Draw upon it as you will, it never runs dry. (#6)

Give your own interpretation of this poem. What is the Valley Spirit and where is the "base from which heaven and earth sprang"? Have you ever experienced the Mysterious Female?

6. Imagine that you are Lao Tzu and that after leaving the gatekeeper with eighty-one verses you remember one that you forgot and one therefore that was not recorded with the others. What was it? What did Lao Tzu remember? Write as Lao Tzu might have the eighty-second verse of the Tao Te Ching.

Chapter 7 ZEN'S ORIGINAL FACE

In a graduate religious studies class, a professor of Chinese Zen Buddhism once asked whether a light projected onto a movie screen symbolized the teachings of Zen.[1] Students who recalled studying the no-self of Buddha and the void of the Tao answered affirmatively. Without speaking, he projected onto the screen the picture of an *enso*, an empty, asymmetrical, spontaneously ink-brushed circle. "This is the emptiness or formless-form of the True Self," he said, "for there is no formlessness with form."

Enso

Buddhist Schools

Before discussing the Ch'an patriarchs Bodhidharma and Hui Neng, and The Diamond and Platform Sutras, let us first take a brief look at the historical trajectory of Buddhism from India to China.

By the first century CE Buddhist missionaries had penetrated into the culture of the later Han Dynasty. Silk trade between China and the West had already produced many merchant colonies from northwest Tun Huang to the Huai Valley. Buddhist businessmen for several generations had settled in China and become bi-lingual; at the same time, intellectual Buddhist monks of various sects began to evangelize and translate Sanskrit texts into Chinese. One way of characterizing this development in Chinese Buddhism is to note its two main branches—the devotion-oriented school, and the wisdom-oriented school.

Devotional Buddhists, by far the most popular school of Buddhism in East Asia today, call Buddha "Amitabha" (immeasurable-light), and chant or recite Buddha's name (A-mi-ta-bha) with honor and devotion. Buddha, along with numerous other Buddhas, abides beyond a trillion Buddha-lands where heavenly music plays and mystical flowers shower the golden ground. In that "Most Happy Land" birds elegantly broadcast the Eightfold Noble Path. Pure Land Buddhists relate to Buddha in a way similar to the way the Vishnavites in India are devoted to Lord Krishna.

Read by almost all Buddhist schools, one of the most important texts for devotional Buddhists is the Lotus Sutra which was probably compiled in Northern India between 250 BCE and the first century CE. The text is based on a cosmic drama in which Sakyamuni Buddha and innumerable Buddhas congregate with Buddha, represented as *Tathagata*, the eternal father of all Buddha-children. Instead of three vehicles (Hinayana, Mahayana and Vajrayana), it teaches one vehicle—the Great Teaching—Mahayana:

> All Buddhas from the very start have taken the vow:
> "The Buddha-way which I walk,
> I desire to enable all living beings
> To attain the same way with me."
> Although Buddhas in future ages
> Preach hundreds of trillions
> Of methods, beyond number,
> In reality there is only the One Vehicle.[2]

Another text often chanted by Pure Land Buddhists—The Heart Sutra—is said to be the heart of the heart of Buddhism. Its mere 16 sentences (262 Chinese characters) summarize Buddha's teaching of emptiness. Recited daily in monasteries, zendos, temples, and households for two millennia, this sutra is used to introduce Buddha's teachings to new students.

THE MAHA PRAJNA PARAMITA HRIDAYA SUTRA

Avalokiteshvara Bodhisattva
when practicing deeply the Prajna Paramita
perceived that all five Skandas are empty
and was saved from all suffering and distress.

"Shariputra, form does not differ from emptiness;
emptiness does not differ from form.
that which is form is emptiness:
that which is emptiness, form.
the same is true of feelings, perceptions, impulses,
consciousness.

Shariputra, all dharmas are marked with emptiness:
they do not appear nor disappear,
are not tainted nor pure,
do not increase nor decrease.

Therefore in emptiness, no form,
no feelings, perceptions, impulses, consciousness:
no eyes, no ears, no nose, no tongue, no body, no mind:
no color, no sound, no smell, no taste, no touch, no object of mind:
no realm of eyes and so forth until no realm of mind consciousness:
no ignorance and also no extinction of it, and so forth
until no old-age-and-death and also no extinction of them:
no suff'ring, no origination, no stopping, no path:
no cognition, also no attainment.
with nothing to attain the Bodhisattva depends on Prajna Paramita
and his mind is no hindrance.
Without any hindrance no fears exist:
far apart from every perverted view he dwells in Nirvana.

In the three worlds all Buddhas depend on Prajna Paramita
and attain Anuttara-Samyaksambodhi.
Therefore know the Prajna Paramita
is the great transcendant mantra,
is the great bright mantra,
is the utmost mantra,
is the supreme mantra,
which is able to relieve all suff'ring
and is true, not false.

So proclaim the Prajna Paramita mantra,
proclaim the mantra that says:
gate, gate, Paragate, Parasamgate! Bodhi! Svaha!"
(Gone, Gone, Gone beyond, Gone altogether beyond, O what
an awakening, All Hail!)[3]

The sutra concludes with an esoteric mantra which, like a finger, points to the moon of true illumination. Like the parables of Jesus, a mantra contains a secret language. Chanting the mantra tunes one's mind to the mind-seal of all the Buddhas. As Edward Conze notes: "A mantra is efficacious because it enshrines a spiritual principle" and because "transcendental wisdom has her being in a mantra, and can thus be apprehended by its repetition and manifold practice."[4]

The wisdom school on the other hand, which is the focus of this chapter, stresses *prajna* (awareness), whether sudden or gradual, whether with or without scriptures, the direct awareness of non-dual Buddha-Mind. The wisdom schools (especially Ch'an in China and Zen in Japan) substitute "just sitting," and resolving *kung-ans* (koan in Japanese, unresolvable problems) for the devotional techniques of chanting the sutras and meritorious actions.

If devotional Buddhism is more popular than Ch'an, why do we focus on the latter here? To put it simply, Ch'an or Zen expresses one of the most unique, most paradoxical and most iconoclastic teachings among all the world's sacred traditions.

Ch'an Buddhism makes a unique claim about itself. Implicitly, if not explicitly, it includes within every transmission of its teachings its own self-negation. In this regard Ch'an has four faces. It appears as a school within Mahayana Buddhism (with distinctive traits, practices, and a sacred canon), as the heart or root-source of all the schools within Buddhism (whether T'ien Tai, Hwa Yen or Pure Land), as the true source of all the great religions East and West, and lastly, as the True Nothingness beyond all "religion."

Here one is presented with the Ch'an beyond Ch'an or what might be called no-Zen Zen. "When Zen in this sense is fully concretized, there is no longer anything to be called Zen, and the uniqueness of Zen is that when it is realized it bows out of being."[5] When one is in harmony with self and world, there is no path, no religion, no Ch'an, just life.

One day a disciple came to a master and asked: "Who is the Buddha?" The master, looking carefully into the disciple's eyes, said: "The God of fire comes asking for fire!" The disciple went away satisfied.

The Story of Bodhidharma (486–593)

The story of Chinese Zen Buddhism is often linked to Bodhidharma, the 28th Patriarch of Indian Buddhism who became the 1st Patriarch of Chinese Buddhism. Legend tells us that after Bodhidharma arrived in Canton, he spent nine years in a mountain temple near Lo Yang gazing at a wall. In fact, the term "wall-gazing" is associated as much with Bodhidharma as the special message which he brought and taught:

> Not relying on words or letters,
> An independent Self-transmitting apart from any teaching;
> Directly pointing to man's Mind,
> Awakening his (Original-) Nature, thereby actualizing his Buddhahood.[6]

These four lines, as D.T. Suzuki points out, distinguish the principles of Ch'an teachings

Bodhidharma

from other schools of Buddhism which were already in existence in China, for they empha-size a direct, radical actualization of one's true nature, an actualization beyond words and ideas. Bodhidharma's expression of the True Source gave rise to a new Buddhist style of expression.

Shortly after Bodhidharma came to China, his reputation as a reclusive, disciplined teacher of meditation reached the Emperor Wu of Laing, who arranged to have an audience with the Indian Buddhist monk. Unlike Chuang Tzu, who preferred to frolic in the muck than to visit a ruler of state, Bodhidharma consented. One can imagine the scene: celibate monk, secular emperor, Confucian protocol. The interview transpired as follows:

> The Emperor Wu of Laing asked Dharma: "Ever since the beginning of my reign I have built so many temples, copied so many sacred books, and supported so many monks and nuns; what do you think my merit might be?"
>
> "No merit whatever, sire!" Dharma bluntly replied.
>
> "Why?" demanded the Emperor astonished.
>
> "All these are inferior deeds . . . which would cause their author to be born in the heavens or on this earth again."
>
> The Emperor Wu thereupon asked Bodhi Dharma again, "What is the first prin-ciple of the holy doctrine?"

"Vast emptiness, and there is nothing in it to be called holy, sire!" answered Dharma.

"Who is it then that is now confronting me?"

"I know not, sire!"[7]

The Emperor asked two questions, one about the merit of his religious building projects, which Bodhidharma dismissed as having "no merit," and the other about Bodhidharma's own *dharma*. "What do you teach?" Wu asked, and when Bodhidharma gave Buddha's answer—nothingness (vast emptiness and there is nothing to learn)—Wu naturally felt one-upped. Not to be shown-up, the emperor fired back with a question to one-up the one-upper: "Who is it then who stands before me now. If Bodhidharma teaches nothing, who then is the teacher before me?" Surely Wu, like the Pharisees who attempted to bind Jesus with trap-questions, thought his question was unanswerable. But Bodhidharma unceremoniously, spontaneously retorts: "I do not know!" Of course the learned emperor, from his unenlightened consciousness, was not enthralled by the illogical-logic of the Bodhidharma's awakening, and dismissed him to a monastery in the state of Wei.

As Bodhidharma's reputation spread, he was visited one day by the monk Shen Kuang who earnestly implored to be instructed in Ch'an. Since Bodhidharma paid no attention to him, the monk stood one evening in the midst of falling snow until buried to the knees. Still Bodhidharma would not see him. At last, after being repeatedly sent away, according to the legend Kuang cut off his left arm and presented it to Bodhidharma as a sign of sincerity. Kuang said:

"My soul is not yet pacified. Pray, master, pacify it." "Bring your soul here, and I will have it pacified." Kuang hesitated for a moment but finally said, "I have sought it these many years and am still unable to get hold of it!" "There! it is pacified once for all." This was Dharma's sentence.[8]

How are we to understand this more or less legendary account of Kuang's sincerity and Bodhidharma's response?

Ch'an's Non-Dualistic Structure

The following fourfold structural analysis of Ch'an Buddhism can be used as an interpretive backdrop for this story: problem, resolution, method, and result.[9]

Kuang's *problem* stems from what Chinese Zen calls the initial human condition (dualistic consciousness) which both affirms its own separate subjectivity and is at the same time objectively-conditioned. He is aware that he is not aware of who he truly is. The "I" who speaks is divided from the "I" with whom he identifies. This, in Zen's view, is the fundamental root of all human problems. All neurosis, anxieties, psychosis, doubts, fears and sufferings arise from this internal division.

Kuang does not know his true nature when he comes to Bodhidharma, for he, like every human, has accepted a number of partial resolutions (whether self-affirmative or object-dependent). Cutting off his arm symbolizes yet another self-affirmative attempt to resolve the question of True Self. According to Bodhidharma, the fundamental question is: Who is the one who cuts off his arm?

A Ch'an master Gutei, who always highlighted his teaching by suddenly raising his right index finger, assigned a disciple to care for the monastery in his absence. While he was away, a Taoist came to learn what the master taught and the disciple enthusiastically raised his right index finger. "This is what my master teaches!" he proudly said.

When his master returned he called for the disciple and said, "I hear that while I was gone we had a visitor to the monastery who wanted to know what I teach. What did you say?" Bursting with pride, the disciple quickly raised his right index finger and just as quickly his master sliced it off with a knife held behind his cloak. As the young man ran off, Gutei called his name. When he turned, Gutei raised his finger. In that instant the young man was enlightened.

The *resolution* to dualistic consciousness is non-dualistic True Self realization in which I am I, I am you and I am not-I (spontaneously and simultemporally). To put it another way, I can only be fully myself when I am the other (whether thing, person or cosmos), and when I am not myself (whether name or form). In China this awakening is called *wu* (*satori* in Japan), which is the Chinese character for the Sanskrit *budh* (the root of *Buddha* and *bodhi*). According to D.T. Suzuki, the chief aspects of this awakening are: irrationality, intuitive insight, authoritativeness, affirmation, a sense of the beyond, impersonal tone, exaltation, and momentariness.[10]

Suzuki himself reports that he tried for years to resolve the philosophical, psychological and spiritual problems posed by the Zen teaching of *Mu* (No; Nothing). The breakthrough occurred when he became "one with *Mu*, identified with *Mu*, so that there was no longer the separateness implied by being conscious of *Mu*." It is from this *samadhi* (formless concentration), as Suzuki adds, that one must awake. "That moment of coming out of the samadhi and seeing it for what it is—that is *satori*. When I came out of that state of *samadhi* during that session I said, I see. This is it!"[11]

The resolution to the human conundrum comes when the human ego (or self-reflective awareness) dies to itself to be reborn no-longer-itself. In Chinese and Japanese Buddhism this is called the "Great Death" or the "Great Doubt Block."

When Bodhidharma challenged Kuang to bring forth his soul or true self, he was attempting to force Kuang to the brink of ego-self-destruction. Introduced in China, this *method* was called *kung-an* (*koan* in Japan). Originally, a *kung-an* meant a public document which set standards of judgment. In Chinese Buddhism it came to mean a statement, question, or challenge which makes no rational sense, and which is used by Ch'an and Zen masters to deliberately trick the seeker out of his or her rational mind into awakening (*wu*). The following *kung-ans* reflect their illogical demand: Show me your Original Face! Before God said "Let there be Light!" who are you? What is the sound of one hand clapping? Without speaking, without remaining silent—Speak! Does a dog have Buddha Nature? *Mu* (No)!

When Bodhidharma presented a *kung-an* to Kuang, the only response possible was not an intellectual statement or an emotional outburst but an intuitive, spontaneous expression of his Original Nature. Students of Chinese Buddhism are challenged by the *kung-an* until its answer spontaneously bursts forth from within the challenge of its illogicality.

Another self-awakening method is "just sitting." Called *zazen* (seated Zen) in Japan, just sitting refers to sitting in a meditative, relaxed posture, back straight, eyes open, gaze downward, fully alert, breathing rhythmically, so that it is the continual breathing itself that sits. Just sitting means that while the aim of *zazen* is threefold—to develop concentration-power, to become awake, and to actualize the awakening-path in daily life activities—the one who is sitting has no conscious aim. The sitter simply is attentive to breath, mind following breath, mind going into breath. In response to the question "Who sits?" a Japanese Zen teacher once said: "When I sit, the earth sits!"

Lastly what is the *result* of this non-dualistic, True Self awakening? How does the awakened person express what Japanese philosopher Nishida calls "Absolutely Contradictory Self-Identity"?[12]

Awakened Compassion

We find ready examples of awakened behavior in Chinese Buddhist literature as well as in Chinese landscaping, flower arrangement and personal demeanor. The well-known ox-herding pictures, for example, illustrate the stages of awakening: searching for the ox (or True Self), seeing, catching, herding, and riding the ox, forgetting the ox in sleep, and forgetting both ox and self. The empty circle (enso) illustrates a return to one's original source. The penultimate picture—the Solitary Moon, or Reaching the Source—shows the seeker at-one with the sought, for the ox is nowwhere to be seen, and the river flows tranquil under a serene moon. Upon awakening, the mountains are green, the waters are blue. Fully transformed, the sage enters the market place bare-footed, dusty and with "bliss-bestowing hands" the full expression of self-affirming, self-negating love, or what might be called awakened compassion:

> Bare-chested and bare-footed, he comes out into the market place;
> Daubed with mud and ashes, how broadly he smiles!
> There is no need for the miraculous power of the gods,
> For he touches, and lo! the dead trees are in full bloom.[13]

This expression depicts two aspects of awakened compassion, the aspect of formlessness and the aspect of form. Like the enso, which represents the formless form of True-Self awakening, the person in the last ox-herding picture is true emptiness spontaneously and smilingly expressing itself. Awakening seeks to transmit itself, seeks to trigger awakening in others, to fill every opportunity with *wu*-oriented speech and action which in Buddhism is the heart of love. One can only truly love, the Zen masters say, when one is fully empty of a self who loves, so that one can be alive with self-affirming, self-negating love for all sentient beings.

The Ox-herding Pictures

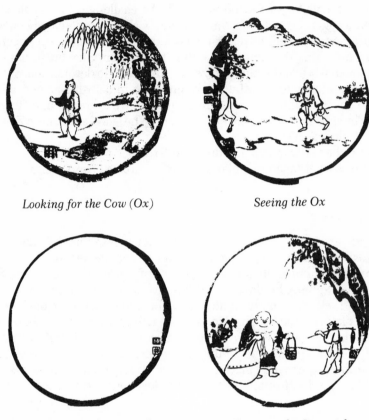

Looking for the Cow (Ox)   *Seeing the Ox*

The Cow (Ox) and the Man   *Entering the City with*
Both Gone Out of Sight   *Bliss-bestowing Hands*

One day Tanzan and Ekido were traveling along a muddy road in the rain and chanced to meet a beautiful girl in a silk kimono who hesitated at the muddy intersection. Tanzan at once lifted her and carried her across. That night Ekido said: "Monks should not look at lovely young females let alone touch them. Why did you do that?" Tanzan replied: "I left her back there; are you still carrying her?"

Conversely, the Japanese Zen master Hakuin was well known to be living a solitary, virtuous life. A beautiful Japanese girl, whose parents owned a nearby food store, suddenly became pregnant, and, after much harassment, named Hakuin as the father. In response to the parents' anger he merely said, "Is that so?" Hakuin, his reputation slandered, raised the child for a year until the mother confessed the truth to her parents. When the girl's mother and father went to Hakuin to ask for forgiveness and to get the child back again, Hakuin merely said as he gave over the child, "Is that so?"[14]

The Story of Hui Neng (638–713)

The sixth, last, and most important of all Chinese Buddhist patriarchs, who is responsible for turning Ch'an from a minor sect to a major school, is Hui Neng (pronounced Hway Lang). "Hui" means to bestow compassion on all beings and "Neng" means the capacity to effect the teachings of Buddha.

We learn from the Platform Sutra that he was born in the southwest of Kwangtung province. When his father died, he and his mother moved to the city of Canton, where the illiterate Hui Neng peddled firewood to support his mother. One day, at age twenty-four, he heard a customer reciting from the Diamond Sutra:

> If a Bodhisattva cherishes the idea of an ego-entity, a personality, a being, or a separated individuality, he is consequently not a Bodhisattva.[15]

After hearing this passage, he reported that his mind became enlightened. Thereupon, when he had provided for his aged mother's security, he left Kwangtung to travel some five hundred miles north to visit Hung Jen, the monastary of the fifth patriarch. At their meeting Hung Jen said: "Southerners have no Buddha-nature; how do you expect to attain it?" Whereupon Hui Neng responded: "There is no north and south in Buddha-nature!" This answer encouraged Hung Jen who sent Hui Neng off to pound rice in the monastery's mill.

Some eight months later, the fifth patriarch announced that he would pass on the Dharma-robe of his authority and patriarchal succession to the monk who composed the most perfect enlightenment stanza (*gatha*). Shen Hsiu, the most learned of the disciples, whom all the other monks felt would be the next master, wrote his stanza on a wall outside the meditation hall:

> The body is the Bodhi-tree,
> The mind is like a clear mirror
> At all times we must strive to polish it,
> And must not let the dust collect.[16]

When Hui Neng heard a servant recite this verse, he knew at once that its composer had not yet realized Mind-Essence; thus he composed his own:

> Bodhi originally has no tree,
> The mirror also has no stand.
> Buddha nature is always clean and pure;
> Where is there room for dust?[17]

The fifth patriarch, as the story is told in the Platform Sutra, recognized Hui Neng's non-dual awakening. At a secret, midnight meeting, using his robe as a screen, he expounded the Diamond-Cutter Sutra. Hui Neng realized that everything is Essence of Mind (Buddha-nature), intrinsically pure, intrinsically free, intrinsically self-sufficient. Then the patriarch bestowed the robe of patriarchal succession upon Hui Neng and sent him away clandestinely so that the other monks, out of loyalty to Shen-hsiu, would not harm him.

Shortly after Hui Neng left, he was pursued by a hot-tempered monk named Ch'en. Every time Hui Neng looked back, Ch'en was there. When about to be caught, Hui Neng threw the robe and begging bowl to the ground and hid. In fact, the pursuer sought the dharma, not the robe, and was immediately enlightened when Hui Neng posed this *kung-an:* "Show me your original face!" At that point Hui Neng realized that the unbroken succession of patriarchs was a symbol not worth perpetuating.

After a period of isolation and travel, Hui Neng decided to break his seclusion, and to propagate the Dharma. He traveled to the Fa Hsin Temple in Canton and arrived without announcing who he was. One day, as a banner blew in the wind, two monks argued as to what moves, the wind or the pennant. Hui Neng suggested that it was neither, that what actually moved was the mind. When head master Yin Tsung heard this, he recognized Hui Neng to be the one who inherited the fifth patriarch's *dharma*. He invited him immediately to take the platform seat of honor.

As part of his instructions, Hui Neng authorized the copying of all his sermons into a volume titled "Sutra Spoken on the High Seat of the Treasure of the Law." Since the *dharma* is non-dual, it must be grasped intuitively by one who realizes Buddha-nature. Therefore, at the time of his death, he warned his disciples not to mourn, but to live, by correct practice, as if he were still alive. After an active life of teaching, in the seventh month of 713 CE, Hui Neng gathered his monks:

> "For whom are you crying?" the master asked. "Are you worrying about me because you think I don't know where I'm going? If I didn't know, I wouldn't be able to leave you this way. What you're really crying about is that you don't know where I'm going. If you actually knew, you couldn't possibly cry because [you would be aware that] the True nature is without birth or death, without going or coming."[18]

Ch'an Sutras

It has been said that since Ch'an awakening is beyond sacred texts, prior to letters and symbols, the sutras are useless, misleading and incomprehensible. A famous Zen painting shows a Patriarch tearing a sutra into pieces and throwing it into the wind. "If you find a sacred canon—burn it!" a Chinese Zen master might say. Yet at the same time, in the traditional Buddhist view, the sutras are a skillful means (*upaya*), a vehicle for the direct transmission of Awakening. Indeed sacred texts are the self-expression of the supreme self-awakening of Buddha-Mind. The truth of the sutras then is both prior to the letters and contained within them in the sense that *wu* and the sutras are transparent to one another.

Hui Neng teaches that all sutras and scriptures were provided to fit the needs and temperaments of various people. While he was against idle lip-repetition of the texts, he says:

> Whether sutra-reciting will enlighten you or not, or benefit you or not, all depends on yourself. He who recites the Sutra with the tongue and puts its teaching into actual practice with his mind "turns round" the Sutra. He who recites it without putting it into practice is "turned round" by the Sutra.[19]

Extrinsic sutra-recitation by itself was of no use to Hui Neng, for it became then an empty habit. It must be accompanied by the intention-realization that the mind reading the sutra is the mind who wrote it, is the mind about whom it is written.

The Mahayanan texts, it may be recalled, include all the Theravadan texts, but also include Tibetan and Chinese writings which came into being as Buddhist teaching was spread by monks and missionaries. The main Mahayanan texts, called the Prajna-Paramitra Sutras (Sutras of Perfect Wisdom), are composed by unknown authors and preserved in Sanskrit, Tibetan and Chinese. These Wisdom Sutras include the Awakening of Faith (attributed to Asvaghosha in the second century BCE), the Heart Sutra (popular, short sutra with concluding mantra often chanted by monks), the Diamond Sutra (Supreme Transcendental Wisdom), and the Platform Sutra (the story of Hui Neng).

Diamond Sutra

The Diamond Sutra, or "The Diamond of the Perfection of Transcendental Wisdom," reflects the dharma which, like a diamond, cuts all other stones and is itself uncut, cuts through all other dharmas and is itself traceless. It was written in Sanskrit, as a part of the larger Maha-Prajna Paramita Sutra in the second or third century CE, perhaps in part by the patriarch Nagarjuna, and was first translated into Chinese about 400 CE.

In the sixteen-foot-long Tun Huang Print of the Diamond Sutra (now in the British Museum), Buddha is pictured sitting cross-legged on a lotus throne, preaching the Diamond-Cutter. Like Christ the teacher in Russian and Greek icons, Buddha's right hand is raised and held in a teaching *mudra* (sacred gesture). Buddha's third eye of Inner Wisdom is a sun super-imposed non-dualistically on the moon. The disciple Subhuti, hands folded, respectfully kneels before Buddha, surrounded by monks, nuns and laity. The Chinese writing to the left says:

> If you want to recite this Sutra, you must first recite the following mantra, so as to purify your mouth, i.e., "Tun-li, tun-li, maha-tun-li, tun-tun-li, svaha."[20]

The body of the Sutra records a dialogue between the Venerable Subhuti and Buddha. Subhuti asks two questions: How should humans abide in this world? How should we control our thoughts? The Buddha's answer is: to be devoid of self, of personality, of ego-entity, and devoid of separate individuality, to practice sutra-reciting or listening to the discourse with a pure, lucid mind and to attain an inner realization of its meaning. To seek the Consummation of Incomparable Enlightenment, one must resolve to liberate all beings and to realize at the same time that not anyone is liberated.

In the crucial section, Buddha asks Subhuti whether Buddha is awake or if he has a system of doctrine which can be recited and memorized. Subhuti responds that Buddha's discourse has neither system nor formulation because it is a transcendental, inexpressible law to be intuited as the law of each disciple's mind. Buddha says that a follower who is attuned through intrinsic faith to a single stanza of the Diamond Sutra, and who enthusiastically retells the text to others, realizes its intrinsic merit.

And why? Because all holy Buddhas owe their awakening to the sacred truth in the canons, and because life otherwise is like a bubble, a glistening shadow, a lightning flash, devoid of permanency, without liberation. Upon hearing this discourse Subhuti had an interior realization that the idea of Fundamental Reality is just a name, that the notion of an ego-entity is erroneous and that thought of a separated individuality is merely an illusion.

Platform Sutra

The full title of Zen's most esteemed sacred text or the Platform Sutra is the "Southern School Sudden Doctrine, Supreme Mahayana Great Perfection of Wisdom: The Platform Sutra preached by the Sixth Patriarch Hui Neng at the Ta Fan Temple in Shao-Chou." There are six extant versions of this Sutra, the oldest and shortest of which was discovered in 1900 in a cave in Northwest China. It was written in Chinese in roughly four types of material: *autobiography*, which appears later in this chapter; *sermons* on the identity of prajna (wisdom) and samadhi (realization of self), on the sudden awakening of no-thought, and seeing directly into one's own nature; *stories* often critical of Pure Land doctrines; and *verse*.

The Platform Sutra is divisible into two basic parts: the sermon at the Ta Fan Temple, which includes the fictionalized autobiography (already reviewed), and the remaining teachings on a variety of subjects: there is no difference between an enlightened man and an ignorant one; reciting and studying the Diamond Sutra enables one to realize Essence of Mind; the distinction between Prajna (Wisdom) and Dhyana (Meditation) and between the Sudden school and the Gradual school does not really exist; everything depends on self-practice; one should speak only what is realized intuitively.

While the historical facts about Hui Neng come to us from naturally biased disciples and followers, it is accepted as certain that he revolutionized Chinese Buddhism with his *kung-an*: "Show me your original face, before you were born!" His unlearned, simple-minded grasp and expression of Buddha-nature had a far-reaching influence, for he gave Indian Buddhism for the first time a truly Chinese expression. "Seeing into one's own nature" was evoked not by abstract formulations, but by a natural, spontaneous, concrete, non-dual self-awakening. As Shin'ichi Hisamatsu remarks, according to Chinese Buddhism "it is precisely the Original Face of man—of any one of us human beings—which is the True-Buddha."[21]

NOTES

1. The Chinese Buddhist word *ch'an* was a transliteration of the Indian Buddhist, Sanskrit word *dhyana* (meditation) and was in turn transliterated into the Japanese Buddhist word Zen. Dhyana, Ch'an and Zen therefore each refer to meditational Buddhism as opposed to devotional Buddhism. When I use the word Zen here I mean Chinese Zen Buddhism, the heart of which was later developed as Japanese Zen Buddhism.

2. Quoted in *The Great Asian Religions,* edited by Chan, Al Faruqi, Kitagawa and Raju (New York: Macmillan Co., 1969), 201.

3. Translator unknown. The mantra in parenthesis is quoted from *Buddhist Scriptures,* translated by Edward Conze (England: Penguin Books, 1959), 162–164. An annotated version of the "Heart Sutra" is found in Edward Conze's *Buddhist Wisdom Books* (New York: Harper Torchbooks, 1958), 77–107.

4. *Ibid.,* 103.

5. Bernard Phillips, "Reflections on Zen and Humanism," *The Humanist* (Nov/Dec. 1968), 14. I am indebted to the late Dr. Bernard Phillips who first introduced me to eastern religions at Temple University.

6. From Shin'ichi Hisamatsu's "Zen: Its Meaning for Modern Civilization," translated by R. DeMartino and Gishin Tokina," The Eastern Buddhist," I, No. 1 (September 65), 22.

7. D.T. Suzuki, *Zen Buddhism* (New York: Doubleday Anchor, 1956), 61.

8. *Ibid.,* 65.

9. For these remarks I am indebted to Richard DeMartino of Temple University who first introduced me to Zen, and to his valuable essay "The Human Situation and Zen Buddhism," in *Zen Buddhism and Psychoanalysis,* by D.T. Suzuki, Erich Fromm and Richard DeMartino (New York: Grove Press, 1960).

10. Suzuki, *ibid.,* 103–108.

11. D.T. Suzuki, *The Field of Zen* (New York: Harper & Row, 1969), 10.

12. DeMartino, 170.

13. D.T. Suzuki, *Manual of Zen Buddhism* (New York: Grove Press, 1960), 134.

14. These stories are found in *Zen Flesh, Zen Bones,* compiled by Paul Reps (New York: Doubleday Anchor, n.d.), 18, 7–8.

15. *The Diamond Sutra and The Sutra of Hui-Neng* translated by A.F. Price and Wong Mou-Lam (Boulder, Colorado: Shambola Publications, 1969), 52.

16. *The Platform Sutra of the Sixth Patriarch,* translated by Philip Yampolski (New York: Columbia University Press, 1967), 130.

17. *Ibid.,* 132.

18. Quoted in Philip Kapleau's *The Wheel of Death* (New York: Harper & Row. 1971), 71–72.

19. Yampolski, 174.

20. Edward Conze, *Buddhist Wisdom Books* (New York: Harper Torchbooks, 1958), 74.

21. Hisamatsu, 32.

Selections

Selections from the Diamond Sutra from sections 1, 2, 3, 8, 10, 12, 13, 14, and 22 translated by A.F. Price, and from the Platform Sutra (all of chapter 1 and portions of chapters 2–5) translated by Wong Mou-Lam.

The Diamond Sutra

SECTION I. THE CONVOCATION OF THE ASSEMBLY

Thus have I heard. Upon a time Buddha sojourned in Anathapindika's Park by Shravasti with a great company of bhikshus, even twelve hundred and fifty.

One day, at the time for breaking fast, the World-honoured enrobed, and carrying His bowl made His way into the great city of Shravasti to beg for His food. In the midst of the city He begged from door to door according to rule. This done, He returned to His retreat and took His meal. When He had finished He put away His robe and begging bowl, washed His feet, arranged His seat, and sat down.

SECTION II. SUBHUTI MAKES A REQUEST

Now in the midst of the assembly was the Venerable Subhuti. Forthwith he arose, uncovered his right shoulder, knelt upon his right knee, and, respectfully raising his hands with palms joined, addressed Buddha thus: World-honoured One, it is most precious how mindful the Tathagata is of all the Bodhisattvas, protecting and instructing them so well! World-honoured One, if good men and good women seek the Consummation of Incomparable Enlightenment, by what criteria should they abide and how should they control their thoughts?

Buddha said: Very good, Subhuti! Just as you say, the Tathagata is ever-mindful of all the Bodhisattvas, protecting and instructing them well. Now listen and take my words to heart: I will declare to you by what criteria good men and good women seeking the Consummation of Incomparable Enlightenment should abide, and how they should control their thoughts.

Said Subhuti: Pray, do, World-honoured One. With joyful anticipation we long to hear.

SECTION III. THE REAL TEACHING OF THE GREAT WAY

Buddha said: Subhuti, all the Bodhisattva-Heroes should discipline their thoughts as follows: All living creatures of whatever class, born from eggs, from wombs, from moisture, or by transformation, whether with form or without form, whether in a state of thinking or exempt from thought-necessity, or wholly beyond all thought realms—all these are caused by Me to attain Unbounded Liberation Nirvana. Yet when vast, uncountable, immeasurable numbers of beings have thus been liberated, verily no being has been liberated. Why is this, Subhuti? It is because no Bodhisattva who is a real Bodhisattva cherishes the idea of an ego-entity, a personality, a being, or a separated individuality.

SECTION VI. RARE IS TRUE FAITH

Subhuti said to Buddha: World-honoured One, will there always be men who will truly believe after coming to hear these teachings?

Buddha answered: Subhuti, do not utter such words! At the end of the last five-hundred-year period following the passing of the Tathagata, there will be self-controlled men, rooted in merit, coming to hear these teachings, who will be inspired with belief. But you should realize that such men have not strengthened their root of merit under just one Buddha, or two Buddhas, or three, or four, or five Buddhas, but under countless Buddhas; and their merit is of every kind. Such men, coming to hear these teachings, will have an immediate uprising of pure faith, Subhuti; and the Tathagata will recognize them. Yes, He will clearly perceive all these of pure heart, and the magnitude of their moral excellences. Wherefore? It is because such men will not fall back to cherishing the idea of an ego-entity, a personality, a being, or a separated individuality. They will neither fall back to cherishing the idea of things as having intrinsic qualities, nor even of things as devoid of intrinsic qualities.

Wherefore? Because if such men allowed their minds to grasp and hold on to anything they would be cherishing the idea of an ego-entity, a personality, a being, or a separated individuality; and if they grasped and held on to the notion of things as having intrinsic qualities they would be cherishing the idea of an ego-entity, a personality, a being, or a separated individuality. Likewise, if they grasped and held on to the notion of things as devoid of intrinsic qualities they would be cherishing the idea of an ego-entity, a personality, a being, or a separated individuality. So you should not be attached to things as being possessed of, or devoid of, intrinsic qualities.

This is the reason why the Tathagata always teaches this saying: My teaching of the Good Law is to be likened unto a raft. The Buddha-teaching must be relinquished; how much more so misteaching!

SECTION VII. GREAT ONES, PERFECT BEYOND
LEARNING, UTTER NO WORDS OF TEACHING

Subhuti, what do you think? Has the Tathagata attained the Consummation of Incomparable Enlightenment? Has the Tathagata a teaching to enunciate?

Subhuti answered: As I understand Buddha's meaning there is no formulation of truth called Consummation of Incomparable Enlightenment. Moreover, the Tathagata has no formulated teaching to enunciate. Wherefore? Because the Tathagata has said that truth is uncontainable and inexpressible. It neither *is* nor is it *not*.

Thus it is that this unformulated Principle is the foundation of the different systems of all the sages.

SECTION X. SETTING FORTH PURE LANDS

Buddha said: Subhuti, what do you think? In the remote past when the Tathagata was with Dipankara Buddha, did he have any degree of attainment in the Good Law?

No, World-honoured One. When the Tathagata was with Dipankara Buddha he had no degree of attainment in the Good Law.

Subhuti, what do you think? Does a Bodhisattva set forth any majestic Buddha-lands?

No, World-honoured One. Wherefore? Because setting forth majestic Buddha-lands is not a majestic setting forth; this is merely a name.

[Then Buddha continued:] Therefore, Subhuti, all Bodhisattvas, lesser and great, should develop a pure, lucid mind, not depending upon sound, flavour, touch, odour or any quality. A Bodhisattva should develop a mind which alights upon no thing whatsoever; and so should he establish it.

Subhuti, this may be likened to a human frame as large as the mighty Mount Sumeru. What do you think? Would such a body be great?

Subhuti replied: Great indeed, World-honoured One. This is because Buddha has explained that no body is called a great body.

SECTION XIII. HOW THIS TEACHING SHOULD BE
RECEIVED AND RETAINED

At that time Subhuti addressed Buddha, saying World-honoured One, by what name should this Discourse be known, and how should we receive and retain it?

Buddha answered: Subhuti, this Discourse should be known as "The Diamond of the Perfection of Transcendental Wisdom"—thus should you receive and retain it. Subhuti, what is the reason herein? According to the Buddha-teaching the Perfection of Transcendental Wisdom is not really such. "Perfection of Transcendental Wisdom" is just the name given to it. Subhuti, what do you think? Has the Tathagata a teaching to enunciate?

Subhuti replied to Buddha: World-honoured One, the Tathagata has nothing to teach.

Subhuti, what do you think? Would there be many molecules in [the composition of] three thousand galaxies of worlds?

Subhuti said: Many, indeed, World-honoured One!

Subhuti, the Tathagata declares that all these molecules are not really such; they are called "molecules." [Furthermore,] the Tathagata declares that a world is not really a world; it is called "a world."

Subhuti, what do you think? May the Tathagata be perceived by the thirty-two physical peculiarities [of an outstanding sage]?

No, World-honoured One, the Tathagata may not be perceived by these thirty-two marks. Wherefore? Because the Tathagata has explained that the thirty-two marks are not really such; they are called "the thirty-two marks."

Subhuti, if on the one hand a good man or a good woman sacrifices as many lives as the sand-grains of the Ganges, and on the other hand anyone receives and retains even only four lines of this Discourse, and teaches and explains them to others, the merit of the latter will be the greater.

SECTION XIV. PERFECT PEACE LIES IN FREEDOM
FROM CHARACTERISTIC DISTINCTIONS

Upon the occasion of hearing this Discourse Subhuti had an interior realization of its meaning and was moved to tears. Whereupon he addressed Buddha thus: It is a most precious thing, World-honoured One, that you should deliver this supremely profound Discourse. Never have I heard such an exposition since of old my eye of wisdom first opened. World-honoured One, if anyone listens to this Discourse in faith with a pure, lucid mind, he will thereupon conceive an idea of Fundamental Reality. We should know that such an one establishes the most remarkable virtue. World-honoured One, such an idea of Fundamental Reality is not, in fact, a distinctive idea; therefore the Tathagata teaches: "Idea of Fundamental Reality" is merely a name.

World-honoured One, having listened to this Discourse, I receive and retain it with faith and understanding. This is not difficult for me, but in ages to come—in the last five hundred years, if there be men coming to hear this Dis-

course who receive and retain it with faith and understanding, they will be persons of most remarkable achievement. Wherefore? Because they will be free from the idea or an ego-entity, free from the idea of a personality, free from the idea of a being, and free from the idea of a separated individuality. And why? Because the distinguishing of an ego-entity is erroneous. Likewise the distinguishing of a personality, or a being, or a separated individuality is erroneous. Consequently those who have left behind every phenomenal distinction are called Buddhas all.

Buddha said to Subhuti: Just as you say! If anyone listens to this Discourse and is neither filled with alarm nor awe nor dread, be it known that such an one is of remarkable achievement. Wherefore? Because, Subhuti, the Tathagata teaches that the First Perfection [the Perfection of Charity] is not, in fact, the First Perfection: such is merely a name.

Subhuti, the Tathagata teaches likewise that the Perfection of Patience is not the Perfection of Patience: such is merely a name. Why so? It is shown thus, Subhuti: When the Rajah of Kalinga mutilated my body, I was at that time free from the idea of an ego-entity, a personality, a being, and a separated individuality. Wherefore? Because then when my limbs were cut away piece by piece, had I been bound by the distinctions aforesaid, feelings of anger and hatred would have been aroused within me. Subhuti, I remember that long ago, sometime during my last past five hundred mortal lives, I was an ascetic practising patience. Even then was I free from those distinctions of separated selfhood. Therefore, Subhuti, Bodhisattvas should leave behind all phenomenal distinctions and awaken the thought of the Consummation of Incomparable Enlightenment by not allowing the mind to depend upon notions evoked by the sensible world—by not allowing the mind to depend upon notions evoked by sounds, odours, flavours, touch-contacts or any qualities. The mind should be kept independent of any thoughts which arise within it. If the mind depends upon anything it has no sure haven. This is why Buddha teaches that the mind of a Bodhisattva should not accept the appearances of things as a basis when exercising charity. Subhuti, as Bodhisattvas practise charity for the welfare of all living beings they should do it in this manner. Just as the Tathagata declares that characteristics are not characteristics, so He declares that all living beings are not, in fact, living beings.

SECTION XXXII. THE DELUSION OF APPEARANCES

Subhuti, someone might fill innumerable worlds with the seven treasures and give all away in gifts of alms, but if any good man or any good woman awakens the thought of Enlightenment and takes even only four lines from this Discourse, reciting, using, receiving, retaining and spreading them abroad and explaining them for the benefit of others, it will be far more meritorious.

Now in what manner may he explain them to others? By detachment from appearances—abiding in Real Truth.—So I tell you—

Thus shall ye think of all this fleeting world:
A star at dawn, a bubble in a stream;
A flash of lightning in a summer cloud,
A flickering lamp, a phantom, and a dream.

When Buddha finished this Discourse the venerable Subhuti, together with the bhikshus, bhikshunis, lay-brothers and sisters, and the whole realms of Gods, Men and Titans, were filled with joy by His teaching, and, taking it sincerely to heart they went their ways.

*   *   *

Sutra Spoken by the Sixth Patriarch on the High Seat of "The Treasure of the Law"

CHAPTER I
AUTOBIOGRAPHY

Once, when the Patriarch had arrived at Pao Lin Monastery, Prefect Wei of Shao Chou and other officials went there to ask him to deliver public lectures on Buddhism in the hall of Ta Fan Temple in the City (of Canton).

In due course, there were assembled (in the lecture hall) Prefect Wei, government officials and Confucian scholars, about thirty each, and bhikkhus, bhikkhunis, Taoists and laymen to the number of about one thousand. After the Patriarch had taken his seat, the congregation in a body paid him homage and asked him to preach on the fundamental laws of Buddhism. Whereupon, His Holiness delivered the following address:

Learned Audience, our Essence of Mind (literally, self-nature) which is the seed or kernel of enlightenment (Bodhi) is pure by nature, and by making use of this mind alone we can reach Buddhahood directly. Now let me tell you something about my own life and how I came into possession of the esoteric teaching of the Dhyana (or the Zen) School.

My father, a native of Fan Yang, was dismissed from his official post and banished to be a commoner in Hsin Chou in Kwangtung. I was unlucky in that my father died when I was very young, leaving my mother poor and miserable. We moved to Kwang Chou (Canton) and were then in very bad circumstances.

I was selling firewood in the market one day, when one of my customers ordered some to be brought to his shop. Upon delivery being made and payment received, I left the shop, outside of which I found a man reciting a sutra. As soon as I heard the text of this sutra my mind at once became enlightened. Thereupon I asked the man the name of the book he was reciting and was told that it was the Diamond Sutra (Vajracchedika or Diamond Cutter). I further enquired whence he came and why he recited this particular sutra. He replied that he came from Tung Ch'an Monastery in the Huang Mei District of Ch'i Chou; that the Abbot in charge of this temple was Hung Yen, the Fifth Patriarch; that there were about one thousand disciples under him; and that when he went there to pay homage to the Patriarch, he attended lectures on this sutra. He further told me that His Holiness used to encourage the laity as well as the monks to recite this scripture, as by doing so they might realise their own Essence of Mind, and thereby reach Buddhahood directly.

It must be due to my good karma in past lives that I heard about this, and that I was given ten taels for the maintenance of my mother by a man who advised me to go to Huang Mei to interview the Fifth Patriarch. After arrangements had been made for her, I left for Huang Mei, which took me less than thirty days to reach.

I then went to pay homage to the Patriarch, and was asked where I came from and what I expected to get from him. I replied, "I am a commoner from Hsin Chou of Kwangtung. I have travelled far to pay you respect and I ask for nothing but Buddhahood." "You are a native of Kwangtung, a barbarian? How can you expect to be a Buddha?" asked the Patriarch. I replied, "Although there are northern men and southern men, north and south make no difference to their Buddha-nature. A barbarian is different from Your Holiness physically, but there is no difference in our Buddha-nature." He was going to speak further to me, but the presence of other disciples made him stop short. He then ordered me to join the crowd to work.

"May I tell Your Holiness," said I, "that Prajna (transcendental Wisdom) often rises in my mind. When one does not go astray from one's own Essence of Mind, one may be called the 'field of merits.' I do not know what work Your Holiness would ask me to do."

"This barbarian is too bright," he remarked. "Go to the stable and speak no more." I then withdrew myself to the backyard and was told by a lay brother to split firewood and to pound rice.

More than eight months after, the Patriarch saw me one day and said, "I know your knowledge of Buddhism is very sound, but I have to refrain from speaking to you lest evil doers should do you harm. Do you understand?" "Yes, Sir, I do," I replied. "To avoid people taking notice of me, I dare not go near your hall."

The Patriarch one day assembled all his disciples and said to them, "The question of incessant rebirth is a momentous one. Day after day, instead of trying to free yourselves from this bitter sea of life and death, you seem to go after tainted merits only (*i.e.*, merits which will cause rebirth). Yet merits will be of no help, if your Essence of Mind is obscured. Go and seek for Prajna (wisdom) in your own mind and then write me a stanza (*gatha*) about it. He who understands what the Essence of Mind is will be given the robe (the insignia of the Patriarchate) and the Dharma (*i.e.*, the esoteric teaching of the Dhyana School), and I shall make him the Sixth Patriarch. Go away quickly. Delay not in writing the stanza, as deliberation is quite unnecessary and of no use. The man who has realised the Essence of Mind can speak of it at once, as soon as he is spoken to about it; and he cannot lose sight of it, even when engaged in battle."

Having received this instruction, the disciples withdrew and said to one another, "It is of no use for us to concentrate our mind to write the stanza and submit it to His Holiness, since the Patriarchate is bound to be won by Shen Hsiu, our instructor. And if we write perfunctorily, it will only be a waste of energy." Upon hearing this, all of them made up their minds not to write and said, "Why should we take the trouble? Hereafter, we will simply follow our instructor, Shen Hsiu, wherever he goes, and look to him for guidance."

Meanwhile, Shen Hsiu reasoned thus with himself. "Considering that I am their teacher, none of them will take part in the competition. I wonder whether I should write a stanza and submit it to His Holiness. If I do not, how can the Patriarch know how deep or superficial my knowledge is? If my object is to get the Dharma, my motive is a pure one. If I were after the Patriarchate, then it would be bad. In that case, my mind would be that of a worldling and my action would amount to robbing the Patriarch's holy seat. But if I do not submit the stanza, I shall never have a chance of getting the Dharma. A very difficult point to decide, indeed!"

In front of the Patriarch's hall there were

three corridors, the walls of which were to be painted by a court artist, named Lu Chen, with pictures from the Lankavatara (Sutra) depicting the transfiguration of the assembly, and with scenes showing the genealogy of the five Patriarchs for the information and veneration of the public.

When Shen Hsiu had composed his stanza he made several attempts to submit it to the Patriarch, but as soon as he went near the hall his mind was so perturbed that he sweated all over. He could not screw up courage to submit it, although in the course of four days he made altogether thirteen attempts to do so.

Then he suggested to himself, "It would be better for me to write it on the wall of the corridor and let the Patriarch see it for himself. If he approves it, I shall come out to pay homage, and tell him that it is done by me; but if he disapproves it, then I shall have wasted several years in this mountain in receiving homage from others which I by no means deserve! In that case, what progress have I made in learning Buddhism?"

At 12 o'clock that night he went secretly with a lamp to write the stanza on the wall of the south corridor, so that the Patriarch might know what spiritual insight he had attained. The stanza read:

Our body is the Bodhi-tree,
And our mind a mirror bright.
Carefully we wipe them hour by hour,
And let no dust alight.

As soon as he had written it he left at once for his room; so nobody knew what he had done. In his room he again pondered: "When the Patriarch sees my stanza tomorrow and is pleased with it, I shall be ready for the Dharma; but if he says that it is badly done, it will mean that I am unfit for the Dharma, owing to the misdeeds in previous lives which thickly becloud my mind. It is difficult to know what the Patriarch will say about it!" In this vein he kept on thinking until dawn, as he could neither sleep nor sit at ease.

But the Patriarch knew already that Shen Hsiu had not entered the door of enlightenment, and that he had not known the Essence of Mind.

In the morning, he sent for Mr. Lu, the court artist, and went with him to the south corridor to have the walls there painted with pictures. By chance, he saw the stanza. "I am sorry to have troubled you to come so far," he said to the artist. "The walls need not be painted now, as the Sutra says, 'All forms or phenomena are transient and illusive.' It will be better to leave the stanza here, so that people may study it and recite it. If they put its teaching into actual practice, they will be saved from the misery of being born in these evil realms of existence (*gatis*). The merit gained by one who practises it will be great indeed!"

He then ordered incense to be burnt, and all his disciples to pay homage to it and to recite it, so that they might realise the Essence of Mind. After they had recited it, all of them exclaimed, "Well done!"

At midnight, the Patriarch sent for Shen Hsiu to come to the hall, and asked him whether the stanza was written by him or not. "It was, Sir," replied Shen Hsiu. "I dare not be so vain as to expect to get the Patriarchate, but I wish Your Holiness would kindly tell me whether my stanza shows the least grain of wisdom."

"Your stanza," replied the Patriarch, "shows that you have not yet realised the Essence of Mind. So far you have reached the 'door of enlightenment,' but you have not yet entered it. To seek for supreme enlightenment with such an understanding as yours can hardly be successful.

"To attain supreme enlightenment, one must be able to know spontaneously one's own nature or Essence of Mind, which is neither created nor can it be annihilated. From ksana to ksana (thought-moment to thought-moment), one should be able to realise the Essence of Mind all the time. All things will then be free from restraint (*i.e.*, emancipated). Once the Tathata (Suchness, another name for the Essence of Mind) is known, one will be free from delusion for ever; and in all circumstances one's mind will be in a state of 'Thusness.' Such a state of mind is absolute Truth. If you can see things in such a frame of mind you will have known the Essence of Mind, which is supreme enlightenment.

"You had better go back to think it over again for a couple of days, and then submit me another stanza. If your stanza shows that you have entered the 'door of enlightenment,' I will transmit you the robe and the Dharma."

Shen Hsiu made obeisance to the Patriarch and left. For several days, he tried in vain to write another stanza. This upset his mind so much that he was as ill at ease as if he were in a nightmare, and he could find comfort neither in sitting nor in walking.

Two days after, it happened that a young boy who was passing by the room where I was pounding rice recited loudly the stanza written by Shen Hsiu. As soon as I heard it, I knew at once that the composer of it had not yet realised the Essence of Mind. For although I had not been taught about it at that time, I already had a general idea of it.

"What stanza is this?" I asked the boy. "You barbarian," he replied, "don't you know about it? The Patriarch told his disciples that the question of incessant rebirth was a momentous one, that those who wished to inherit his robe and Dharma should write him a stanza, and that the one who had an understanding of the Essence of Mind would get them and be made the Sixth Patriarch. Elder Shen Hsiu wrote this 'Formless' Stanza on the wall of the south corridor and the Patriarch told us to recite it. He also said that those who put its teaching into actual practice would attain great merit, and be saved from the misery of being born in the evil realms of existence."

I told the boy that I wished to recite the stanza too, so that I might have an affinity with its teaching in future life. I also told him that although I had been pounding rice there for eight months I had never been to the hall, and that he would have to show me where the stanza was to enable me to make obeisance to it.

The boy took me there and I asked him to read it to me, as I am illiterate. A petty officer of the Chiang Chou District named Chang Tih-Yung, who happened to be there, read it out to me. When he had finished reading I told him that I also had composed a stanza, and asked him to write it for me. "Extraordinary indeed," he exclaimed, "that you also can compose a stanza!"

"Don't despise a beginner," said I, "if you are a seeker of supreme enlightenment. You should know that the lowest class may have the sharpest wit, while the highest may be in want of intelligence. If you slight others, you commit a very great sin."

"Dictate your stanza," said he. "I will take it down for you. But do not forget to deliver me, should you succeed in getting the Dharma!"

My stanza read: There is no Bodhi-tree,
                 Nor stand of a mirror bright.
                 Since all is void,
                 Where can the dust alight?

When he had written this, all disciples and others who were present were greatly surprised. Filled with admiration, they said to one another, "How wonderful! No doubt we should not judge people by appearance. How can it be that for so long we have made a Bodhisattva incarnate work for us?"

Seeing that the crowd was overwhelmed with amazement, the Patriarch rubbed off the stanza with his shoe, lest jealous ones should do me injury. He expressed the opinion, which they took for granted, that the author of this stanza had also not yet realised the Essence of Mind.

Next day the Patriarch came secretly to the room where the rice was pounded. Seeing that I was working there with a stone pestle, he said to me, "A seeker of the Path risks his life for the Dharma. Should he not do so?" Then he asked, "Is the rice ready?" "Ready long ago," I replied, "only waiting for the sieve." He knocked the mortar thrice with his stick and left.

Knowing what his message meant, in the third watch of the night I went to his room. Using the robe as a screen so that none could see us, he expounded the Diamond Sutra to me. When he came to the sentence, "One should use one's mind in such a way that it will be free from any attachment," I at once became thoroughly enlightened, and realised that all things in the universe are the Essence of Mind itself.

"Who would have thought," I said to the Patriarch, "that the Essence of Mind is intrinsically pure! Who would have thought that the Essence of Mind is intrinsically free from becoming or annihilation! Who would have thought that the Essence of Mind is intrinsically self-sufficient! Who would have thought that the Essence of Mind is intrinsically free from change! Who would have thought that all things are the manifestation of the Essence of Mind!"

Knowing that I had realised the Essence of Mind, the Patriarch said, "For him who does not know his own mind there is no use learning Buddhism. On the other hand, if he knows his own mind and sees intuitively his own nature, he is a Hero, a 'Teacher of gods and men,' 'Buddha'."

Thus, to the knowledge of no one, the Dharma was transmitted to me at midnight, and consequently I became the inheritor of the teaching of the 'Sudden' School as well as of the robe and the begging bowl.

"You are now the Sixth Patriarch," said he. "Take good care of yourself, and deliver as many sentient beings as possible. Spread and preserve the teaching, and don't let it come to an end. Take note of my stanza:

Sentient beings who sow the seeds of enlightenment
In the field of causation will reap the fruit of Buddhahood.
Inanimate objects void of Buddha-nature
Sow not and reap not.

He further said, "When the Patriarch Bodhidharma first came to China, most Chinese had no confidence in him, and so this robe was handed down as a testimony from one Patriarch to another. As to the Dharma, this is transmitted from heart to heart, and the recipient must realise it by his own efforts. From time immemorial it has been the practice for one Buddha to pass to his successor the quintessence of the Dharma, and for one Patriarch to transmit to another the esoteric teaching from heart to heart. As the robe may give cause for dispute, you are the last one to inherit it. Should you hand it down to your successor, your life would be in imminent danger. Now leave this place as quickly as you can, lest some one should do you harm."

"Whither should I go?" I asked. "At Huai you stop and at Hui you seclude yourself," he replied.

Upon receiving the robe and the begging bowl in the middle of the night, I told the Patriarch that, being a Southerner, I did not know the mountain tracks, and that it was impossible for me to get to the mouth of the river (to catch a boat). "You need not worry," said he. "I will go with you."

He then accompanied me to Kiukiang, and there ordered me into a boat. As he did the rowing himself, I asked him to sit down and let me handle the oar. "It is only right for me to carry you across," he said (an allusion to the sea of birth and death which one has to go across before the shore of Nirvana can be reached). To this I replied, "While I am under illusion, it is for you to get me across; but after enlightenment, I should cross it by myself. (Although the term 'to go across' is the same, it is used differently in each case). As I happen to be born on the frontier, even my speaking is incorrect in pronunciation, (but in spite of this) I have had the honour to inherit the Dharma from you. Since I am now enlightened, it is only right for me to cross the sea of birth and death myself by realising my own Essence of Mind."

"Quite so, quite so," he agreed. "Beginning from you the Dhyana School will become very popular. Three years after your departure from me I shall leave this world. You may start on your journey now. Go as fast as you can towards the South. Do not preach too soon, as Buddhism is not so easily spread."

After saying good-bye, I left him and walked towards the South. In about two months' time, I reached the Ta Yü Mountain. There I noticed that several hundred men were in pursuit of me with the intention of robbing me of my robe and begging bowl.

Among them there was a monk named Hui Ming, whose lay surname was Ch'en. He was a general of the fourth rank in lay life. His manner was rough and his temper hot. Of all the pursuers, he was the most vigilant in search of me. When he was about to overtake me, I threw the robe and the begging bowl on a rock, saying, "This robe is nothing but a symbol. What is the use of taking it away by force?" (I then hid myself). When he got to the rock, he tried to pick them up, but found he could not. Then he shouted out, "Lay Brother, Lay Brother, (for the Patriarch had not yet formally joined the Order) I come for the Dharma, not for the robe."

Whereupon I came out from my hiding place and squatted on the rock. He made obeisance and said, "Lay Brother, preach to me, please."

"Since the object of your coming is the Dharma," said I, "refrain from thinking of anything and keep your mind blank. I will then teach you." When he had done this for a considerable time, I said, "When you are thinking of neither good nor evil, what is at that particular moment, Venerable Sir, your real nature (literally, original face)?"

As soon as he heard this he at once became enlightened. But he further asked, "Apart from those esoteric sayings and esoteric ideas handed down by the Patriarch from generation to generation, are there any other esoteric teachings?" "What I can tell you is not esoteric," I replied. "If you turn your light inwardly, you will find what is esoteric within you."

"In spite of my staying in Huang Mei," said he, "I did not realise my self-nature. Now thanks to your guidance, I know it as a water-drinker knows how hot or how cold the water is. Lay Brother, you are now my teacher."

ZEN JOURNAL EXERCISES

1. Take a few deep breaths as if you have just completed a set of *t'ai chi*. Spontaneously, without thinking, answer as many of the following questions as you have answers for.

    1. What does Zen taste like?
    2. What color is Zen?
    3. How does Zen feel?
    4. Can you imagine yourself awake (in a Zen sense)?
    5. What is the essence of Zen?
    6. What is the sound of one hand clapping?
    7. Who is the Buddha?
    8. Where do I come from?
    9. What is my Original Face?
    10. Who is Zen?

2. The Diamond Sutra is essentially a dialogue between Venerable Subhuti and Buddha, the "World-honoured One." In the second section Subhuti asks two questions which provide direction for the remainder of the Sutra:

    ". . . if good men and good women seek the Consummation of Incomparable Enlightenment, by what criteria should they abide and how should they control their thoughts?"

    How does Buddha answer these questions? Give an answer that is expressed in today's language, in contemporary jargon or even slang—as basic as you can. How would you answer the twin questions of abiding (being) and of controlling thoughts (doing)?

3. In a section of the Diamond-Cutter the World-honoured One uttered this verse:

    > Who sees me by form,
    > Who seeks me in sound
    > Perverted are his footsteps upon the Way,
    > For he cannot perceive the Tathagata.
    > (Section XXVI)

    a. What does this mean to you?
    b. Compare and contrast what Buddha says here about himself with what Lord Krishna said about himself in the Bhagavad Gita.

4. Imagine yourself sitting in a cave with Bodhidharma when he first came to China. Imagine not speaking for two years—living that close to someone and not speaking at all for

two years. What did you learn about Bodhidharma during that time. Is he as fierce as this picture appears?

5. The following is an awakening-poem in which the writer cleverly used typographical symbols to indicate what was said. This exercise asks you to substitute words for the symbols. What do you think the disciple said and how did the awakened master respond? Make a line-by-line transliteration of the poem as if you understood how to translate his typological symbolese into English.

SATORI

    (a short poetic effort to be played in the
    Marabhar
    Caves utilizing all available natural
    lighting)
    Cast
    Zen Master
    Student
    S. (%)
    ZM: . . .
    S: (%)?
    ZM: # = *
    S: (?)
    ZM: " ; ?"
    S: (!)
    ZM:
    S: !!
    ZM: !
    S:
    ZM:

K.E. Ishibashi

6. In the Platform Sutra Hui Neng says:

> He who recites the Sutra with the tongue and puts its teaching into actual practice with his mind "turns round" the Sutra.

What does Hui Neng mean by " 'turns round' the Sutra"? Can you give an example of a person (possibly yourself) turning round a sutra? Which sutra do you turn round?

7. Imagine that you are in the fifth patriarch's monastery. Describe the scene. Having heard the Diamond Sutra, you are now feeding and caring for pigs. You are illiterate, and so someone has to read you a four-line enlightenment poem written on a wall—

> The body is like the bodhi tree
> The mind a mirror bright
> One must wipe it clean each day
> And let no dust (*karma*) alight!

What would your enlightenment *gatha* be? How would you express the heart of Ch'an Buddhism in four lines?

8. Based on your understanding of Hui Neng and Ch'an Buddhism, discuss the following selection from the Platform Sutra. What is the relation between the reader/hearer, the text and awakening?

> Learned Audience . . . all sutras and scriptures of the Mahayana and Hinayana Schools, as well as the twelve sections of the canonical writings, were provided to suit the different needs and temperaments of various people. Through this the ignorant may attain sudden enlightenment, and their mind thereby becomes illuminated. Then they are no longer different from the wise men.

Chapter 8   THE COVENANT OF ISRAEL

An old rabbi, about to die, is surrounded by his students. "Why are you sad?" he asks. "Because you are about to die!" they reply. "But that is the way of all human life" he answers. "But, before you die, please give us one more teaching," they implore. He answers, "When you are about to die, repent!" "But," they ask, "how do we know when we are going to die?" "Repent every day," he replies, "and then you'll be ready!"[1]

As we travel from Hindu/Buddhist/Chinese sacred stories to Hebraic/Christian/Muslim ones, from traditions which practice silence and stillness, to those who enunciate the Divine Word, we arrive in Jerusalem (City of Peace), the religious center of the world for Jews and Christians, and sacred to Muslims as well. At an altitude of twenty-six hundred feet above sea level, the city seems like a fortress between the desert to the east and the Mediterranean to the west, and is called Queen of the Palestinian plains.

The Temple at Jerusalem

Entering its narrow streets and outdoor markets, the mental traveler becomes aware of a religious atmosphere which connects almost four thousand years of sacred history: from Abraham's attempted sacrifice of Isaac on Mount Moriah in 1750 BCE to King David's purchase of the fifteen acre "Threshing Floor" in 960 BCE; from the first and second temple periods (950–586 BCE, and 515 BCE–70 CE) to the birth, death and resurrection of Jesus (4 BCE–30 CE); from the destruction of the second temple (70 CE) to the building of the Dome of the Rock near where the second temple stood in 691 CE. In this and the ensuing two chapters we will encounter each of the three major Semitic sacred traditions—Judaism, Christianity and Islam.

We come first to the unique story of G-d's revelation to a "chosen people," to the descendants of Abraham, Isaac, and Jacob (Israel), to Moses, David, and to the heirs of the Prophets and Sages.[2] The Hebrew Scriptures (Torah), while similar in parts to other sacred texts (e.g., to the Vedas), uniquely introduce the dynamics of "salvation history." For whereas in India history was cyclic and illusory, and in China it harmonized with nature, the Jewish, Christian and Islamic faiths are shaped by the G-d who participates in human history through a salvific, covenantal relationship.

Jewish novelist Elie Wiesel tells a moving story in *The Gates of the Forest* of the founder of the Hasidic movement, the great Rabbi Israel Baal Shem-Tov who, when misfortune threatened the Jews, customarily went into a special part of the forest where he would light a special fire and say a special prayer. Always a miracle was accomplished, and the potential misfortune was averted.

> Later, when his disciple, the celebrated Magid of Mezeritch, had occasion, for the same reason, to intercede with heaven, he would go to the same place in the forest and say: "Master of the Universe, listen! I do not know how to light the fire, but I am still able to say the prayer." And again the miracle would be accomplished.

> Still later, Rabbi Moshe-Leib of Sassov, in order to save his people once more, would go into the forest and say: "I do not know to light the fire, I do not know the prayer, but I know the place and this must be sufficient." It was sufficient and the miracle was accomplished.

> Then it fell to Rabbi Israel of Rizhin to overcome misfortune. Sitting in his armchair, his head in his hands, he spoke to God: "I cannot even find the place in the forest. All I can do is to tell the story, and this must be sufficient." And it was sufficient. God made man because he loves stories.[3]

Before retelling the Hebrew that stands behind this story, let us look first at three irreducible characteristics of the Hebraic covenant—G-d, Torah and Israel.

YHWH

In the Torah we read:

> "Shema Yisrael Adonai Elohaynu
> Adonai echad."

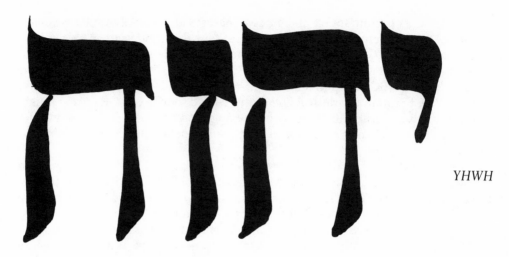

YHWH

"Hear, O Israel! The LORD is our God,
The LORD is One."[4]

This prayerful first affirmation of Hebrew faith is the first commandment. G-d is One (mono-theism); there is none other in heaven or on earth to be worshiped. Though one, G-d has many names in Hebrew scriptures, the most important of which include El, Elohim, YHWH, and Adonai (LORD). Yet G-d is ultimately beyond any name. It is this awareness of G-d's namelessness which caused Rabbi Zossima to become rapturously ecstatic every time the cantor chanted: "And G-d said . . ." As Elie Wiesel notes, "One can be a Jew with G-d, one can be a Jew against G-d, but one cannot be a Jew without G-d."[5]

In Genesis, there are two accounts of the beginning. In the first, Elohim, the Powerful and Mighty One, the one who alone is worthy of worship, praise and adoration, creates (*bara*) the heavens and the earth, and creates humans in G-d's image. In the second account, YHWH (G-d of thunder and lightening, he who causes to be) creates humans from the earth and breathes life-spirit into them. Since YHWH is ultimate, and since the Hebrew canon originally was without vowels, G-d's name was represented by four consonants—Y-H-W-H—the so-called tetragramaton. To protect against blasphemy, irreverence and misuse, this name was pronounced by the high priest in the temple, and was forbidden to others.

The high point of the story occurs when G-d suddenly appears to the prophet Moses at Sinai in a flaming bush that does not burn out. G-d tells Moses to announce to the Israelites their exodus from Pharaoh's control. Moses of course is astounded. Who is this? By what name shall he be known? G-d's answer avoided any final definition or interpretation and remains a unique theological mystery.

And God said to Moses, "Ehyeh-Asher-Ehyeh." (I will be who I will be.) He continued, "Thus shall you say to the Israelites, 'Ehyeh sent me to you.' " And God said further to Moses, "Thus shall you speak to the Israelites: The LORD, the God of your fathers, the God of Abraham, the God of Isaac, and the God of Jacob, has sent me to you:

This shall be My name forever,
This My appellation for all eternity.[6]

Elohim, the abstract plural, is here identified with YHWH, the one who was, is and will be. The G-d of Abraham, Isaac and Jacob is YHWH, the G-d who will be who He will be.

Torah

To fully describe Torah (the Divine Law), the principal repository of G-d's self-revelation, at least four meanings have been developed in Israel's history. Torah means the first five books of Moses, also called the Pentateuch or books of Jewish law (Genesis, Exodus, Leviticus, Numbers, Deuteronomy). Torah means also the Hebrew Scriptures as a whole, including the Law, the Prophets and the Writings. Third, the term applies to the entirety of G-d's revelation to Israel which includes the history of rabbinic interpretation and scriptural commentary (e.g., the Talmud and Midrashim). And last, in a mystical sense, Torah describes an inner attitude toward G-d and world—being Torah. It is said that one should go to a rabbi not to hear him read Torah, but to watch him lace and unlace his boots—not to speak about Torah, but to be Torah.

By Torah we will refer here to the entire Hebrew Bible passed orally from age to age, written by scribes on goat skin scrolls, and finally canonized at Jamnia in 90 CE. Written by hand in black ink on a parchment scroll without vowel points and mounted on wooden rollers, it is kept in a sacred ark behind a curtain-closed recess at the east end of the synagogue. Written without verses or chapters, it is said that when all the letters of Torah are taken together they spell G-d's name. At the central point of each sabbath service, the scroll is brought forth from the ark. It is then processed through the synagogue to be touched and kissed, and then the weekly portion is chanted.

Israel

The Israelites are named by G-d's angel in one of Jacob's dreams (he who struggles with G-d and wins). In Genesis, we are told that Jacob wrestles with an angel until daybreak and does not let go even after his hip is dislocated. The angel says: "Your name shall no longer be Jacob, but Israel; because you have been strong against G-d, you shall prevail against men" (Gen 32:26–30). Israel therefore became the name of a people chosen to enter a convenantal relation with G-d. The Israelites were chosen because they responded positively to G-d's call; they chose to be chosen. Whether patriarch, tribal judge, monarch, prophet, priest or sage, the descendants of Jacob became, though not always willingly, instruments of G-d's purpose.

The seal of being chosen was the covenant (*b'rith*), a bilateral agreement between YHWH and Israel which revealed a Divine message, set forth a promise and demand and included a sign. For example God promised: to Noah never again to destroy the earth by water (Gen 9:9–13); to Abraham that his descendants would enter the promised land (Gen 15:18); to Moses that he would deliver the Israelites safely, and that they would become a kingdom of priests, a holy nation (Ex 19:56–20); to Joshua, at Shechem, to renew the covenant in the promised land (Jos 24:25); to Jeremiah, to establish a new, covenant in the heart (Jer 31:31).

The Israelites were identified by the importance they placed on observance of the sabbath (*Shabbat*) or every seventh setting of the sun, and by their insistence on circumcision. Once every week the Israelites rested from all normal secular activities, and celebrated the holiness of all time. On the sabbath all over the Hebrew world, the Torah is read, the "Shema" ("Hear, O Israel, the Lord our G-d, the Lord is one") is sung and prayed and the covenant with the fathers of Israel is remembered. On the sabbath everything ceases, and the people of G-d reflect upon the truth that G-d is one, that humans are free and are called to serve G-d, and that G-d has promised in return to grant *shalom*.[7]

The Hebrew Story

The biblical story is a story of G-d's entrance into history through appearances, dreams, visions, natural phenomena, angels, miraculous events and inspired, prophetic words. It is the story of an on-going dialogue between the Israelites and G-d's Word. We can understand this pregnant and often-discussed phrase—the "Word of G-d"—in two ways: as G-d *speaks* (e.g., in the garden, to Moses, through angels and prophets), and as the inspired *words* spoken about G-d. Because of the unique, almost uncanny nature of the biblical narrative, we will briefly retell the major touchstones of Israel's salvation history with a special focus upon the covenant. At the same time, we will view the story of Israel's evolution according to the three main literary forms of the Hebrew Bible (*Tenakh*): law and teaching (Torah), prophets (*Nevi'im*) and collected writings (*Ketubim*).

TOUCHSTONES OF SALVATION HISTORY

1) CREATION: Humans created (*Imago Dei*) (Gen. 1 & 2) Adam & Eve/Tree of Life/Knowledge of Good & Evil/the Serpent, the Fall, Exit from the Garden/Cain murders Abel (Gen 4)

2) COVENANT: FLOOD (Gen 6–8) Noah's Ark/Rainbow Covenant/New World Order Tower of Babel/Confusion of Tongues/Dispersion of People

PATRIARCHS

1850................Call of Abram (Abraham), Father of Faith (Gen 12) Circumcision
Covenant (Gen 17)—Chosen People
1700................Isaac, Jacob (Israel) & twelve sons (Gen 46) to Egypt and slavery

3) EXODUS

1290................Moses' call/God's name: "I WILL BE" (Ex 2–3)
1250................Passover & Deliverance through Red Sea (Ex 13–15) Wilderness,
Trials & Purification (Ex 16ff) G-d's Law—The Decalogue (Ex 20;
Lv 19, 23; Dt 6, 26, 30, 32) Journey to the Promised Land—Canaan

4) KINGDOM/PROMISED LAND

1210................Joshua—Ark & People cross the Jordan (Jos 1–5) Conquest of Jericho (Jos 6)
1210–1020..........Judges: Charismatic Warrior Heroes (Jgs 1–21)

MONARCHY

1020................Samuel Anoints Saul King of Israel (1 Sam 10)
1000–961............David/The Ark & Jerusalem (2 Sam 2–21, 1 Kgs 2)
961–922.............Solomon/Builds Temple at Jerusalem (1 Kgs 3–11)
750–701.............Prophets: (Amos & Hosea & First Isaiah)
922.................Idolatry & Divided Kingdom
Northern Ten Tribes (Israel)
Southern Two Tribes (Judah)

5) EXILE

721.................Assyria Conquers Israel (2 Kgs 17)
621.................Book of Deuteronomy "discovered"; Josiah's reforms (2 Kgs 22–23)
625–539.............Prophets: Jeremiah Warnings & Promises/Doom & Salvation
587.................Nebuchadnezzar destroys Jerusalem/Temple destroyed (2 Kgs 24)

6) RETURN

538.................Jewish remnant returns to Jerusalem (Ezr 1)
520–515.............The Second Temple Built (Ezr 6)
445ff................Ezra & Nehemiah's Religious Reforms/Torah Promulgated (Neh 8)

FOREIGN RULE

330ff . . . . .Egypt, Syria Greek and Roman
170–50 . . . . .Jewish Apocalypse (Dan 7, 12)
70 CE . . . . .Second Temple Destroyed by Romans
90 CE . . . . .Rabbis Formulate Hebrew Canon at Jamnia

Genesis

The first book of Torah, "Genesis" (*Bereshit*—"In the Beginning"), contains both primordial, mythic, prehistoric stories (the Creation, the Flood and the Tower of Babel) as well as the beginnings of the historic story (covenant; exodus; promised land; kingdoms; exile; return). Genesis begins one unbroken saga of the birth and pilgrimage of a people of faith in the uncreated Creator, the G-d of Abraham, Isaac and Jacob.

While there are at least four creation accounts in Hebrew scriptures (Gen 1:1ff and 2:4ff, Prv 8:22ff, and Job 38ff), the first two Genesis accounts are the most often remembered. The first, actually written later than the second and by a different author, begins with *Elohim's* command: "Let there be" and there was. Elohim says:

"I will make man in My image, after My likeness. They shall rule the fish of the sea, the birds of the sky, the cattle, the whole earth, and all the creeping things that creep on earth." And God created man in His image, in the image of God He created him; male and female He created them.[8]

In the second account YHWH creates Adam (all men) from the dust, molds him into a human shape and breathes into his nostrils a breath of life; thus humans become living beings. After Eden is planted and the animals named by Adam, which gives him power over them, no helpmate was found so YHWH put Adam into a deep sleep, and from his rib made woman. Adam exclaims:

> This one at last
> Is bone of my bones
> And flesh of my flesh.
> This one shall be called Woman (*Ishshah*),
> For from man (*Ish*) was she taken.[9]

The two creation accounts written by different authors in different periods might be outlined as follows:

Genesis 1–2:4a	Genesis 2:4aff.
light from dark from chaos	heaven and earth
firmament from waters	mist waters ground

vegetative earth from sea	man from the dust
day from night in seasons	Eden planted
living creatures in air & sea	animals named by man
living creatures on earth & man	male & female created
rest on the seventh day	

While there are differences of sequence and of Holy name in these accounts, each story communicates that G-d created humans through an act of separation, whether from Nothing, Void or Chaos.

Immediately after creation however there is trouble in paradise. G-d gives Adam and Eve power to name everything in the garden, but also he gives them an admonition against eating the fruit from the tree at the center of the garden. In her naked innocence, Eve encounters the most subtle serpent who tempts her and Adam to eat of the fruit. "You will not die!" The serpent lies. "God knows in fact that on the day you eat it your eyes will be opened and you will be like gods, knowing good and evil" (Gen 3:4–5). Once they eat, their eyes are opened and they realize their nakedness. When in the cool of day YHWH appears, they hid in the trees. But YHWH calls out, "Where are you?" (Gen 3:9). Adam and Eve confess that they have eaten the forbidden fruit whereupon they are banished from the garden and punished to labor in sorrow.

According to a Hasidic story, while Rabbi Zalman (who died in 1813) was awaiting trial in a Petersburg prison, one day the chief jailer entered his cell. Just as Sri Aurobindo practiced yoga during his Indian imprisonment, so the majestic rav spent hours in deep meditation in his cell. This is how the jailer found him. When at last the rav was ready to converse, the jailer posed a number of questions about scriptures. Finally he asked: "How are we to understand an all-knowing G-d who asks Adam, 'Where art thou?'" The rav answered, "Do you believe that the Scriptures are eternal and that every era, every generation and every (person) is included in them?" When the jailer agreed the zaddik (one who is proven true) said, "So where are you in your world?"[10] From the Chinese Zen standpoint, everything depends upon how a person responds to that question.

If we were hearing the Adam and Eve story for the first time, we would naturally wonder at this point, "What will G-d do next?"

First G-d makes clothes for Adam and Eve and then mercifully expels them from the garden, lest they eat next from the tree of life and live forever. Imagine how different the story would have been if they had eaten from the tree of everlasting life and were condemned to live eternally in alienation from G-d. By choosing to experience the knowledge of good and evil, they choose a life which ironically introduced death into the world, for G-d stationed cherubim with firey revolving swords to guard the way back to the tree of life. Expelled from the garden, human experience begins in the world.

As John Steinbeck notes in *East of Eden* the story of Cain and Abel, Adam and Eve's immediate descendants, contains the whole history of humankind, in any age, in any culture, in any race—the primordial murder of brother by brother. Cain, the first son, the farmer (who brought grain as his sacrifice to the Lord), kills Abel, the second son, the shepherd, the nomad (who brought a lamb for the sacrifice). When human wickedness multiplies beyond endurance, YHWH instructs Noah to prepare an ark so that he, his family, and selected animals and birds can escape the forty-day, forty-night flood. After the water subsided and Noah and his family disembark, Noah builds an altar for YHWH and offers a burnt sacrifice.

Again the earth is populated with people who speak the same vocabulary. They agree to construct a town to make a name for themselves, and to build a brick tower with its top reaching heaven. In response to this arrogance, G-d confuses their language so that they no longer understand each other. Then YHWH scatters human cultures by separating peoples into many tongues and races. It is from within one such culture, in the land of Ur of the Chaldaeans, that Abram was called by G-d to leave country, family and his father's house for the unknown land of Canaan. With the story of Abram we shift from primeval history to patriarchal history.

Abraham

Between Baghdad and the Persian Gulf lay the ancient city of Ur with up to half a million inhabitants who enjoyed a high level of civilization. Toward the beginning of the second millennium, Abram (who became Abraham), originally from Haran in northwest Mesopotamia, migrated from Ur, the Sumerian capital of agriculture and commerce. Surrounded by Sumerian and Babylonian gods, Abram left his home with a radical faith in El Shaddai the Highest G-d. How he arrived at this faith we do not know, but following G-d's lead Abram, his wife Sarai (who became Sarah), and their Aramean nomadic family crossed the Jordan River and traveled to Canaan. They become known as Hebrews, the people from the other side (of the Euphrates).

We first read of Jerusalem when Abraham, during his wanderings, gave a tithe to Melchizedek, King of Ir/Shalem (Jerusalem). Later, settling in Hebron, after a sojourn in Egypt to avoid a famine, Abram received a revelation from YHWH:

> When Abram was ninety-nine years old, the LORD (YHWH) appeared to Abram and said to him, "I am El Shaddai. Walk in My ways and be blameless. I will establish My covenant between Me and you, and I will make you exceedingly numerous."[11]

To more fully understand the Hebraic concept of "covenant" it will be helpful to note the difference between the two types of law found in Torah: conditional and absolute. Conditional law referred to contracts which stated a condition: if "A" happens then "B" follows. Whereas such secular contracts are breakable, the covenant between G-d and the people is absolute and indissoluble. Once Abram says "yes" to G-d's offer, he receives a new name—Abraham (father of the many)—and accepts circumcision as the sign of the covenant. Sarai too receives a new name, Sarah, and is promised a child, Isaac. His birth and childhood were a great joy to his parents.[12]

As it was customary among ancient Semitic peoples to sacrifice the life of the first born son to propitiate the gods, Abraham agreed to G-d's later demand that he sacrifice his first born son Isaac. After the altar was built on Mount Moriah (today's Jerusalem) and the sacrifice prepared, in the dramatic moment before the knife descended, an angel of the Lord interceded to preserve Isaac's life. This site took on a special sacredness and was subsequently called the Foundation Stone of the World. It later became the site at which the first and second temples were built.

Isaac's son Jacob, named Israel, had twelve sons who became progenitors of the twelve tribes of the Hebrews. Through Joseph, one of the twelve sons, a major part of Jacob's family migrated to Egypt to avoid a famine, and were eventually enslaved by the Egyptian Pharaoh. Against this backdrop, one of the leading characters in the story appears.

Moses

Moses' life was filled with miraculous circumstances. To begin with, in order to protect her son from the Pharaoh's edict that new-born Hebrew children were to be killed, his mother abandoned him so that he would be found by the Egyptian royalty, and be raised by the oppressors of his own people. Then, around 1250 BCE, in Exodus (*Shemot*-Names) we read of Moses' encounters with Pharaoh, the ten plagues and the escape route to the Red Sea, the Egyptian pursuit, YHWH's miraculous parting of the sea, the Hebrews' escape and the death of the Egyptian pursuers. Israel's most holy annual ritual, Passover, commemorates deliverance from this tenth and final plague sent by G-d against Pharaoh and his people. The last plague was a visit by the angel of death to claim the lives of all first born males and beasts alike except in houses marked with sacrifical blood. Those the angel passed over. Once in the desert, on a pilgrimage that was to last forty years, YHWH sends manna and quail from the heavens, brings forth water from a rock, and then, at Sinai, enters into a new covenantal relationship with Moses and the people.

One of the most sacred moments in all of Hebrew history is Moses' encounter with G-d at Sinai. While tending the flock of Jethro, his father-in-law, he was called by G-d from the heart of a burning bush. "I am the G-d of your father, of Abraham, Isaac and Jacob," G-d said. He continued that He wanted Moses to lead the Israelites from their bondage to Pharaoh. "But who am I to say has sent me?" Moses replied. The importance of this question is highlighted when we recall that for the Hebrew people to know someone's name was to be intimate with that person, and when we recall it was one of the first gifts G-d gave Adam in the Garden. G-d's reply, as we have seen, is profoundly enigmatic—"Ehyeh-Asher-Ehyer"—"I will be who I will be (Ex 3:13–15). Just as the Tao that can be named is not the real Tao, G-d reveals His nameless name to Moses. G-d is the one who is always coming to meet his creation from an unpredictable future, known only to G-d.

After forty days and forty nights of fasting on Mount Sinai, Moses received the most holy gift G-d had even given on two tablets of stone. In an awesome description we read that YHWH descended in the form of fire, and the whole mountain shook. In "peals of thunder," G-d called Moses to the top together with Aaron to give him the decalogue. As the rainbow was a sign of Noah's covenant, and circumcision a sign of Abraham's, the tablets become the sign that G-d will lead Moses to the promised land. The first five describe the human-divine relationship and the last five, ideal human behavior. In Exodus 20, the commandments are listed:

1. You shall have no other G-d beside me.
2. You shall not swear falsely by YHWH's name.
3. You shall keep the sabbath day holy.
4. You shall honor your father and your mother.
5. You shall not murder.
6. You shall not commit adultery.
7. You shall not steal.
8. You shall not bear false witness against your neighbor.
9. You shall not covet your neighbor's wife.
10. You shall not covet your neighbor's posessions.

After reading them to the people, Moses sprinkled blood from a bullock sacrifice, half on the tablets and half on the people, and said: "This is the blood of the covenant that YHWH makes with you, containing all these rules" (Ex 24:8).

According to the sages, the writings which follow the Sinai revelation recede in sanctity and holy power. Leviticus, Numbers and Deuteronomy, the last three books of Torah, further explain the laws and rules by which the people are to live. Tassels were to be worn on prayer shawls to remind the Israelites to pray (Num 15), and they were to keep their covenantal agreements with YHWH (Dt 4:32ff, 7:11), to keep to their social and individual identity (Dt 26:16), and to live in the promised land (Dt 4:32, 11:10). Observing the law brought forth holiness, for as YHWH says:

> Speak to the whole Israelite community and say to them: You shall be holy, for I, the LORD your God, am holy. You shall each revere his mother and his father, and keep My sabbaths: I the LORD am your God.[13]

Each Israelite was called to be holy, to live righteously and to love justice. Just as there cannot be sacred myths without the representational power of rituals, neither can there be a covenant without laws, for it is through lawful obedience that the Israelites were to keep their covenant with YHWH.

At the end of his life, after Moses had the Book of Law put beside the ark of the covenant he, like Jacob, gave an individual blessing and a specific task to each of the twelve tribes. When Moses finished his benediction he implored Israel to keep and observe all the words of this Law. Then he climbed Mount Nebo to receive a glimpse of the land which YHWH had promised but which Moses was not allowed to enter. Moses died as decreed and YHWH buried him in the land of Moab so that none would know his grave site.

It is important here to remember the narrative's structure. The Book of Genesis ends with Jacob's blessing of his twelve sons who become the leaders of the twelve tribes of Israel.

This blessing transferred the course of salvation history from the family to the nation. With this blessing, the tribes, now on the border of a new beginning, enter the promised land.

The Promised Land

Within the second group of books, the *Nevi'im*, the prophets (including Joshua, Judges, 1 and 2 Samuel, 1 and 2 Kings, and the later prophets Amos, Hosea, Isaiah, Jeremiah, and Ezekiel), the story continues.

After marching around the city walls seven times behind the ark of YHWH, and encouraged by the faith and leadership of Joshua, the Hebrews crossed the Jordan and defeated the armies of Jericho. Through Joshua, YHWH told the people: "I gave you a land where you never toiled, you live in towns you never built; you eat now from vineyards and olive groves you never planted" (Jos 24:13). And the people replied:

> "We will serve none but the LORD our God, and we will obey none but Him." On that day at Shechem, Joshua made a covenant for the people and he made a fixed rule for them. Joshua recorded all this in a book of divine instruction.[14]

Although Joshua set up a central sanctuary containing the Ark and partitioned captured lands to the tribes according to its numbers, this federation was too unstable to survive. From 1210 BCE to 1020 the Israelites were lead by a series of Judges (including Ehud, Deborah, Gideon, Jephtah, Samson and Samuel). The tribes unified in Canaan under the decisive and charismatic leadership of these Judges who, because of their wisdom and charismatic personalities, became national heroes.

By the end of Samuel's time (1020 BCE), when practically all the surrounding Canaanites had been subdued, the Israelites had begun to drift toward Canaanite deities. There was growing civil discontent among the tribes. Finally, when Samuel had grown old, and his sons had judged poorly, the people came to him and said: "We want a king, so that we in our turn can be like the other nations; our king shall rule us and be our leader and fight our battles" (1 Sam 8:19–20). The Israelites were no longer willing to be ruled by YHWH's charismatic leaders, but instead chose human rule over divinely inspired leadership.

David and Solomon

Around 1020 BCE, during a period when neighboring nations were growing into stronger kingdoms, Saul became Israel's first theocratic king. While the anointing ritual had been previously reserved to the priests, Samuel privately anointed Saul with a vial of oil as the prince of YHWH's heritage. While Saul was a gifted military leader, as was his dedicated son Jonathan, he did not respond kindly to the ascending popularity of young David, who had been secretly anointed by Samuel as the next king at YHWH's direction. David, the youngest son of Jesse (of Bethlehem), accepted the challenge to fight Goliath, the Philistine's leader. It is well known how this shepherd boy, "a boy of fresh complexion, with fine eyes and pleasant bearing" (1 Sam 16:12), with a stone and a sling defeated Goliath who was armed with sword, spear and javelin. From that time till his death, Saul remained uneasy in David's presence, and was at times aggressively jealous toward him.

Around 1000 BCE David, the warrior and the poet, the womanizer and the seer, became Israel's greatest king. Shortly after he was anointed (a second time) at thirty years of age, he conquered Jerusalem and made it the political and religious center of the monarchy. When the ark of the covenant was brought from Judah, David danced before YHWH in a linen loin cloth, and sang with all his might. In response to David's wish to build a house of cedar so that the ark can be removed from its tent, YHWH had the prophet Nathan say:

> Go and say to My servant David: Thus said the LORD: Are you the one to build a house for Me to dwell in? From the day that I brought the people of Israel out of Egypt to this day I have not dwelt in a house, but have moved about in Tent and Tabernacle. As I moved about wherever the Israelites went, did I ever reproach any of the tribal leaders whom I appointed to care for My people Israel: Why have you not built Me a house of cedar?[15]

David clearly was *the* king of the chosen people. Not only was he an able warrior and shrewd politician, he was also a bard and musician. Some of the great psalms are attributed to David, psalms of theological majesty. Yet at the same time David is pictured in weakness. One day he sees Bathsheba from his roof bathing below, sends for her, knowing she is married, sleeps with her and impregnates her. Cleverly, David has her husband sent to the battle front where he is killed. He then takes her as his wife and she bears their son, Solomon. Though David centralized Israelite worship and allegiance as never before, and though he wanted to build a sanctuary on Mount Moriah, on orders from YHWH he left the task of building the temple to his son Solomon. He did nonetheless purchase the threshing floor of Arunah which was the place of the attempted sacrifice of Isaac, land which is where the temples were built.

Considered the wisest of rulers, it was Solomon who constructed the temple on Mount Moriah. Constructed of brass, copper and the cedars of Lebanon, it was built through forced labor and heavy taxation. Once completed, he brought the ark of the covenant to the temple and placed it in the *Debir* (Holy of Holies) in the innermost sanctuary where priests offered sacrifices of sheep and oxen. More importantly, it was believed to house the invisible presence of YHWH as well. "There was nothing inside the Ark but the two tablets of stone which Moses placed there at Horeb, when the LORD made [a covenant] with the Israelites after their departure from the land of Egypt" (1 Kgs 8:9).

When Solomon died, the people were not satisfied with his successor, Rehoboam, and as a result of many unanswered complaints, ten of the twelve tribes seceded to the north to form the kingdom of Israel. Only Judah, the royal lineage, and Benjamin remained with the Davidic ancestry. Both kingdoms experienced continuing difficulties. Israel was more willing to acculturate itself into non-Hebrew cultures and in 721 BCE was destroyed by the Assyrians, its ten tribes lost. From then on there remained only the descendants of Judah—the Jews—who still possessed the national sanctuary at Jerusalem. It was during this period, beginning in the eighth century BCE and stretching into the Babylonian exile, that the great prophets arose.

The Prophets

The prophet was one who spoke forth for YHWH, not so much as a foreteller but as a forth-teller, not as one who told of future events, but as one who spoke in the place of the Divine ("Thus says the Lord"). Prophets were called to a life of religious radicalism in which they spelled out a dual message—doom (for those who turned practice of the covenant into formal rituals and wrong conduct) and salvation (for those who repented, who turned back to G-d and awaited the Messianic age to come).

Of necessity, prophets became the people's representative before G-d, and before the people, G-d's voice. Prophets were frontiersmen of a renewed faith, trailblazers of new moral paths. They challenged the advance of the pagan civilization of their day by their unyielding demands for right conduct and moral living. The prophets criticized rituals without moral character and re-emphasized an ethical monotheism. As a Talmudic rabbi expounded:

> Six hundred and thirteen commandments were given to Moses, three hundred and sixty-five negative ones, corresponding to the number of the days of the solar year, and two hundred forty-eight positive commandments, corresponding to the (bones in the human) body. . . .
> Isaiah came and reduced them to six [Isaiah 33:25–26]: (i) He who walks right-eously and (ii) speaks uprightly, (iii) he who despises the gain of oppressions, (iv) shakes his hand from holding bribes, (v) stops his ear from hearing of blood (vi) and shuts his eyes from looking upon evil, he shall dwell on high. Micah came and re-duced them to three [Micah 6:8]: It has been told you, man, what is good, and what the Lord demands from you, (i) only to do justly, and (ii) to love mercy, and (iii) to walk humbly before God. . . . Isaiah again came and reduced them to two [Isaiah 56:1]: Thus says the Lord, (i) keep justice and (ii) do righteousness.
> Amos came and reduced them to a single one, as it said, For thus says the Lord to the house of Israel. Seek Me and live.
> Habakkuk further came and based them on one, as it is said [Habakkuk 2:4], But the righteous shall live by his faith.[16]

Obedience to the law is transformed and fulfilled in the prophets by untiring trust and com-mitment.

Around 850 BCE Elijah, the prototypical prophet, suddenly appeared from the desert consumed with zeal to confront the king of Israel, Ahab, who worshiped the Canaanite idol Baal. He challenged Ahab to assemble the prophets of Baal on Mount Carmel. Each was to prepare a wooden altar upon which two bulls were placed for sacrifice. When Baal does not ignite the sacrifice made to him, Elijah has water poured three times over his bull and wood, and then calls out to YHWH. YHWH's fire consumes the holocaust, the wood and the water in the trench around the offering. Elijah then enters into a cave on Sinai, perhaps the crevice where Moses crouched when G-d's glory passed him by, and YHWH appears to him, not in a mighty wind, not in an earthquake, not in a fire, but in the sound of "a gentle breeze" (1 Kgs 19:13). YHWH tells him to anoint Elisha as the prophet to succeed him. As Elisha stands beside Elijah, at the Jordan River, Elijah asks Elisha to make a request. Elisha requests a double portion of Elijah's spirit and then watches as Elijah ascends to heaven in a chariot of fire.

As the moral degeneration of Israel deepened, the rich disenfranchised the poor, debauchery and sexual excesses increased along with idolatry and oppression. In the voice of Amos, a zealous spirit flared up. Amos (750 BCE, northern kingdom) once dramatically interrupted the high priest Amaziah's solemn service, and cried out in G-d's name: "I hate, I despise your feasts. . . . How ill I look upon the peace offerings of your fatted beasts. . . . But let justice roll down as waters, and righteousness as a mighty stream" (Am 5:21–25). For Amos, ethical behavior and righteous activity were more important in G-d's sight than ritual performance.

A hundred years after the fall of the Northern Kingdom, the prophet Jeremiah (625–586 BCE) called Israel to a new, inner covenant:

> See, a time is coming—declares the LORD—when I will make a new covenant with the House of Israel and the House of Judah. It will not be like the covenant I made with their fathers, when I took them by the hand to lead them out of the land of Egypt, a covenant which they broke, so that I rejected them, declares the LORD. But such is the covenant I will make with the House of Israel after these days—declares the LORD: I will put My Teaching into their inmost being and inscribe it upon their hearts.[17]

As Jeremiah and the prophets before him had predicted, doom came to Judah in 587–586 BCE. Through a series of calamities and ill-advised military campaigns against the Babylonians (who had replaced the Assyrians as the Eastern Power), in July 587 BCE the enemy broke through the walls of Jerusalem. Priests were tortured, families were deported to Babylonia and Jerusalem, and the Holy City of Peace and home of the ark of the covenant was burned to the ground in August 587. First Israel, then Judah fell; what was left of the nation was shocked, despairing and virtually without hope.

Prophecy climaxed in Second Isaiah, an unknown figure of the exile whose words are found in Isaiah 40–55. Here we find one of the most elevated expressions of ethical monotheism in Hebrew scriptures. In the face of the total destruction of the homeland, government and temple, he eloquently intoned: "Comfort ye, comfort ye, my people, says your God" (Isaiah 40:1). For this Isaiah, Israel was to communicate to the nations that universal salvation involved, paradoxically, suffering and service:

> This is My servant, whom I uphold,
> My chosen one, in whom I delight.
> I have put My spirit upon him,

He shall teach the true way to the nations.
He shall not cry out or shout aloud,
Or make his voice heard in the streets.
He shall not break even a bruised reed,
Or snuff out even a dim wick.
He shall bring forth the true way.
He shall not grow dim or be bruised
Till he has established the true way on earth;
And the coastlands shall await his
     teaching.[18]

Ezra and Nehemiah

While exiled in Babylon (587–538 BCE) with the temple destroyed, the Israelites developed local synagogues, stressed prayer and Torah study as ways of worshiping, and produced *rabbis* (teachers) to teach and interpret tradition. As the threat of intermarriage increased, Israel began to interpret holiness as ground for separatistic attitudes. Strict prohibition against intermarriage, elaborate dietary restrictions, and vigilant observance of the sabbath and of the covenant kept them from integrating into Babylonian culture. In 539, after Cyrus the Persian defeated the Babylonians, he issued a decree allowing Jews to return to their land.

The books of Ezra and Nehemiah narrate the arrival of the scribe Ezra in 445 BCE, who brought with him the law of Moses (either all or most of the Pentateuch, compiled by priests in Babylonia). In a dramatic moment, after the former king's cupbearer, Nehemiah, rebuilt Jerusalem's walls, Ezra stood on a raised dais, like Hui Neng the sixth patriarch of Ch'an Buddhism, and read "from the Law of G-d, translating and giving the sense, so that the people understood what was read" (Neh 8:8). Interestingly, we are told that he interpreted the text into Aramaic so that the people would understand what they heard.

With the temple rebuilt, the Law was again studied, translated, explained to foreigners, and quickly became again the focusing symbol of a covenanted people. It was during this period that the Torah received a firm identity. The righteous Jew became one whose "delight is in the Law (Torah) of the Lord; and on his law he meditates day and night" (Ps 1:2).

Wisdom

Along with prophets and priests, among returning Jews were the sages (*Hakhamim*) who provided counsel in practical and moral matters, and who speculated upon the nature of truth, meaning and value. Much of our information about this period is housed in the third portion of Hebrew scriptures–the *Ketubim* (Collected Writings). It is comprised of history, poetry, proverbs, chronicles and apocalyptic literature and includes Psalms, Proverbs, Job, Song of Solomon, Ruth, Lamentations, Ecclesiastes, Esther, Daniel, Ezra, Nehemiah and 1 and 2 Chronicles. The fundamental mark characterizing Hebrew is that G-d's creation is grounded on a moral foundation. Seeming hardly interested in the covenant and with little concern for history, the sages were predominantly interested in the individual religious consciousness.

While priests were specialists in correct ritual performance who enjoyed the authority of the *cultus,* and the prophets specialized in attacking these cultic rituals, the sages and seers specialized in providing specific instructions, maxims, aphorisms, lessons, poetry and music. The Book of Proverbs, for example, is an anthology of terse, vivid, aphoristic, popular sayings, not particularly Jewish in character. In fact they may remind the reader of Confucius' Analects or of Buddha's Dhammapada, and provide advice about proper conduct and warnings against over-indulgences. Ecclesiastes and Job both speculate about the meaning and purpose of human life. For Qoheleth (the preacher) in Ecclesiastes, death is the great equalizer, while the drama of Job addresses the mystery of human suffering. The one hundred and fifty Psalms provide congregational hymns, individual praise, ritual hymns for the enthronement of a king, and miscellaneous laments, to and glorifications of G-d.

Canonization

According to classical Judaism, a *Beth ha Midrash* (a house of study) could also be used as a *Beth ha Knesset* (a house of assembly, a synagogue), but not vice versa. The study of sacred texts was a required higher form of worship for Jews. So deeply did the Hebrews revere their sacred books that when old or damaged beyond use they were not to be destroyed or thrown away, but were buried in a vault beneath the synagogue. Every aspect of Jewish life was regulated by these sacred texts—from prayer and worship to commerce, from marital obligations to family relations. Like the Muslims, the Jews are a people of the Holy Book, one could even say a Torah-intoxicated community of faith.

It should be remembered that until after the fall of Jerusalem in 70 CE, the Jews had no complete, fixed text. Each scribe recorded his own version. The earliest indications we have of a written record was in Exodus 17:14, where Moses was told by YHWH to write the Torah for a memorial in the book, and in Deuteronomy 31:9, where Moses wrote the Law and gave it to the priests who placed it in the ark of the covenant. Later, after the Jewish nation had been exiled in Babylon, the priest-scribe Ezra brought a copy of the Torah with him back to Jerusalem. As we have seen, Ezra publicly promulgated the Mosaic Law, translated it and interpreted its meaning. No one knows exactly what form of Torah Ezra presented; it may well have been based upon Deuteronomy, the book discovered in the temple walls in 621 BCE during Josiah's reforms. His text became the standard by which a national reform in Jewish religious consciousness was achieved.

By 200 BCE, a collection of prophetic writings were accepted as canonical including the former Prophets (Joshua, Judges, Samuel and Kings) and the later Prophets (the three major and twelve Minor Prophets). As the Hebrew community developed, prophetic voices became more revered and were often quoted and discussed in the synagogue. Soon the prophets' teachings took a position alongside the books of Moses, and still later, in about 100 BCE, there is evidence that a collection of liturgical writings, the prayers and poetic hymns of David, the proverbs of Solomon, which were used in worship, formed the third major division of the

שְׁמוֹת בְּנֵי יִשְׂרָאֵל הַבָּאִים מִצְרָיְמָה אֵת יַעֲקֹב אִישׁ וּבֵיתוֹ בָּאוּ ׃ רְאוּבֵן שִׁמְעוֹן לֵוִי וִיהוּדָה ׃ יִשָּׂשכָר זְבוּלֻן וּבִנְיָמִן ׃ דָּן וְנַפְתָּלִי גָּד וְאָשֵׁר ׃ וַיְהִי כָּל־נֶפֶשׁ יֹצְאֵי יֶרֶךְ־יַעֲקֹב שִׁבְעִים נָפֶשׁ וְיוֹסֵף הָיָה בְמִצְרָיִם ׃ וַיָּמָת יוֹסֵף וְכָל־אֶחָיו וְכֹל הַדּוֹר הַהוּא ׃ וּבְנֵי יִשְׂרָאֵל פָּרוּ וַיִּשְׁרְצוּ וַיִּרְבּוּ וַיַּעַצְמוּ בִּמְאֹד מְאֹד וַתִּמָּלֵא הָאָרֶץ אֹתָם ׃

וַיָּקָם מֶלֶךְ־חָדָשׁ עַל־מִצְרָיִם אֲשֶׁר לֹא־יָדַע אֶת־יוֹסֵף ׃ וַיֹּאמֶר אֶל־עַמּוֹ הִנֵּה עַם בְּנֵי יִשְׂרָאֵל רַב וְעָצוּם מִמֶּנּוּ ׃ הָבָה נִתְחַכְּמָה לוֹ פֶּן־יִרְבֶּה וְהָיָה כִּי־תִקְרֶאנָה מִלְחָמָה וְנוֹסַף גַּם־הוּא עַל־שֹׂנְאֵינוּ וְנִלְחַם־בָּנוּ וְעָלָה מִן־הָאָרֶץ ׃ וַיָּשִׂימוּ עָלָיו שָׂרֵי מִסִּים לְמַעַן עַנֹּתוֹ בְּסִבְלֹתָם וַיִּבֶן עָרֵי מִסְכְּנוֹת לְפַרְעֹה אֶת־פִּתֹם וְאֶת־רַעַמְסֵס ׃ וְכַאֲשֶׁר יְעַנּוּ אֹתוֹ כֵּן יִרְבֶּה וְכֵן יִפְרֹץ וַיָּקֻצוּ מִפְּנֵי בְּנֵי יִשְׂרָאֵל ׃ וַיַּעֲבִדוּ מִצְרַיִם אֶת־בְּנֵי יִשְׂרָאֵל בְּפָרֶךְ ׃ וַיְמָרְרוּ אֶת־חַיֵּיהֶם בַּעֲבֹדָה קָשָׁה בְּחֹמֶר וּבִלְבֵנִים וּבְכָל־עֲבֹדָה בַּשָּׂדֶה אֵת כָּל־עֲבֹדָתָם אֲשֶׁר־עָבְדוּ בָהֶם בְּפָרֶךְ ׃ וַיֹּאמֶר מֶלֶךְ מִצְרַיִם לַמְיַלְּדֹת הָעִבְרִיֹּת אֲשֶׁר שֵׁם הָאַחַת שִׁפְרָה וְשֵׁם הַשֵּׁנִית פּוּעָה ׃ וַיֹּאמֶר בְּיַלֶּדְכֶן אֶת־הָעִבְרִיּוֹת וּרְאִיתֶן עַל־הָאָבְנָיִם אִם־בֵּן הוּא וַהֲמִתֶּן אֹתוֹ וְאִם־בַּת הִיא וָחָיָה ׃ וַתִּירֶאןָ הַמְיַלְּדֹת אֶת־הָאֱלֹהִים וְלֹא עָשׂוּ כַּאֲשֶׁר דִּבֶּר אֲלֵיהֶן מֶלֶךְ מִצְרָיִם וַתְּחַיֶּיןָ אֶת־הַיְלָדִים ׃ וַיִּקְרָא מֶלֶךְ־מִצְרַיִם לַמְיַלְּדֹת וַיֹּאמֶר לָהֶן מַדּוּעַ עֲשִׂיתֶן הַדָּבָר הַזֶּה וַתְּחַיֶּיןָ אֶת־הַיְלָדִים ׃ וַתֹּאמַרְןָ הַמְיַלְּדֹת אֶל־פַּרְעֹה כִּי לֹא כַנָּשִׁים הַמִּצְרִיֹּת הָעִבְרִיֹּת כִּי־חָיוֹת הֵנָּה בְּטֶרֶם תָּבוֹא אֲלֵהֶן הַמְיַלֶּדֶת וְיָלָדוּ ׃ וַיֵּיטֶב אֱלֹהִים לַמְיַלְּדֹת וַיִּרֶב הָעָם וַיַּעַצְמוּ מְאֹד ׃ וַיְהִי כִּי־יָרְאוּ הַמְיַלְּדֹת אֶת־הָאֱלֹהִים וַיַּעַשׂ לָהֶם בָּתִּים ׃

First Rabbinical Bible—Venice, 1517
(Courtesy of the Library of the Jewish Theological Seminary of America,
New York, N.Y.)

Hebrew Bible. It was not until the council of Jamnia (90 CE) that their number was firmly established.

After the fall of Jerusalem, the Pharisees, scribes and rabbis decided to preserve their sacred writings. Using the Torah and prophets as guidelines, they assembled on the Palestinian coast at Jamnia in 90 CE and finally fixed the Hebrew canon. Prior to canonization, a text might be miscopied or added to, or words inadvertently deleted. Once canonized, however, it was copied with fidelity. Since Hebrew was for so long a spoken language, and, since as we have noted, G-d's name cannot be written, the original text was simply a consonantal outline without vowels, a shorthand notation. It was not until the seventh and eighth centuries CE that a group of Jewish scholars known as Masoretes (traditionalists) revised the text and with great patience added the vowel points. Thus the standard text of Hebrew scriptures was called the Masoretic Text from which all subsequent copies both Jewish and Christian have been made.

NOTES

1. Talmud B Shabath 153a.

2. The chosen people were originally called Hebrews, the people from the other side (of the Jordan), Semites who entered Canaan (a name used by inhabitants before the arrival of Hebrews) and who after Jacob were given the name Israel ("one who has struggled with G-d"). As Israelites, they fought the Palestinian Philistines for possession of Canaan. The term Jew (in Hebrew, *Yehudi*) means one who lives in Judah. According to Orthodox Judaism, G-d's name is too holy, too sacrosanct to utter, let alone to write, and so I follow the Orthodox practice of deleting the vowel to indicate respect for the unutterable mystery of G-d's reality.

3. Elie Wiesel, *The Gates of the Forest* (New York: Holt Rinehart and Winston, 1966), preface.

4. Deuteronomy 6:4. The translation is found in *The Torah* (Philadelphia: The Jewish Publication Society, 1962). All scripture quotations in this chapter are from the Jewish Publication Society editions.

5. Elie Wiesel in The Long Search Film "Israel: The Chosen People," one of thirteen films produced by the BBC and first transmitted in the winter of 1977.

6. Exodus 3:14–15.

7. As Abraham Heschel has suggested, Judaism is a constant pilgrimage to the sabbath. Abraham Heschel, *The Earth Is the Lord's and the Sabbath* (New York: Harper & Row, 1951), 90.

8. Genesis 1:26–27. Historical biblical criticism has developed a multiple-author theory for the Torah, namely "J" (Jahwist), "E" (Elohist), "D" (Deuteronomist), and "P" (Priestly) authors. The Torah was originally built from these four sources which are woven together in the first five books of Hebrew scripture. In the northern kingdom authors of the "E" source (which used Elohim for G-d), and of the "D" source (largely the Book of Deuteronomy) were both against the king who resided in the south. In the southern kingdom, the

"J" source (which called G-d YHWH or Yahweh), and the "P" source (which focused on priestly duties) supported the king. For example, the opening creation account is a priestly version which was written largely to justify keeping the sabbath holy.

9. Genesis 2:23.

10. Martin Buber, *The Way of Man* (New Jersey: Citadel Press, Inc., 1966), 9–10.

11. Genesis 17:1–8.

12. Actually when it looked as if Sarah would remain barren, Abraham had a son Ishmael with his maid-servant Haggar. After Isaac was born Sarah insisted that Haggar and Ishmael be sent out into the desert. Arabs consider Ishmael their spiritual forefather, a similar status afforded by Jews to Isaac. Thus Abraham is the spiritual forefather of the three major western religions.

13. Leviticus 19:1–3.

14. Joshua 214:24–26.

15. Samuel 7:5–7.

16. Quoted by Jacob Neusner in *The Way of Torah* (Belmont, California: Wadsworth Publishing Co., 1979), 22 (parentheses mine).

17. Jeremiah 31:31–34.

18. Isaiah 42:1–4.

Selections

Selections from the Torah (largely from Genesis and Exodus) and from the Historical (Joshua, Judges, 1 and 2 Samuel and Kings, Ezra and Nehemiah) and the Prophetic Books (1 and 2 Isaiah, Jeremiah and Ezekiel), translated by the Jewish Publication Society of America.

Genesis

1 When God began to create the heaven and the earth—²the earth being unformed and void, with darkness over the surface of the deep and a wind from God sweeping over the water—³God said, "Let there be light"; and there was light. ⁴God saw how good the light was, and God separated the light from the darkness. ⁵God called the light Day, and the darkness He called Night. And there was evening and there was morning, a first day.

⁶God said, "Let there be an expanse in the midst of the water, that it may separate water from water." ⁷God made the expanse, and it separated the water which was below the expanse from the water which was above the expanse. And it was so. ⁸God called the expanse Sky. And there was evening and there was morning, a second day.

⁹God said, "Let the water below the sky be gathered into one area, that the dry land may appear." And it was so. ¹⁰God called the dry land Earth, and the gathering of waters He called Seas. And God saw how good this was. ¹¹And God said, "Let the earth sprout vegetation: seed-bearing plants, fruit trees of every kind on earth that bear fruit with the seed in it." And it was so. ¹²The earth brought forth vegetation: seed-bearing plants of every kind, and trees of every kind bearing fruit with the seed in it. And God saw how good this was. ¹³And there was evening and there was morning, a third day.

¹⁴God said, "Let there be lights in the expanse of the sky to separate day from night; they shall serve as signs for the set times—the days and the years; ¹⁵and they shall serve as lights in the expanse of the sky to shine upon the earth." And it was so. ¹⁶God made the two great lights, the greater light to dominate the day and the lesser light to dominate the night, and the stars. ¹⁷And God set them in the expanse of the sky to shine upon the earth, ¹⁸to dominate the day and the night, and to separate light from darkness. And God saw how good this was. ¹⁹And there was evening and there was morning, a fourth day.

²⁰God said, "Let the waters bring forth swarms of living creatures, and birds that fly above the earth across the expanse of the sky." ²¹God created the great sea monsters, and all the living creatures of every kind that creep, which the waters brought forth in swarms; and all the winged birds of every kind. And God saw how good this was. ²²God blessed them, saying, "Be fertile and increase, fill the waters in the seas, and let the birds increase on the earth." ²³And there was evening and there was morning, a fifth day.

²⁴God said, "Let the earth bring forth every kind of living creature: cattle, creeping things, and wild beasts of every kind." And it was so. ²⁵God made wild beasts of every kind and cattle of every kind, and all kinds of creeping things of the earth. And God saw how good this was. ²⁶And God said, "I will make man in My image, after My likeness. They shall rule the fish of the sea, the birds of the sky, the cattle, the whole earth, and all the creeping things that creep on earth." ²⁷And God created man in His image, in the image of God He created him; male and female He created them. ²⁸God blessed them and God said to them, "Be fertile and increase, fill the earth and master it; and rule the fish of the sea, the birds of the sky, and all the living things that creep on earth."

²⁹God said, "See, I give you every seed-bearing plant that is upon all the earth, and every tree that has seed-bearing fruit; they shall be yours for food. ³⁰And to all the animals on land, to all the birds of the sky, and to everything that creeps on earth, in which there is the breath of life, [I give] all the green plants for food." And it was so. ³¹And God saw all that He had made, and found it very good. And there was evening and there was morning, the sixth day.

2 The heaven and the earth were finished, and all their array. [2]And on the seventh day God finished the work which He had been doing, and He ceased on the seventh day from all the work which He had done. [3]And God blessed the seventh day and declared it holy, because on it God ceased from all the work of creation which He had done. [4]Such is the story of heaven and earth as they were created.

When the LORD God made earth and heaven—[5]no shrub of the field being yet in the earth and no grains having yet sprouted, because the LORD God had not sent rain upon the earth and there was no man to till the soil, [6]but a flow would well up from the ground and water the whole surface of the earth—[7]the LORD God formed man from the dust of the earth, and He blew into his nostrils the breath of life; and man became a living being.

[8]The LORD God planted a garden in Eden, in the east, and placed there the man whom He had formed. [9]And from the ground the LORD God caused to grow every tree that was pleasing to the sight and good for food, with the tree of life in the middle of the garden, and the tree of knowledge of good and bad.

[10]A river issues from Eden to water the garden, and from there it divides and becomes four branches. [11]The name of the first is Pishon, the one that winds through the whole land of Havilah, where the gold is. [12]The gold of that land is good; bdellium is there, and lapis lazuli. [13]The name of the second river is Gihon, the one that winds through the whole land of Cush. [14]The name of the third river is Tigris, the one that flows east of Asshur; and the fourth river is the Euphrates.

[15]The LORD God took the man and placed him in the garden of Eden, to till it and tend it. [16]And the LORD God commanded the man, saying, "Of every tree of the garden you are free to eat; [17]but as for the tree of knowledge of good and bad, you must not eat of it; for as soon as you eat of it, you shall be doomed to die."

[18]The LORD God said, "It is not good for man to be alone; I will make a fitting helper for him." [19]And the LORD God formed out of the earth all the wild beasts and all the birds of the sky, and brought them to the man to see what he would call them; and whatever the man called each living creature, that would be its name. [20]And the man gave names to all the cattle and to the birds of the sky and to all the wild beasts; but for Adam no fitting helper was found. [21]So the LORD God cast a deep sleep upon the man and he slept; and He took one of his ribs and closed up the flesh at that spot. [22]And the LORD God fashioned into a woman the rib that He had taken from the man, and He brought her to the man. [23]Then the man said,

"This one at last
Is bone of my bones
And flesh of my flesh.
This one shall be called Woman,
For from man was she taken."

[24]Hence a man leaves his father and mother and clings to his wife, so that they become one flesh.

[25]The two of them were naked, the man and his 3 wife, yet they felt no shame. [1]Now the serpent was the shrewdest of all the wild beasts that the LORD God had made. He said to the woman, "Did God really say: You shall not eat of any tree of the garden?" [2]And the woman said to the serpent, "We may eat of the fruit of the other trees of the garden. [3]It is only about fruit of the tree in the middle of the garden that God said: You shall not eat of it or touch it, lest you die." [4]And the serpent said to the woman, "You are not going to die. [5]God knows that, as soon as you eat of it, your eyes will be opened and you will be like God, who knows good and bad." [6]When the woman saw that the tree was good for eating and a delight to the eyes, and that the tree was desirable as a source of wisdom, she took of its fruit and ate; and she gave some to her husband also, and he ate. [7]Then the eyes of both of them were opened and they perceived that they were naked; and they sewed together fig leaves and made themselves loincloths.

⁸They heard the sound of the LORD God moving about in the garden at the breezy time of day; and the man and his wife hid from the LORD God among the trees of the garden. ⁹The LORD God called out to the man and said to him, "Where are you?" ¹⁰He replied, "I heard the sound of You in the garden, and I was afraid because I was naked, so I hid." ¹¹Then He said, "Who told you that you were naked? Did you eat of the tree from which I had forbidden you to eat?" ¹²The man said, "The woman You put at my side—she gave me of the tree, and I ate." ¹³And the LORD God said to the woman, "What is this you have done!" The woman replied "The serpent duped me, and I ate." ¹⁴And the LORD God said to the serpent,

"Because you did this,
Banned shall you be from all cattle
And all wild beasts;
On your belly shall you crawl
And dirt shall you eat
All the days of your life.
¹⁵I will put enmity
Between you and the woman,
And between your offspring and hers;
They shall strike at your head,
And you shall strike at their heel."

¹⁶And to the woman He said,

"I will make most severe
Your pangs in childbearing;
In pain shall you bear children.
Yet your urge shall be for your husband,
And he shall rule over you."

¹⁷To Adam He said, "Because you heeded your wife and ate of the tree about which I commanded you, saying, 'You shall not eat of it,'

Cursed be the ground because of you;
In anguish shall you eat of it
All the days of your life.
¹⁸Thorns and thistles
Shall it bring forth for you,
And you shall feed on the grains of the field.
¹⁹By the sweat of your brow
Shall you get bread to eat,
Until you return to the ground,
For from it you were taken:

For dust you are,
And to dust you shall return."

²⁰The man named his wife Eve, because she was the mother of all the living. ²¹And the LORD God made for Adam and his wife garments of skins, and He clothed them.

²²And the LORD God said, "Now that the man has become like one of us, knowing good and bad, what if he should stretch out his hand and take also from the tree of life and eat, and live forever!" ²³So the LORD God banished him from the garden of Eden, to till the soil from which he was taken. ²⁴He drove the man out, and stationed east of the garden of Eden the cherubim and the fiery ever-turning sword, to guard the way to the tree of life.

11 All the earth had the same language and the same words. ²And as men migrated from the east, they came upon a valley in the land of Shinar and settled there. ³They said to one another, "Come, let us make bricks and burn them hard."—Brick served them as stone, and bitumen served them as mortar.—⁴And they said, "Come, let us build us a city, and a tower with its top in the sky, to make a name for ourselves; else we shall be scattered all over the world." ⁵The LORD came down to look at the city and tower which man had built, ⁶and the LORD said, "If, as one people with one language for all, this is how they have begun to act, then nothing that they may propose to do will be out of their reach. ⁷Let Me, then, go down and confound their speech there, so that they shall not understand one another's speech." ⁸Thus the LORD scattered them from there over the face of the whole earth; and they stopped building the city. ⁹That is why it was called Babel, because there the LORD confounded the speech of the whole earth; and from there the LORD scattered them over the face of the whole earth.

they set out together from Ur of the Chaldeans for the land of Canaan; but when they had come as far as Haran, they settled there. ³²The days of Terah came to 205 years; and Terah died in Haran.

12 The LORD said to Abram, "Go forth from your native land and from your father's house to the land that I will show you.

> [2]I will make of you a great nation,
> And I will bless you;
> I will make your name great,
> And you shall be a blessing:
> [3]I will bless those who bless you,
> And curse him that curses you;
> All the families of the earth
> Shall bless themselves by you."

[4]Abram went forth as the LORD had spoken to him, and Lot went with him. Abram was seventy-five years old when he left Haran. [5]Abram took his wife Sarai and his brother's son Lot, and all the wealth that they had amassed, and the persons that they had acquired in Haran; and they set out for the land of Canaan. When they arrived in the land of Canaan, [6]Abram passed through the land as far as the site of Shechem, at the terebinth of Moreh. The Canaanites were then in the land.

[7]The LORD appeared to Abram and said, "I will give this land to your offspring." And he built an altar there to the LORD who had appeared to him. [8]From there he moved on to the hill country east of Bethel and pitched his tent, with Bethel on the west and Ai on the east; and he built there an altar to the LORD and invoked the LORD by name. [9]Then Abram journeyed by stages toward the Negeb.

17 When Abram was ninety-nine years old, the LORD appeared to Abram and said to him, "I am El Shaddai. Walk in My ways and be blameless. [2]I will establish My covenant between Me and you, and I will make you exceedingly numerous."

[3]Abram threw himself on his face, as God continued speaking to him, [4]"As for Me, this is My covenant with you: You shall be the father of a multitude of nations. [5]And you shall no longer be called Abram, but your name shall be Abraham, for I make you the father of a multitude of nations. [6]I will make you exceedingly fertile, and make nations of you; and kings shall come forth

from you. [7]I will maintain My covenant between Me and you, and your offspring to come, as an everlasting covenant throughout the ages, to be God to you and to your offspring to come. [8]I give the land you sojourn in to you and your offspring to come, all the land of Canaan, as an everlasting possession. I will be their God."

[9]God further said to Abraham, "As for you, you shall keep My covenant, you and your offspring to come, throughout the ages. [10]Such shall be the covenant, which you shall keep, between Me and you and your offspring to follow: every male among you shall be circumcised. [11]You shall circumcise the flesh of your foreskin, and that shall be the sign of the covenant between Me and you. [12]At the age of eight days, every male among you throughout the generations shall be circumcised, even the homeborn slave and the one bought from an outsider who is not of your seed.—[13]The slave that is born in your household or bought with your money must be circumcised!—Thus shall My covenant be marked in your flesh as an everlasting pact. [14]An uncircumcised male who does not circumcise the flesh of his foreskin—such a person shall be cut off from his kin; he has broken My covenant."

[15]And God said to Abraham, "As for your wife Sarai, you shall not call her Sarai, but her name shall be Sarah. [16]I will bless her; indeed, I will give you a son by her. I will bless her so that she shall give rise to nations; rulers of peoples shall issue from her." [17]Abraham threw himself on his face and laughed, as he said to himself, "Can a child be born to a man a hundred years old, or can Sarah bear a child at ninety?" [18]And Abraham said to God, "Oh that Ishmael might live by Your favor!" [19]God said, "Nevertheless, Sarah your wife shall bear you a son, and you shall name him Isaac, and I will maintain My covenant with him as an everlasting covenant for his offspring to come. [20]As for Ishmael, I have heeded you. I hereby bless him. I will make him fertile and exceedingly numerous. He shall be the father of twelve chieftains, and I will make of him a great nation. [21]But My covenant I will

maintain with Isaac, whom Sarah shall bear to you at this season next year." [22]And when He was done speaking with him, God was gone from Abraham.

[23]Then Abraham took his son Ishmael, and all his homeborn slaves and all those he had bought, every male among Abraham's retainers, and he circumcised the flesh of their foreskins on that very day, as God had spoken to him. [24]Abraham was ninety-nine years old when he circumcised the flesh of his foreskin [25]and his son Ishmael was thirteen years old when he was circumcised in the flesh of his foreskin. [26]Thus Abraham and his son Ishmael were circumcised on that very day; [27]and all his retainers, his homeborn slaves and those that had been bought from outsiders, were circumcised with him.

22 Some time afterward, God put Abraham to the test. He said to him, "Abraham," and he answered, "Here I am." [2]And He said, "Take your son, your favored one, Isaac, whom you love, and go to the land of Moriah, and offer him there as a burnt offering on one of the heights which I will point out to you." [3]So early next morning, Abraham saddled his ass and took with him two of his servants and his son Isaac. He split the wood for the burnt offering, and he set out for the place of which God had told him. [4]On the third day Abraham looked up and saw the place from afar. [5]Then Abraham said to his servants, "You stay here with the ass. The boy and I will go up there; we will worship and we will return to you."

[6]Abraham took the wood for the burnt offering and put it on his son Isaac. He himself took the firestone and the knife; and the two walked off together. [7]Then Isaac said to his father Abraham, "Father!" And he answered, "Yes, my son." And he said, "Here is the firestone and the wood; but where is the sheep for the burnt offering?" [8]And Abraham said, "God will see to the sheep for His burnt offering, my son." And the two of them walked on together.

[9]They arrived at the place of which God had told him. Abraham built an altar there; he laid out the wood; he bound his son Isaac; he laid him on the altar, on top of the wood. [10]And Abraham picked up the knife to slay his son. [11]Then an angel of the LORD called to him from heaven: "Abraham! Abraham!" And he answered, "Here I am." [12]And he said, "Do not raise your hand against the boy, or do anything to him. For now I know that you fear God, since you have not withheld your son, your favored one, from Me." [13]When Abraham looked up, his eye fell upon a ram, caught in the thicket by its horns. So Abraham went and took the ram and offered it up as a burnt offering in place of his son. [14]And Abraham named that site Adonai-yireh, whence the present saying, "On the mount of the LORD there is vision."

[15]The angel of the LORD called to Abraham a second time from heaven, [16]and said, "By Myself I swear, the LORD declares: because you have done this and have not withheld your son, your favored one, [17]I will bestow My blessing upon you and make your descendants as numerous as the stars of heaven and the sands on the seashore; and your descendants shall capture the gates of their enemies. [18]All the nations of the earth shall bless themselves by your descendants, because you have obeyed My command." [19]Abraham then returned to his servants, and they departed together for Beer-sheba; and Abraham stayed in Beer-sheba.

*   *   *

Exodus

2 [23]A long time after that, the king of Egypt died. The Israelites were groaning under the bondage and cried out; and their cry for help from the bondage rose up to God. [24]God heard their moaning, and God remembered His covenant with Abraham and Isaac and Jacob. [25]God looked upon the Israelites, and God took notice of them.

3 Now Moses, tending the flock of his father-in-law Jethro, the priest of Midian, drove the flock into the wilderness, and came to Horeb, the mountain of God. [2]An angel of the LORD appeared to him in a blazing fire out of a bush. He gazed, and there was a bush all aflame, yet the bush was not consumed. [3]Moses said, "I must turn aside to look at this marvelous sight; why is the bush not burnt?" [4]When the LORD saw that he had turned aside to look, God called to him out of the bush: "Moses! Moses!" He answered, "Here I am." [5]And He said, "Do not come closer. Remove your sandals from your feet, for the place on which you stand is holy ground. [6]I am," He said, "the God of your father, the God of Abraham, the God of Isaac, and the God of Jacob." And Moses hid his face, for he was afraid to look at God.

[7]And the LORD continued, "I have marked well the plight of My people in Egypt and have heeded their outcry because of their taskmasters; yes, I am mindful of their sufferings. [8]I have come down to rescue them from the Egyptians and to bring them out of that land to a good and spacious land, a land flowing with milk and honey, the home of the Canaanites, the Hittites, the Amorites, the Perizzites, the Hivites, and the Jebusites. [9]Now the cry of the Israelites has reached Me; moreover, I have seen how the Egyptians oppress them. [10]Come, therefore, I will send you to Pharaoh, and you shall free My people, the Israelites, from Egypt."

[11]But Moses said to God, "Who am I that I should go to Pharaoh and free the Israelites from Egypt?" [12]And He said, "I will be with you, and it shall be your sign that it was I who sent you. And when you have freed the people from Egypt, you shall worship God at this mountain."

[13]Moses said to God, "When I come to the Israelites and say to them 'The God of your fathers has sent me to you,' and they ask me, 'What is His name?' what shall I say to them?" [14]And God said to Moses, "Ehyeh-Asher-Ehyeh." He continued, "Thus shall you say to the Israelites, 'Ehyeh sent me to you.' " [15]And God said further to Moses, "Thus shall you speak to the Israelites: The LORD, the God of your fathers, the God of Abraham, the God of Isaac, and the God of Jacob, has sent me to you:

This shall be My name forever,
This My appellation for all eternity.

[16]"Go and assemble the elders of Israel and say to them: the LORD, the God of your fathers, the God of Abraham, Isaac, and Jacob, has appeared to me and said, 'I have taken note of you and of what is being done to you in Egypt, [17]and I have declared: I will take you out of the misery of Egypt to the land of the Canaanites, the Hittites, the Amorites, the Perizzites, the Hivites, and the Jebusites, to a land flowing with milk and honey.' [18]They will listen to you; then you shall go with the elders of Israel to the king of Egypt and you shall say to him, 'The LORD, the God of the Hebrews, manifested Himself to us. Now therefore, let us go a distance of three days into the wilderness to sacrifice to the LORD our God.' [19]Yet I know that the king of Egypt will not let you go except by force. [20]So I will stretch out My hand and smite Egypt with various wonders which I will work upon them; after that he shall let you go. [21]And I will dispose the Egyptians favorably toward this people, so that when you go, you will not go away empty-handed. [22]Each woman shall borrow from her neighbor and the lodger in her house objects of silver and gold, and clothing, and you shall put these on your sons and daughters, thus stripping the Egyptians."

4 But Moses spoke up and said, "What if they do not believe me and do not listen to me, but say: The LORD did not appear to you?" [2]The LORD said to him, "What is that in your hand?" And he replied, "A rod." [3]He said, "Cast it on the ground." He cast it on the ground and it became a snake; and Moses recoiled from it. [4]Then the LORD said to Moses, "Put out your hand and grasp it by the tail"—he put out his hand and seized it, and it became a rod in his hand—[5]"that they may believe that the LORD, the God of their fathers, the God of Abraham, the God of Isaac, and the God of Jacob, did appear to you."

11 And the LORD said to Moses, "I will bring but one more plague upon Pharaoh and upon Egypt; after that he shall let you go from here; indeed, when he lets you go, he will drive you out of here one and all. ²Tell the people that each man shall borrow from his neighbor, and each woman from hers, objects of silver and gold." ³The LORD disposed the Egyptians favorably toward the people. Moreover, Moses himself was much esteemed in the land of Egypt, among Pharaoh's courtiers and among the people.

⁴Moses said, "Thus says the LORD: Toward midnight I will go forth among the Egyptians, ⁵and every first-born in the land of Egypt shall die, from the first-born of Pharaoh who sits on his throne to the first-born of the slave girl who is behind the millstones; and all the first-born of the cattle. ⁶And there will be a loud cry in all the land of Egypt, such as has never been or will ever be again; ⁷but not a dog shall snarl at any of the Israelites, at man or beast—in order that you may know that the LORD makes a distinction between Egypt and Israel. ⁸Then all these courtiers of yours shall come down to me and bow low to me, saying, 'Depart, you and all the people who follow you!' After that I will depart." And he left Pharaoh's presence in hot anger.

⁹Now the LORD had said to Moses, "Pharaoh will not heed you, in order that My marvels may be multiplied in the land of Egypt." ¹⁰Moses and Aaron had performed all these marvels before Pharaoh, but the LORD had stiffened the heart of Pharaoh so that he would not let the Israelites go from his land.

12 The LORD said to Moses and Aaron in the land of Egypt: ²This month shall mark for you the beginning of the months; it shall be the first of the months of the year for you. ³Speak to the whole assembly of Israel and say that on the tenth of this month each of them shall take a lamb to a family, a lamb to a household. ⁴But if the household is too small for a lamb, then let him share one with the neighbor closest to his household in the number of persons: you shall apportion the lamb according to what each person should eat. ⁵Your lamb shall be without blemish, a yearling male; you may take it from the sheep or from the goats. ⁶You shall keep watch over it until the fourteenth day of this month; and all the aggregate community of the Israelites shall slaughter it at twilight. ⁷They shall take some of the blood and put it on the two doorposts and the lintel of the houses in which they are to eat it. ⁸They shall eat the flesh that same night; they shall eat it roasted over the fire, with unleavened bread and with bitter herbs. ⁹Do not eat any of it raw, or cooked in any way with water, but roasted—head, legs, and entrails—over the fire. ¹⁰You shall not leave any of it over until morning; whatever is left of it until morning you shall burn.

¹¹This is how you shall eat it: your loins girded, your sandals on your feet, and your staff in your hand; and you shall eat it hurriedly: it is a passover offering to the LORD. ¹²For that night I will go through the land of Egypt and strike down every first-born in the land of Egypt, both man and beast; and I will mete out punishments to all the gods of Egypt, I the LORD. ¹³And the blood on the houses in which you dwell shall be a sign for you: when I see the blood I will pass over you, so that no plague will destroy you when I strike the land of Egypt.

¹⁴This day shall be to you one of remembrance: you shall celebrate it as a festival to the LORD throughout the generations; you shall celebrate it as an institution for all time. ¹⁵Seven days you shall eat unleavened bread; on the very first day you shall remove leaven from your houses, for whoever eats leavened bread from the first day to the seventh day, that person shall be cut off from Israel.

19 On the third new moon after the Israelites had gone forth from the land of Egypt, on that very day, they entered the wilderness of Sinai. ²Having journeyed from Rephidim, they entered the wilderness of Sinai and encamped in the wilderness. Israel encamped there in front of the mountain, ³and Moses went up to God. The LORD called to him from the mountain, saying,

"Thus shall you say to the house of Jacob and declare to the children of Israel: ⁴'You have seen what I did to the Egyptians, how I bore you on eagles' wings and brought you to Me. ⁵Now then, if you will obey Me faithfully and keep My covenant, you shall be My treasured possession among all the peoples. Indeed, all the earth is Mine, ⁶but you shall be to Me a kingdom of priests and a holy nation.' These are the words that you shall speak to the children of Israel."

⁷Moses came and summoned the elders of the people and put before them all the words that the LORD had commanded him. ⁸All the people answered as one, saying, "All that the LORD has spoken we will do!" And Moses brought back the people's words to the LORD. ⁹And the LORD said to Moses, "I will come to you in a thick cloud, in order that the people may hear when I speak with you and so trust you thereafter." Then Moses reported the people's words to the LORD, ¹⁰and the LORD said to Moses, "Go to the people and warn them to stay pure today and tomorrow. Let them wash their clothes. ¹¹Let them be ready for the third day; for on the third day the LORD will come down, in the sight of all the people, on Mount Sinai. ¹²You shall set bounds for the people round about, saying, 'Beware of going up the mountain or touching the border of it. Whoever touches the mountain shall be put to death: ¹³no hand shall touch him, but he shall be either stoned or pierced through; beast or man, he shall not live.' When the ram's horn sounds a long blast, they shall come up unto the mountain."

¹⁴Moses came down from the mountain to the people and warned the people to stay pure, and they washed their clothes. ¹⁵And he said to the people, "Be ready for the third day: do not go near a woman."

¹⁶On the third day, as morning dawned, there was thunder, and lightning, and a dense cloud upon the mountain, and a very loud blast of the horn; and all the people who were in the camp trembled. ¹⁷Moses led the people out of the camp toward God, and they took their places at the foot of the mountain.

¹⁸Now Mount Sinai was all in smoke, for the LORD had come down upon it in fire; the smoke rose like the smoke of a kiln, and the whole mountain trembled violently. ¹⁹The blare of the horn grew louder and louder. As Moses spoke, God answered him in thunder. ²⁰The LORD came down upon Mount Sinai, on the top of the mountain, and the LORD called Moses to the top of the mountain and Moses went up. ²¹The LORD said to Moses, "Go down, warn the people not to break through to the LORD to gaze, lest many of them perish. ²²The priests also, who come near the LORD, must purify themselves, lest the LORD break out against them." ²³But Moses said to the LORD, "The people cannot come up to Mount Sinai, for You warned us saying, 'Set bounds about the mountain and sanctify it.' ²⁴So the LORD said to him, "Go down, and come back together with Aaron; but let not the priests or the people break through to come up to the LORD, lest He break out against them." ²⁵And Moses went down to the people and spoke to them.

20 God spoke all these words saying:

²I the LORD am your God who brought you out of the land of Egypt, the house of bondage: ³You shall have no other gods beside Me.

⁴You shall not make for yourself a sculptured image, or any likeness of what is in the heavens above, or on the earth below, or in the waters under the earth. ⁵You shall not bow down to them or serve them. For I the LORD your God am an impassioned God, visiting the guilt of the fathers upon the children, upon the third and upon the fourth generations of those who reject Me, ⁶but showing kindness to the thousandth generation of those who love Me and keep My commandments.

⁷You shall not swear falsely by the name of the LORD your God; for the LORD will not clear one who swears falsely by His name.

⁸Remember the sabbath day and keep it holy. ⁹Six days you shall labor and do all your work, ¹⁰but the seventh day is a sabbath of the LORD your God: you shall not do any work—you, your son or daughter, your male or female slave,

or your cattle, or the stranger who is within your settlements. [11]For in six days the LORD made heaven and earth and sea, and all that is in them, and He rested on the seventh day; therefore the LORD blessed the sabbath day and hallowed it.

[12]Honor your father and your mother, that you may long endure on the land which the LORD your God is giving you.

[13]You shall not murder.

You shall not commit adultery.

You shall not steal.

You shall not bear false witness against your neighbor.

[14]You shall not covet your neighbor's house: you shall not covet your neighbor's wife, or his male or female slave, or his ox or his ass, or anything that is your neighbor's.

[15]All the people witnessed the thunder and lightning, the blare of the horn and the mountain smoking; and when the people saw it, they fell back and stood at a distance. [16]"You speak to us," they said to Moses, "and we will obey; but let not God speak to us, lest we die." [17]Moses answered the people, "Be not afraid; for God has come only in order to test you, and in order that the fear of Him may be ever with you, so that you do not go astray." [18]So the people remained at a distance, while Moses approached the thick cloud where God was.

[19]The LORD said to Moses:

Thus shall you say to the Israelites: You yourselves saw that I spoke to you from the very heavens: [20]With Me, therefore, you shall not make any gods of silver, nor shall you make for yourselves any gods of gold. [21]Make for Me an altar of earth and sacrifice on it your burnt offerings and your sacrifices of well-being, your sheep and your oxen; in every place where I cause My name to be mentioned I will come to you and bless you. [22]But if you make for Me an altar of stones, do not build it of hewn stones; for by wielding your tool upon them you have profaned them. [23]Do not ascend My altar by steps, that your nakedness may not be exposed upon it.

*   *   *

Joshua

1 After the death of Moses the servant of the LORD, the LORD said to Joshua son of Nun, Moses' attendant:

[2]"My servant Moses is dead. Prepare to cross the Jordan, together with all this people, into the land which I am giving to the Israelites. [3]Every spot on which your foot treads I give to you, as I promised Moses. [4]Your territory shall extend from the wilderness and the Lebanon to the Great River, the River Euphrates [on the east]— the whole Hittite country—and up to the Mediterranean Sea on the west. [5]No man shall be able to resist you as long as you live. As I was with Moses, so I will be with you; I will not fail you or forsake you.

[6]"Be strong and resolute, for you shall apportion to this people the land that I swore to their fathers to give them. [7]But you must be very strong and resolute to observe faithfully all the Teaching that My servant Moses enjoined upon you. Do not deviate from it to the right or to the left, that you may be successful wherever you go. [8]Let not this Book of the Teaching cease from your lips, but recite it day and night, so that you may observe faithfully all that is written in it. Only then will you prosper in your undertakings and only then will you be successful.

[9]"I charge you: Be strong and resolute; do not be terrified or dismayed, for the LORD your God is with you wherever you go."

6 Now Jericho was shut up tight because of the Israelites; no one could leave or enter.

[2]The LORD said to Joshua, "See, I will deliver Jericho and her king [and her] warriors into your hands. [3]Let all your troops march around the city and complete one circuit of the city. Do this six days, [4]with seven priests carrying seven ram's horns preceding the Ark. On the seventh day, march around the city seven times, with the priests blowing the horns. [5]And when a long blast is sounded on the horn—as soon as you

hear that sound of the horn—all the people shall give a mighty shout. Thereupon the city wall will collapse, and the people shall advance, every man straight ahead."

⁶Joshua son of Nun summoned the priests and said to them, "Take up the Ark of the Covenant, and let seven priests carrying seven ram's horns precede the Ark of the LORD." ⁷And he instructed the people, "Go forward, march around the city, with the vanguard marching in front of the Ark of the LORD." ⁸When Joshua had instructed the people, the seven priests carrying seven ram's horns advanced before the LORD, blowing their horns; and the Ark of the LORD's Covenant followed them. ⁹The vanguard marched in front of the priests who were blowing the horns, and the rear guard marched behind the Ark, with the horns sounding all the time. ¹⁰But Joshua's orders to the rest of the people were, "Do not shout, do not let your voices be heard, and do not let a sound issue from your lips until the moment that I command you, 'Shout!' Then you shall shout."

¹¹So he had the Ark of the LORD go around the city and complete one circuit; then they returned to camp and spent the night in camp. ¹²Joshua rose early the next day; and the priests took up the Ark of the LORD, ¹³while the seven priests bearing the seven ram's horns marched in front of the Ark of the LORD, blowing the horns as they marched. The vanguard marched in front of them, and the rear guard marched behind the Ark of the LORD, with the horns sounding all the time. ¹⁴And so they marched around the city once on the second day and returned to the camp. They did this six days.

¹⁵On the seventh day, they rose at daybreak and marched around the city, in the same manner, seven times; that was the only day that they marched around the city seven times. ¹⁶On the seventh round, as the priests blew the horns, Joshua commanded the people, "Shout! For the LORD has given you the city. ¹⁷The city and everything in it are to be proscribed for the LORD; only Rahab the harlot is to be spared, and all who are with her in the house, because she hid the messengers we sent. ¹⁸But you must beware of that which is proscribed, or else you will be proscribed: if you take anything from that which is proscribed, you will cause the camp of Israel to be proscribed; you will bring calamity upon it. ¹⁹All the silver and gold and objects of copper and iron are consecrated to the LORD; they must go into the treasury of the LORD."

²⁰So the people shouted when the horns were sounded. When the people heard the sound of the horns, the people raised a mighty shout and the wall collapsed. The people rushed into the city, every man straight in front of him, and they captured the city. ²¹They exterminated everything in the city with the sword: man and woman, young and old, ox and sheep and ass. ²²But Joshua bade the two men who had spied out the land, "Go into the harlot's house and bring out the woman and all that belong to her, as you swore to her." ²³So the young spies went in and brought out Rahab, her father and her mother, her brothers and all that belonged to her—they brought out her whole family and left them outside the camp of Israel.

²⁴They burned down the city and everything in it. But the silver and gold and the objects of copper and iron were deposited in the treasury of the HOUSE of the LORD. ²⁵Only Rahab the harlot and her father's family were spared by Joshua, along with all that belonged to her, and she dwelt among the Israelites—as is still the case. For she had hidden the messengers that Joshua sent to spy out Jericho.

²⁶At that time Joshua pronounced this oath: "Cursed of the LORD be the man who shall undertake to fortify this city of Jericho: he shall lay its foundations at the cost of his firstborn, and set up its gates at the cost of his youngest."

²⁷The LORD was with Joshua, and his fame spread throughout the land.

²⁴,²⁵On that day at Shechem, Joshua made a covenant for the people and he made a fixed rule for them. ²⁶Joshua recorded all this in a book of divine instruction. He took a great stone and set it up at the foot of the oak in the sacred precinct

of the LORD; [27]and Joshua said to all the people, "See, this very stone shall be a witness against us, for it heard all the words that the LORD spoke to us; it shall be a witness against you, lest you break faith with your God." [28]Joshua then dismissed the people to their allotted portions.

[29]After these events, Joshua son of Nun, the servant of the LORD, died at the age of one hundred and ten years. [30]They buried him on his own property, at Timnath-serah in the hill country of Ephraim, north of Mount Gaash. [31]Israel served the LORD during the lifetime of Joshua and the lifetime of the elders who lived on after Joshua, and who had experienced all the deeds that the LORD had wrought for Israel.

[32]The bones of Joseph, which the Israelites had brought up from Egypt, were buried at Shechem, in the piece of ground which Jacob had bought for a hundred *kesitahs* from the children of Hamor, Shechem's father, and which had become a heritage of the Josephites.

[33]Eleazar son of Aaron also died, and they buried him on the hill of his son Phinehas, which had been given to him in the hill country of Ephraim.

2 Samuel

7 When the king was settled in his palace and the LORD had granted him safety from all the enemies around him, [2]the king said to the prophet Nathan: "Here I am dwelling in a house of cedar, while the Ark of the LORD abides in a tent!" [3]Nathan said to the king, "Go and do whatever you have in mind, for the LORD is with you."

[4]But that same night the word of the LORD came to Nathan: [5]"Go and say to My servant David: Thus said the LORD: Are you the one to build a house for Me to dwell in? [6]From the day that I brought the people of Israel out of Egypt to this day I have not dwelt in a house, but have moved about in Tent and Tabernacle. [7]As I moved about wherever the Israelites went, did I ever reproach any of the tribal leaders whom I

appointed to care for My people Israel: Why have you not built Me a house of cedar?

[8]"Further, say thus to My servant David: Thus said the LORD of Hosts: I took you from the pasture, from following the flock, to be ruler of My people Israel, [9]and I have been with you wherever you went, and have cut down all your enemies before you. Moreover, I will give you great renown like that of the greatest men on earth. [10]I will establish a home for My people Israel and will plant them firm, so that they shall dwell secure and shall tremble no more. Evil men shall not oppress them any more as in the past, [11]ever since I appointed chieftains over My people Israel. I will give you safety from all your enemies.

"The LORD declares to you that He, the LORD, will establish a house for you. [12]When your days are done and you lie with your fathers, I will raise up your offspring after you, one of your own issue, and I will establish his kingship. [13]He shall build a house for My name, and I will establish his royal throne forever. [14]I will be a father to him, and he shall be a son to Me. When he does wrong, I will chastise him with the rod of men and the affliction of mortals; [15]but I will never withdraw My favor from him as I withdrew it from Saul, whom I removed to make room for you. [16]Your house and your kingship shall ever be secure before you; your throne shall be established forever."

Isaiah

6 In the year that King Uzziah died, I beheld my Lord seated on a high and lofty throne; and the skirts of His robe filled the Temple. [2]Seraphs stood in attendance on Him. Each of them had six wings: with two he covered his face, with two he covered his legs, and with two he would fly.

[3]And one would call to the other,
"Holy, holy, holy!
The LORD of Hosts!"
His presence fills all the earth!"

⁴The doorpost would shake at the sound of the one who called, and the House kept filling with smoke. ⁵I cried,

"Woe is me; I am lost!
For I am a man of unclean lips
And I live among a people
Of unclean lips;
Yet my own eyes have beheld
The King LORD of Hosts.

⁶Then one of the seraphs flew over to me with a live coal, which he had taken from the altar with a pair of tongs. ⁷He touched it to my lips and declared,

"Now that this has touched your lips,
Your guilt shall depart
And your sin be purged away."

⁸Then I heard the voice of my LORD saying, "Whom shall I send? Who will go for us?" And I said, "Here am I; send me." ⁹And He said, "Go, say to that people:

'Hear, indeed, but do not understand;
See, indeed, but do not grasp.'
¹⁰Dull that people's mind,
Stop its ear,
And seal its eyes—
Lest, seeing with its eyes
And hearing with its ears,
It also grasp with its mind,
And repent and save itself."

¹¹I asked, "How long, my Lord?" And He replied:

"Till towns lie waste without inhabitants
And houses without people,
And the ground lies waste and desolate—
¹²For the LORD will banish the
population—
And deserted sites are many
In the midst of the land.

¹³"But while a tenth part yet remains in it, it shall repent. It shall be ravaged like the terebinth and the oak, of which stumps are left even when they are felled: its stump shall be a holy seed."

11 But a shoot shall grow out of the stump of Jesse,

A twig shall sprout from his stock.
²The spirit of the LORD shall alight upon him:
A spirit of wisdom and insight,
A spirit of counsel and valor,
A spirit of devotion and reverence for the LORD.
³He shall sense the truth by his reverence for the LORD:
He shall not judge by what his eyes behold,
Nor decide by what his ears perceive.
⁴Thus he shall judge the poor with equity
And decide with justice for the lowly of the land.
He shall strike down a land with the rod of his mouth
And slay the wicked with the breath of his lips.
⁵Justice shall be the girdle of his loins,
And faithfulness the girdle of his waist.
⁶The wolf shall dwell with the lamb,
The leopard lie down with the kid;
The calf, the beast of prey, and the fatling together,
With a little boy to herd them.
⁷The cow and the bear shall graze,
Their young shall lie down together,
And the lion, like the ox, shall eat straw.
⁸A babe shall play
Over a viper's hole,
And an infant pass his hand
Over an adder's den.
⁹In all of My sacred mount
Nothing evil or vile shall be done;
For the land shall be filled with devotion to the LORD
As water covers the sea.

42 This is My servant, whom I uphold,

My chosen one, in whom I delight.
I have put My spirit upon him,
He shall teach the true way to the nations.
²He shall not cry out or shout aloud,

Or make his voice heard in the streets.
³He shall not break even a bruised reed,
Or snuff out even a dim wick.
He shall bring forth the true way.
⁴He shall not grow dim or be bruised
Till he has established the true way on earth;
And the coastlands shall await his teaching.
⁵Thus said God the LORD,
Who created the heavens and stretched them out,
Who spread out the earth and what it brings forth,
Who gave breath to the people upon it
And life to those who walk thereon:
⁶I the LORD, in My grace, have summoned you,
And I have grasped you by the hand.
I created you, and appointed you
A covenant-people, a light of nations
⁷Opening eyes deprived of light,
Rescuing prisoners from confinement,
From the dungeon those who sit in darkness.
⁸I am the LORD, that is My name;
I will not yield My glory to another,
Nor My renown to idols.
⁹See, the things once predicted have come,
And now I foretell new things,
Announce to you ere they sprout up.
That her term of service is over,
That her iniquity is expiated;
For she has received at the hand of the LORD
Double for all her sins.

Psalms

1 Happy is the man who has not followed the counsel of the wicked,
or taken the path of sinners,
or joined the company of the insolent;
²rather, the teaching of the LORD is his delight,
and he studies that teaching day and night.
³He is like a tree planted beside streams of water,
that yields its fruit in season,
whose foliage never fades,
and whatever it produces thrives.
⁴Not so the wicked;

rather, they are like chaff that wind blows away.
⁵Therefore the wicked will not survive judgment,
nor will sinners, in the assembly of the righteous.
⁶For the LORD cherishes the way of the righteous,
but the way of the wicked is doomed.

100 A psalm for praise.
Raise a shout for the LORD, all the earth;
²worship the LORD in gladness;
come into His presence with shouts of joy.
³Acknowledge that the LORD is God;
He made us and we are His,
His people, the flock He tends.
⁴Enter His gates with praise,
His courts with acclamation.
Praise Him!
Bless His name!
⁵For the LORD is good;
His steadfast love is eternal;
His faithfulness is for all generations.

Ecclesiastes

3 A season is set for everything, a time for every experience under heaven:
²A time for being born and a time for dying,
A time for planting and a time for uprooting the planted;
³A time for slaying and a time for healing,
A time for tearing down and a time for building up;
⁴A time for weeping and a time for laughing,
A time for wailing and a time for dancing;
⁵A time for throwing stones and a time for gathering stones,
A time for embracing and a time for shunning embraces;
⁶A time for seeking and a time for losing,
A time for keeping and a time for discarding;
⁷A time for ripping and a time for sewing,
A time for silence and a time for speaking;
⁸A time for loving and a time for hating;
A time for war and a time for peace.

TORAH JOURNAL EXERCISES

1. Write your own creation story. Let your imaginative mind wander back in time and history, back to the beginning of things, and begin your creation account exactly as Genesis does:

    "In the beginning God . . ."

    Continue from these first four words to formulate your own version of the Genesis account. It may be close to, or have little to do with, the Genesis version. You may wish to select either the Genesis 1:1 or the Genesis 2:4 account of creation and rewrite it. One purpose might be to retrieve the original meaning and intention in today's language (e.g., street-talk, or newspaper talk, or academic-talk, or video-talk, or hip-talk, etc.).

2. Where were Adam and Eve after the fall? What differences were experienced before and after the fall? What does the writer mean when he says "then the eyes of both of them were opened and they realized that they were naked"? Imagine that you hear the sound of YHWH. You are scared and you hide but YHWH's voice reaches you. "Where are you?" G-d asks. What would your answer be?

3. Recall the story of Abram, how G-d called him to leave his home, his security, his past, and to wander off into an unknown frontier. What if you heard or felt a call to leave your home and to follow the promptings of a revelational G-d? How would you respond? How fast would you leave or would you refuse to go? If you went off, what would you take with you?

4. To better understand the Ten Commandments, write short answers to the following:
    a. If you were G-d giving Moses the Ten Commandments all over again, would you change any of them. Would you rearrange or eliminate any of them? Why?
    b. Update the Ten Commandments. Imagine that you are a twentieth century Moses. How would you word the commandments to catch the spirit of our age? Write spontaneously, as the ideas come to you. When finished prioritize them and then compare them to Moses'.
    c. Compare the Exodus account with what you, as Moses, just wrote. Any differences? What did you include? What did you leave out? Did you learn anything about the commandments or yourself in the process?

5. Reread some of G-d's calls to Abram (Gen 12:1–9), Moses (Ex 3:1–15), Elisha (1 Kgs 19:19–21), Isaiah (Is 6), Jeremiah (Jer 1) and Ezekiel (Ez 2). What do all of these Divine-calls have in common? In what ways are they distinctive? What would it be like to be called by G-d? Imagine that G-d intended to call you forth for a task. How would G-d reach you (through what means or medium) and what task would G-d ask of you? How would you reply?

6. If you felt called by G-d to be a twentieth century prophet, what would your message be? Pick a contemporary social issue (e.g., nuclear arms, the death penalty, abortion, busing, video-games, pollution, starvation, etc.) and speak out about it as if you were directly inspired by the G-d of Abraham, Isaac and Jacob.

7. Record your oracle (of doom or salvation) as if YHWH is speaking through you! Start with typical prophetic beginning "Thus says YHWH . . ." What would you be inspired to say next?
8. If you were to write the 151st Psalm, what would you say? Would you write a hymn of praise or a lament, an appeal against your enemies, or a song of the glories of creation? Pick a subject and then reread a few Psalms to absorb the style, the poetic rhythms and the musical tones. Imitate the scriptural style as much as possible when you write your own Psalm. When you are finished, compare it to one of the original 150.
9. In a similar fashion, write your own Proverb in the style of the following:

> A good man is more desirable than great wealth,
> the respect of others is better than silver or gold (Prv 22:1).

You may also wish to personify Wisdom and have her speak through you. For instance you may wish to rewrite Proverbs 8:22–31. Compare what Wisdom says here to what Yahweh says to Job when Yahweh speaks out of the whirlwind.

Chapter 9 THE JESUS STORY

One day Abbot Ammonas, a fourth century Egyptian desert father, said to a monk whom he saw wearing a hairshirt: "That won't help you a bit!" The monk replied that he was continually troubled by three options: whether to withdraw into the wilderness, to move to a foreign land where he would be unknown, or to remain in his cell and eat only once every second day. Abbot Ammonas promptly told him to forget all three, and to sit in his cell, eat once a day, and "have always in your heart the words which are read in the Gospel and were said by the Publican."[1] The question this story raises is: Why did the abbot render this particular advice? Who is this Jesus whom Christians claim brings salvation? What sets Jesus of Nazareth apart from other holy teachers?

While it is impossible to know what Jesus looked like, it is helpful to begin answering these questions by looking at ways in which Jesus has been pictured.

The first face is not a picture of what Jesus might actually have looked like, but rather an idealized icon of Divine Transcendence. Through the use of color and light, iconographers attempt to catch the light of the Divine Presence in the face. A Christ-icon therefore is not a signed painting, but an anonymous meditation on the mystery of the incarnation. Used by the Greek and Russian Orthodox communities in private meditation and liturgy, the icon face of Jesus pictures, paradoxically, the unpicturable. It pictures the mysterious identification between Jesus the Son and God the Father. This is an image of Jesus as the second person of the Holy Trinity, as pre-existent Word of God.

If the first face depicts the God-man, the second picture portrays a fully human Jesus. I vividly remember a stained glass image of Jesus in the Andover Newton Seminary Chapel whose white hands and face were painted black by a student civil-rights advocate. At that time (1963–66) the second face, the "Wanted" poster of Jesus, was circulating in the Boston area. Aside from its purpose and point of view, the image depicts a socially concerned, ultrahuman Jesus who identifies with common working people and the unemployed, and who associates with the disenfranchised, the sick, the sinners, the lost. This is an image of Jesus the liberator, of Jesus as the one who seeks to emancipate the prisoner, the prostitute and the poor.

The last face appears on the Shroud of Turin kept by the Catholic Church in Italy, and which some have claimed contains an impression made by the body and face of Jesus.[2] On the cloth is the imprint of a well-built man in his mid-thirties, 5 feet 11 inches tall, approximately 170 pounds, with shoulder-length hair and a short beard. Body markings evidence severe beatings on the face and back, and show nail punctures in the hands and feet.

Leaving aside arguments for and against the shroud's authenticity, the question re-

Icon Face

WANTED

JESUS of NAZARETH

ALIAS — SUBJECT IS KNOWN TO APPEAR UNDER THE NAMES "SON OF MAN" AND "PRINCE OF PEACE".

Vagrant — Loiters around Synagogues; has a "Hippie" appearance, often seen without shoes. Associates with common working people and the unemployed. Said to work sporadically as a carpenter.

anarchist — Subject is a professional agitator wanted for sedition and conspiring to overthrow the established government.

CHARLATAN — Claims visionary ideas, said to victimize the sick and the blind with stories of miraculous cures.

MARKED — SCARS ON HANDS AND FEET THE RESULT OF NEAR EXECUTION BY AN ANGRY CROWD LED BY RESPECTABLE CITIZENS AND LEGAL AUTHORITIES.

DANGEROUS — This man is a serious threat to established law and order. A substantial reward is being offered for information leading to his apprehension. If you see this man call your local law enforcement agency.

Human Face

Shroud Face

mains: How did the image get into the cloth? Using an image analyzer, scientists have been able to represent the face three dimensionally on a computer screen. This would not be possible if it was a painting or a photograph. One theory (assuming it is the face of Jesus) speculates that the image was produced by an intense burst of radiation-like energy in a millisecond of time. If authentic, this would be an image of the resurrected Christ.

All discussions of Jesus begin with the resurrection, for it is the keystone event and sign for Christians of Christ's eternal living presence. As biblical scholars have noted, the Gospels were written backward, that is from the standpoint of the accomplished fact of the death and resurrection of Jesus. If Jesus did not rise from the tomb, not only, as Paul says, is Christian preaching in vain, but Christianity would lose its major claim to uniqueness among the world's faiths. Neither Buddha nor Confucius before him, nor Muhammad after, claimed to be both human and divine. Jesus did. As he says, "I am the resurrection and the life," or, to put it slightly differently, Jesus is the resurrection in life.

The story of Jesus occurs within three contexts or circles: that of Hebraic culture, that of the Gospels' idiosyncratic language, and that of the Apostolic Church. Beginning with a brief discussion of Jewish groups at the time of Jesus, we will encounter Jesus as portrayed in the synoptic Gospels (Mark, Matthew and Luke), and last as reflected in writings by and about Peter, Paul and John. Each views Jesus from a slightly different angle, with a slightly different camera.

JUDAISM AT THE TIME OF JESUS

Before Jesus we recall, Temple-Judaism had been restored through the efforts of Ezra, Nehemiah and other scribes, priests and laity, who returned to Jerusalem in 538 BCE after forty years in Babylonian exile. The arrival of Alexander the Great of Macedonia, who conquered the then-known world in 336–323 BCE, fueled apocalyptic expectations (cf. Daniel) within an already rigorously lawful religious life. This second temple period was marked by priestly rituals and the Hellenization of Hebrew theology. So strong was the Hellenistic cultural influence on the Jews not only in Palestine (about a half million) but also in the diaspora (about seven million), that the Torah was translated into Greek to guide Jews who did not know Hebrew. Said to be the combined effort of seventy biblical scholars, this early translation of the Torah (called the *Septuagint*) later became the basis of the Christian Old Testament.

In the period from Ezra to the birth of Jesus, the search for the central meaning of both written and oral Torahs intensified. By 200 CE the oral Torah traditions were being written in the *Mishna* (Review) which, along with the *Gemara* (Completion), was collected in the Talmud (compendium of learning). During this time, from unknown origins, a rigorously ethical sect known as the Pharisees ("separated ones") emerged. They may have derived from the *hasidim* ("pious ones") who actively supported the Maccabean revolt against Greek tyranny, or they may have broken away from the apocalyptic Essenes who retreated to the desert to lead the purified life. Convinced that the end of the world was not imminent, the Pharisees soon became the leading exponents, interpreters and molders of the Torah which they held was handed down at Sinai. According to a Pharisaic interpretation, of all the 613 laws only three laws could not be suspended—no murder, no adultery and no idolatry. And most importantly they believed that as the prophets had forecast, the Messiah was to come.

More than any other group, it was the Pharisees whom Jesus constantly encountered, was questioned by and toward whom he aimed his parables of the kingdom. In fact, as has been suggested, Jesus' teachings often echoed those of the Pharisees. Whether this is true or not will be left to scholarly speculation; however, it is true that the Pharisees were the only group to survive the destruction of the second temple (70 CE) and thus are the progenitors of modern Judaism.

The other dominant religious group were the Sadducees, the aristocratic, conservative, largely priestly descendants of Zadok (who anointed Solomon king of Israel, 1 Kgs 1:39). The Sadducees, who collaborated with the Romans in administering national affairs, were primarily concerned with temple ritual. To safeguard and preserve Jewish traditions, they believed only in the exact words of scripture, without any alteration. In opposition to the Pharisees, they minimized the application of law to everyday life, did not accept a resurrection of the dead, denied the validity of oral Torah, and denied divine providence and the Pharisees' belief in angels. It is the Sadducees who come to the fore at the trial of Jesus.

A third group, the Essenes, believing that the end of time was near, withdrew into the desert where they refrained from worldly activities and practiced self-control, poverty and monastic seclusion. Some Essenes, perhaps like John the Baptist, called everyone who would listen "to repent" and "to be baptized." Everyone in the Qumran community followed strict initiation and purification rituals and gathered ritually for breaking bread and sharing wine. They wrote a manual of discipline for their own community and copied scriptures which they placed in clay jars, hiding them from the Romans in caves. Now on display in the National Museum of Israel in Jerusalem, they are among the oldest surviving biblical manuscripts.

A fourth group, the Zealots, also occupied Palestine at this time. They were dramatically opposed to Roman domination, to foreign taxation, and zealously preached the active overthrow, by violence if necessary, of all foreign powers. It is possible that Judas Iscariot, the "betrayer" of Jesus, was a Zealot who was disappointed that Jesus had refused to become a political activist. The deeply religious Zealots were always ready to battle for the Lord, and after Jerusalem fell in 70 CE, some barricaded themselves in Herod's fortress at Masadah at the Dead Sea. After a three-year struggle, when further resistance was impossible, the 967 men, women, and children killed themselves rather than be captured by the Roman armies.

Last were the Samaritans, most of whom settled north of Jerusalem in Judea. They were outcasts from orthodox Jewish circles because they did not acknowledge the Jerusalem temple to be God's dwelling place, and because they limited scripture to the first five books of Moses. The origin of their separation is traced to the time of Nehiemiah (fifth century BCE), and was solidified when they built their own temple on Mount Gerizim, near Shechem (third century BCE), a temple that was later destroyed by the Jewish Maccabean ruler John Hyrcanus (in 128 BCE). When the Romans took control of Palestine (in 64–63 BCE), the Samaritans were allowed to practice their beliefs through their own priesthood. It was in fact a

Samaritan woman whom Jesus met one day at Jacob's well, who was among the first to proclaim Jesus as the Christ, and to evangelize among her people.

Jesus never fit the popular Jewish expectations of the Messiah. Whereas the Pharisees sought a religio-political leader, the Essenes two Messiahs (one religious and one military), and the Zealots a revolutionary figure, Jesus was none of them. As we will see, the Gospel-Jesus became the suffering servant who preached God's kingdom and died tortuously for it.

In what follows we will shift our attention from the Jewish cultural backdrop to the linguistic framework in which the images of Jesus were framed. Then we will conclude with the developing church's portrait.

THE GOSPELS

The English word "Gospel" (God-spell, God-story) is used to translate the Greek word *evangelion* or good tidings. The word Gospel refers to the oral proclamation of tradition concerning the good news, to the one who proclaims it, to the written text (though only later), and to the events in the life of the early church. The Gospels belong to the confessional genre. They are neither history, biography nor accurate observation and reporting, though they include these. Rather they are sequential collections of glad-tidings told to kindle faith.

While it can be argued that Mark pioneered the gospel form as a way of presenting Jesus' teachings, it can also be shown that it was Jesus himself who first used the phrase in a synagogue at Nazareth. There he stood and read from the Prophet Isaiah:

> The spirit of the Lord is upon me;
> therefore he has anointed me.
> He has sent me to bring glad tidings to the poor,
> to proclaim liberty to captives,
> Recovery of sight to the blind and release to prisoners,
> To announce a year of favor from the Lord.[3]

When Jesus sat down he said: "This text is being fulfilled today even as you listen" (Lk 4:22). As we will see momentarily, the one who is sent to bring the "good news" is himself the "good news" he is sent to proclaim. It is important to note here that while the Hebrew scriptures as we know them did not exist as a single text in Jesus' time, copies of Genesis, Exodus, Leviticus, Numbers and Deuteronomy, along with the Prophets were written on separate scrolls and collected in synagogues and in religious centers such as at Qumran where the Dead Sea scrolls were found. Jesus had studied these texts with the learned rabbis and often recalled images from memory which were applicable to his own life, which his own life fulfilled.

Aside from Roman historians Pliny the Younger and Tacitus, and Jewish historian Josephus, our historic picture of Jesus comes primarily from the Gospels which contain sayings by Jesus and stories about him, stories which spread through Palestine during and after his life. Each gospelist organizes them into the same basic pattern: birth and baptism at the Jordan; ministry in Galilee; entry into Jerusalem; and the passion, death and resurrection. Apart from this structure, the Gospels are arranged in various ways. Each paints with different brushes, speaks to different audiences and at times addresses different needs. Mark (65–70 CE), Matthew (70–75) and Luke (75–80) are called the synoptic Gospels ("seen together" or seen with one eye) because they include similar stories, and similar sequences of events. The Fourth Gospel, John (90–95), contains only eight percent of the synoptic material.

Mark (or John Marcus), half Jewish, half Gentile, was a scribe and secretary for Peter. Mark wrote to the Gentile Christians in Rome and depicted Jesus as the "Christ," the hidden "Son of God," the Messianic secret, as a master who is servant to all. Matthew, a Jewish tax collector, was written specifically for the Hebrew Christian audience. In Matthew, Jesus is depicted as the "Son of Abraham," the "Son of David," the "Second Moses." He is a great lawgiver. Luke (Lucas), a Greek physician, historian, artist, who knew Paul in Tarsus, and who wrote specifically to the Greek Gentiles, called Jesus "Lord" (*Kyrios*), "Son of Man," the Savior of the poor and neglected. For Luke, Jesus was the savior of all people, not the Jews alone. John emphasizes what the other gospels leave out. Jesus for John is the pre-existent Logos (Word of God) through whom everything is created and who, at the same time, is one with the Father. For John, Jesus is the way, truth and light for all persons, past or future.

We progress now to two major scriptural images of Jesus—that of the synoptics, and that of Peter, Paul and John. It might be said that the synoptics and Peter present Jesus from a more human standpoint and that Paul and John present him from a more transcendent one. Our intention is not to reduce Jesus to a single perspective, or to a combination of them, but to highlight characterizations by those closest to him. Hopefully what emerges is an animated picture of a real person's actions and attitudes.

The Synoptic Jesus

Jesus was a common name among Jews since it is the Aramaic form of the Hebrew word *Yeshua* (Joshua, YHWH saves). He was called the Christ (Greek for the Aramaic *messiah*, the anointed one, the prophesied king), and was born in Bethlehem (house of bread), David's town, during the reign of Caesar Augustus (30 BCE–4 CE), possibly during the years of Jubilation in 6–4 BCE.[4] Because Matthew, Mark and Luke include similar materials, we will first trace the chronology of his lifestory as it is presented in their writings.

Virgin Birth

According to the Lucan version, the most poetic and literarily descriptive, the pre-announced birth occurred during the first Roman census in fourteen years, during the springtime when shepherds were in the fields protecting their flocks. Joseph, betrothed to Mary who is already pregnant with Jesus, takes her from Nazareth their home, to Bethlehem to register for the census. Unique to Luke's version of the birth of Jesus is the annunciation to the Virgin Mary (from Hebrew Miriam) by the Angel Gabriel that she, an unmarried Jewish teenager, is to become the God-bearer (*theotokos*). When Mary visits her cousin Elizabeth,

who was pregnant with John the Baptist, Elizabeth's child leaps in her womb and Mary rejoices:

> My being proclaims the greatness of the Lord,
> my spirit finds joy in God my savior.
> For he has looked upon his servant in her lowliness;
> all ages to come shall call me blessed.
> God who is mighty has done great things for me;
> holy is his name.
> His mercy is from age to age
> on those who fear him.
> He has shown might with his arm;
> he has confused the proud in their inmost thoughts.
> He has deposed the mighty from their thrones
> and raised the lowly to high places.
> The hungry he has given every good thing,
> while the rich he has sent empty away.[5]

This is the earliest proclamation of the good news and a foretaste of the beatitudes of Jesus.
In fact, Mary can be called the first disciple because she is the first to hear the good news
(Lk 1:26ff), the first to accept the good news (Lk 1:28) and the first to proclaim it (Lk 1:46ff).
For this reason early church writers viewed Mary as a second Eve, whose offspring would
vanquish the serpent (Gen 3:14–15), and as "the woman adorned with the sun" (Rev 12:1–
6). Mary thus came to be viewed as the mother of the church.

At the Temple

Since Jesus is Mary's first born son, according to Jewish custom, after his name is given,
two purifications were performed. At eight days Jesus was circumcised as a sign of the on-
going covenant with YHWH. When Jesus was presented at the temple as a sacrifical offering
to YHWH, (to be then ransomed back according to Torah with a pair of turtle doves), the pious
old Simeon, recognizes Jesus as the one for whom he has been waiting, and says:

> This child is destined to be the downfall and the rise of many in Israel, a sign that
> will be opposed and you yourself shall be pierced with a sword—so that the thoughts
> of many hearts may be laid bare.[6]

Luke tells us next that as a twelve year old, Jesus was lost to his parents for three days
in Jerusalem, where they went each year to celebrate the feast of the Passover. When they
found him, he was discussing Torah with the rabbis and scribes in the temple, as was expected of every Jewish boy just prior to *bar mitzvah*. We have no record of his life and theological training from this event until his baptism, though it is assumed that he worked as a
carpenter with his foster-father Joseph.

Baptism/Temptation

As practiced by the Essene community, baptism was an initiation and purification ritual which signified the identity of the elect. Jesus, on the other hand, was baptized at the hands of John the Baptist, by water and the spirit, in the Jordan River through which years earlier Joshua had led the Hebrews into the Promised Land. When John tried to dissuade him—"It is I who need baptism from you"—Jesus says, "It is fitting that we should, in this way, do all that righteousness (Torah) demands" (Mt 3:13–15). As soon as Jesus was immersed in the river the heavens opened and the Holy Spirit descended like a dove upon him. God said, "This is my Son, the Beloved; my favor rests on him" (Mt 3:16–17).

The Spirit then leads Jesus from the Jordan into a forty-day fast in the wilderness where he overcomes three temptations from Satan. To each he replied with a passage of scripture from the Torah. He was tempted:

1) to turn stones to bread—
A) "Man does not live on bread alone but on every word that comes from the mouth of God";
2) to throw himself down from the temple parapet—
A) "You must not put your Lord God to the test";
3) to worship Satan—
A) "You must worship the Lord your God, and serve him alone."[7]

Teachings of Jesus

Aside from the fact that Jesus is a healer and exorcist, which we will not discuss here, he is often addressed in the Gospels as "Rabbi" (Master), not only by his immediate followers, but also by antagonists. Over fifty times in the Gospels he is referred to as "teacher," though certainly not in the strict rabbinic sense. While the title had not yet become indicative of a formal ordination to teach, it carried an informal acceptance of one as a wisdom teacher. Our question is: What did Jesus teach?

As biblical scholars note, the teachings of Jesus have two primary foci: eschatological (the future and immanent coming of the kingdom of God), and ethical (the new law of love). If the beatitudes are the heart of Jesus ethics of love and service, then it is the kingdom of God which ushers forth this new righteousness. According to Mark, the first proclamation of the "Good News" by Jesus was in Galilee. "The time has come," he said, "and the kingdom of God is close at hand; repent, and believe the good news" (Mk 1:15). The Greek word *meta-noia,* to repent, literally to change one's mind (meta-noeisis), means to turn and to be turned by the transformational nature of God's Spirit. Jesus' first message announced that by denouncing old thoughts, habits and attitudes, one is born new. As we will see, Paul continues this theme by calling for a "renewal of one's mind by a spiritual revolution" (Eph 4:24), and by challenging disciples to have Christ in their mind (Phil 2:5). And Peter carries the trajectory forward when he exorts followers to "free your minds and to trust only in Christ's grace" (1 Pet 1:13).

After Jesus sends out the twelve apostles (Peter and brother Andrew, James and brother John, Philip and Bartholomew, Thomas, Matthew, James and Thaddaeus, Simon and Judas) to "be cunning as serpents and yet as harmless as doves" (Mt 10:16), he begins to preach the parables of the kingdom. As Buddha did, Jesus used parables as didactic stories which both revealed and concealed. Parabolically, the kingdom of God is like a tiny mustard seed which germinates and grows into a large tree, a treasure hidden in a field which one sells everything else to buy, a fine pearl, and a dragnet which collects both the good and the bad fish.

"Have you understood all this?" "Yes," they answered; to which he replied, "Every scribe who is learned in the reign of God is like the head of a household who can bring from his storeroom both the new and the old."[8]

In this condensed parable Jesus compares the disciple who seeks the kingdom of God to a scribe. The scribe was a copyist and at times reader and interpreter of the sacred books. Ezra for example both read and interpreted the Torah for the Jews who returned to Jerusalem under Cyrus' edict. Being a disciple-scribe, according to Jesus, is like going into a storeroom (of the sacred texts) to bring out (*exegesis*) both old and new images of sacred meaning. Like Confucius, Jesus communicated the double element of all spiritual truth, a *recovery* of the old (that which is eternal, universal and of God), and a *discovery* of the new (that which appears from the old in a novel manner) as if for the first time.

What characterizes this new birth is the arrival of what C.H. Dodd calls the zero hour, "the climax of a process, bringing a crisis in which decisive action is called for."[9] This zero hour, the culminating harvest, the fulfillment of promises, is the good news of the "kingdom of God." In Hebrew, this phrase means the "reign of God," that is, the power and majesty of God's presence here and now, and yet to come at the end of time.

This of course thoroughly upset and turned upside down his contemporaries' expectations. The Jews expected a Davidic king, a powerful and wealthy conqueror. But Jesus spoke, instead, in the beatitudes of giving up power and of being childlike:

How blest are the poor in spirit: the reign (kingdom) of God is theirs.
Blest too are the sorrowing; they shall be consoled.
Blest are the lowly; they shall inherit the land.
Blest are they who hunger and thirst for holiness; they shall have their fill.
Blest are they who show mercy; mercy shall be theirs.
Blest are the single-hearted for they shall see God.
Blest too the peacemakers; they shall be called sons of God.
Blest are those persecuted for holiness' sake; the reign of God is theirs.
Blest are you when they insult you and persecute you and utter every kind of slander against you because of me.
Be glad and rejoice, for your reward in heaven is great.[10]

The beatitudes speak powerfully and eloquently of a new righteousness which is poor in spirit, gentle, mourning, hungering and thirsting, merciful, pure-hearted, peacemaking. Jesus presents himself as one who has come to fulfill the Law, not to abolish it, to bring a new standard of virtue—from the rightness of external acts to the rightness of religious attitudes. Like Confucius before him, Jesus does not abolish tradition (the Torah) but reanimates it by at times turning the old upside down.

Jesus teaches that God (as *Abba,* as loving Father) desires an intimate relation with His children. Two of his best known parables—the Good Samaritan and the Prodigal Son—strikingly illustrate this uncontainable love.

In the parable of the Good Samaritan (Lk 10:25–37) a lawyer, trained in the minutiae of Jewish Law, asks Jesus what he must do to inherit eternal life. Jesus skillfully answers with another question: "What does the Law (Torah) say?" The lawyer answers, "Love the Lord with all your heart, and your neighbor as yourself."

"Excellent," Jesus answers. "Do it!" But the lawyer counters, "Who is my neighbor?"

Then Jesus tells him of a Jew who was beaten, robbed, and left for dead. After a priest and Levite pass him by, a Samaritan (whom the Jews rigorously avoided), moved with compassion, carries him to an inn where he can recuperate and pays for his stay. "Now who is the real neighbor?" Jesus asks.

In an equally striking parable (Lk 15:11–32), Jesus tells of a younger son who takes his inheritance and leaves home. The older brother also takes his half of the father's wealth but does not leave. After squandering his money in a foreign country, the younger son is reduced to caring for the swine. When he comes to his senses, he returns to work as a hired hand only to find his father eagerly waiting for him. As the younger son begs for mercy, his father calls for robes, jewelry and a feast to celebrate his son's return. This unexpected behavior expectedly arouses the older son's jealousy. "Why?" he asks his father. "Why the festivities?" His father answers, "All I have is yours, but now your brother who was dead has returned."

Each parable points to the natural result of *metanoia,* namely a compassionate attitude toward other humans, especially those who have been wronged or who have themselves wronged others.

Peter's Confession and The Transfiguration

The apex of each of the synoptics is Peter's confession of faith in the identity of Jesus as the Christ. Like a Shakespearean tragedy which reaches its climax in the third act and then moves toward the final tragic conclusion, so too the Gospels seem to reach a peak when Peter says, "You are the Christ . . . the Son of the living God" (Mk 8:27–30; Mt 16:17; Lk 9:18–21). In Matthew's version, Jesus replies, "You are Peter (*petros*) and on this rock (*petra*) I will build my church (*ecclesia*). . . . I will give you the keys of the kingdom of heaven. Whatever you declare bound on earth shall be bound in heaven; whatever you declare loosed on earth shall be loosed in heaven" (Mt 16:18–19). A short time later, Peter, James and his brother John accompany Jesus to a mountain. There they see Jesus glowingly transfigured, in dazzling white, elevated with Moses (the Law) on one side and Elijah (the Prophets) on the other. As at his baptism, a voice from heaven says, "This is my beloved Son on whom my favor rests. Listen to him" (Mt 17:5). In Mark's account (Mk 9:2ff) we are told, interestingly, that the disciples afterward discussed among themselves what "rising from the dead" could mean. The early church theologians interpreted this entire scene as prefiguring the resurrection.

Passion

The Jerusalem ministry begins with the final week of his life. Jesus enters the city on a donkey to fulfill his Passover obligations. Controversy about his person and purpose has been building not only in the Sanhedrin (Jewish courts) and among synagogue leaders, but as well among the Roman political leaders who are already watching the Zealots carefully. The scribes, Pharisees and Sadducees all question points of his teaching and the source of his authority. After being anointed at Bethany, Jesus celebrates the passover meal (6:00 P.M.) in the upper room of a house which tradition ascribes to Mark's mother:

> During the meal he took bread, blessed and broke it, and gave it to them. "Take this," he said; "this is my body." He likewise took a cup, gave thanks and passed it to them, and they all drank from it. He said to them: "This is my blood, the blood of the covenant, to be poured out on behalf of many. I solemnly assure you, I will never again drink of the fruit of the vine until the day when I drink it new in the reign of God."[11]

Jesus further establishes a new covenant (testament) by expanding the meaning of the Passover meal (which celebrated deliverance from Egyptian oppression) to include forgiveness for personal sins, and by identifying his body with the unleavened bread, his blood with the Passover wine.

According to Mark, at 9:00 P.M. Jesus prays alone at Gethsemane. At midnight he is arrested, at 3:00 A.M. he stands before the Sanhedrin and at 6:00 A.M. he is delivered by the Sanhedrin to Pilate for trial as "king of the Jews." Pilate's initial response is to find Jesus without blame, but when he is reminded that freeing Jesus (who "makes himself king") would be to defy Caesar (king of the Roman empire), he hands him over to be crucified. Jesus is taken from the praetorium, led through the streets of Jerusalem to Golotha Hill just outside the city walls, and crucified between two thieves. The inscription on the placard above his head reads: "The King of the Jews."

Between 9:00 and 3:00 P.M. on Friday, before Jesus dies, he speaks his last words (not necessarily in this order):

> Eloi, Eloi, lama sabachthani—My God, my God, why hast thou forsaken me? (Mt 27:46; Mk 15:34).
> Father, forgive them; they do not know what they are doing (Lk 23:34).
> This day you will be with me in paradise (Lk 23:43).

Father, into your hands I commit my spirit (Lk 23:46).
Woman, behold your son. Son, behold your mother (Jn 19:27).
I am thirsty (Jn 19:28).
It is finished (Jn 19:30).

Each in its context witnesses to the powerful nuances of his good news, even in death. Whereas Buddha enlightened a truth-seeker who came to him as he was dying, Jesus, by the way he died, converts one of two thieves and a Roman centurion who witnesses his death. Meanwhile, the disciples have fled.

Resurrection

When the Jewish sabbath was over, when Jews could again travel and work after a day of rest, the two Marys (the mother of Jesus and Magdalene) and Salome discover the burial tomb to be empty. An angel appears to announce that Jesus of Nazareth has risen. On the road to Emmaus, Jesus appears to two disciples but they do not recognize him at first. Then referring to Moses, the Prophets and the Psalms, he "explained to them the passages throughout the scriptures that were about himself" (Lk 24:27). After opening "their minds to understand the scriptures" (Lk 24:46), the resurrected Jesus speaks his final words: "And now I am sending down to you what the Father has promised. Stay in the city then, until you are clothed with the power from on high" (Lk 24:49).

The resurrection of Christ was disputed by some from earliest times. It was believed that either the Jews or the disciples stole the body though Matthew reports that the Jews had Pilate secure the grave, and we know that Roman centurions were executed if they failed at their task. After the tomb was found empty (reported by all four evangelists), and after Jesus appeared to individuals, to groups and to five hundred (as Paul reports), Jesus appears to the eleven, breathes on them and says: "Receive the Holy Spirit. If you forgive men's sins, they are forgiven them; if you hold them bound, they are bound" (Jn 20:22–23). This direct transformation of spiritual grace foreshadows the descent of the Holy Spirit at Pentecost.

As we have seen, the resurrection is the central mystery of Christianity. When the apostles were first told by the women and Mary, the mother of Jesus, "this story of theirs seemed (like) pure nonsense, and they did not believe them" (Lk 24:11). Only after their eyes were opened did recognition burn within them. But the question remains: What actually happened?

Writing to the Church in Corinth some fifteen years later, St. Paul answered this question by comparing the body to a seed that is sown in the ground, and which must die before it can have new life. In a similar fashion the perishable body of Jesus died and became imperishable. What was on earth a living soul, had now become a heavenly body, a life-giving spirit (1 Cor 15:35–49). At the same time what really happened transformed the disciples' experience of Christ. He became a new, spirit-giving presence, risen from the dead. It was by the power of this spirit that the church was to be initiated, animated and guided.

THE EARLY CHURCH

Aside from Mary and John the Baptist, the three most important figures in the New Testament church after Jesus are Peter, Paul and John—Peter the leader of the twelve and first bishop of Rome, Paul the "apostle to the Gentiles," and John the last living eyewitness. In the remainder of the chapter we will briefly look at their reflections of the identity of Jesus.

Peter's Jesus

Luke begins the Acts account where he concluded his Gospel, with Jesus' promise of the Holy Spirit's coming. The book really begins with Pentecost (a harvest festival fifty days after Passover), with the birth of the church and the inauguration of the apostolic age. The Pentecost festival was especially important to the Essenes because it celebrates God's revelations to Moses at Sinai. Luke tells us in his dramatic historic narrative:

> When the day of Pentecost came it found them gathered in one place. Suddenly from up in the sky there came a noise like a strong, driving wind which was heard all through the house where they were seated. Tongues as of fire appeared, which parted and came to rest on each of them. All were filled with the Holy Spirit. They began to express themselves in foreign tongues and make bold proclamation as the Spirit prompted them.[12]

According to the early church theologians, the experiences of Pentecost, in which the disciples understood many different tongues, reversed the Babel experience in which human tongues were confused. Directly Peter interprets what has happened and his words have an immediacy and intimacy similar to the words of Jesus. "You must repent," Peter says, "and everyone of you must be baptized in the name of Jesus Christ for the forgiveness of your sins, and you will receive the gift of the Holy Spirit" (Acts 2:37–39). To the first words of Jesus— "Repent; the kingdom of God is at hand"—Peter adds: "Be baptized." Here we notice the first organizational decision of the early church, for to follow Christ one had to repent *and* to receive an acceptable sign.

Actually we know very little of the fisherman apostle who became the leader of the twelve disciples. According to the Acts account, Peter's early preaching, often referred to as the *kerygma* (proclamation; message), includes seven affirmations of faith in Christ which present the early church's image of Jesus, and which eventually became the backbone of the church's creedal statements:

- the dawn of the promised age (Acts 3:18–24); the life, death, and resurrection of Christ (Acts 2:22–31);
- the authority of the resurrection for the faithful (Acts 2:33–36; 4:2);
- the new community (church) as the sign of the new age (Acts 2:33; 5:32);
- the present power of the Holy Spirit;

- the promise of Christ's coming again as Judge and Savior (Acts 3:21);
- an appeal for repentance (Acts 2:38–39).[13]

As might be expected, Peter's image of Jesus is strongly influenced by the Torah and Prophets. The writer of 1 Peter calls Jesus "the (Passover) lamb without spot or stain" who is sacrificed as a ransom for all (1 Pet 1:18–20), and the suffering servant through whose wounds his followers are healed (1 Pet 2:21–25). Interestingly he also calls Jesus "the living stone, rejected by men but chosen by God" (1 Pet 2:4). For Peter, Jesus is the risen witness to Torah and prophecy, as well as the messianic herald of God's kingdom on earth.

The author of John provides a wonderful vignette which summarizes Peter's view of Jesus. After Jesus taught that he was the eternal bread, and that disciples should eat his flesh and drink his blood, some of the disciples found this language intolerable and departed. "What about you?" Jesus says to the twelve. "Do you want to leave too?" But Peter answers, "Lord, where shall we go? You have eternal life. You are the Holy One of God" (Jn 6:64–69).

Paul's Jesus

If Peter's image of Jesus is flavored by his Jewish culture, Paul's is more colored by Greek idealism. Paul was born Saul (5–7 CE) to a devout Pharisaic family in Tarsus, Cilicia, a Roman province north of Jerusalem, beyond the borders of Palestine. Named after Israel's first king, he belonged to the tribe of Benjamin (Acts 13:21; 23:6) and grew up in Tarsus, a commercial and intellectual center. He studied the Torah under Rabbi Gamaliel, a leading rabbinic figure of the day (Acts 23:3), and became a fanatical persecutor of Christians. But after witnessing the stoning of Stephen (Acts 7:58), he experienced on the road to Damascus a radical conversion (Acts 9:1–19; 22:1–21; 26:1–23; Gal 1:12–16). As Paul himself tells the story:

> As I was traveling along, approaching Damascus around noon, a great light from the sky suddenly flashed all about me. I fell to the ground and heard a voice say to me, "Saul, Saul, why do you persecute me?" I answered, "Who are you, sir?" He said to me, "I am Jesus the Nazorean whom you are persecuting." My companions saw the light but did not hear the voice speaking to me. "What is it I must do, sir?" I asked, and the Lord replied, "Get up and go into Damascus. There you will be told about everything you are destined to do."[14]

Psychologically speaking, Saul experienced the death of his ethnocentric, legalistic, anti-Christian "I," and was resurrected into the mystery of Christ's "I." He experienced utter emptiness toward Christ and became transformed by the renewal of his mind in Christ.

Subsequently Paul took three separate missionary journeys: with Barnabas to Cyprus, Asia Minor and Antioch (Acts 13:1–14:28), with Silas and Timothy to Asia Minor, Greek cities, Caesarea and Judea (Acts 15:36–18:22), and to Asia Minor, Europe, Tyre, Caesarea and Jerusalem (Acts 18:23–21:16). Twenty-one of the twenty-seven books of the New Testament are letters, almost half of which were traditionally attributed to Paul's correspondences to various churches in Asia Minor and in Europe which he either visited or helped organize.[15]

Paul's image of Christ is Greco-Hebraic. His highest Christology is reflected in two early Christian hymns. In the first, Christ is pictured as:

> The image of the unseen God
> and the first-born of all creation,
> for in him were created,
> all things in heaven and on earth:
> everything visible and everything invisible,
> Thrones, Dominations, Sovereignties, Powers—
> all things were created through him and for him.
> Before anything was created, he existed,
> and he holds all things in unity.
> Now the Church is his body,
> he is its head.[16]

Here Paul identifies Jesus with the Hebrew notion of the Messiah as the suffering servant, but extends his image to include Christ as a pre-existent figure (as John was later to do)— "the power of God and the wisdom of God" (1 Cor 2:24). Not only is Christ with the Father at creation, but now the church is an extension of Christ's body into history.

In the second hymn, Jesus is called *Kyrios* (Lord), the term that Greek-speaking, Hellenistic Jews used for *Adonai* (the name substituted for YHWH when Torah was read). As Lord, Christ makes all things new through his surrender to and victory over death.

> His state was divine,
> yet he did not cling
> to his equality with God
> but emptied himself
> to assume the condition of a slave,
> and became as men are;
> and being as all men are,
> he was humbler yet,
> even to accepting death,
> death on a cross.
> But God raised him high
> and gave him the name
> which is above all other names
> so that all beings,
> in the heavens, on earth and in the underworld,
> should bend the knee at the name of Jesus
> and that every tongue should acclaim

A Fragment of the Fourth Gospel
(The John Rylands Library)

> Jesus Christ as Lord (Kyrios),
> to the glory of God the Father.[17]

The divine became human through a self-emptying (*kenosis*) and freely accepted crucifixion; the resurrected Christ therefore is to be accorded the name above all names—*Kyrios* (Lord). From a Chinese Zen standpoint one might say that this hymn expresses a Christian *kung-an,* namely that the crucifixion is the resurrection.

In these two early church hymns Paul develops one of the highest Christologies in the New Testament—Christ Jesus is identical with Adonai. In this sense, Paul and John are often linked because of their common emphasis on the transcendent (Christology from above), whereas the synoptics share with Peter an emphasis on the humanness of Jesus (Christology from below).

John's Jesus

Son of Zebedee, brother to James, who alone reports the beloved disciple at the foot of the cross with Mary, John is the most deliberately theological Gospel. John's Gospel must be read therefore with a more concentrated attention to the mystical inter-connections between and among God, Christ and the believer. John (and his community) were asked by the church to write his Gospel because according to tradition he was the last eye-witness. In response he became the first to adapt and apply to Jesus a Greek philosophical term—Logos (reason). John is the only evangelist who presents Jesus as a divine figure who becomes man, and who talks about his pre-existence.

While the *Tao Te Ching* begins with a logical contradiction—"The Tao that can be tao-ed (named) is not the real Tao"—John begins with a theological one:

> In the beginning was the Word:
> the Word was with God's presence,
> and the Word was God.
> He was present to God in the beginning.[18]

Like Paul, John depicts a pre-existent Christ, the *Logos* (Word, Reason, Purpose). While in Greek culture Logos meant Word, or Purpose, or Reason, in Hebrew the association was with Wisdom (the pre-existent divine feminine). For John, Jesus was not just the Davidic Messiah, not just the pre-existent *Logos,* but also a cosmic figure who, like Lord Krishna in the Bhagavad Gita, identified himself with the phenomenal world. For example, there are seven so-called "I am" statements in John which provide us with seven Messianic self-reflections:

> I am the Bread of Life (6:35, 41, 48, 51);
> I am the Light of the World (8:12);
> I am the Door (10:7);
> I am the Good Shepherd (10:11, 13);
> I am the Resurrection (11:25);
> I am the Way, Truth and Life (14:6);
> I am the True Vine (15:1,5).

Each of these of course must be understood in its fuller context. Jesus is true vine and his disciples are branches by means, as Jesus says, of "the word that I have spoken to you" (Jn 15:3). For instance, what did Jesus mean when he identified himself with the "bread of life"? Minimally one should read all of John 6 before attempting to answer.

The chapter begins shortly before Passover by the Sea of Galilee with the miracle of the loaves and fishes. The next day when the crowds find Jesus he tells them to seek eternal food which the Son of Man offers. Associating himself with the manna which God gave the Jews in the desert, Jesus says further:

> Let me solemnly assure you,
> if you do not eat the flesh of the Son of Man
> and drink his blood,
> you have no life in you.
> He who feeds on my flesh
> and drinks my blood
> has life eternal,
> and I will raise him up on the last day.
> For my flesh is real food
> and my blood real drink.[19]

Jesus completes this connection with his disciples by initiating a transformation in the Passover meal. The early church saw in this eucharistic passage a vital immanence between and within Christ and the believers.

We have seen that whereas in Mark Jesus is the son of God (the servant), in Matthew the son of David (the teacher), and in Luke the son of Adam (Perfect Man), in John Jesus is the Logos, given to the world because God loved the world so much, that he sent his Son, that through him the world might be saved (Jn 3:16–17). And whereas Paul emphasized *pistis* (faith), John emphasizes *agape* (Divine, self-surrendering love), for God is *agape*. Each indicates that faith includes an inner, mystical union with the Christ. This union is transpersonal, transcultural and transhistoric, and at the same time depends upon an inner grasping and being grasped by Christ's presence. John portrays Jesus as *with, in* and *one with* the Father, just as the authentic follower is *with, in* and *one with* Christ.

> The Son does only what the Father does (5:20).
> I am from above; I am he (8:24).
> Before Abraham ever was, I am (8:58).
> The Father is in me and I am in the Father (10:38).
> I am in my Father and you are in me and I in you (14:20).
> Father, may they be one in us, as you are in me and I am in you (17:21).

Finally, as the author of John's Gospel indicates, after Jesus foretells his death and subsequent glorification, he compares himself to a grain of wheat which must die first before yielding the "rich harvest." Jesus tellingly says: "Unless the grain of wheat falling into the ground dies, it alone remains; but if it dies, much fruit it bears."[20] We end therefore where we began, with a dying-rising man-God, with an impossible possibility.

Canonization

If the Hebrew scriptures are viewed as a continuing revelation of God's prehistoric and historic activity, from the patriarchs through the prophets and seers, then it can be said that the New Testament continues the same story. Beginning with the Prophet John (the Baptizer), the life and teachings and resurrection of Jesus are told along with the birth and spread of the early Church. The Christian scriptures thus contain both the Hebrew canon (Old Testament) and the New Testament comprised of twenty-seven books—Gospels, Letters, Epistles, and Apocalypse. It was not finally canonized until the publication of Jerome's Latin Vulgate edition early in the fifth century.

While Paul's letters to the churches (written between 50–62) and the Gospels (written between 65–95) were in circulation among the early church members, most early Christians never saw or read them. There were also at that time dozens of Gospels and letters like that of 1 Clement and teachings like the *Didache,* all of which made canonical claims. However, the idea of establishing a second canon alongside the Torah did not occur in the apostolic age because Jesus had not come to replace but to fulfill Torah, and because the earliest Christians expected Jesus' imminent return. It was Paul's letters which first circulated among the major churches (Rome, Corinth, Antioch, Ephesus), copies of which increased as the number of new church communities increased. It became apparent, as more converts entered the church, how valuable written records about the life of Jesus were. The need for creating a canon became evident as the early church moved further away from the earliest apostles, and as leaders like Marcion proposed a canon which excluded the entire Hebrew Scriptures and included only Luke and ten of Paul's letters.

By 150, Irenaeus named and quoted from the New Testament books as we have them today except for a few short epistles. By the end of the second century the church had provided a prologue to four Gospels to legitimize them, and officially accepted as authentic: Acts, thirteen Pauline letters, three so-called Catholic Epistles (1 and 2 Timothy and Titus) which deal with Church structure, Revelation and the Apocalypse of Peter. After further discussions, in 367 Athanasius in his *Festal Letter 39* named the twenty-seven books which appear in Jerome's Latin Vulgate edition (405 CE). That version fixed what we today recognize as the New Testament. Selection of the books included in the canon was based on authenticity of apostolic authorship, true kerygmatic teaching, and universal usage.

From its initial formulation the New Testament incorporated entirely and quoted freely from the Hebrew scripture. In fact, it has been noted that the Christian canon is one of the only major scriptures of the world which includes the complete canon of another tradition. Other sacred texts, as we have noted, offer self-descriptive images within their texts (e.g., the cosmic bow in the Upanishads, a leaf on an upside-down cosmic tree in the Gita, the most precious flower in the Dhammapada, and the stone tablet in Judaism). In the "New Testament," sacred scripture is said to cut "like any double-edged sword" (Heb 4:12–13), and its purpose is to teach holiness, to refute errors and to guide people's lives (2 Timothy 3:14–17).

NOTES

1. From *the Wisdom of the Desert*, translated by Thomas Merton (New York: New Directions, 1960), 41.

2. The fourteen foot long cloth contains the full-bodied imprint of a crucified man said to be Jesus. The Shroud was last displayed publicly in 1978 (only the third time in this century) in the Cathedral of San Giovanni Baptista in Turin.

3. Luke 4:18, quoting Isaiah 61:1–2. Unless otherwise noted, all New Testament references come from *The New American Bible* (New York: Collier-Macmillan, 1970).

4. Every forty-ninth year (seven times seven) the Hebrews took a year off, and every second forty-ninth year they took two years off. Scholars estimate that this happened during Jesus' time on earth. The date of his birth is not known for certain, though he was born during the rule of King Herod the Great who died 4 BCE. During the sixth century a Roman abbot, Dionysius Exiquus, who began to date historic events from Jesus' birth, miscalculated that date by four years. The December 25 date was a later adaptation of the church to coincide with the Roman celebration of the birthday of the sun after the winter solstice.

5. Luke 1:46–53.

6. Luke 2:34–35. In Matthew's account, we are told of the astrologers who have noted a once-in-every-700-year configuration of stars and who have followed their celestial studies to Bethlehem and also of the flight of the Holy Family into Egypt to avoid Herod's slaughter of all newborn Hebrew sons.

7. Deuteronomy 8:3; Psalms 91:11–12; Deuteronomy 6:13.

8. Matthew 13:51–52.

9. C.H. Dodd, *The Founder of Christianity* (New York: Macmillan Co., 1970), 54.

10. Matthew 5:3–12.

11. Mark 14:22–25.

12. Acts 2:1–4.

13. This list is a slight modification of one developed by C.H. Dodd in *The Apostolic Preaching* (New York: Harper & Brothers, 1962). Luke pictures the early Christian *koinonia* (community) as those who are faithful to the apostolic teaching, faithful to the community, to the breaking of bread, and to prayers (Acts 2:42). In fact the early church existed in a double matrix—*koinonia* and *Didache*. The *koinonia* was shared ritualistic practices, beliefs and attitudes toward life, with special attention to Baptism and Eucharistic meals; and the *Didache* was an early catechetical handbook of practical instructions and basic guidelines in Christian faith and practice which included instruction in church organization, worship, creedal statements, and doctrines.

14. Acts 22:6–10.

15. Paul's letters modify the typical Greek-letter form of the day by beginning with an acknowledgment of his Christian allegiance and then by substituting "peace" and "grace" for customary greetings. Of course the letters were written with specific, practical purposes in mind, and not with a thought toward canonization. Thus it is incorrect to call them "Epistles" (a letter-form assigned to a general audience), for each letter was intended solely for the one addressed. Most scholars assign at least the following seven letters to Paul:

1 Thessalonians	51/52 CE
Galatians	53/54 CE
1 Corinthians	55 CE
2 Corinthians	56 CE
Romans	57/58 CE
Philippians	62 CE
Philemon	62 CE

16. Colossians 1:15–20. This and the following passage are quoted from *The Jerusalem Bible*, edited by Alexander Jones (New York: Doubleday & Co., 1966).

17. Philippians 2:6–11.

18. John 1:1–2.

19. John 6:53–55.

20. John 12:24. Quoted from *The Interlinear Greek-English New Testament* (Grand Rapids, Michigan: Zondervan Publishing House, 1958).

Selections

Selections from the Gospels, Acts and selected letters of Paul (1 Corinthians, Romans, Galatians, and Philippians), taken from the Revised Standard Version.

The Gospel According to Mark

THE BEGINNING OF THE GOSPEL of Jesus Christ, the Son of God. ²As it is written in Isaiah the prophet,

"Behold, I send my messenger before thy face,
who shall prepare thy way;
³the voice of one crying in the wilderness:
Prepare the way of the Lord,
make his paths straight—"

⁴John the baptizer appeared in the wilderness, preaching a baptism of repentance for the forgiveness of sins. ⁵And there went out to him all the country of Judea, and all the people of Jerusalem; and they were baptized by him in the river Jordan, confessing their sins. ⁶Now John was clothed with camel's hair, and had a leather girdle around his waist, and ate locusts and wild honey. ⁷And he preached, saying, "After me comes he who is mightier than I, the thong of whose sandals I am not worthy to stoop down and untie. ⁸I have baptized you with water; but he will baptize you with the Holy Spirit."

⁹In those days Jesus came from Nazareth of Galilee and was baptized by John in the Jordan. ¹⁰And when he came up out of the water, immediately he saw the heavens opened and the Spirit descending upon him like a dove; ¹¹and a voice came from heaven, "Thou art my beloved Son; with thee I am well pleased."

¹²The Spirit immediately drove him out into the wilderness. ¹³And he was in the wilderness forty days, tempted by Satan; and he was with the wild beasts; and the angels ministered to him.

¹⁴Now after John was arrested, Jesus came into Galilee, preaching the gospel of God, ¹⁵and saying, "The time is fulfilled, and the kingdom of God is at hand; repent, and believe in the gospel."

¹⁶And passing along by the Sea of Galilee, he saw Simon and Andrew the brother of Simon casting a net in the sea; for they were fishermen. ¹⁷And Jesus said to them, "Follow me and I will make you become fishers of men." ¹⁸And immediately they left their nets and followed him. ¹⁹And going on a little farther, he saw James the son of Zebedee and John his brother, who were in their boat mending the nets. ²⁰And immediately he called them; and they left their father Zebedee in the boat with the hired servants, and followed him.

²¹And they went into Caper′-na-um; and immediately on the sabbath he entered the synagogue and taught. ²²And they were astonished at his teaching, for he taught them as one who had authority, and not as the scribes. ²³And immediately there was in their synagogue a man with an unclean spirit; ²⁴and he cried out, "What have you to do with us, Jesus of Nazareth? Have you come to destroy us? I know who you are, the Holy One of God." ²⁵But Jesus rebuked him, saying, "Be silent, and come out of him!" ²⁶And the unclean spirit, convulsing him and crying with a loud voice, came out of him. ²⁷And they were all amazed, so that they questioned among themselves, saying, "What is this? A new teaching! With authority he commands even the unclean spirits, and they obey him." ²⁸And at once his fame spread everywhere throughout all the surrounding region of Galilee.

²⁹And immediately he left the synagogue, and entered the house of Simon and Andrew, with James and John. ³⁰Now Simon's mother-in-law lay sick with a fever, and immediately they told him of her. ³¹And he came and took her by the hand and lifted her up, and the fever left her; and she served them.

³²That evening, at sundown, they brought to him all who were sick or possessed with demons. ³³And the whole city was gathered together about the door. ³⁴And he healed many who were sick with various diseases, and cast out many demons; and he would not permit the demons to speak, because they knew him.

³⁵And in the morning, a great while before

day, he rose and went out to a lonely place, and there he prayed. [36]And Simon and those who were with him pursued him, [37]and they found him and said to him, "Every one is searching for you." [38]And he said to them, "Let us go on to the next towns, that I may preach there also; for that is why I came out." [39]And he went throughout all Galilee, preaching in their synagogues and casting out demons.

* * *

14It was now two days before the Passover and the feast of Unleavened Bread. And the chief priests and the scribes were seeking how to arrest him by stealth, and kill him; [2]for they said, "Not during the feast, lest there be a tumult of the people."

[3]And while he was at Bethany in the house of Simon the leper, as he sat at table, a woman came with an alabaster flask of ointment of pure nard, very costly, and she broke the flask and poured it over his head. [4]But there were some who said to themselves indignantly, "Why was the ointment thus wasted? [5]For this ointment might have been sold for more than three hundred denarii, and given to the poor." And they reproached her. [6]But Jesus said, "Let her alone; why do you trouble her? She has done a beautiful thing to me. [7]For you always have the poor with you, and whenever you will, you can do good to them; but you will not always have me. [8]She has done what she could; she has anointed my body beforehand for burying. [9]And truly, I say to you, wherever the gospel is preached in the whole world, what she has done will be told in memory of her."

[10]Then Judas Iscariot, who was one of the twelve, went to the chief priests in order to betray him to them. [11]And when they heard it they were glad, and promised to give him money. And he sought an opportunity to betray him.

[12]And on the first day of Unleavened Bread, when they sacrificed the passover lamb, his disciples said to him, "Where will you have us go and prepare for you to eat the passover?" [13]And he sent two of his disciples, and said to them, "Go into the city, and a man carrying a jar of water will meet you; follow him, [14]and wherever he enters, say to the householder, 'The Teacher says, Where is my guest room, where am I to eat the passover with my disciples?' [15]And he will show you a large upper room furnished and ready; there prepare for us." [16]And the disciples set out and went to the city, and found it as he had told them; and they prepared the passover.

[17]And when it was evening he came with the twelve. [18]And as they were at table eating, Jesus said, "Truly, I say to you, one of you will betray me, one who is eating with me." [19]They began to be sorrowful, and to say to him one after another, "Is it I?" [20]He said to them, "It is one of the twelve, one who is dipping bread into the dish with me. [21]For the Son of man goes as it is written of him, but woe to that man by whom the Son of man is betrayed! It would have been better for that man if he had not been born."

[22]And as they were eating, he took bread, and blessed, and broke it, and gave it to them, and said, "Take; this is my body." [23]And he took a cup, and when he had given thanks he gave it to them, and they all drank of it. [24]And he said to them, "This is my blood of the covenant, which is poured out for many. [25]Truly, I say to you, I shall not drink again of the fruit of the vine until that day when I drink it new in the kingdom of God."

* * *

15[16]And the soldiers led him away inside the palace (that is, the praetorium); and they called together the whole battalion. [17]And they clothed him in a purple cloak, and plaiting a crown of thorns they put it on him. [18]And they began to salute him, "Hail, King of the Jews!" [19]And they struck his head with a reed, and spat upon him, and they knelt down in homage to him. [20]And when they had mocked him, they stripped him of the purple cloak, and put his own clothes on him. And they led him out to crucify him.

[21]And they compelled a passer-by, Simon of

Cyre'ne, who was coming in from the country, the father of Alexander and Rufus, to carry his cross. ²²And they brought him to the place called Gol'gotha (which means the place of a skull). ²³And they offered him wine mingled with myrrh; but he did not take it. ²⁴And they crucified him, and divided his garments among them, casting lots for them, to decide what each should take. ²⁵And it was the third hour, when they crucified him. ²⁶And the inscription of the charge against him read, "The King of the Jews." ²⁷And with him they crucified two robbers, one on his right and one on his left. ²⁹And those who passed by derided him, wagging their heads, and saying, "Aha! You who would destroy the temple and built it in three days, ³⁰save yourself, and come down from the cross!" ³¹So also the chief priests mocked him to one another with the scribes, saying, "He saved others; he cannot save himself. ³²Let the Christ, the King of Israel, come down now from the cross, that we may see and believe." Those who were crucified with him also reviled him.

³³And when the sixth hour had come, there was darkness over the whole land until the ninth hour. ³⁴And at the ninth hour Jesus cried with a loud voice, "E'lo-i, E'lo-i, la'ma sabach-tha'ni?" which means, "My God, my God, why hast thou forsaken me?" ³⁵And some of the bystanders hearing it said, "Behold, he is calling 'Eli'jah." ³⁶And one ran and, filling a sponge full of vinegar, put it on a reed and gave it to him to drink, saying, "Wait, let us see whether Eli'jah will come to take him down." ³⁷And Jesus uttered a loud cry, and breathed his last. ³⁸And the curtain of the temple was torn in two, from top to bottom. ³⁹And when the centurion, who stood facing him, saw that he thus breathed his last, he said, "Truly this man was the Son of God!"

⁴⁰There were also women looking on from afar, among whom were Mary Mag'dalene, and Mary the mother of James the younger and of Joses, and Salo'me, ⁴¹who, when he was in Galilee, followed him, and ministered to him; and also many other women who came up with him to Jerusalem.

⁴²And when evening had come, since it was the day of Preparation, that is, the day before the sabbath, ⁴³Joseph of Arimathe'a, a respected member of the council, who was also himself looking for the kingdom of God, took courage and went to Pilate, and asked for the body of Jesus. ⁴⁴And Pilate wondered if he were already dead; and summoning the centurion, he asked him whether he was already dead. ⁴⁵And when he learned from the centurion that he was dead, he granted the body to Joseph. ⁴⁶And he bought a linen shroud, and taking him down, wrapped him in the linen shroud, and laid him in a tomb which had been hewn out of the rock; and he rolled a stone against the door of the tomb. ⁴⁷Mary Mag'dalene and Mary the mother of Jesus saw where he was laid.

* * *

16And when the sabbath was past, Mary Mag'dalene, and Mary the mother of James, and Salo'me, bought spices, so that they might go and anoint him. ²And very early on the first day of the week they went to the tomb when the sun had risen. ³And they were saying to one another, "Who will roll away the stone for us from the door of the tomb?" ⁴And looking up, they saw that the stone was rolled back—it was very large. ⁵And entering the tomb, they saw a young man sitting on the right side, dressed in a white robe; and they were amazed. ⁶And he said to them, "Do not be amazed; you seek Jesus of Nazareth, who was crucified. He has risen, he is not here; see the place where they laid him. ⁷But go, tell his disciples and Peter that he is going before you to Galilee; there you will see him, as he told you." ⁸And they went out and fled from the tomb; for trembling and astonishment had come upon them; and they said nothing to any one, for they were afraid.

Matthew

3¹³Then Jesus came from Galilee to the Jordan to John, to be baptized by him. ¹⁴John would have prevented him, saying, "I need to be baptized by you, and do you come to me?" ¹⁵But Jesus answered him, "Let it be so now; for thus it is fitting for us to fulfil all righteousness." Then he consented. ¹⁶And when Jesus was baptized, he went up immediately from the water, and behold, the heavens were opened and he saw the Spirit of God descending like a dove, and alighting on him; ¹⁷and lo, a voice from heaven, saying, "This is my beloved Son, with whom I am well pleased."

4 Then Jesus was led up by the Spirit into the wilderness to be tempted by the devil. ²And he fasted forty days and forty nights, and afterward he was hungry. ³And the tempter came and said to him. "If you are the Son of God, command these stones to become loaves of bread." ⁴But he answered, "It is written,

'Man shall not live by bread alone,
but by every word that proceeds from the mouth of God.' "

⁵Then the devil took him to the holy city, and set him on the pinnacle of the temple, ⁶and said to him, "If you are the Son of God, throw yourself down; for it is written,
'He will give his angels charge of you,'
and
'On their hands they will bear you up,
lest you strike your foot against a stone.' "
⁷Jesus said to him, "Again it is written, 'You shall not tempt the Lord your God.' " ⁸Again, the devil took him to a very high mountain, and showed him all the kingdoms of the world and the glory of them; ⁹and he said to him, "All these I will give you, if you will fall down and worship me."
¹⁰Then Jesus said to him, "Begone, Satan! for it is written,
'You shall worship the Lord your God
and him only shall you serve.' "
¹¹Then the devil left him, and behold, angels came and ministered to him.

¹²Now when he heard that John had been arrested, he withdrew into Galilee; ¹³and leaving Nazareth he went and dwelt in Caper′na-um by the sea, in the territory of Zeb′ulun and Naph′tali, ¹⁴that what was spoken by the prophet Isaiah might be fulfilled:

¹⁵"The land of Zeb′ulun and the land of Naph′tali,
toward the sea, across the Jordan,
Galilee of the Gentiles—
¹⁶the people who sat in darkness have seen a great light,
and for those who sat in the region
and shadow of death
light has dawned."
¹⁷From that time Jesus began to preach, saying, "Repent, for the kingdom of heaven is at hand."

¹⁸As he walked by the Sea of Galilee, he saw two brothers, Simon who is called Peter and Andrew his brother, casting a net into the sea; for they were fishermen. ¹⁹And he said to them, "Follow me, and I will make you fishers of men." ²⁰Immediately they left their nets and followed him. ²¹And going on from there he saw two other brothers, James the son of Zeb′edee and John his brother, in the boat with Zeb′edee their father, mending their nets, and he called them. ²²Immediately they left the boat and their father, and followed him.

²³And he went about all Galilee, teaching in their synagogues and preaching the gospel of the kingdom and healing every disease and every infirmity among the people. ²⁴So his fame spread throughout all Syria, and they brought him all the sick, those afflicted with various diseases and pains, demoniacs, epileptics, and paralytics, and he healed them. ²⁵And great crowds followed him from Galilee and the Decap′olis and Jerusalem and Judea and from beyond the Jordan.

* * *

5 Seeing the crowds, he went up on the mountain, and when he sat down his disciples came to him. ²And he opened his mouth and taught them, saying:
³"Blessed are the poor in spirit, for theirs is the kingdom of heaven.

[4]"Blessed are those who mourn, for they shall be comforted.

[5]"Blessed are the meek, for they shall inherit the earth.

[6]"Blessed are those who hunger and thirst for righteousness, for they shall be satisfied.

[7]"Blessed are the merciful, for they shall obtain mercy.

[8]"Blessed are the pure in heart, for they shall see God.

[9]"Blessed are the peacemakers, for they shall be called sons of God.

[10]"Blessed are those who are persecuted for righteousness' sake, for theirs is the kingdom of heaven.

[11]"Blessed are you when men revile you and persecute you and utter all kinds of evil against you falsely on my account. [12]Rejoice and be glad, for your reward is great in heaven, for so men persecuted the prophets who were before you.

[13]"You are the salt of the earth; but if salt has lost its taste, how shall its saltness be restored? It is no longer good for anything except to be thrown out and trodden under foot by men.

[14]"You are the light of the world. A city set on a hill cannot be hid. [15]Nor do men light a lamp and put it under a bushel, but on a stand, and it gives light to all in the house. [16]Let your light so shine before men, that they may see your good works and give glory to your Father who is in heaven.

[17]"Think not that I have come to abolish the law and the prophets; I have come not to abolish them but to fulfil them. [18]For truly, I say to you, till heaven and earth pass away, not an iota, not a dot, will pass from the law until all is accomplished. [19]Whoever then relaxes one of the least of these commandments and teaches men so, shall be called least in the kingdom of heaven; but he who does them and teaches them shall be called great in the kingdom of heaven. [20]For I tell you, unless your righteousness exceeds that of the scribes and Pharisees, you will never enter the kingdom of heaven.

[43]"You have heard that it was said, 'You shall love your neighbor and hate your enemy.'

[44]But I say to you, Love your enemies and pray for those who persecute you, [45]so that you may be sons of your Father who is in heaven; for he makes his sun rise on the evil and on the good, and sends rain on the just and on the unjust. [46]For if you love those who love you, what reward have you? Do not even the tax collectors do the same? [47]And if you salute only your brethren, what more are you doing than others? Do not even the Gentiles do the same? [48]You, therefore, must be perfect, as your heavenly Father is perfect.

*　　*　　*

6"Beware of practicing your piety before men in order to be seen by them; for then you will have no reward from your Father who is in heaven.

[9]Pray then like this:
Our Father who art in heaven,
Hallowed be thy name.
[10]Thy kingdom come.
Thy will be done,
On earth as it is in heaven.
[11]Give us this day our daily bread,
[12]And forgive us our debts,
As we also have forgiven our debtors;
[13]And lead us not into temptation,
But deliver us from evil.

[14]For if you forgive men their trespasses, your heavenly Father also will forgive you; [15]but if you do not forgive men their trespasses, neither will your Father forgive your trespasses.

*　　*　　*

16[13]Now when Jesus came into the district of Caesare'a Philip'pi, he asked his disciples, "Who do men say that the Son of man is?" [14]And they said, "Some say John the Baptist, others say Eli'jah, and others Jeremiah or one of the prophets." [15]He said to them, "But who do you say that I am?" [16]Simon Peter replied, "You are the Christ, the Son of the living God." [17]And Jesus answered him, "Blessed are you, Simon Bar-

Jona! For flesh and blood has not revealed this to you, but my Father who is in heaven. [18]And I tell you, you are Peter, and on this rock I will build my church, and the powers of death shall not prevail against it. [19]I will give you the keys of the kingdom of heaven, and whatever you bind on earth shall be bound in heaven, and whatever you loose on earth shall be loosed in heaven." [20]Then he strictly charged the disciples to tell no one that he was the Christ.

[21]From that time Jesus began to show his disciples that he must go to Jerusalem and suffer many things from the elders and chief priests and scribes, and be killed, and on the third day be raised. [22]And Peter took him and began to rebuke him, saying, "God forbid, Lord! This shall never happen to you." [23]But he turned and said to Peter, "Get behind me, Satan! You are a hindrance to me; for you are not on the side of God, but of men."

[24]Then Jesus told his disciples, "If any man would come after me, let him deny himself and take up his cross and follow me. [25]For whoever would save his life will lose it, and whoever loses his life for my sake will find it. [26]For what will it profit a man, if he gains the whole world and forfeits his life? Or what shall a man give in return for his life? [27]For the Son of man is to come with his angels in the glory of his Father, and then he will repay every man for what he has done. [28]Truly, I say to you, there are some standing here who will not taste death before they see the Son of man coming in his kingdom."

*   *   *

17 And after six days Jesus took with him Peter and James and John his brother, and led them up a high mountain apart. [2]And he was transfigured before them, and his face shone like the sun, and his garments became white as light. [3]And behold, there appeared to them Moses and Eli'jah, talking with him. [4]And Peter said to Jesus, "Lord, it is well that we are here; if you wish, I will make three booths here, one for you and one for Moses and one for Eli'jah." [5]He was still speaking, when lo, a bright cloud overshadowed them, and a voice from the cloud said, "This is my beloved Son, with whom I am well pleased; listen to him." [6]When the disciples heard this, they fell on their faces, and were filled with awe. [7]But Jesus came and touched them, saying, "Rise, and have no fear." [8]And when they lifted up their eyes, they saw no one but Jesus only.

[9]And as they were coming down the mountain, Jesus commanded them, "Tell no one the vision, until the Son of Man is raised from the dead."

*   *   *

18 [10]And the disciples asked him, "Then why do the scribes say that first Eli'jah must come?" [11]He replied, " Eli'jah does come, and he is to restore all things; [12]but I tell you that Eli'jah has already come, and they did not know him, but did to him whatever they pleased. So also the Son of man will suffer at their hands." [13]Then the disciples understood that he was speaking to them of John the Baptist.

Luke

1 [26]In the sixth month the angel Gabriel was sent from God to a city of Galilee named Nazareth, [27]to a virgin betrothed to a man whose name was Joseph, of the house of David; and the virgin's name was Mary. [28]And he came to her and said, "Hail, O favored one, the Lord is with you!" [29]But she was greatly troubled at the saying, and considered in her mind what sort of greeting this might be. [30]And the angel said to her, "Do not be afraid, Mary, for you have found favor with God. [31]And behold, you will conceive in your womb and bear a son, and you shall call his name Jesus.

[32]He will be great, and will be called the Son of the Most High;

and the Lord God will give to him the throne of his father David,

[33]and he will reign over the house of Jacob for ever;

and of his kingdom there will be no end."

³⁴And Mary said to the angel, "How shall this be, since I have no husband?" ³⁵And the angel said to her,

"The Holy Spirit will come upon you,
and the power of the Most High will overshadow you;
therefore the child to be born will be called holy, the Son of God.

³⁶And behold, your kinswoman Elizabeth in her old age has also conceived a son; and this is the sixth month with her who was called barren. ³⁷For with God nothing will be impossible." ³⁸And Mary said, "Behold, I am the handmaid of the Lord; let it be to me according to your word." And the angel departed from her.

³⁹In those days Mary arose and went with haste into the hill country, to a city of Judah, ⁴⁰and she entered the house of Zechari'ah and greeted Elizabeth. ⁴¹And when Elizabeth heard the greeting of Mary, the babe leaped in her womb; and Elizabeth was filled with the Holy Spirit ⁴²and she exclaimed with a loud cry, "Blessed are you among women, and blessed is the fruit of your womb! ⁴³And why is this granted me, that the mother of my Lord should come to me? ⁴⁴For behold, when the voice of your greeting came to my ears, the babe in my womb leaped for joy. ⁴⁵And blessed is she who believed that there would be a fulfilment of what was spoken to her from the Lord." ⁴⁶And Mary said,

"My soul magnifies the Lord,
⁴⁷and my spirit rejoices in God my Savior,
⁴⁸for he has regarded the low estate of his handmaiden.
For behold, henceforth all generations will call
  me blessed;
⁴⁹for he who is mighty has done great things for
  me,
and holy is his name.
⁵⁰And his mercy is on those who fear him
from generation to generation.
⁵¹He has shown strength with his arm, he has
  scattered the proud in the imagination of their
  hearts,
⁵²he has put down the mighty from their thrones,

and exalted those of low degree;
⁵³he has filled the hungry with good things,
and the rich he has sent empty away,
⁵⁴He has helped his servant Israel,
in remembrance of his mercy,
⁵⁵as he spoke to our fathers,
to Abraham and to his posterity for ever."

*   *   *

2In those days a decree went out from Caesar Augustus that all the world should be enrolled. ²This was the first enrollment, when Quirin'i-us was governor of Syria. ³And all went to be enrolled, each to his own city. And Joseph also went up from Galilee, from the city of Nazareth, to Judea, to the city of David, which is called Bethlehem, because he was of the house and lineage of David, ⁵to be enrolled with Mary, his betrothed, who was with child. ⁶And while they were there, the time came for her to be delivered. ⁷And she gave birth to her first-born son and wrapped him in swaddling cloths, and laid him in a manger, because there was no place for them in the inn.

⁸And in that region there were shepherds out in the field, keeping watch over their flock by night. ⁹And an angel of the Lord appeared to them, and the glory of the Lord shone around them, and they were filled with fear. ¹⁰And the angel said to them, "Be not afraid; for behold, I bring you good news of a great joy which will come to all the people; ¹¹for to you is born this day in the city of David a Savior, who is Christ the Lord. ¹²And this will be a sign for you: you will find a babe wrapped in swaddling cloths and lying in a manger." ¹³And suddenly there was with the angel a multitude of the heavenly host praising God and saying,

¹⁴"Glory to God in the highest, and on earth peace among men with whom he is pleased!"

¹⁵When the angels went away from them into heaven, the shepherds said to one another, "Let us go over to Bethlehem and see this thing that has happened, which the Lord has made known to us." ¹⁶And they went with haste, and found Mary and Joseph, and the babe lying in a

manger. ¹⁷And when they saw it they made known the saying which had been told them concerning this child; ¹⁸and all who heard it wondered at what the shepherds told them. ¹⁹But Mary kept all these things, pondering them in her heart. ²⁰And the shepherds returned, glorifying and praising God for all they had heard and seen, as it had been told them.

²¹And at the end of eight days, when he was circumcised, he was called Jesus, the name given by the angel before he was conceived in the womb.

²²And when the time came for their purification according to the law of Moses, they brought him up to Jerusalem to present him to the Lord ²³(as it is written in the law of the Lord, "Every male that opens the womb shall be called holy to the Lord") ²⁴and to offer a sacrifice according to what is said in the law of the Lord, "a pair of turtledoves, or two young pigeons." ²⁵Now there was a man in Jerusalem, whose name was Simeon, and this man was righteous and devout, looking for the consolation of Israel, and the Holy Spirit was upon him. ²⁶And it had been revealed to him by the Holy Spirit that he should not see death before he had seen the Lord's Christ. ²⁷And inspired by the Spirit he came into the temple; and when the parents brought in the child Jesus, to do for him according to the custom of the law, ²⁸he took him up in his arms and blessed God and said,

²⁹"Lord, now lettest thou thy servant depart in peace,
according to thy word;
³⁰for mine eyes have seen thy salvation
³¹which thou hast prepared in the presence of all peoples,
³²a light for revelation to the Gentiles, and for glory to thy people Israel."

³³And his father and his mother marveled at what was said about him; ³⁴and Simeon blessed them and said to Mary his mother,

"Behold, this child is set for the fall and rising of many in Israel,
and for a sign that is spoken against

³⁵(and a sword will pierce through your own soul also),
that thoughts out of many hearts may be revealed."

* * *

10²¹In that same hour he rejoiced in the Holy Spirit and said, "I thank thee, Father, Lord of heaven and earth, that thou hast hidden these things from the wise and understanding and revealed them to babes; yea, Father, for such was thy gracious will. ²²All things have been delivered to me by my Father; and no one knows who the Son is except the Father, or who the Father is except the Son and any one to whom the Son chooses to reveal him."

²³Then turning to the disciples he said privately, "Blessed are the eyes which see what you see! ²⁴For I tell you that many prophets and kings desired to see what you see, and did not see it, and to hear what you hear, and did not hear it."

²⁵And behold, a lawyer stood up to put him to the test, saying, "Teacher, what shall I do to inherit eternal life?" ²⁶He said to him, "What is written in the law? How do you read?" ²⁷And he answered, "You shall love the Lord your God with all your heart, and with all your soul, and with all your strength, and with all your mind; and your neighbor as yourself." ²⁸And he said to him, "You have answered right; do this, and you will live."

²⁹But he, desiring to justify himself, said to Jesus, "And who is my neighbor?" ³⁰Jesus replied, "A man was going down from Jerusalem to Jericho, and he fell among robbers, who stripped him and beat him, and departed, leaving him half dead. ³¹Now by chance a priest was going down that road; and when he saw him he passed by on the other side. ³²So likewise a Levite, when he came to the place and saw him, passed by on the other side. ³³But a Samaritan, as he journeyed, came to where he was; and when he saw him, he had compassion, ³⁴and went to him and bound up his wounds, pouring

on oil and wine; then he set him on his own beast and brought him to an inn, and took care of him. [35]And the next day he took out two denarii and gave them to the innkeeper, saying, 'Take care of him; and whatever more you spend, I will repay you when I come back.' [36]Which of these three, do you think, proved neighbor to the man who fell among the robbers?" [37]He said, "The one who showed mercy on him." And Jesus said to him, "Go and do likewise."

*   *   *

15 Now the tax collectors and sinners were all drawing near to hear him. [2]And the Pharisees and the scribes murmured, saying, "This man receives sinners and eats with them."

[3]So he told them this parable: [4]"What man of you, having a hundred sheep, if he has lost one of them, does not leave the ninety-nine in the wilderness, and go after the one which is lost, until he finds it? [5]And when he has found it, he lays it on his shoulders, rejoicing. [6]And when he comes home, he calls together his friends and his neighbors, saying to them, 'Rejoice with me, for I have found my sheep which was lost.' [7]Just so, I tell you, there will be more joy in heaven over one sinner who repents than over ninety-nine righteous persons who need no repentance.

[8]"Or what woman, having ten silver coins, if she loses one coin, does not light a lamp and sweep the house and seek diligently until she finds it? [9]And when she has found it, she calls together her friends and neighbors, saying, 'Rejoice with me, for I have found the coin which I had lost.' [10]Just so, I tell you, there is joy before the angels of God over one sinner who repents."

[11]And he said, "There was a man who had two sons; [12]and the younger of them said to his father, 'Father, give me the share of property that falls to me.' And he divided his living between them. [13]Not many days later, the younger son gathered all he had and took his journey into a far country, and there he squandered his property in loose living. [14]And when he had spent everything, a great famine arose in that country, and he began to be in want. [15]So he went and joined himself to one of the citizens of that country, who sent him into his fields to feed swine. [16]And he would gladly have fed on the pods that the swine ate; and no one gave him anything. [17]But when he came to himself he said, 'How many of my father's hired servants have bread enough and to spare, but I perish here with hunger! [18]I will arise and go to my father, and I will say to him, "Father, I have sinned against heaven and before you; [19]I am no longer worthy to be called your son; treat me as one of your hired servants." ' [20]And he arose and came to his father. But while he was yet at a distance, his father saw him and had compassion, and ran and embraced him and kissed him. [21]And the son said to him, 'Father, I have sinned against heaven and before you; I am no longer worthy to be called your son.' [22]But the father said to his servants, 'Bring quickly the best robe, and put it on him; and put a ring on his hand, and shoes on his feet; [23]and bring the fatted calf and kill it, and let us eat and make merry; [24]for this my son was dead, and is alive again; he was lost, and is found.' And they began to make merry.

[25]"Now his elder son was in the field; and as he came and drew near to the house, he heard music and dancing. [26]And he called one of the servants and asked what this meant. [27]And he said to him, 'Your brother has come, and your father has killed the fatted calf, because he has received him safe and sound.' [28]But he was angry and refused to go in. His father came out and entreated him, [29]but he answered his father, 'Lo, these many years I have served you, and I never disobeyed your command; yet you never gave me a kid, that I might make merry with my friends. [30]But when this son of yours came, who has devoured your living with harlots, you killed for him the fatted calf!' [31]And he said to him, 'Son, you are always with me, and all that is mine is yours. [32]It was fitting to make merry and be glad, for this your brother was dead, and is alive; he was lost, and is found.' "

John

In the beginning was the Word, and the Word was with God, and the Word was God. ²He was in the beginning with God; ³all things were made through him, and without him was not anything made that was made. ⁴In him was life, and the life was the light of men. ⁵The light shines in the darkness, and the darkness has not overcome it.

⁶There was a man sent from God, whose name was John. ⁷He came for testimony, to bear witness to the light, that all might believe through him. ⁸He was not the light, but came to bear witness to the light.

⁹The true light that enlightens every man was coming into the world.¹⁰ He was in the world, and the world was made through him, yet the world knew him not. ¹¹He came to his own home, and his own people received him not. ¹²But to all who received him, who believed in his name, he gave power to become children of God; ¹³who were born, not of blood nor of the will of the flesh nor of the will of man, but of God.

¹⁴And the Word became flesh and dwelt among us, full of grace and truth; we have beheld his glory, glory as of the only Son from the Father. ¹⁵(John bore witness to him, and cried, "This was he of whom I said, 'He who comes after me ranks before me, for he was before me.' ") ¹⁶And from his fulness have we all received, grace upon grace. ¹⁷For the law was given through Moses; grace and truth came through Jesus Christ. ¹⁸No one has ever seen God; the only Son, who is in the bosom of the Father, he has made him known.

* * *

6³⁵Jesus said to them, "I am the bread of life; he who comes to me shall not hunger, and he who believes in me shall never thirst. ³⁶But I said to you that you have seen me and yet do not believe. ³⁷All that the Father gives me will come to me; and him who comes to me I will not cast out.

³⁸For I have come down from heaven, not to do my own will, but the will of him who sent me; ³⁹and this is the will of him who sent me, that I should lose nothing of all that he has given me, but raise it up at the last day. ⁴⁰For this is the will of my Father, that every one who sees the Son and believes in him should have eternal life; and I will raise him up at the last day."

⁴¹The Jews then murmured at him, because he said, "I am the bread which came down from heaven." ⁴²They said, "Is not this Jesus, the son of Joseph, whose father and mother we know? How does he now say, 'I have come down from heaven'?" ⁴³Jesus answered them, "Do not murmur among yourselves. ⁴⁴No one can come to me unless the Father who sent me draws him; and I will raise him up at the last day. ⁴⁵It is written in the prophets, 'And they shall all be taught by God.' Every one who has heard and learned from the Father comes to me. ⁴⁶Not that any one has seen the Father except him who is from God; he has seen the Father. ⁴⁷Truly, truly, I say to you, he who believes has eternal life. ⁴⁸I am the bread of life. ⁴⁹Your fathers ate the manna in the wilderness, and they died. ⁵⁰This is the bread which comes down from heaven, that a man may eat of it and not die. ⁵¹I am the living bread which came down from heaven; if any one eats of this bread, he will live for ever; and the bread which I shall give for the life of the world is my flesh."

⁵²The Jews then disputed among themselves, saying, "How can this man give us his flesh to eat?" ⁵³So Jesus said to them, "Truly, truly, I say to you, unless you eat the flesh of the Son of man and drink his blood, you have no life in you; ⁵⁴he who eats my flesh and drinks my blood has eternal life, and I will raise him up at the last day. ⁵⁵For my flesh is food indeed, and my blood is drink indeed. ⁵⁶He who eats my flesh and drinks my blood abides in me, and I in him. ⁵⁷As the living Father sent me, and I live because of the Father, so he who eats me will live because of me. ⁵⁸This is the bread which came down from heaven, not such as the fathers ate and died; he who eats this bread will live for ever." ⁵⁹This he

said in the synagogue, as he taught at Caper'naum.

[60] Many of his disciples, when they heard it, said, "This is a hard saying; who can listen to it?" [61] But Jesus, knowing in himself that his disciples murmured at it, said to them, "Do you take offense at this? [62] Then what if you were to see the Son of man ascending where he was before? [63] It is the spirit that gives life, the flesh is of no avail; the words that I have spoken to you are spirit and life. [64] But there are some of you that do not believe." For Jesus knew from the first who those were that did not believe, and who it was that would betray him. [65] And he said, "This is why I told you that no one can come to me unless it is granted him by the Father."

[66] After this many of his disciples drew back and no longer went about with him. [67] Jesus said to the twelve, "Do you also wish to go away?" [68] Simon Peter answered him, "Lord, to whom shall we go? You have the words of eternal life; [69] and we have believed, and have come to know, that you are the Holy One of God." [70] Jesus answered them, "Did I not choose you, the twelve, and one of you is a devil?" [71] He spoke of Judas the son of Simon Iscariot, for he, one of the twelve, was to betray him.

*   *   *

8 They went each to his own house, [1] but Jesus went to the Mount of Olives. [2] Early in the morning he came again to the temple; all the people came to him, and he sat down and taught them. [3] The scribes and the Pharisees brought a woman who had been caught in adultery, and placing her in the midst [4] they said to him, "Teacher, this woman has been caught in the act of adultery. [5] Now in the law Moses commanded us to stone such. What do you say about her?" [6] This they said to test him, that they might have some charge to bring against him. Jesus bent down and wrote with his finger on the ground. [7] And as they continued to ask him, he stood up and said to them, "Let him who is without sin among you be the first to throw a stone at her." [8] And once

more he bent down and wrote with his finger on the ground. [9] But when they heard it, they went away, one by one, beginning with the eldest, and Jesus was left alone with the woman standing before him. [10] Jesus looked up and said to her, "Woman, where are they? Has no one condemned you?" [11] She said, "No one, Lord." And Jesus said, "Neither do I condemn you; go, and do not sin again."

*   *   *

16 "I have said all this to you to keep you from falling away. [2] They will put you out of the synagogues; indeed, the hour is coming when whoever kills you will think he is offering service to God. [3] And they will do this because they have not known the Father, nor me. [4] But I have said these things to you, that when their hour comes you may remember that I told you of them.

"I did not say these things to you from the beginning, because I was with you. [5] But now I am going to him who sent me; yet none of you asks me, 'Where are you going?' [6] But because I have said these things to you, sorrow has filled your hearts. [7] Nevertheless I tell you the truth: it is to your advantage that I go away, for if I do not go away, the Counselor will not come to you; but if I go, I will send him to you. [8] And when he comes, he will convince the world concerning sin and righteousness and judgment: [9] concerning sin, because they do not believe in me; [10] concerning righteousness, because I go to the Father, and you will see me no more; [11] concerning judgment, because the ruler of this world is judged.

[12] "I have yet many things to say to you, but you cannot bear them now. [13] When the Spirit of truth comes, he will guide you into all the truth; for he will not speak on his own authority, but whatever he hears he will speak, and he will declare to you the things that are to come. [14] He will glorify me, for he will take what is mine and declare it to you. [15] All that the Father has is mine; therefore I said that he will take what is mine and declare it to you.

* * *

17 When Jesus had spoken these words, he lifted up his eyes to heaven and said, "Father, the hour has come; glorify thy Son that the Son may glorify thee, ²since thou hast given him power over all flesh, to give eternal life to all whom thou hast given him. ³And this is eternal life, that they know thee the only true God, and Jesus Christ whom thou hast sent. ⁴I glorified thee on earth, having accomplished the work which thou gavest me to do; ⁵and now, Father, glorify thou me in thy own presence with the glory which I had with thee before the world was made.

²⁰"I do not pray for these only, but also for those who believe in me through their word, ²¹that they may all be one; even as thou, Father, art in me, and I in thee, that they also may be in us, so that the world may believe that thou hast sent me. ²²The glory which thou hast given me I have given to them, that they may be one even as we are one, ²³I in them and thou in me, that they may become perfectly one, so that the world may know that thou hast sent me and hast loved them even as thou hast loved me. ²⁴Father, I desire that they also, whom thou hast given me, may be with me where I am, to behold my glory which thou hast given me in thy love for me before the foundation of the world. ²⁵O righteous Father, the world has not known thee, but I have known thee; and these know that thou hast sent me. ²⁶I made known to them thy name, and I will make it known, that the love with which thou hast loved me may be in them, and I in them."

* * *

20 Now on the first day of the week Mary Mag'dalene came to the tomb early, while it was still dark, and saw that the stone had been taken away from the tomb. ²So she ran, and went to Simon Peter and the other disciple, the one whom Jesus loved, and said to them, "They have taken the Lord out of the tomb, and we do not know where they have laid him." ³Peter then came out with the other disciple, and they went toward the tomb. ⁴They both ran, but the other disciple outran Peter and reached the tomb first; ⁵and stooping to look in, he saw the linen cloths lying there, but he did not go in. ⁶Then Simon Peter came, following Him, and went into the tomb; he saw the linen cloths lying, ⁷and the napkin, which had been on his head, not lying with the linen cloths but rolled up in a place by itself. ⁸Then the other disciple, who reached the tomb first, also went in, and he saw and believed; ⁹for as yet they did not know the scripture, that he must rise from the dead. ¹⁰Then the disciples went back to their homes.

¹¹But Mary stood weeping outside the tomb, and as she wept she stooped to look into the tomb; ¹²and she saw two angels in white, sitting where the body of Jesus had lain, one at the head and one at the feet. ¹³They said to her, "Woman, why are you weeping?" She said to them, "Because they have taken away my Lord, and I do not know where they have laid him." ¹⁴Saying this, she turned round and saw Jesus standing, but she did not know that it was Jesus. ¹⁵Jesus said to her, "Woman, why are you weeping? Whom do you seek?" Supposing him to be the gardener, she said to him, "Sir, if you have carried him away, tell me where you have laid him, and I will take him away." ¹⁶Jesus said to her, "Mary." She turned and said to him in Hebrew, "Rab-bo'ni!" (which means Teacher). ¹⁷Jesus said to her, "Do not hold me, for I have not yet ascended to the Father; but go to my brethren and say to them, I am ascending to my Father and your Father, to my God and your God." ¹⁸Mary Mag'dalene went and said to the disciples, "I have seen the Lord"; and she told them that he had said these things to her.

¹⁹On the evening of that day, the first day of the week, the doors being shut where the disciples were, for fear of the Jews, Jesus came and stood among them and said to them, "Peace be with you." ²⁰When he had said this, he showed them his hands and his side. Then the disciples were glad when they saw the Lord. ²¹Jesus said to them again, "Peace be with you. As the Father has sent me, even so I send you." ²²And when he

had said this, he breathed on them, and said to them, "Receive the Holy Spirit. [23]If you forgive the sins of any, they are forgiven; if you retain the sins of any, they are retained."

[24]Now Thomas, one of the twelve, called the Twin, was not with them when Jesus came. [25]So the other disciples told him, "We have seen the Lord." But he said to them, "Unless I see in his hands the print of the nails, and place my finger in the mark of the nails, and place my hand in his side, I will not believe."

[26]Eight days later, his disciples were again in the house, and Thomas was with them. The doors were shut, but Jesus came and stood among them, and said, "Peace be with you." [27]Then he said to Thomas, "Put your finger here, and see my hands; and put out your hand, and place it in my side; do not be faithless, but believing." [28]Thomas answered him, "My Lord and my God!" [29]Jesus said to him, "Have you believed because you have seen me? Blessed are those who have not seen and yet believe."

[30]Now Jesus did many other signs in the presence of the disciples, which are not written in this book; [31]but these are written that you may believe that Jesus is the Christ, the Son of God, and that believing you may have life in his name.

Romans

8There is therefore now no condemnation for those who are in Christ Jesus. [2]For the law of the Spirit of life in Christ Jesus has set me free from the law of sin and death. [3]For God has done what the law, weakened by the flesh, could not do: sending his own Son in the likeness of sinful flesh and for sin, he condemned sin in the flesh, [4]in order that the just requirement of the law might be fulfilled in us, who walk not according to the flesh but according to the Spirit. [5]For those who live according to the flesh set their minds on the things of the flesh, but those who live according to the Spirit set their minds on the things of the Spirit. [6]To set the mind on the flesh is death, but to set the mind on the Spirit is life and peace. [7]For the mind that is set on the flesh is

hostile to God; it does not submit to God's law, indeed it cannot; [8]and those who are in the flesh cannot please God.

[9]But you are not in the flesh, you are in the Spirit, if in fact the Spirit of God dwells in you. Any one who does not have the Spirit of Christ does not belong to him. [10]But if Christ is in you, although your bodies are dead because of sin, your spirits are alive because of righteousness. [11]If the Spirit of him who raised Jesus from the dead dwells in you, he who raised Christ Jesus from the dead will give life to your mortal bodies also through his Spirit which dwells in you.

[12]So then, brethren, we are debtors; not to the flesh, to live according to the flesh—[13]for if you live according to the flesh you will die, but if by the Spirit you put to death the deeds of the body you will live. [14]For all who are led by the Spirit of God are sons of God. [15]For you did not receive the spirit of slavery to fall back into fear, but you have received the spirit of sonship. When we cry, "Abba! Father!" [16]it is the Spirit himself bearing witness with our spirit that we are children of God, [17]and if children, then heirs, heirs of God and fellow heirs with Christ, provided we suffer with him in order that we may also be glorified with him.

[18]I consider that the sufferings of this present time are not worth comparing with the glory that is to be revealed to us. [19]For the creation waits with eager longing for the revealing of the sons of God; [20]for the creation was subjected to futility, not of its own will but by the will of him who subjected it in hope; [21]because the creation itself will be set free from its bondage to decay and obtain the glorious liberty of the children of God. [22]We know that the whole creation has been groaning in travail together until now; [23]and not only the creation, but we ourselves, who have the first fruits of the Spirit, groan inwardly as we wait for adoption as sons, the redemption of our bodies. [24]For in this hope we were saved. Now hope that is seen is not hope. For who hopes for what he sees? [25]But if we hope for what we do not see, we wait for it with patience.

[26]Likewise the Spirit helps us in our weakness; for we do not know how to pray as we ought, but the Spirit himself intercedes for us with sighs too deep for words. [27]And he who searches the hearts of men knows what is the mind of the Spirit, because the Spirit intercedes for the saints according to the will of God.

[28]We know that in everything God works for good with those who love him, who are called according to his purpose. [29]For those whom he foreknew he also predestined to be conformed to the image of his Son, in order that he might be the first-born among many brethren. [30]And those whom he predestined he also called; and those whom he called he also justified; and those whom he justified he also glorified.

[31]What then shall we say to this? If God is for us, who is against us? [32]He who did not spare his own Son but gave him up for us all, will he not also give us all things with him? [33]Who shall bring any charge against God's elect? It is God who justifies; [34]who is to condemn? Is it Christ Jesus, who died, yes, who was raised from the dead, who is at the right hand of God, who indeed intercedes for us? [35]Who shall separate us from the love of Christ? Shall tribulation, or distress, or persecution, or famine, or nakedness, or peril, or sword? [36]As it is written,

"For thy sake we are being killed all the day long;

we are regarded as sheep to be slaughtered."

[37]No, in all these things we are more than conquerors through him who loved us. [38]For I am sure that neither death, nor life, nor angels, nor principalities, nor things present, nor things to come, nor powers, [39]nor height, nor depth, nor anything else in all creation, will be able to separate us from the love of God in Christ Jesus our Lord.

1 Corinthians

2 [17]But in the following instructions I do not commend you, because when you come together it is not for the better but for the worse. [18]For, in the first place, when you assemble as a church, I hear that there are divisions among you; and I partly believe it, [19]for there must be factions among you in order that those who are genuine among you may be recognized. [20]When you meet together, it is not the Lord's supper that you eat. [21]For in eating, each one goes ahead with his own meal, and one is hungry and another is drunk. [22]What! Do you not have houses to eat and drink in? Or do you despise the church of God and humiliate those who have nothing? What shall I say to you? Shall I commend you in this? No, I will not.

[23]For I received from the Lord what I also delivered to you, that the Lord Jesus on the night when he was betrayed took bread, [24]and when he had given thanks, he broke it, and said, "This is my body which is for you. Do this in remembrance of me." [25]In the same way also the cup, after supper, saying, "This cup is the new covenant in my blood. Do this, as often as you drink it, in remembrance of me." [26]For as often as you eat this bread and drink the cup, you proclaim the Lord's death until he comes.

[27]Whoever, therefore, eats the bread or drinks the cup of the Lord in an unworthy manner will be guilty of profaning the body and blood of the Lord. [28]Let a man examine himself, and so eat of the bread and drink of the cup. [29]For any one who eats and drinks without discerning the body eats and drinks judgment upon himself. [30]That is why many of you are weak and ill, and some have died. [31]But if we judged ourselves truly, we should not be judged. [32]But when we are judged by the Lord, we are chastened so that we may not be condemned along with the world.

*   *   *

12 Now concerning spiritual gifts, brethren, I do not want you to be uninformed. [2]You know that when you were heathen, you were led astray to dumb idols, however, you may have been moved. [3]Therefore I want you to understand that no one speaking by the Spirit of God ever says

"Jesus be cursed!" and no one can say "Jesus is Lord" except by the Holy Spirit.

[4]Now there are varieties of gifts, but the same Spirit; [5]and there are varieties of service, but the same Lord; [6]and there are varieties of working, but it is the same God who inspires them all in every one. [7]To each is given the manifestation of the Spirit for the common good. [8]To one is given through the Spirit the utterance of wisdom, and to another the utterance of knowledge according to the same Spirit, [9]to another faith by the same Spirit, to another gifts of healing by the one Spirit, [10]to another the working of miracles, to another prophecy, to another the ability to distinguish between spirits, to another various kinds of tongues, to another the interpretation of tongues. [11]All these are inspired by one and the same Spirit, who apportions to each one individually as he wills.

[12]For just as the body is one and has many members, and all the members of the body, though many, are one body, so it is with Christ. [13]For by one Spirit we were all baptized into one body—Jews or Greeks, slaves or free—and all were made to drink of one Spirit.

[27]Now you are the body of Christ and individually members of it. [28]And God has appointed in the church first apostles, second prophets, third teachers, then workers of miracles, then healers, helpers, administrators, speakers in various kinds of tongues. [29]Are all apostles? Are all prophets? Are all teachers? Do all work miracles? [30]Do all possess gifts of healing? Do all speak with tongues? Do all interpret? [31]But earnestly desire the higher gifts.

And I will show you a still more excellent way.

*   *   *

13If I speak in the tongues of men and of angels, but have not love, I am a noisy gong or a clanging cymbal. [2]And if I have prophetic powers, and understand all mysteries and all knowledge, and if I have all faith, so as to remove mountains, but have not love, I am nothing. [3]If

I give away all I have, and if I deliver my body to be burned, but have not love, I gain nothing.

[4]Love is patient and kind; love is not jealous or boastful; [5]it is not arrogant or rude. Love does not insist on its own way; it is not irritable or resentful; [6]it does not rejoice at wrong, but rejoices in the right. [7]Love bears all things, believes all things, hopes all things, endures all things.

[8]Love never ends; as for prophecies, they will pass away; as for tongues, they will cease; as for knowledge, it will pass away. [9]For our knowledge is imperfect and our prophecy is imperfect; [10]but when the perfect comes, the imperfect will pass away. [11]When I was a child, I spoke like a child, I thought like a child, I reasoned like a child; when I became a man, I gave up childish ways. [12]For now we see in a mirror dimly, but then face to face. Now I know in part; then I shall understand fully, even as I have been fully understood. [13]So faith, hope, love abide, these three; but the greatest of these is love.

*   *   *

15Now I would remind you, brethren, in what terms I preached to you the gospel, which you received, in which you stand, [2]by which you are saved, if you hold it fast—unless you believed in vain.

[3]For I delivered to you as of first importance what I also received, that Christ died for our sins in accordance with the scriptures, [4]that he was buried, that he was raised on the third day in accordance with the scriptures, [5]and that he appeared to Cephas, then to the twelve. [6]Then he appeared to more than five hundred brethren at one time, most of whom are still alive, though some have fallen asleep. [7]Then he appeared to James, then to all the apostles. [8]Last of all, as to one untimely born, he appeared also to me. [9]For I am the least of the apostles, unfit to be called an apostle, because I persecuted the church of God. [10]But by the grace of God I am what I am, and his grace toward me was not in vain. On the contrary, I worked harder than any of them, though it was not I, but the grace of God which

is with me. [11]Whether then it was I or they, so we preach and so you believed.

[12]Now if Christ is preached as raised from the dead, how can some of you say that there is no resurrection of the dead? [13]But if there is no resurrection of the dead, then Christ has not been raised; [14]if Christ has not been raised, then our preaching is in vain and your faith is in vain. [15]We are even found to be misrepresenting God, because we testified of God that he raised Christ, whom he did not raise if it is true that the dead are not raised. [16]For if the dead are not raised, then Christ has not been raised. [17]If Christ has not been raised, your faith is futile and you are still in your sins. [18]Then those also who have fallen asleep in Christ have perished. [19]If for this life only we have hoped in Christ, we are of all men most to be pitied.

[20]But in fact Christ has been raised from the dead, the first fruits of those who have fallen asleep. [21]For as by a man came death, by a man has come also the resurrection of the dead. [22]For as in Adam all die, so also in Christ shall all be made alive. [23]But each in his own order: Christ the first fruits, then at his coming those who belong to Christ. [24]Then comes the end, when he delivers the kingdom to God the Father after destroying every rule and every authority and power. [25]For he must reign until he has put all his enemies under his feet. [26]The last enemy to be destroyed is death. [27]"For God has put all things in subjection under his feet." But when it says, "All things are put in subjection under him," it is plain that he is excepted who put all things under him. [28]When all things are subjected to him, then the Son himself will also be subjected to him who put all things under him, that God may be everything to every one.

[29]Otherwise, what do people mean by being baptized on behalf of the dead? If the dead are not raised at all, why are people baptized on their behalf? [30]Why am I in peril every hour? [31]I protest, brethren, by my pride in you which I have in Christ Jesus our Lord, I die every day! [32]What do I gain if, humanly speaking, I fought with beasts at Ephesus? If the dead are not raised,

"Let us eat and drink, for tomorrow we die." [33]Do not be deceived: "Bad company ruins good morals." [34]Come to your right mind, and sin no more. For some have no knowledge of God. I say this to your shame.

[35]But some one will ask, "How are the dead raised? With what kind of body do they come?" [36]You foolish man! What you sow does not come to life unless it dies. [37]And what you sow is not the body which is to be, but a bare kernel, perhaps of wheat or of some other grain. [38]But God gives it a body as he has chosen, and to each kind of seed its own body. [39]For not all flesh is alike, but there is one kind for men, another for animals, another for birds, and another for fish. [40]There are celestial bodies and there are terrestrial bodies; but the glory of the celestial is one, and the glory of the terrestrial is another. [41]There is one glory of the sun, and another glory of the moon, and another glory of the stars; for star differs from star in glory.

[42]So is it with the resurrection of the dead. What is sown is perishable, what is raised is imperishable. [43]It is sown in dishonor, it is raised in glory. It is sown in weakness, it is raised in power. [44]It is sown a physical body, it is raised a spiritual body. If there is a physical body, there is also a spiritual body. [45]Thus it is written, "The first man Adam became a living being"; the last Adam became a life-giving spirit. [46]But it is not the spiritual which is first but the physical, and then the spiritual. [47]The first man was from the earth, a man of dust; the second man is from heaven. [48]As was the man of dust, so are those who are of the dust; and as is the man of heaven, so are those who are of heaven. [49]Just as we have borne the image of the man of dust, we shall also bear the image of the man of heaven. [50]I tell you this, brethren: flesh and blood cannot inherit the kingdom of God, nor does the perishable inherit the imperishable.

[51]Lo! I tell you a mystery. We shall not all sleep, but we shall all be changed, [52]in a moment, in the twinkling of an eye, at the last trumpet. For the trumpet will sound, and the dead will be raised imperishable, and we shall be

changed. [53]For this perishable nature must put on the imperishable, and this mortal nature must put on immortality. [54]When the perishable puts on the imperishable, and the mortal puts on immortality, then shall come to pass the saying that is written:

"Death is swallowed up in victory." [55]"O death, where is thy victory?

O death, where is thy sting?"

[56]The sting of death is sin, and the power of sin is the law. [57]But thanks be to God, who gives us the victory through our Lord Jesus Christ.

[58]Therefore, my beloved brethren, be steadfast, immovable, always abounding in the work of the Lord knowing that in the Lord your labor is not in vain.

Galatians

3[15]We ourselves, who are Jews by birth and not Gentile sinners, [16]yet who know that a man is not justified by works of the law but through faith in Jesus Christ, even we have believed in Christ Jesus, in order to be justified by faith in Christ, and not by works of the law, because by works of the law shall no one be justified. [17]But if, in our endeavor to be justified in Christ, we ourselves were found to be sinners, is Christ then an agent of sin? Certainly not! [18]But if I build up again those things which I tore down, then I prove myself a transgressor. [19]For I through the law died to the law, that I might live to God. [20]I have been crucified with Christ; it is no longer I who live, but Christ who lives in me; and the life I now live in the flesh I live by faith in the Son of God, who loved me and gave himself for me. [21]I do not nullify the grace of God; for if justification were through the law, then Christ died to no purpose.

Philippians

2So if there is any encouragement in Christ, any incentive of love, any participation in the Spirit, any affection and sympathy, [2]complete my joy by being of the same mind, having the same love, being in full accord and of one mind. [3]Do nothing from selfishness or conceit, but in humility count others better than yourselves. [4]Let each of you look not only to his own interests, but also to the interests of others. [5]Have this mind among yourselves, which is yours in Christ Jesus, [6]who, though he was in the form of God, did not count equality with God a thing to be grasped, [7]but emptied himself, taking the form of a servant, being born in the likeness of men. [8]And being found in human form he humbled himself and became obedient unto death, even death on a cross. [9]Therefore God has highly exalted him and bestowed on him the name which is above every name, [10]that at the name of Jesus every knee should bow, in heaven and on earth and under the earth, [11]and every tongue confess that Jesus Christ is Lord, to the glory of God the Father.

[12]Therefore, my beloved, as you have always obeyed, so now, not only as in my presence but much more in my absence, work out your own salvation with fear and trembling; [13]for God is at work in you, both to will and to work for his good pleasure.

[14]Do all things without grumbling or questioning, [15]that you may be blameless and innocent, children of God without blemish in the midst of a crooked and perverse generation, among whom you shine as lights in the world, [16]holding fast the word of life, so that in the day of Christ I may be proud that I did not run in vain or labor in vain. [17]Even if I am to be poured as a libation upon the sacrificial offering of your faith, I am glad and rejoice with you all. [18]Likewise you also should be glad and rejoice with me.

*   *   *

3If then you have been raised with Christ, seek the things that are above, where Christ is, seated at the right hand of God, [2]Set your minds on things that are above, not on things that are on earth. [3]For you have died, and your life is hid with Christ in God. [4]When Christ who is our life appears, then you also will appear with him in glory.

⁵Put to death therefore what is earthly in you: fornication, impurity, passion, evil desire, and covetousness, which is idolatry. ⁶On account of these the wrath of God is coming. ⁷In these you once walked, when you lived in them. ⁸But now put them all away: anger, wrath, malice, slander, and foul talk from your mouth. ⁹Do not lie to one another, seeing that you have put off the old nature with its practices ¹⁰and have put on the new nature, which is being renewed in knowledge after the image of its creator. ¹¹Here there cannot be Greek and Jew, circumcised and uncircumcised, barbarian, Scyth′ian, slave, free man, but Christ is all, and in all.

¹²Put on then, as God's chosen ones, holy and beloved, compassion, kindness, lowliness, meekness, and patience, ¹³forbearing one another and, if one has a complaint against another, forgiving each other; as the Lord has forgiven you, so you also must forgive. ¹⁴And above all these put on love, which binds everything together in perfect harmony. ¹⁵And let the peace of Christ rule in your hearts, to which indeed you were called in the one body. And be thankful. ¹⁶Let the word of Christ dwell in you richly, teach and admonish one another in all wisdom, and sing psalms and hymns and spiritual songs with thankfulness in your hearts to God. ¹⁷And whatever you do, in word or deed, do everything in the name of the Lord Jesus, giving thanks to God the Father through him.

NEW TESTAMENT JOURNAL EXERCISES

1. Who is the real Jesus? Based on your reading of the New Testament materials, and on the difference in testimonies (Jesus about himself, the gospelists about Jesus and his opposition's opinions) what is your image of Jesus? Who did he think he was, and was he right? Support your image of Jesus with passages from the New Testament (and from Hebrew scriptures where appropriate).

2. Have a dialogue with Jesus in which you ask Jesus to clarify points of his teaching which are not clear to you. You may wish to ask Jesus about how he sees himself, about his purpose and mission, or about his teachings concerning repentance, the kingdom of God, sin, hell, marriage, forgiveness, etc. After each question pause and imagine that you are Jesus. How would Jesus have responded to your questions?

3. Reread Mark 4:1–20, the parable of the sower and the parable which explains why Jesus speaks in parables!

    Recall that a parable is a story with hidden truths, told to initiates which both reveals and conceals at the same time, and which is told specifically to the Jews so as not to be understood by the Gentiles.

    Imagine that you are Mark, and that you remember one very important parable of Jesus which you had not included in your Gospels. Write that parable.

4. Select your favorite parable of Jesus and retell it in updated language. Select a particular audience and address your language update to them in particular. For example, here's how a southern preacher, Clarence Jordan, retells the story of the Good Samaritan:

    "You recall the story of the man who was traveling along the road in his car. He was stopped—beaten, robbed, stripped of clothes, and left bleeding.

    "Along comes a white minister in his '63 Buick. He sees the man and is about to step on his power brakes when he recalls that he must go to a revival meeting at eight. He has promised, and if he stops, he may be late. He may have to go to court. He may get blood on his new upholstery. So he steps on the gas and as he passes he says: "God bless you, brother, God bless you!"

    "Next comes a gospel singer in a '59 Chevy. He was about to stop but he recalls that he must be at church a half hour early to lead the choir. A meeting can start without the preacher, but not without the song leader. So he goes on singing—"Brighten the corner where you are"—and drives on by.

    "Lastly comes a man in an old Ford. He sees the beaten man and pulls over. He is black. He doesn't know him or what happened but he helps. He puts him in the car and takes him to town. On the way he passes the gospel singer's church where revival is held. He reads the sign: 'All are welcome,' and he knows what that means. At the hospital he gets a nurse and says that he has found a man beaten and bloody. He only has $2 to offer but he will return on Saturday after being paid, to furnish the rest.

    " 'Now,' said Jesus, 'which one did right?' "

5. Imagine that you are Jesus, and that you are about to address an assembly of your con-

temporaries. Imagine that you wanted to convey the true spirit of the Hebrew law. How would you rephrase the ten commandments so that today's audience would pay attention?

6. After the death/resurrection of Jesus, imagine yourself at a caucus of disciples, in John Mark's mother's, upper room, where you had once been for the last supper, and where you are now gathered on Pentecost sabbath with other members of the inner circle of followers when suddenly . . .

    What actually happened? Imagine yourself there in the midst of that transforming experience. Describe the Pentecost experience, in any way you can.

7. If you were Peter or James or one of the early Jewish-born apostles, and you were confronting other religious Jews (temple-Jews, Pharisaic-Jews), how would you attempt to convince them of your faith? What would you say if, for example, you were asked to speak in a local synagogue? Imagine yourself being singled out and called to the front and asked to deliver a homily on Jesus. What would you say?

8. Reread Paul's conversion experience in Acts 9 and try to imagine it. Have you ever experienced a transformational experience analogous to this? If so, describe it. What is the major revolution that occurred in Saul of Tarsus on the road to Damascus which produced St. Paul? What is the source point or origin of his experience?

9. Imagine what would have happened if Paul and Jesus would have met each other while Jesus was still alive. How would they have met? What would they have said to each other? Construct an imaginary dialogue in which you act as if you are in turn each of them.

Chapter 10 THE MUSLIM WITNESS

The story of the Islamic faith begins when Adam submitted to Allah and is last revealed to and through the Prophet Muhammad. From these events onward, a great monotheistic faith arose in the center of the Arabian peninsula. Islam grew initially in the towns of Mecca and Medina which are situated on the caravan trade route across the peninsula. Along these trade routes then traveled not only silks and spices, rugs and jewels, but also Jewish and Christian teachings. Being the youngest western faith, Al-Islam comes from the Arabic root *slm*, which means to enter into the Peace of Allah through a radical submission to God's will. Just as a Jew is greeted with "*Shalom*," and a Christian with the "Peace of Christ," when a Muslim greets another Muslim, he or she might say "*Salaam Aleikum*"—peace be unto you.

Al-Islam

When we come to Islam, we come to the only major sacred story that we have studied which contains its own word for religion, *din*. Whereas Hinduism takes its name from the Indus River, Buddhism, Confucianism, and Christianity from their founders, Taoism from the Tao, and Judaism from a people (Hebrews-Israelites-Jews), Islam is not a proper noun, but a way of living, a way of practicing peace. Islam was the name ascribed to the doer of *Salam* (Muslim). To be a Muslim means therefore to be gathered together as the universal people of Allah, a people who radically submit in peace to the absolute oneness of God.

As Seyyed Hossein Nasar indicates, Islam claims to be both the final religion, the fulfillment of all other religions, and also a "primordial religion (*al-din al-hanif*) because it is based on the doctrine of Unity which has always existed and which lies in the nature of things."[1] This unity is based on three personalities—Adam, Abraham and Muhammad—all monotheists (*muwahhid*). Adam and Abraham are fathers of the Semites, and Muhammad, the "Seal of Prophecy."

There are no churches, temples or priests, no outside authorities who determine "Islamicity"; to enter the house of Islam is to enter the mosque. Unlike a church, a mosque is an empty building, void of icons, symbols or any external religious artifacts, where the faithful assemble for prayer. Before entering a mosque, one washes hands, feet, face, ears, nose, and mouth, and is required to leave sandals and shoes outside. On Friday, the leader reads from the Qur'an and the people read silently. After the leader chants "Allah Akbar" (God is great), he and the people bow toward Mecca on hands and knees, and touch forehead and nose to their rug in prayer.

Islam begins in Arabia in the seventh century when Muhammad first preached a universal monotheism which refuted existing Semitic tribal injustices and polytheistic cults.

Muhammad was conscious of having precursors in Judaism and in Christianity. In fact Islam views itself as the final fulfillment of the biblical revelation, views Muhammad as the seal of prophecy, and regards the Qur'an as the final revelation of God:

Today those who disbelieve despair about your religion, so do not dread them, and (rather) dread Me.

(Today I have perfected your religion for you, and completed My favor towards you, and have consented to grant you [Islām] as a religion: a commitment to live in peace.)

Anyone who is obliged to do so while (he is) starving, yet without deliberately sinning, [will find] God is Forgiving, Merciful.[2]

Like the Jews, Muslims believe in one God who alone is to be worshiped, who alone is the transcendent, sovereign Lord of history, and who alone provides humans with divine imperatives to act justly. As God spoke through Abraham, Moses and the prophets, so too Allah speaks through Muhammad; as God speaks in the Torah so too Allah speaks in the Qur'an. In both faiths, it is the prophet who speaks for God. In fact, of the twenty-eight prophets mentioned in the Qur'an four are Arabian, eighteen are Hebrew and three Christian—Zechariah, John the Baptizer and Jesus. But Islam refuses to acknowledge the Torah as the only law, the Jews as the only chosen people, Isaac as the rightful heir of Abraham, and Jewish prophecy as complete.[3] While accepting the teachings of Hebrew prophets, Muslims claim that impurities have been allowed to accumulate, and that the Jews have abandoned the prophetic covenant. Muhammad has been sent therefore as the "seal" of prophecy, to revive universal monotheism.

Like Christianity, Muslims accept the life of Jesus, his virgin birth, baptism, teachings, miracles and ascension but not his death upon the cross and therefore his resurrection. Muslims deny that Jesus was anything more than a human prophet. Like Moses or Muhammad, Jesus was completely human. Only Allah is divine. Islam rejects the church as the house of God while at the same time accepting the last judgment, heaven and hell and sin. With regard to the "Apostles' Creed," Orthodox Islam rejects those affirmations which are italicized and accepts the rest.

> I believe in God
> The Father Almighty,
> Maker of heaven and earth:
> And in Jesus Christ
> *His only Son, our Lord,*
> Who was conceived by the Holy
> Ghost,
> Born of the Virgin Mary
> *Suffered under Pontius Pilate,*
> *Was crucified,* died and *was buried.*

He descended into hell;
The third day
He rose again from the dead.
He ascended into heaven,
And sitteth on the right hand of God
The Father Almighty;
From thence He shall come
To judge the quick and the dead.
I believe in the Holy Ghost;
The Holy Catholic Church;
The Communion of Saints;
The forgiveness of sins;
The Resurrection of the body,
And the life everlasting.

To simplify, as the following chart illustrates, a Muslim might say that whereas Judaism is monotheistic and ethnocentric, and Christianity trinitarian and universalistic, Islam alone is monotheistic and universal. Islam therefore claims to be the final revelation of the indivisible, non-parochial, monotheistic, otherness of Allah to all peoples.

ISLAM	JUDAISM	CHRISTIANITY
1. Monotheistic	Monotheistic	Trinitarian
2. Universalistic	Ethno-Centric (Nationalistic)	Universalistic

The Story of Muhammad (570–632)

The witness of Islam begins with the story of Muhammad. In fact, the Muslim calendar dates events *Anno Hegirae* (A.H.—in the year of the Hijra) and begins therefore from July 16, 622 CE when Muhammad migrated from Mecca (city of his birth) to Medina where he strengthened his forces and developed a community of faithful followers. In 8 A.H. (630 CE) he, like Joshua, led his people, the people of Allah, back to Mecca which he conquered. While Muhammad was not an *avatar* or *messiah,* he was *Rasuliyyah* (in "the state of being sent"). As Torah is for the Jews and Christ for Christians, the Qur'an is the singular event which gives Islam its meaning and direction.

Muhammad, son of Abdallah, was born in a Hashemite clan of the Quraysh Tribe in about 570 CE. His father died before his birth and his mother Amina was left with only an elderly female slave and five camels. According to orthodox teachings, she experienced none of the difficulties of pregnancy. Instead she heard a voice one day which told her that her son was to be a ruler and prophet, and that she should name the child Ahmad, that is Muhammad, the illustrious. As with the births of other spiritual persons, miraculous signs accompanied his. When Muhammad was delivered a brilliant light as from a star illumined the skies from east to west. He was born clean, circumcised and with the navel-cord already cut. Shortly after his birth he was entrusted to a Bedouin family and to a foster mother Halimah who raised him until, at the age of six, his mother too died. He was then given to his grandfather Abd al Muttalib, and two years later, upon his death, to his uncle Abdu Talib who loved him greatly.

At the age of twelve, Muhammad accompanied his uncle on a trade caravan to Syria where he was singled out by a monk named Bahira who possessed esoteric knowledge. The monk noticed how a tree lowered its branches over the boy to provide him with shade at a resting place. When he examined Muhammad more closely, he found a seal of his prophetic office between his shoulders. Immediately he warned his uncle to return to his country and to guard Muhammad against those who might try to harm him.

Said to be uneducated, Muhammad grew up in relative poverty in Mecca, a busy commercial hub controlling the Indian Ocean, the Mediterranean, Yemen and Egyptian trade routes. Like all wealthy, commercially-oriented societies, Mecca also exposed Muhammad to poverty, slavery, social-class barriers, fraud, injustice, economic greed, and a variety of religious cults. Aside from Judaism, Christianity, Zoroastrianism, and polytheistic, native Arabian practices, the city also contained *hanifs* ("monotheists"), *kahins* (soothsayers) and *shairs* (spirit-poets).

When Muhammad was twenty-five, his uncle said to him: "Since we are poor, and since times are so difficult for us, you should offer your services to the wealthy widow Khadijah who is sending a caravan to Syria." Khadijah was the noblest and richest woman among the Quraish and she happily accepted his offer. The caravan was highly successful and when they returned to Mecca she sent a message to him to inquire whether he intended to marry. When Muhammad pleaded poverty he was told that Khadijah herself who was then forty was offering to marry him. He quickly accepted. That their twenty-five year marriage was a happy and prosperous one can be seen from the fact that, although in later years Muhammad had nine wives, he took no other woman as long as she lived. They had four daughters and two sons, but only Fatimah had descendants who reached adulthood. It was Khadijah who stood by him when others denounced him, and it was she who was the first to believe in his mission, even before he himself believed in it.

Now forty, independent, respected by his countrymen as Al-Amin (the reliable), Muhammad began to experience dreams and visions as bright as the morning skies. A lover of solitude, he often wandered far from the city in reverie, and once a year retired to a cave on Mount Hira where he spent a month in meditation.

According to tradition, Muhammad's initial revelatory experience took place in a cave in a desert hill not far from Mecca. Like the ascetic Syrian Christians, he practiced solitary reflection. Muhammad had become a *hanif* (those who turn away) which came to mean the upright, the person of truthful or right conduct, who wandered the hills about Mecca to brood privately. Toward the end of an evening's meditation, while asleep, or in a sleep-like trance, he hears a voice say, "Recite!" When he answers that he cannot, the voice again says, "Recite (read)!" Again Muhammad answers that he cannot.

Thereupon the angel seemed to seize Muhammad by the throat and began to strangle

him while repeating the command to recite. Squeezing and shaking him with such vigor that
his life seemed threatened, Muhammad finally submitted and received the first of the revelations which comprise the Qur'an:

> In the name of God, the Mercy-giving, the Merciful!
>
> READ in the name of your Lord Who creates,
> creates man from a clot!
> READ, for your Lord is most Generous;
> [it is He] Who teaches
> by means of the pen,
> teaches man what he does not know.
>
> However man acts so arrogant,
> for he considers he is self-sufficient.
> Yet to your Lord will be the Return![4]

Muhammad's initial refusal to recite is not interpreted as a lack or failure of faith, but
rather as a function of his illiteracy combined with fear and confusion. Remember, Muhammad had not actively sought a revelation. Rather it came in spite of himself through a force
beyond his own invention. Like the Hebrew prophets before him. Muhammad had been chosen to be an instrument for transmitting a Divine message. The Qur'an reinforces the transcendent power of his revelational experiences:

> In the name of God, the Mercy-giving, the Merciful!
>
> By The Star as it sets, your companion
> has neither strayed nor is he misguided.
> He does not speak from some whim;
> it is merely inspiration
> that is revealed [to him].
>
> Someone firm in strength has taught him,
> someone possessing such ability
> that he soared up and stood,
> poised at the highest [point on the] horizon.
> Then he approached and came right down,
> and stood two bow-lengths off
> or even closer. He inspired
> whatever he inspired in His servant.
> His vitals did not deny whatever he saw.
> Yet will you (all) distrust him
> about what he [actually] saw?[5]

When he left the cave it was as if the message was written in his heart. The same voice says, "Muhammad—you are Allah's messenger and I am Gabriel!" When Muhammad lifted his eyes he saw the Angel Gabriel in the likeness of a man at the horizon of heaven. No matter where Muhammad turned his eyes, there stood the angel confronting him. When finally the angel vanished, he distraughtly returned to his wife Khadijah.

Sensitive to her husband's condition, she encouraged him to become a prophet to the people, and upon their return to Mecca she took him to her cousin who knew Jewish and Christian scriptures. When he heard of Muhammad's experiences, he declared that the same heavenly messenger who had come to Moses in Torah had come to Muhammad. Muhammad, the solitary-loving, illiterate *hanif*, became "The Slave of Allah," a "witness," a "warner," a "caller unto God." After preaching his message privately to his own family, he was commanded to "arise and warn" (74:2), whereupon he began preaching in public. Resistance to him in Mecca was politically and economically based. The Meccan business interests worried that his pure monotheism might "tempt" people away from their economic sanctuaries. Thus began a ten-year struggle to convert the Meccan oligarchy.

Pre-Islamic, Arab culture was arranged in tribal groupings and was marked by family and clan solidarity. Characteristic of the desert life was a disorganized collection of gods, heavenly bodies and demons associated with natural elements and shrines like the Ka'bah located in the center of Mecca. Meccan polytheism was tied as well to social status and economic position. Therefore influential leaders attempted to bribe Muhammad at first with the promise of wealth in exchange for a withdrawal of Allah's demand that all Meccans worship the one God. But Muhammad's response was that God wanted nothing less than complete submission.

The arguments and disputes intensified and were accompanied by an increased persecution of the Prophet's followers. Every day Muhammad went to the Ka'ba to pray and to rally support, but most of his followers were slaves and members of the lower classes. In 620, the Qur'an (17:1) reveals that Muhammad, who was resting in prayer at the Ka'ba in Mecca, was taken by the angel Gabriel on a white steed to the hill of Moriah in Jerusalem, site of Solomon's temple which was rebuilt under Ezra and Nehemiah in 515 BCE, restored by Herod at the time of Jesus, and destroyed by the Emperor Titus in 70 CE. In his Night Journey, the Prophet is taken to the seventh heaven where, as we read in a later Hadith, he encounters the scintillating throne of Allah. "My sight was so dazzled by it that I feared blindness. Therefore I shut my eyes, which was by Allah's good favour. When I thus veiled my sight Allah shifted my sight [from my eyes] to my heart, so with my heart I began to look at what I had been looking at with my eyes. It was a light so bright in its scintillation that I despair of ever describing to you what I saw of His majesty. . . . There He was, when the veil had been lifted from Him, seated on His Throne, in His dignity, His might, His glory, His exaltedness, but beyond that it is not permitted me to describe Him to you. Glory be to Him! How majestic is He! How brilliant is His light!"[6] Allah reveals to Muhammad that each Muslim should pray fifty times a day which Moses interprets as five prayers a day since each prayer counts as ten.

In 621, during the pilgrimage season, the Prophet was able to convert some prominent members of Yathrib (later called Medina), some two hundred miles north of Mecca. After ten years of opposition, leaders from Medina, which had been weakened by civil wars, besought Muhammad to come there as a mediator and peacekeeper. For several years he negotiated with them, and after he secured a position of authority, he and his followers escaped from Mecca on June 20, 622 CE.

The *Hijra* (the emigration as the escape is called) took many days travel by unfrequented paths, and ironically, when they reached the outskirts of Yathrib, it was a Jew who announced to the Medians that the expected one had arrived. The *Hijra* marks a division in the story: until then he had been a preacher; thereafter he was to be a ruler of State.

When Muhammad reached Medina, his first act was to institute a document (later called the Constitution of Medina) which declared that all Medinese—Muslims, Jews, Christians and pagans alike—were to form one community under his leadership. With skillful diplomacy and shrewd political maneuverings, Muhammad created a network of alliances with the Bedouin tribes in the countryside as well as with the political powers in Medina itself. Several times during the ensuing years Muhammad courageously managed to save his outnumbered army from attacks by larger Meccan forces. By introducing new defensive tactics—digging trenches and raising barricades—and through his indefatigable faith he inspired a great zeal in his followers.

Finally, eight years after Muhammad originally left Mecca, he negotiated his return. With ten thousand men, he led a march on the temporarily evacuated city on Wednesday, the tenth of Ramadan, in the eighth year of the Hijrah. This was to be his greatest triumph. He freely forgave the Meccans for the years of hostility he endured and granted a general amnesty to all her citizens. His army entered peaceably—no home was looted, no human indignities suffered. Going straight to the Ka'ba, Muhammad purged the stone of its three hundred and sixty idols. Thus was Mecca converted to Islam.

In the tenth year of the *Hijra* the Prophet made his last pilgrimage to Mecca and delivered his farewell speech to a gathering of forty thousand Muslims. At the end of the address and as his final word he recited this revelation: "Today I (Allah) have perfected your religion for you, and I have completed My blessing upon you, and I have approved Islam for your religion" (Qur'an 5:5). When the prophet died in 632 CE, after joining in public prayer for the last time, Abu Bakr, a close disciple, said to the people gathered at a mosque in prayer:

Muhammad is only a messenger. Messengers have passed away before him. If he should die or be killed, will you (all) revert to your old ways? Anyone who turns on his heels will never injure God in any way, while God will reward the grateful.[7]

In the ten years from his *Hijra* Muhammad was transformed from a rejected fugitive to the most revered man in Arabia who had founded a community that was to become a major religious movement in the world.

Allah

Allah

Having discussed the term "Islam" and having retold the story of Muhammad's revelation and *Hijra* we will now examine four interdependent realities which comprise the heart of the Islamic story: Allah, *Umma* (community), *shari'a* (Law) and Qur'an.

The Arabic word Allah (from al-ilah, *the* God) is not a name but rather a term for the supreme singular which negates all pluralisms. While Muhammad, it will be remembered, was surrounded by polytheistic, dehumanizing beliefs and practices, his God was the highest development of a universal, ethical monotheism. Islamic ritual and teaching affirm both *Allah akbar* (Greater is God), and *Hasbuna Allah* ("God is our enough").

In the name of God, the Mercy-giving, the Merciful!

SAY: "God is <u>Unique!</u>
God is the Source [for everything];
He has not fathered anyone
nor was He fathered, and there
is nothing comparable to Him!"[8]

Traditionally there are said to be ninety-nine names for God; the hundreth, the name beyond all names, the truest name, is not a name. Attar of Nishapur, one of the greatest Sufi literary masters, tells of a madman passing by a minaret when the muezzin was giving the call to prayer. Someone asked the madman what the muezzin was doing. He replied, "Shaking a nutshell which has nothing in it!" When you speak any of the ninety-nine names of God, you are shaking a hollow nutshell. About God, it is said, it is best not to speak at all.[9] Neither feminine nor masculine, neither singular nor plural, Allah is said to be Seer, Hearer, Bestower, Pardoner, Keeper, and Guide. One of the most eloquent depictions of Allah is of the Light (of heaven and earth), which is compared to a "lamp" or to a "shining star"—the "light upon light":

> God is the Light of Heaven and Earth!
> His light may be compared to a niche
> in which there is a lamp; the lamp
> is in a glass; the glass
> is just as if it were a glittering star
> kindled from a blessed olive tree,
> [which is] neither Eastern nor Western,
> whose oil will almost glow though fire
> has never touched it. Light upon light,
> God guides anyone He wishes to His light.
> God composes parables for mankind;
> God is Aware of everything![10]

There are four main symbols in this parable, which combine in the profound metaphor of Allah as Light upon Light. The niche refers to a shallow recess in the wall where a lamp was placed, high enough to reflect the light throughout the whole room. The lamp provides the source of the illumination and is analogous to God's light. The glass is the transparent medium which both protects the light source and transmits it. The fuel is a mystical olive oil, neither of the east or west, but cosmically pure. Just as each element is necessary to light a room, so the illumitable Light of Allah, which transcends all other lights, shines through each element of the parable. Allah is the True Light which cannot be described, the quintessential Light of which all others lights are weak reflections.

The opening *sura* in the Qur'an is the quintessence of the entire book, and is often called the "Lord's Prayer" of Islam:

> In the name of God, the Mercy-giving, the Merciful!

> Praise be to God, Lord of the Universe,
> the Mercy-giving, the Merciful!
> Ruler on the Day for Repayment!
> You do we worship and You do we call on for help,

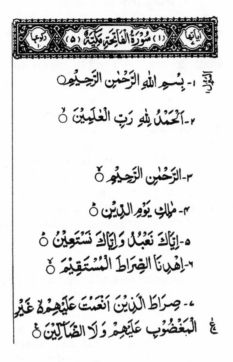

بِسۡمِ اللّٰهِ الرَّحۡمٰنِ الرَّحِيۡمِ ۔١

اَلۡحَمۡدُ لِلّٰهِ رَبِّ الۡعٰلَمِيۡنَ ۙ ۔٢

الرَّحۡمٰنِ الرَّحِيۡمِ ۙ ۔٣

مٰلِكِ يَوۡمِ الدِّيۡنِ ؕ ۔٤

اِيَّاكَ نَعۡبُدُ وَاِيَّاكَ نَسۡتَعِيۡنُ ؕ ۔٥

اِهۡدِنَا الصِّرَاطَ الۡمُسۡتَقِيۡمَ ۙ ۔٦

صِرَاطَ الَّذِيۡنَ اَنۡعَمۡتَ عَلَيۡهِمۡ ۙ غَيۡرِ ۔٧

الۡمَغۡضُوۡبِ عَلَيۡهِمۡ وَلَا الضَّآلِّيۡنَ

Guide us along the Straight Road,
the road of those whom You have favored,
with whom You are not angry,
nor who are lost![11]

Called a comprehensive summation of the entire Qur'an, these lines are repeated five times a day as a part of every believer's prayers. The first two verses invoke God's name as Most Gracious and Most Merciful, and establish the believer's relation to God as one of absolute, self-surrendering praise. The next two verses proclaim various attributes of Allah—the All-merciful, the All-compassionate, the Master of the Day of Judgment. Verse five establishes the commensurate attitude of worship as service and prayer. In verse six the believer beseeches Allah for guidance upon the straight path, and, in verse seven, contemplates what that guidance means. Humans worship Allah their creator because it is Allah who continues to create. As in the Genesis account, humans are created out of clay:

We created man from an extract of clay; then We placed him as a drop of semen in a secure resting-place. Then We turned the semen into a clot; next We turned the clot into tissue; and then We turned the tissue into bones and clothed the bones with flesh.

Then We reproduced him as a fresh creation. Blessed be God, the Best of Creators!

Then later on you shall die. Next you will be raised up again on Resurrection Day.[12]

Allah is unlike anything known or imagined, for while humans are subject to natural laws, Allah is transcendently unbound, beyond all attributes, yet closer to us than our jugular vein.

The Qur'an, as we see, depicts a close relationship between life and death, and are just as close between death and creation and death and resurrection. Just as Allah brings life into being, so too Allah determines the span of a person's life, causes death, and brings about a new creation (resurrection). As in the Gospels, so too in the Qur'an death is depicted as a sleep prior to judgment. At that point we are either condemned to a second death (eternal punishment suffered by the unbelievers), or a second birth (eternal life with Allah).

Umma

As already mentioned, to be a Muslim means to submit to Allah and to be a member of the Islamic community (*umma*). The term *umma* is difficult to translate with one word because it refers at once to a nation, a community of people and a religious grouping. *Umma* thus might be characterized as the Islamic community whose solidarity is with all humans and all living creatures in united submission to Allah and Allah's messenger. Originally, according to the Qur'an, humankind lived in a single, united *umma*.

By the time of the *Hijra,* the *umma* had already formed and was solidified when Muhammad arrived in Medina with a charter of guiding principles for believers, be they Medinans, Meccans, Jews, Christians or pagans. According to the charter, which has been described as the germ of the Islamic state, the Muslims formed one *umma* against all humankind. After the community became established, those who had not adopted Islam were excluded. And as the nation and the religion developed, the *umma* became the ideological, not geographical, gathering of the people around common beliefs: in Allah, in the Messenger, Muhammad; in angels; in the Day of Judgment; and in the so-called "Five Pillars" of Islam which we will elaborate.

Shari'a

The general term for both religion and law, the *dharma,* or the Torah of Islam is *shari'a* (the straight path), which theoretically governs all aspects of every Muslim's life. The *shari'a* represents God's will; thus it is not only a crime but also a sin to violate it. This initiated a radical change from pre-Islamic society (based on tribal, kinship and family customs and unwritten rules) to the Muslim *umma* (based on the equality of all Muslims before Allah).

In response to the problem of what to do about customs and laws which were not noted in the Qur'an, the orthodox Sunni answered that customary law must continue to be enforced unless altered by the Qur'an, while the Shi'i answered that customary laws were abrogated unless specifically sanctioned by the Qur'an. Shi'ite Muslims, partisans of Ali, the cousin, foster brother and son-in-law of Prophet Muhammad, held that descendants of Ali had exclusive rights to the Caliphal office. It was the Caliphs or "successors" who were given the military and political authority of Muhammad, not his prophetic role. This institution of succession began with the nomination of Abu Bakr as the first Caliph, a "Commander of the Believers." To this day shi͞ite Muslims oppose the first three Caliphs who were elected.

Sunni Muslims on the other hand speak of themselves as *ahl al-sunnah wa al-jama'at*, the people of established custom, all of whom received the same collections of traditions known as the "six correct books." Sunnis, who characterize themselves as traditionalists, the bearers of true Islam, today comprise roughly eighty-five percent of the Muslim world. A major difference between the two schools concerns their view of the *imam* (leader) who conducts the community in prayer and who is a learned teacher. The Shi'ah believe that the *imam* is also inspired by Allah, and the most extreme Shi͞ite sects believe the *imam* to be virtually an incarnation of God.

Despite their differences, all Muslims are united by the "Five Pillars." To be a Muslim in any way, one must observe and practice these five elements of Islamic faith (*iman*):

1. Confession (*Shahada*)
2. Prayer (*Salat*)
3. Alms (*Zakat*)
4. Fasting (*Saum*)
5. Pilgrimage (*Hajj*)

These words *"La ilaha illa-allah: Muhammadun rasul Allah,"* "There is no God but Allah, and Muhammad is his Rasul" (prophet, messenger, apostle), are the first words an orthodox Muslim child learns. The emphasis is solely upon the Divine Otherness of Allah; Muhammad is simply a chosen vehicle, mouthpiece, for God's final revelation.

Second, Muslims are called to prayer (by a *muezzin* from a *minaret* tower) five times a day: before sunrise (while the world sleeps); at noon (in the middle of business); in the afternoon; after sunset, and before sleep. There are usually a fixed number of bowings (facing Mecca with one's back to the world) accompanied by recitation of *Allah akbar* with hands open on each side of the face. The opening *sura* of the Qur'an (already cited) is recited before a full prostration with one's face (nose and forehead) to the ground is made. To the given set of prayers are added voluntary, informal ones. The purpose of the prayers is not the ritual recitation but a total concentration on conversing with Allah submissively.

Third, although giving alms is an act of voluntary charity, *zakat* is in fact a religious taxation, and its collection and redistribution are determined by a variety of factors. The giving of one's wealth, as much as twenty percent of it to the poor, was regarded as a loan made to *Allah* which he will repay manifold. Paying the tax, which originally was fixed in proportion to a Muslim's worth, was an outward sign and manifestation of one's support of the *umma*. The monies were distributed to relations, orphans, travelers, the poor, the needy, slaves, prisoners, and debtors. And as the Qur'an warns the giver:

You who believe, do not cancel your acts of charity by [making] any reproach or scolding like someone who spends his money simply for people to see it while he does not believe in God and the Last Day. He may be compared to a boulder covered with some soil which a rainstorm strikes and leaves bare. They cannot do anything with whatever they have earned. God does not guide such disbelieving folk.[13]

Fourth during the ninth month on the Islamic calendar (Ramadan, the month when the Qur'an came down), orthodox Muslims abstain from eating, drinking, smoking and sex from first light, "when the white thread is discernible from the black" (2:183), until sunset. Fasting is looked upon not as a burdensome, obligatory deprivation, but as a God-given opportunity for each human being to experience poverty, hunger, self-discipline and dedication. Through fasting it is hoped that one will be freed from material desires and more conscious of the poor. As the Qur'an tells us:

You who believe, fasting has been prescribed for you just as it was prescribed for those before you, so that you may do your duty, on days which have been planned ahead. Any of you who is ill or on a journey [should choose] a number of other days. For those who can [scarcely] afford it, making up for it means feeding a poor man. It is even better for anyone who can volunteer some wealth; although it is better yet for you to fast, if you only knew.[14]

Over the thirty-night span, each evening in mosques the Qur'an is recited in its entirety, which concludes at the end of the month with the festival of 'id al-fitr (festival of the breaking of the fast).

The last pillar—the *hajj* (Pilgrimage)—commemorates Muhammad's migration from Mecca to Medina. Once in each Muslim's lifetime, he or she is required, if physically and financially able, to visit the sacred mosque at Mecca during the twelfth month. Only committed Muslims take part in the *hajj* which requires a spirit of sacrifice. Muhammad said that if one performs the pilgrimage with a surrendering spirit (without sex, material gain or wrongful acts), then the pilgrim returns as innocent as on the day of birth.

The *hajj* dramatically reinforces the communal bond of the *umma* for every pilgrim, of every race, language and culture, of every status and educational achievement, all travel dressed in two pieces of white, unsewn cloth. The white dress signifies commonality of intention, action and surrender to Allah. Everyone becomes equal before God; everyone comes with the same intentions. As part of the pilgrimage, on the third of nine days, each Muslim must destroy the idols of head and heart (i.e., force, deception and wealth). In his well-known autobiography, Malcolm X movingly reports his experience at Mecca which caused him to rearrange his thought-patterns, to toss aside previous conclusions, and to realize that he belonged to a community which included the whitest of the white.[15]

The symbolic goal of the journey is located at the center of the Meccan mosque. As a part of the pilgrimage every pilgrim properly circles and kisses the *Ka'ba* (House of God), a cube-shaped building in the great mosque at Mecca which encloses the sacred Black Stone.

The *Ka^cba* is a masonry cube, open to the sky, which is linked to similar houses built by Adam and later rebuilt by Abraham. Originally built in heaven, it has remained intact as the axis upon which the whole world turns. In 630 Muhammad purified the Black Stone of all idols and reaffirmed Islamic faith in Allah. As Allah reveals to Muhammad:

> Thus We set up the House as a resort for mankind and a sanctuary, and [said]: "Adopt Abraham's station as a place for prayer." We entrusted Abraham and Ishmael with cleaning out My house for those who circle around it and are secluded [praying] there, and who bow down on their knees in worship.[16]

While not one of the "Five Pillars" *per se, Jihad* (Holy War) has often been construed as an essential Muslim belief. The conditions for Holy War are carefully spelled out in the Qur'an: there must first be an enemy who threatens one's freedom; one must then try to avoid fighting by faith and prayer; then reason and meditation must be employed to shape moral action; and then, only as a last resort, armed action is to be taken. As the Qur'an says:

> Fight those who fight against you along God's way, yet do not initiate hostilities; God does not love aggressors. Kill them wherever you may catch them, and expel them from anywhere they may have expelled you. Sedition is more serious than killing! Yet do not fight them at the Hallowed Mosque unless they fight you there. If they should fight you, then fight them back; such is the reward for disbelievers. However if they stop, God will be Forgiving, Merciful.[17]

As for those who die fighting in the cause of *Allah,* though they die, they live in the presence of *Allah,* for it is considered a highest honor to so die.

Qur'an

When we come to the Qur'an, we come to the source and central subject of the Muslim story. The word Qur'an comes from a Semitic root which means to recite, to read, to proclaim. The Qur'an is the story of Allah's revelatory discourses transmitted through Gabriel and the messenger Muhammad, and is considered by Muslims to be the literal Word of God (*Kalam Allah*), words with immaculate verbal accuracy from Allah to Gabriel to Muhammad. Called the only standing miracle in all Islam, the Qur'an is referred to as the "well-preserved tablet," the "Criterion," or simply "The Book" (*al-Kitab*), and Muslims as "People of the Book." According to the Qur'an, Moses was given the first covenant, Jesus gave the second (or new covenant) and Muhammad in the Qur'an is given the third (or last covenant).

So holy and so sacrosanct is the Qur'an that to memorize it (*hafiz*) was a mark of the highest piety, to interpret it (*tafsir*) was a religious honor, to recite it was a trained profession, to touch it was a ritual, and to copy it was a sacred task. In fact, no one is to read or touch the Qur'an without first washing ritualistically as before entering a mosque, and when it is read it should rest on a stand. It is the Holy Book because of its divine origin—its miraculous revelation to an illiterate, brooding recluse who spent long hours alone in prayer. Muhammad was chosen, as the Israelites were chosen, to receive and to retransmit, without any conscious interference or manipulation, the speech of God (*Kalam Allah*). The heavenly text of the Qur'an therefore is to Muslims what Christ is to Christians, what Torah is to Jews.

While an authorized version was not established until between 644 and 656 CE, twelve to twenty-four years after the death of the prophet, Muslims claim that it is the only sacred text in all the world's major, classical religions that evolved in the full light of history, that can be authentically attributed to one person, and that stands as an irrepeatable, singularly eloquent, inspired script. In fact, Muslim practitioners claim that the Arabic Qur'an is the most profoundly eloquent and sublimely illuminating script of all canons, and that therefore it must not be read in translation if one is to glean the full resonance of God's voice. As Isma'il Al Faruqi writes: "The Qur'an is the totality of the law of Islam (shariah). . . . There is no path to God except through it, no salvation without it and no holding to anything that diverges from it."[18]

Just as the Qur'an is an assemblage of styles, it also contains an assortment of teachings: religious and scientific; spiritual and mathematical; legal and social. There are doctrinal messages and practices, stories of the prophets and saints whose message is like that of Muhammad, exhortations and laws (toward regulating outer and inner life), and autobiographical details of Muhammad's religious experience. Like a pattern which arabesques through the various *suras,* each teaching is written by God before creation, and then recited, written on bones, skin and paper and memorized by millions of followers.

The Qur'an contains a collection of 114 chapters (*suras*), arranged according to length, from the longest (286 verses) to the shortest. The division into *suras* probably dates back to Muhammad himself, but the further division of *suras* into verses (*ayahs*) came later. The *suras* were written at various times during Muhammad's mission—the shorter *suras* first in Mecca and the longer ones later in Medina. As the number and variety of social and political problems arrived, and as the problem of relating to non-Muslims increased, the *suras* grew longer. Except for *sura* nine, they all begin: "In the name of *Allah,* most gracious and most merciful," and are arranged, less chronologically than to reflect the movement of Muhammad between Medina and Mecca. The titles of each *sura* are taken from the *sura* itself, for originally there were no titles.

There are indications that at the death of Muhammad, some of the passages had already been written down under his supervision, but that he left no instructions about their order. The text we have today was collected and ordered by the third caliph, Uthman, who appointed Zayd ibn Thabit, one of Muhammad's secretaries, to prepare an official text. While there were other versions in circulation, eventually the Uthmanic Qur'an, based on a document in the possession of the daughter of the second caliph Umar, with the aid of governmental pressure, became the officially recognized version.

The Cow

The *sura* which contains the most self-reflection, and which is also the longest, is "The Cow." Said to be "a Qur'an for people who understood" (41:3), a "confirmation of revelations that went before it, and a fuller explanation of the Book" (10:37), the Cow begins with the letters "A", "L" and "M", which are mystical symbols of the esoteric nature of God. These letters are also found prefixed to five other *suras* (2,3,29,30,31,32).[19] Some say that each letter represents an attribute of God. Others say that the letters indicate three names: *Allah*, Jibril (Gabriel) and Muhammad—the source (word) of the Qur'an, the angelic messenger and the earthly prophet. If we look at the nature of the sound which the letters represent, we see that "A" is breathed from the throat, "L" is a palatal from the middle of the mouth and "M" is a labial or lip sound. Symbolically they can be taken as the beginning, middle and end of life which is indeed the content of the *suras*, creation, growth and death.

The Qur'an is said to be sure, true guidance, as in the Hebrew Book of Proverbs a guidance which comes to those who "fear" God. This is the fear of awe, majesty, reverence, and humility before the transcendent glory and almighty majesty of *Allah*. The opening seven verses of this *sura* sum up its remaining verses:

In the name of God, the Mercy-giving, the Merciful!

A.L.M.
    This is the Book which contains no doubt; it means guidance for those who do their duty
    who believe in the Unseen, keep up prayer, and spend something from whatever We have provided them with;
    who believe in what has been sent down to you as well as what was sent down before you,
    While they are convinced about the Hereafter; such people hold on to guidance from their Lord; those will be successful.[20]

What follows is a brief outline of "The Cow," of the distinct statements in the *sura* which present the believer's proper attitude toward the book. The Qur'an, it is said, is:

1. not to be doubted; a guide for the righteous;
2. given to Moses so that the people might be rightly guided;
3. not to be imitated or claimed to be written by man;
4. Allah's revelation through Gabriel written for the faithful and to confirming previous scriptures;
5. not to be denied—those who deny the Book will be surely lost;
6. the revelation of what has already been revealed to Abraham, Ishmael, Isaac, Jacob, Moses, Jesus and other prophets;
7. revealed in the month of Ramadan, a book of guidance with proofs;

8. called the "Book of Allah" and believers the "People of the Book."

The Qur'an is clearly the central axis around which all Muslim teaching and practice revolves and to which all Muslims return whether in prayer, pilgrimage, or silent meditation. In this sense the Qur'an has three nuances: the act of recitation or reminding, the giving of the whole revelation through a recitation, and as any particular revelation that is recited. As we are told in the Qur'an:

> Do not try to hurry it up with your tongue; it is up to Us to collect it, as well as [to know how] to recite it. So whenever We do read it, follow in its reading; * it is then We Who must explain it![21]

NOTES

1. Seyyed Hossein Nasar, *Ideals and Realities of Islam* (Boston: Beacon Press, 1966), 32–33.

2. *Qur'an* 5:5. Unless otherwise noted, all references from the *Qur'an* will be from T.B. Irving's *The Qur'an* (Battleboro, Vermont: Amana Books, 1985.)

3. Muslims trace their spiritual lineage from Abraham through Abraham's "first" son Ishmael by his handmaiden Hagar (Genesis 16), not through Isaac who was born later to Abraham's wife Sarah. Islam is not ethnocentric; in fact only twenty-five percent of its present population is Arabic. Muslims are also comprised of Spaniards, Africans, Turks, Indians, and Palestinians to name a few.

4. *Qur'an* 96:1–5.

5. *Qur'an* 53:1–12.

6. Quoted in *Sacred Texts of the World,* edited by Ninian Smart and Richard Hecht (New York: Crossroad Publishing Company, 1982), 120–71.

7. *Qur'an* 3:138.

8. *Qur'an* 112:1–4.

9. Indries Shah, *The Way of the Sufi* (New York: E.P. Dutton & Co., 1970), 66.

10. *Qur'an* 24:35.

11. *Qur'an* 1:1–7.

12. *Qur'an* 23:11–16.

13. *Qur'an* 2:264.

14. *Qur'an* 2:183–184.

15. Malcolm X, *The Autobiography of Malcolm X* (New York: Ballantine Books, 1973), 340.

16. *Qur'an* 2:118–125.

17. *Qur'an* 2:190–192.

18. Isma'il Ragi Al Faruqi, "The Moment of Islam in the History of Revelation," in *The Great Asian Religions,* 336.

19. A cognate group of letters—"A", "L", "R"—are used to begin other *suras*. The letters

Alif, Lam, Ra) are said to refer to the beginning, middle and final end of a person's spiritual history—one's creation from clots of blood, one's present condition of submission to the will of Allah, and the final judgment which all humans face.

20. *Qur'an* 2:1–5.
21. *Qur'an* 75:16–18.

ISLAMIC JOURNAL EXERCISES

1. Imagine that you, like Muhammad, are the spiritually sensitive, brooding type, who has gone into a desert to meditate in solitude. You are still in the darkness as hours pass by. You seem to lose consciousness momentarily, for when the visionary light appears, you wake up, as if having just awakened from a dream. Imagine that feeling and then without thinking about it, what does the voice in the light say to you? First complete this portion of the exercise and then compare what you have written with Muhammad's own call to recite (in *Sura* 96).

2. Select one of your favorite passages from the Qur'an, silently re-read it, and then write a spontaneously-unthought-out paragraph about that passage. Then re-read the passage aloud and more slowly than normal. When you have finished, write a paragraph about what you realize reading aloud (reciting) that you did not reading silently. You may wish to discuss any insights or ideas or questions you may have about the text.

3. Imagine that you are Muhammad's cousin. You've known him all his life, both before and after marriage. Imagine that you, like Muhammad before his transformational vision, are a non-believer, an agnostic, a secular humanist, whatever; and all of a sudden your cousin Muhammad tries to convert you to the revelation of Allah. What is your immediate response? Have a dialogue with Muhammad in which you question his teaching (e.g., on the Five Pillars; Last Judgment; Prayer; Fasting; Sin; etc.).

4. It is said that there are two ways to interpret the Qur'an—literally or figuratively—and that some passages should be interpreted one way, some the other. How would you interpret the following passage? Can it be interpreted both ways? If so what holds the two interpretations together?

DEFRAUDING
Revealed at Mecca
In the name of Allah, the Beneficent, the Merciful.

1. Woe unto the defrauders:
2. Those who when they take the measure from mankind demand it full,
3. But if they measure unto them or weigh for them, they cause them loss.
4. Do such (men) not consider that they will be raised again.
5. Unto an awful Day,
6. The day when (all) mankind stand before the Lord of the Worlds?

5. Review the discussion and scripture which applies to Holy War. Do you agree with this process or would you alter it in some way or do you totally disagree with it? Provide a response of some kind to the issue of a God-sanctioned war.

6. Compare and contrast the first pillar of Islam ("There is no God but Allah, and Muhammad is his prophet") with the first commandment in Exodus ("I am Yahweh your God . . . you shall have no other Gods before me"). Is the God of Abraham one and the same? Discuss by using quotations from the Qur'an and the Hebrew and Christian scriptures.

7. Re-read the following *sura* slowly to see if you hear a meaning you might not have considered:

> "God is the Light
> Of the heavens and the earth.
> The parable of His Light
> Is as if there were a niche
> And within it a Lamp:
> The Lamp enclosed in Glass.
> The glass as it were
> A brilliant star . . .
> Light upon Light!
> God doth guide
> Whom He will
> To His Light:

8. What is the deepest insight you have gained from reading the Qur'an? Have a dialogue with Muhammad in which you discuss your insight with him to see if it can be deepened.

9.   > God doth set forth parables
>   For me: and God
>   Doth know all things."
>   (XXIV:35)

Discuss the different dimensions of this parable: the niche; the lamp; and the glass. What do each symbolize and how do they create a meaning in union with the other two which would be impossible without such a union? What does the verse mean toward the end which says that God sets forth parables?

10. Reread the events surrounding Muhammad's death. What did he say and what was said about him? How would you compare the way Muhammad died to the way Jesus died or Buddha died?

Selections

Selections from the Qur'an from suras 1, 2, 7, 10, 14, 17, 22, 24, 32, 43, 61, 87, 96, and 110–114 translated by T.B. Irving (Al-Hajj Ta'lim °Ali)

The Qur'an

I

The Opening

In the name of God, the Mercy-giving, the Merciful!

Praise be to God, Lord of the Universe,
the Mercy-giving, the Merciful!
Ruler on the Day for Repayment!
You do we worship and You do we call on for
    help.
Guide us along the Straight Road,
the road of those whom You have favored,
with whom You are not angry,
nor who are lost!

                        [Amen.]

In the name of God, the Mercy-giving, the Merciful!

A.L.M.

1 This is the Book which contains no doubt;
it means guidance for those who do their
duty

    who believe in the Unseen, keep up
prayer, and spend something from whatever We have provided them with;

    who believe in what has been sent
down to you as well as what was sent down
before you,

    While they are convinced about the
Hereafter; such people hold on to guidance
from their Lord; those will be successful.

    It is all the same whether you warn
those who disbelieve or do not warn them;
they still will not believe: God has sealed off
their hearts and their hearing, while over
their sight there hangs a covering; they will
have severe torment.

8 Some people say: "We believe in God and
the Last Day," while they are not believers.

They would like to deceive God and those
who believe, while they merely outwit
themselves and do not even notice it! Their
hearts contain malice so God has increased
their [share of] malice. They will have painful torment because they have been lying.

10 Whenever someone tells them: "Don't act
so depraved on earth," they say: "We are
only improving matters!" They are indeed
mischief makers, but they are not aware of
it. When someone tells them: "Believe just
as other people believe," they say: "Are we
to believe just as simpletons believe?"
Surely they are the fools even though they
do not realize it!

15 Whenever they meet those who believe,
they say: "We believe;" while once they go
off alone with their ringleaders, they say:
"We are with you; we were only joking!"
God will joke with them and let them go on
acting arrogantly in their blind fashion!
Those are the ones who have purchased error at the price of guidance, while their bargain does not profit them nor have they
been guided.

    They may be compared to someone
who kindles a fire, and once it lights up
whatever lies around him, God takes away
their light and leaves them in darkness.
They do not see: deaf, dumb and blind, they
will never respond!

    Or to a raincloud from the sky containing darkness, thunder and lightning; they
stick their fingers in their ears to ward off
death because of the thunderclaps, for God
will soon be rounding up disbelievers.

    Lightning almost snatches their sight
away: each time it lights things up for
them, they walk along in it, while when
darkness settles down on them, they stand
stockstill. If God wanted, He would take
away their hearing and eyesight; God is Capable of everything!

21 Mankind, worship your Lord Who created
you as well as those before you, so that you
may do your duty! [He is] the One Who has

made the earth a carpet for you and had the sky built above you, and sent water to pour down from the sky and brought forth fruit by means of it as sustenance for you. Do not set up rivals for God while you know [better].

If you (all) are in any doubt about what We have sent down to Our servant, then bring a chapter like it and call in your witnesses besides God if you are so truthful. If you do not—and you will never do so—then heed the Fire which has been prepared for disbelievers whose fuel is mankind and stones! Proclaim to those who believe and perform honorable deeds that they will have gardens through which rivers flow. Each time they are provided with fruits from it for their sustenance, they will say: "This is what we were provided with before!" They will be given similar things and have clean-living spouses there. They will live in it for ever!

God does not hesitate to compare things to a mosquito nor to anything bigger than it. Those who believe realize that it is the Truth from their Lord, while those who disbelieve say: "What does God want in such a comparison?" He lets so many go astray through it, and guides many by means of it. Yet only immoral persons are led astray by it! Those who break God's covenant after they have pledged to keep it, and sever whatever God has ordered to be joined, and act depraved on earth, will be the losers. How can you disbelieve in God when you once were dead and He furnished you with life? Soon He will let you die once more, then bring you back to life again; then unto Him will you return! He is the One Who has created everything that is on earth for you; then He soared up to Heaven and perfected it as seven heavens. He is Aware of everything!

30 So when your Lord told the angels: "I am placing an overlord on earth", they said: "Will You place someone there who will corrupt it and shed blood, while we hymn Your praise and sanctify You?" He said: "I know something you do not know."

He taught Adam all the names of everything; then presented them to the angels, and said: "Tell me the names of these if you are so truthful." They said: "Glory be to You; we have no knowledge except whatever You have taught us. You are the Aware, the Wise!" He said: "Adam, tell them their names."

Once he had told them their names, He said: "Did I not tell you that I know the Unseen in Heaven and Earth? I know whatever you disclose and whatever you have been hiding."

So We told the angels: "Bow down on your knees before Adam." They [all] knelt down except for Diabolis. He refused and acted proudly, and became a disbeliever.

We said: "Adam, settle down in the Garden, both you and your wife, and eat freely from it anywhere either of you may wish. Yet do not approach this tree lest you become wrongdoers."

Satan made them stumble over it and had them both expelled from where they had been [living]. We said: "Clear out! Some of you will [become] enemies of others. You will have a resting place on earth and enjoyment for a while."

Adam received words [of inspiration] from his Lord and he turned towards Him. He is the Relenting, the Merciful!

We said: "Clear out from it together! If you should be handed guidance from Me, then anyone who follows My guidance will have no fear nor will they be saddened; while those who disbelieve and reject Our signs will become inmates of the Fire; they shall remain in it!"

40 Children of Israel, remember My favor which I have shown you, and fulfil My agreement! I shall fulfil your covenant. I am the One you should revere! Believe in what I have sent down to confirm what you

already have, and do not be the first to disbelieve in it. Do not sell My signs for a paltry price. I am the One you should heed! Do not cloak Truth with falsehood nor hide the Truth while you realize it.

Keep up prayer, pay the welfare tax, and worship along with those who bow their heads. Are you ordering people to be virtuous while forgetting it yourselves, even as you recite the Book? Will you not use your reason?

46 Seek help through patience and prayer, since it is exacting except for the submissive who assume they will meet their Lord, and that they will return to Him.

118 Those who do not know (anything) say: "If God would only speak to us, or a sign were brought us!" Likewise those before them said the same as they are saying; their hearts are all alike. We have explained signs for folk who are certain. We have sent you with the Truth as a herald and a warner: you will not be questioned about the inmates of Hades.

120 Neither the Jews nor the Christians will ever be satisfied with you until you follow their sect. SAY:

"God's guidance means [real] guidance!"

If you followed their whims after the knowledge which has come to you, you would not have any patron nor supporter against God. Those whom We have brought the Book, recite it in the way it should be recited; such men believe in it. Those who disbelieve in it will be the losers.

122 O Children of Israel, remember My favor which I bestowed on you, and how I preferred you over [everyone in] the Universe. Heed a day when no soul will make amends in any way for any other soul and no adjustment will be accepted from it nor any intercession benefit it. They will not be supported.

When his Lord tested Abraham by means of [certain] words, and he fulfilled

them, He said: "I am going to make you into a leader for mankind." He said: "What about my offspring?"; He said: "My pledge does not apply to evildoers."

125 Thus We set up the House as a resort for mankind and a sanctuary, and [said]: "Adopt Abraham's station as a place for prayer." We entrusted Abraham and Ishmael with cleaning out My house for those who circle around it and are secluded [praying] there, and who bow down on their knees in worship.

So Abraham said: "My Lord, make this countryside safe and provide any of its people who believe in God and the Last Day with fruit from it." He said: "Even anyone who disbelieves, I'll let enjoy things for a while, then drive him along towards the torment of Fire. How awful is such a goal!"

Thus Abraham along with Ishmael laid the foundations for the House: "Our Lord, accept this from us! Indeed You are the Alert, the Aware! Our Lord, leave us peacefully committed to You, and make our offspring into a nation which is at peace with You. Show us our ceremonies and turn towards us. You are so Relenting, the Merciful! Our Lord, send a messenger in among them from among themselves who will recite Your verses to them and teach them the Book and wisdom! He will purify them, for You are the Powerful, the Wise!"

130 Who would shrink from [joining] Abraham's sect except someone who fools himself? We selected him during worldly life, while in the Hereafter he will be among the honorable ones. So when his Lord told him: "Commit yourself to [live in] peace"; he said: "I have already committed myself peacefully to the Lord of the Universe!"

Abraham commissioned his sons with it [as a legacy], and [so did] Jacob: "My sons, God has selected your religion for you. Do not die unless you are Muslims." Or were you present as death appeared for Jacob, when he said to his sons: "What will you serve after I am gone?" They said: "We shall worship your God and the God of your forefathers Abraham, Ishmael and Isaac: God Alone! We are committed peacefully to Him."

That is a nation which has already passed away: there awaits it whatever it has earned, while you will have what you have earned. You will not be questioned about what they have been doing.

135 They say: "Become Jews or Christians; you will [then] be guided." SAY: "Rather Abraham's sect, [for he was] a seeker [after Truth]; he was no associator [of others with God Alone]." SAY: "We believe in God and what has been sent down to us, and what was sent down to Abraham, Ishmael, Isaac, Jacob and their descendants, and what was given Moses and Jesus, and what was given the [other] prophets by their Lord. We do not discriminate against any one of them and are committed [to live] in peace to Him."

3
The House of ᶜImrān

In the name of God, the Mercy-giving, the Merciful!

1 A.L.M.

God, there is no deity except Him,

the Living, the Eternal!

4 He has sent down the Book to you with Truth to confirm whatever existed before it. He sent down the Torah and the Gospel in the past as guidance for mankind; He has (also) sent down the Standard. Those who disbelieve in God's signs will have severe torment; God is Powerful, the Master of Retribution!

5 Nothing is hidden from God, on Earth nor in Heaven. He it is Who shapes you just as He wishes in [your mothers'] wombs. There is no deity except Him, the Powerful, the

Wise! He is the One Who sent you down the Book which contains decisive verses. They [form] the basis of the Book; while others are allegorical.

Those whose hearts are prone to falter follow whatever is allegorical in it, seeking to create dissension by giving [their own] interpretation of it. Yet only God knows its interpretation; those who are versed in knowledge say: "We believe in it; it all comes from our Lord!" However only prudent persons bear it in mind.

Our Lord, do not let our hearts falter once You have guided us; grant us mercy from Your presence, for You are the Bountiful! Our Lord, You will be gathering mankind together on a day there is no doubt about; God will never go back on the Promise!

16 God testifies there is no deity except Himself, and so do the angels and persons possessing knowledge. Maintaining fairplay, there is no deity except Him, the Powerful, the Wise.

Religion with God means [Islam:]
a commitment to [live in] peace.

Those who have already been given the Book did not disagree until after knowledge had come to them, out of envy for one another. Anyone who disbelieves in God's signs [will find] God is Prompt in reckoning!

20 If they should argue with you, then say: "I have committed my person peacefully to God, and [so has] anyone who follows me. Tell both those who have been given the Book as well as the unlettered: "Have you become Muslims?" If they commit themselves to [live in] peace, then they are guided; while if they turn away, you need merely to state things plainly. God is Observant of [His] worshippers.

41 So the angels said: "Mary, God has selected you and purified you. He has selected you over [all] the women in the Universe. Mary,

devote yourself to your Lord; fall down on your knees and bow alongside those who so bow down."

Such is some information about the Unseen We have revealed to you. You were not in their presence as they cast [lots with] their pens [to see] which of them would be entrusted with Mary. You were not in their presence while they were so disputing.

45 Thus the angels said: "Mary, God announces word to you about someone whose name will be Christ Jesus, the son of Mary, [who is] well regarded in this world and the Hereafter, and one of those drawn near [to God] He will speak to people while still an infant and as an adult, and will be an honorable person." She said: "My Lord, how can I have a child while no human being has ever touched me?"

50 He said: "That is how God creates anything He wishes. Whenever He decides upon some matter, He merely tells it: 'Be!', and it is. He will teach him the Book and wisdom, plus the Torah and the Gospel as a messenger to the Children of Israel: 'I have brought you a sign from your Lord. I shall create something in the shape of a bird for you out of clay, and blow into it so it will become a [real] bird with God's permission. I shall cure those who are blind from birth and lepers, and revive the dead with God's permission. I shall announce to you what you may eat and what you should store up in your houses. That will serve as a sign for you if you are believers, confirming what I have already [learned] from the Torah. I shall permit you some things which have been forbidden you. I have brought you a sign from your Lord, so heed God and obey me!

God is both my Lord and your Lord, so serve Him. This is a Straight Road!' "

4

Women

150 Those who disbelieve in God and His mes-

sengers, and want to distinguish between God and His messengers, and say: "We believe in some and disbelieve in others"; wanting to adopt a course in between, are really disbelievers. We have reserved humiliating torment for disbelievers. Those who believe in God and His messengers, and do not single out any one of them [especially], will be given their earnings. God is Forgiving, Merciful.

153 The People of the Book ask you to have a book sent down from Heaven for them. They asked Moses for something even greater than that, and said: "Show us God directly." The Thunderbolt caught them in their wrongdoing.

Then they adopted the Calf even after explanations had come to them. We still pardoned that, and gave Moses clear authority. We raised the Mountain up over them as their charter, and told them: "Enter the gate while on your knees." We told them [further]: "Do not go too far on the Sabbath," and made a solemn pledge with them.

Because of their breaking the charter, their disbelief in God's signs, their killing the prophets without any right to do so, and their saying: "Our hearts are covered over," instead, God has stamped them with their disbelief. They only believe a little because of their disbelief and their talking such terrible slander about Mary and (also) for their saying: "We killed God's messenger Christ Jesus, the son of Mary!" They neither killed nor crucified him, even though it seemed so to them. Those who disagree about it are in doubt concerning it; they have no [real] knowledge about it except by following conjecture. No one is certain they killed him! Rather God lifted him up towards Himself. God is Powerful, Wise!

160 There is nobody from the People of the Book but who will believe in him before his death, while on Resurrection Day he will act as a witness against them. Because of

wrongdoing on the part of those who are Jews, We have forbidden them certain wholesome things which had been permitted them; and because they blocked off so many people from God's way and took usury although they had been forbidden to, and idly consumed other people's wealth, We have reserved painful torment for those among them who are disbelievers. Yet those of them who are versed in knowledge, as well as believers, believe in what is sent down to you and what has been sent down [to those] before you; and We shall give a splendid wage to those who keep up prayer and pay the welfare tax, and who believe in God and the Last Day.

163 We have inspired you just as We inspired Noah and the prophets following him, and as We inspired Abraham, Ishmael, Isaac, Jacob and the patriarchs, and Jesus, Job, Jonah, Aaron and Solomon; and just as We gave David the Psalms.

We have told you about some messengers [sent] previously, while other messengers We have not yet told you about—God spoke directly to Moses—messengers bringing good news plus a warning so that mankind would have no argument against God once the messengers [had come]. God is Powerful, Wise.

170 Nevertheless God bears witness through what He has sent down to you; He sent it down with His (own full) knowledge. And angels so testify, though God suffices as a Witness. Those who disbelieve and obstruct God's way have strayed far afield. Those who disbelieve and act wrongfully will not find that God will forgive them nor guide them along any road except the road to Hell, to remain there for ever. That will be so easy for God [to do]! O mankind, the Messenger has brought you the Truth from your Lord, so believe, since it is best for you. If you should disbelieve, God still holds whatever is in Heaven and Earth; God is Aware, Wise.

People of the Book, do not exaggerate in [practising] your religion and tell nothing except the Truth about God. Christ Jesus, the son of Mary, was merely God's messenger and His word which He cast into Mary, and a spirit [proceeding] from Him.

Believe in God [Alone] and His messengers, and do not say: "Three!" Stopping [it] will be better for you. God is only One God; glory be to Him, beyond His having any son! He owns whatever is in Heaven and whatever is on Earth; God suffices as a Trustee.

17
The Night Journey
(Glory!; or The Children of Israel)

In the name of God, the Mercy-giving, the Merciful!

1 Glory be to Him, Who had His servant travel by night from the Hallowed Mosque to the Further Mosque whose surroundings We have blessed, so We might show him some of Our signs! He is the Alert, the Observant!

We gave Moses the Book and granted it as guidance for the Children of Israel: "Do not accept any defender except Me!" [They were] offspring [of those] whom We put on board with Noah; he was a grateful servant. We decreed in the Book concerning the Children of Israel: "You will create havoc on earth twice, and display great haughtiness."

5 When the first of both warnings came, we despatched servants of Ours to inflict severe violence upon you (all). They rampaged through [your] homes, and it served as a warning which was acted upon. Then We offered you another chance against them, and reinforced you with wealth and children, and granted you more manpower. If you have acted kindly, you acted kindly

towards yourselves, while if you committed any evil, it was towards [yourselves] as well.

Thus the warning about the next one came along to trouble your persons, and so they would enter the Mosque just as they had entered it in the first place, so they might utterly annihilate anything they overcame.

Perhaps your Lord may show mercy to you. If you should turn back, We will go back (too) and turn Hell into a confinement for disbelievers!

10 This Qur'ān guides one to something that is more straightforward and reassures believers who perform honorable actions; they shall have great earnings. Nevertheless We have reserved painful torment for those who do not believe in the Hereafter.

19
Mary

16 Mention in the Book how Mary withdrew from her people to an Eastern place. She chose to be secluded from them. We sent her Our spirit, who presented himself to her as a full-grown human being. She said: "I take refuge with the Mercy-giving from you, unless you are someone who does his duty."

20 He said: "I am only your Lord's messenger to bestow a clean-living boy on you." She said: "How shall I have a boy when no human being has ever touched me, nor am I a loose woman?" He said: "Thus your Lord has said: 'It is a simple matter for Me [to do]. We will grant him as a sign for mankind and a mercy from Ourself.' It is a matter that has been decided."

So she conceived him, and withdrew to a remote place to have him. Labor pains came over her by the trunk of a datepalm. She said: "If only I had died before this, and been forgotten, overlooked!"

25 Someone called out to her from below where she was: "Don't feel so sad! Your Lord has placed a brook at your feet. Shake the trunk of the datepalm towards you so it will drop some fresh dates on you. Eat and drink, and refresh yourself. Should you see even a single human being, then say: "I have vowed to keep a fast to the Mercy-giving whereby I'll never speak to any person today!" "

She carried him back to her family. They said: "Mary, you have brought something hard to believe! Kinswoman of Aaron, your father was no evil man, nor was your mother a loose woman." She pointed to him. They said: "How shall we talk to someone who is a child in the cradle?"

30 He said: "I am God's servant. He has given me the Book and made me a prophet. He has made me blessed wherever I may be, and commissioned me to pray and [pay] the welfare tax so long as I live; and [to act] considerate towards my mother. He has not made me domineering, hard to get along with. Peace be on the day I was born, and the day I shall die and the day I am raised to life again!"

Such was Jesus, the son of Mary; [it is] a true statement which they are still puzzling over. It is not God's role to adopt a son. Glory be to Him! Whenever He determines upon some matter, He merely tells it: "Be!", and it is. God is my Lord and your Lord, so worship Him [Alone]. This is a Straight Road [to follow].

24
Light

In the name of God, the Mercy-giving, the Merciful!

1 [This is] a chapter We have sent down and ordained.
We send clear signs down in it
so that you (all) may be reminded.

Flog both the adulterous woman and the adulterous man with a hundred lashes, and do not let any pity for either party distract you from [complying with] God's religion if you believe in God and the Last Day. Have a group of believers witness their punishment. An adulterous man may only marry an adulterous woman or one who associates [others with God]; while an adulterous woman may only be married to an adulterous man or one who associates [others with God]. Such [conduct] is forbidden to believers.

32 Marry off any single persons among you, as well as your honorable servants and maids. If they are poor, God will enrich them from His bounty. God is Boundless, Aware. Yet let those who do not find [any way to] marry, hold off until God enriches them out of His bounty.

Should those whom your right hands control desire their freedom, then draw up such a writ for them if you recognize anything worthwhile in them. Give them some of God's wealth which He has given you. Do not force your girls [whom you control] into prostitution so that you may seek the display of worldly life, if they want to preserve their chastity. Anyone who forces them (to do otherwise) [will find] God is Forgiving, Merciful, even after forcing them to. We have sent you down clarifying signs and an example in those who have passed on before you, as well as instruction for the heedful.

35 God is the Light of Heaven and Earth! His light may be compared to a niche in which there is a lamp; the lamp is in a glass; the glass is just as if it were a glittering star kindled from a blessed olive tree, [which is] neither Eastern nor Western, whose oil will almost glow though fire has never touched it. Light upon light, God guides anyone He wishes to His light. God composes parables for mankind; God is Aware of everything!

There are houses God has permitted to be built where His name is mentioned; in them

He is glorified morning and evening by men whom neither business nor trading distract from remembering God, keeping up prayer, and paying the welfare tax. They fear a day when their hearts and eyesight will feel upset unless God rewards them for the finest things they may have done, and gives them even more out of His bounty. God provides for anyone He wishes without any reckoning!

Those who disbelieve [will find] their deeds [will disappear] like a mirage on a desert; the thirsty man will reckon it is water till, as he comes up to it, he finds it is nothing. Yet he finds God [stands] beside him and he must render Him his account; God is Prompt in reckoning!

40 Or like darkness on the unfathomed sea: one wave covers up another wave, over which there [hang] clouds; layers of darkness, one above the other! When he stretches out his hand, he can scarcely see it. Anyone whom God does not grant light to will have no light!

56
The Inevitable

In the name of God, the Mercy-giving, the Merciful!

When the Inevitable arrives no one will deny its happening, humbling, exalting!

10 The earth will be rocked with a jolt and the mountains crumble to pieces and become dust that is scattered about. You will form three groups: the Companions on the Right (What do the Companions on the Right

[mean]?); the Companions on the Left (What do the Companions on the Unlucky side [mean]?); and the Pioneers will be out there leading!

20 Those will be the nearest in gardens of bliss, a multitude from early men and a few from later ones on couches set close together, leaning back on them, facing one another. Immortal youths will stroll around them with glasses, pitchers, and a cup from a fountain which will not upset them nor dull their senses; and any fruit that they may choose, and the meat from any fowl they may desire; and bright-eyed damsels [chaste] just like treasured pearls, as a reward for what they have been doing. They will not hear any idle talk there nor any fault-finding, merely people saying: "Peace! Peace!"

30 The Companions on the Right—what about

40 the Companions on the Right? [They will be] among hawthorns trimmed of their thorns, and bananas piled bunch on bunch, with their shade spread out, water pouring forth, and plenty of fruit which is neither rationed nor forbidden, and padded furniture raised [off the floor]. We have produced special women and made them (ever) virgins, easy to get along with and of their same age, for the Companions on the Right, a multitude from early men as well as a multitude from later ones.

41 The Companions on the Unlucky side, what about the Companions on the Left? In a scorching wind, scalding water, and the shade of pitch-black smoke, which is neither cool nor refreshing. They had been luxuriating before that happened and persisted in awesome blasphemy, and kept on saying: "When we have died and become dust and bones, will we be raised up again? Along with our earliest forefathers?"

50 SAY: "The earlier and the later ones will be gathered together for an appointment on a well-known day. Then you mistaken rejectors will be eating something from the In-fernal Tree, filling (your) bellies with it and drinking scalding water in addition, lapping it up, the way thirsty [camels] drink."

60 Such will be their fare on the Day for Repayment! We created you, if you would only acknowledge it. Have you ever considered what you emit? Did you create it, or are We its Creators? We have ordained death for (all of) you; no one will get ahead to prevent Us from changing your attributes, and transforming you into something you would never recognize.

You know about the first transformation, if you will only recall it. Have you considered what you plant as crops? Do you farm it or are We the Farmers? If We so wished, We would turn it into chaff so you would do nothing but exclaim: "We are debt-ridden; in fact, we are destitute!"

70 Have you ever considered the water you drink? Do you pour it down from the rain-clouds or are We its Pourers? If We so wished, We might make it brackish. If you would only act grateful!

Have you considered the Fire you kindle? Are you the ones who grow its trees [for firewood] or are We their Growers? We have granted it as a Reminder and enjoyment for those living in the wilderness.

So celebrate your Lord's almighty name!

75 Yet I swear by the stars' positions (it is a serious oath, if you only knew it!) that it is a Noble Qur'ān [kept] as a treasured Book which none but the purified may touch, something sent down by the Lord of the Universe.

Are you (all) trying to dodge this report? Are you making [the fact] that you reject it into your means of livelihood? Why not

—when [your soul] leaps to your throat [at death] and you are then observing, (We are even Nearer to it than you are, even though you do not notice it)—

provided you are not under any obligation, answer back if you are so truthful . . . !

90 Thus if he is one of those who are drawn close [he will have] contentment, fragrance, and a garden of bliss—while if he is one of the Companions on the Right: "Peace be on you" [will be the greeting] from the Companions on the Right.

However if he is one of the mistaken rejectors a welcome of scalding water plus a roasting in Hades [will await him]. This is the absolute Truth;

69

Reality

In the name of God, the Mercy-giving, the Merciful!

1 Reality!
What is reality?
What will make you recognize
what reality is like?

Thamūd and ᶜĀd denied [they would face] disaster. As for Thamūd, they were wiped out by the Thunderbolt. As for ᶜĀd, they were wiped out by a furiously howling gale. He loosed it on them for seven grueling nights and eight days. You would see folk collapsing in it as if they were hollow palm trunks. Do you see any survivors from them?

10 Pharaoh came, as well as those before him, and the places Overthrown through [their own] misdeeds; they defied their Lord's messenger, so He seized them with a tightening grip. When the water overflowed, We loaded you on the vessel, so We might set it up as a Reminder for you and so (your) attentive ears might retain it.

When a single blast is blown on the Trumpet and the earth is lifted up along with the mountains and they are both flattened by a single blow, the Event will take place on that day! The sky will split open and seem flimsy that day while angels [will stand] along its edges. Eight [in all] will bear your Lord's throne above them on that day.

20 On that day you will (all) be arraigned; no secret of yours will remain hidden. Anyone who is given his book in his right hand will say: "Here, read my book! I always thought I would face my reckoning!" He will be in pleasant living in a lofty garden whose clusters [of fruit] will hang within easy reach. "Eat and drink to your heart's content because of what you sent on ahead in bygone days."

However anyone who is given his book in his left hand will say: "It's too bad for me; if only my book had not been given me, I would not have known my reckoning! If it had only been the Sentence [once and for all]! My money has not helped me out; my authority has been wiped out on me."

30 "Take him off and handcuff him! Then let Hades roast him! Then padlock him to a chain gang seventy yards long. He did not believe in God Almighty nor ever urge [others] to feed the needy. He has no close friend here today, nor any food except for some garbage which only sinners eat."

40 Yet I swear by whatever you observe and what you do not observe, that it is a statement [made] by a noble messenger. It is no poet's statement; how little do you believe! Nor is it some fortune teller's statement; how little do you think things over! [It is] something sent down by the Lord of the Universe.

If he had mouthed some [false] statements about Us, We would have seized him by the right hand; then cut off his main artery. Not one of you would have prevented it!

50 It is a Reminder for the heedful:
We know too that some of you will reject it.
It means despair for disbelievers;
yet it is the absolute Truth!
So hymn your Lord's almighty name!

75
Resurrection

In the name of God, the Mercy-giving, the Merciful!

I do swear by Resurrection Day,
as I swear by the rebuking soul,
does man reckon We shall never
gather his bones together [again]?

Of course We are Capable of reshaping
even his fingertips. Yet man wants to carouse right out in the open. He asks: "When
will Resurrection Day be?"

10 When one's sight is dazzled,
and the moon is eclipsed,
as the sun and moon are brought together,
on that day (every)man will say:
"Where is there any escape?"

Of course there will be no sanctuary;
recourse will be only with your Lord on that
day. Man will be notified that day about
anything he has sent on ahead or else held
back. Indeed man holds evidence even
against himself although he may proffer his
excuses.

Do not try to hurry it up with your
tongue; it is up to Us to collect it, as well as
[to know how] to recite it. So whenever We
do read it, follow in its reading; it is then We
Who must explain it!

20 Indeed how you (all) love the fleeting present while you neglect the Hereafter! Some
faces will be radiant on that day, looking
toward their Lord; while other faces will be
scowling on that day, thinking that some
impoverishing blow will be dealt them. Indeed when it reaches as high as one's collarbone and someone says: "Who is such a
wizard?", he will suppose that it means
leave-taking while one shin will twist
around the other shin [to keep it from moving]; towards your Lord will the Drive be on
that day!

30 He was not trusting and did not pray,
but said: "No!" and turned away.
Then he stalked off haughtily
to his family, [though] closer to you
and even closer! Then closer
to you [lies your doom]
and still closer!

40 Does man reckon
he'll be left forlorn?
Was he not once a drop
of ejected semen? Then he became
a clot, so [God]
created and fashioned [him]
and made him into two sexes,
male and female. Is such a Being
not Able to revive the dead?

96
The Clot
(or Read!)

In the name of God, the Mercy-giving, the Merciful!

1 READ in the name of your Lord Who creates,
creates man from a clot!
READ, for your Lord is most Generous;
[it is He] Who teaches
by means of the pen,
teaches man what he does not know.

5 However man acts so arrogant,
for he considers he is self-sufficient.
Yet to your Lord will be the Return!

Have you seen someone who stops a
worshipper as he prays?

Have you considered whether he is
[looking] for guidance or ordering heedfulness? Have you seen whether he has rejected [the message] and turned away?

Does he not know that God sees [everything]? Of course not! Yet if he does not
stop, We shall catch him by his forelock!
Such a lying sinful forelock!

Let him appeal to his henchmen: We
shall appeal to the avenging [angels]. Of

course, do not obey him; <u>bow down</u> on your knees, and come closer!

97
Power (or Fate)

These 5 Meccan verses were revealed after He Frowned! 80 and before <u>The Sun</u> 91. This chapter is thus one of the first to be revealed.

    The 'Night of Power' refers to one of the last ten days during the month of Ramadān, when the Qur'ān was first sent down to Muhammad. This passage might be compared with 24:v for a similar hymn to God's power or glory, as this is manifested in His light.

In the name of God, the Mercy-giving, the Merciful!

*We have sent it down on the Night of <u>Power</u>!
*What will make you realize
what the Night of <u>Power</u> is like?

*The Night of <u>Power</u> is better
than a thousand months. Angels and the Spirit descend on it on every errand

with their Lord's permission; [it means] peace till the approach of daybreak.

112
Sincerity
(or [God's] Oneness)

In the name of God, the Mercy-giving, the Merciful!

SAY: "God is <u>Unique</u>!
God is the Source [for everything];
He has not fathered anyone
nor was He fathered, and there
is nothing comparable to Him!"

113
Dawn

In the name of God, the Mercy-giving, the Merciful!

SAY: "I take refuge with the Lord of <u>Dawn</u>
from the mischief which He has created,
and from the evil of dusk
as it settles down, and from the mischief
of women spitting on knots and from
the evil of some envier when <u>he envies</u>."

Conclusion ENCOUNTER OF SACRED SCRIPTURES

Religious scholars have insightfully called the latter part of the twentieth century the second axial age. The term "axial" derives from the Greek word for "value," and refers to the first time in human history that local customs and beliefs were replaced by universal values. The philosopher Karl Jaspers in *The Origin and Goal of History* locates the first axial age between the ninth and the sixth centuries BCE. This represented to him a time when the spiritual foundations of China, India, Persia, Palestine and Greece were being formed (e.g., Hindu Rishis and Hebrew Prophets, 800 BCE, Confucius, Lao Tzu, and Gautama Buddha, 500 BCE, and Socrates and Plato, 400 BCE, while Jesus 3 BCE to 30 CE and Mohammad 570 to 632 CE are seen as developments of Judaism). The point is that by the sixth century BCE human wisdom and achievement reached a pinnacle in its evolution.

If this period represents the first religiously pivotal age in human history, we are now entering a second in which the universal values of unique sacred traditions are now entering into vital dialogues with one another.[1] It is now impossible to study any single faith tradition without being aware of, and understanding, the world religious context. We are currently entering a multinational, pan-cultural epoch in world history in which spiritual and religious insights and teachings have begun to influence and cross-fertilize each other. As Astronaut Russell Schweikart of the Apollo 9 flight crew said while on mission to the moon: "From out here there are no limits, no frames, no boundaries; from here the earth is a whole."

In the opening chapter, it was noted that one studies sacred traditions and sacred texts in a way analogous to making a pilgrimage. First the traveler must depart from what is most familiar (location, worldview) to enter into a new matrix (the primary texts). Then, after crossing over into another cultural self-expression, the reader returns with new insights. It is with this return that we will conclude because finally the question we want to answer is: So what? Of what personal value is the study of sacred scriptures?

It is necessary, at this point, to answer the question from a personal perspective. In what follows I will outline ways in which reading and understanding eastern texts has both clarified and extended my perceptions of the Gospel images of Jesus. This is not to suggest that my viewpoints are any more interesting or important than anyone else's. I am suggesting rather that it is important for the reader to reflect upon personal worldviews and deepest convictions in light of these sacred stories. It is only then that the interpretative process is completed, only then that intrapersonal learning occurs.

Facing East

As I look back at my initial introduction to the world's sacred traditions, what first inspired me to read more were their inner actualizations of mystery and ritual. India deeply impressed me with its openness to the righteous action of other faiths, with its substitution of both/and for either/or ways of thinking, with its emphasis on actualized, spiritual teachers, and with its correlating insistence upon actualizing true self.

I was immediately and am still grasped by the Hindu understanding that despite anything we say about the ultimate Brahman, we must also say "not this," "not that" (*neti, neti*). Brahman cannot be named and has no attributes, yet is given three hundred and thirty million names and has the attributes of being (*sat*), consciousness (*chit*) and bliss (*ananda*). Brahman is thus both with and without description, for Brahman breathes breathlessly and speaks wordlessly. India showed me the need to balance theological analogies with mystical negations.

As a teacher of religious studies, I was subsequently impressed with Confucius' method of reanimating tradition, with his transformal attitude toward ritual behavior, and his harmonization of the sacred and the secular. Confucius selectively investigated the classics, transmitted them with reanimated meanings, and thereby restored an ancient harmony between teacher, taught and the teaching. After reading the Analects, I realized that this reanimation process is a key for understanding sacred texts, for until I can repeat a story in my own words, I have not fully integrated it.

Equally and oppositely, Taoism carried me back into the hollow root of nature. Its flow invigorated my awareness of nature's inner face, of her ever-changing rhythms. Whether in the Tao Te Ching or in Chuang Tzu's stories, I was magnetized by the image of what Eliot calls "the still point at the center of the turning world." Taoist mysticism provided me with a bridge to the ch'an patriarchs who point directly to a pathless path, a dharmaless dharma, a ch'an beyond ch'an. The more I pondered Bodhidharma's four truths—not depending on words or letters; beyond scriptures; direct pointing; heart-mind to heart-mind—the more I understood the teachings of the sixth and last patriarch, Hui Neng. In the Platform Sutra, he notes that there is nothing inherently wrong with sutra-reciting; rather, it is necessary to turn round the sutra, not to be turned round by it.[2]

Upon hearing this, Fa Ta was enlightened to the necessity of approaching scriptures without holding any pre-conceived, arbitrary beliefs. I realized that as long as I tried to understand any sacred text through its own theological interpretations, I was, in Hui Neng's terms, being turned round by the text. And I realized that one could turn round (understand) one's own scriptures by reading them alongside similar texts from other traditions.

CROSS-REANIMATION OF SACRED TEXTS

In this section I want to indicate ways in which my dialogue with eastern texts has helped me to understand the Gospels, especially through the cross-reanimation of key texts. First however let me clarify what I mean by the cross-reanimation process.

In this procedure one sacred text inner-faces with another (whether two selections from the same canon, or two texts from differing canons). That is, two texts meet and dialogue within the reader's educated imagination. Each text is therein reanimated, more available to interpretation.

The writings of Samuel Beckett suggest an analogical example of this process in my life. After composing two novels in his native tongue, Beckett decided to write in French and then to translate his own words back into English. *Waiting for Godot,* his translation of *En Attendant Godot* for example, has a precision and a potency that the English without the French original would never have had. In other words he conceived the play in French so that his own English became foreign, became aesthetically distanced.

In a similar way, it was necessary for my native religious tongue (Christianity) to become foreign, and for a foreign tongue (the eastern) to become, for a time, as if native. When I then viewed eastern insights alongside New Testament images of Jesus, those images gained a transformational potency for me. As will be illustrated, this cross-reanimational level of scriptural interpretation involves placing two different texts side-by-side, reading them in each other's light, and, in that associative framework, discovering a revitalized understanding of one through the other. I will now briefly describe the results of three such cross-reanimational dialogues: the Aum of Jesus, the Tao of Jesus, and the Zen of Jesus.

THE AUM OF JESUS

India has always been attracted to Jesus as another *avatar,* like Krishna, like Buddha. One day while walking in a grove of trees, Sri Ramakrishna, a nineteenth century Hindu saint, had a vision of Christ. Four days earlier he had experienced a living and effulgent vision of the Madonna and Child. Ramakrishna realized from these visions that "this is Jesus, who poured out his heart's blood for the redemption of mankind. . . . The Son of Man then embraced Sri Ramakrishna and entered into him, and Sri Ramakrishna went into *samadhi,* the state of transcendental consciousness."[3] This is one of many such stories the religious pilgrim hears in India, stories which acknowledge the avataric power of the Christ.

Theologically speaking, Abhishiktananda in the *Hindu-Christian Meeting Point* further suggests a correlation between "Aum" in the Upanishads and the "Logos" in St. John's "Prologue." As we recall, the Gospel of John begins:

> In the beginning was the Word;
> the Word was with in God's presence,
> and the Word was God.
> He was present to God in the beginning.[4]

Vac (Word, Speech) is the closest Sanskrit equivalent to Logos, if Logos is understood as "Word." Grammatically feminine, Vac is primordial mystery, the whole of the *sruti* (the Hindu's sacred texts). Before creation, Vac is the sound Aum (the undifferentiated sound or breath of Brahman).

HARIH AUM! AUM, the word, is all this. A clear explanation of it is as follows: All that is past, present, and future is, indeed, Aum. And whatever else there is, beyond the threefold division of time—that also is truly Aum.[5]

Beyond waking consciousness, dream consciousness, and deep sleep consciousness, Aum is essence of supreme consciousness (the Atman to be realized). One who actualizes Atman hears the soundless sound of aum which yogins hear in deep meditation, a sound whose vibrational pitches induce profound mediative states.

When I reread John's "Prologue" with this in mind, I realized that there is a wordless dimension to the Logos, what can be called the Aum of Logos, and that the Logos may well be manifested, though unnamed, within other cultural expressions. I came to experience the presence of Christ in the silence of a wordless sound.

In the Bhagavad Gita this wordless sound becomes the Light which becomes Krishna. Lord Krishna says I am: The Father and Mother of this Universe (9:17); The Way (9:18); The beginning, the middle, and the end of all that lives (10:20); Life immortal and death; What is and I am what is not (9:19). Viewing Christ in light of Krishna, Christ grows more cosmically profound on the one hand, and Jesus, in contradistinction, grows more historically real, for while both ask disciples to take up their yoga (yoke), Jesus is finally an historic Messiah, while Krishna's historicity is uncertain and unnecessary.

Reflection upon the cosmic nature of Krishna's self-manifestations to Arjuna in the Bhagavad Gita instigated two theological insights for me: a trans-historicized Christ and a re-historicized Jesus. Christ Jesus becomes what Teilhard de Chardin calls the cosmic Christ, present in and through all creation, in all creative acts, in all persons and in this very thought. At the same time, when I reflect that Krishna's historicity is not as important to a Hindu as his eternal teachings, I realize again the astounding, paradoxical, salvific significance of the Christian's claim that the Logos in the historic Jesus was and is the God of Abraham, Isaac and Jacob. I realize that when Jesus speaks, the entire cosmos, all humanity, all animals, all nature, speaks.

THE TAO OF JESUS

The classical Chinese texts do not speak of an avatar or Messiah, but rather of the sage who walks in the Tao (the mysterious valley spirit, the Mother of all). As Lao Tzu says:

> Tao gave birth to the One;
> the One gave birth successively
> to two things, three things,
> up to ten thousand.[6]

All that is created is traced back to the One which comes from the Tao. I saw that the Tao which can be told of is not an unvarying Tao, and that Tao is "darker than any Mystery, the Doorway whence issued all Secret Essences." The Tao cannot be frozen into a static pattern of understanding. As day yields to night, earth to heaven, receptivity to action, yin to yang, as all nature manifests incessant fluctuation and evolutionary transfigurations, Tao, the mysterious feminine, is forever becoming new.

Often Lao Tzu returns to the image of *p'u* (uncarved block) to express the paradoxical reversal of the Tao's courseway. *P'u* is virginal or original nature, child-like purity, prior to the imprint of culture. To actualize the uncut-block-nature of Tao, he advises us to banish wisdom, to discard knowledge, to forget, and to let go of our preconceptions. The only motion is returning, a returning to the state of infancy. The sage is one who has advanced beyond the ordinary human condition by reanimating the spontaneous inactivity of a sleeping infant, the uninhibited joy of a child at play.

> All (humans), indeed, are wreathed in smiles,
> As though feasting after the Great Sacrifice,
> As though going up to the Spring Carnival.
> I alone am inert, like a child that has not yet given sign;
> Like an infant that has not yet smiled.[7]

Through this understanding, I was able for the first time to grasp an element of Christ's central teaching. Biblical scholars have noted that to enter the kingdom of God, the *telos* of Christ's message, one must be helpless "like a little child." Jesus says in Matthew:

> Just then the disciples came up to Jesus with the question, "Who is of greatest importance in the kingdom of God?" He called a little child over and stood him in their midst and said: "I assure you, unless you change and become like little children, you will not enter the kingdom of God. Whoever makes himself lowly, becoming like this child, is of greatest importance in that heavenly reign.[8]

I had always pondered and questioned the meaning of this passage because I had limited myself to thinking of childhood as an autobiographical stage of innocent Becoming, just as a little child in Taoist images means becoming soft, yielding, unknowing, like an "uncarved block" (*p'u*), ready for any imprint. It occurred to me that this pure potentiality was like the condition of "absolute trust" which Jesus teaches:

> Look at the birds in the sky. They do not sow or reap, they gather nothing into barns; yet your heavenly Father feeds them. Are not you more important than they? Which of you by worrying can add a moment to his life-span? As for clothes, why be concerned? Learn a lesson from the way the wild flowers grow. They do not work; they do not spin. Yet I assure you, not even Solomon in all his splendor was arrayed like one of these.[9]

A Taoist master could also have said what Jesus said: forget to worry; do not be concerned with appearances; study the birds who are always fed and the flowers which never work.

Whereas the Taoist is empty in the Tao, the Christian is enspirited by faith. This cross-reanimation of images revealed a new dimension of Jesus' message for me—that faith is like the trust of the birds, the toilsomeness of the flowers, that faith, like the Tao, does not worry about tomorrow, or about yesterday, but dwells naturally, effortlessly and gracefully in the present moment. I realized that I had to relax into faith rather than to will-it-forth, that I had to accept the Tao of faith to experience the Logos of faith.

Returning to the root of quietness, as Lao Tzu says, where the warm breath of the sun and the cool breath of the shade are blended (#42), where teaching is wordless and action actionless (#43), returning to the infancy of the Uncarved Block (#28), I saw a new inner connection between Christian faith (*pistis*) and the Taoist practice of "subtracting day by day" until inactivity is reached (#48). Of course this is not the inactivity of doing nothing, or of interfering with what anyone else is doing, but rather acting as if lower than others in order to guide them (#46). Through these images I was gently reminded that to have faith, like *wu wei*, is to act without striving (#81), is to become empty of knowledge so as to allow the grace of true wisdom to enter.

Paul clearly pictures the essence of this Christian/Taoist reversal of ordinary human expectations when he writes to the Corinthians: "My power is at its best in weakness . . . it is when I am weak that I am strong."[10] I discovered that, for me, the secret to becoming childlike (and hence to having a courageous faith) was to trust that through the gate of weakness and seeming foolishness, the kingdom is entered.

THE ZEN OF JESUS

As I review these reanimational insights, I realize how much eastern teachings and texts have deepened my understanding of the Gospel image of Jesus. Nowhere is this more true for me than looking at Christ through the Chinese Zen sutras.

In John's Gospel, Jesus identified himself with a series of substantial and insubstantial terms through a single, self-equating "I am." He says: I am: the Christ (4:26); the Bread of Life (6:35); the Light of the World (8:12); before Abraham (8:58); the Door (10:7); the Good Shepherd (10:11); One with the Father (10:30/38); the Resurrection and the Life (11:25); Teacher and Lord (13:13); the Way, the Truth, the Life (14:6); in the Father and in you (14:20); the True Vine (15:1). In Zen's story the fundamental question is: Who is the "I" who says "I am"? This question bypasses the *what* and *how* of ordinary questioning in which the questioner himself is not questioned, in which the questioner's ideological finitude is simply assumed. And the answer, twistingly, is always no one!

Siddhartha Gautama, who became the Buddha (the Awakened One), taught a provocative equation—Not/I equals I. That is, when Buddha was asked—Are you an angel? A holy man? An inspired philosopher? A man? —he answered: "I am not. I am Awake!" And when Bodhidharma, who came from India to China, was asked by the Emperor Wu, "Who now stands before me?" Bodhidharma answered, "I do not know!" It was the same when Tung Shan crossed a body of water and saw for the first time his "real face" reflected:

> I meet him wherever I go.
> He is the same as me.
> Yet I am not he!
> Only if you understand this
> Will you identify with what you are.[11]

In Zen's view, the Jesus-I who says follow *me*, or take *my* yoke upon you—his incarnational "I"—is non-dualistically and co-extensively "not-I." Paul pointed to this equation when he wrote that although Jesus was in the form of God, he "did not count equality with God a thing to be grasped but emptied himself, taking the form of a servant, being born in the likeness of men."[12] This *kenotic* awakening, the perfecting of Jesus' humanity, is connatural with the death of I-consciousness. So the answer to the question "Who speaks?" when Jesus speaks makes it impossible for us to hold onto any one image of the speaker. The one who speaks is, finally, beyond images since the one who speaks is speaking through "the image of the imageless God."

Through contemplating ko'ans and their solutions, and through applying their insights to the person of Jesus, I realized that Jesus was the God-man in a way analogous to the Zen master's being-without-being. I began to understand that each ko'an demanded the spontaneous, natural expression of the not-I "I," of the "I" who is simultemporally "you" and "not-I." I was profoundly moved by the last Ox-herding picture of the man who entered the market place with "bliss bestowing hands," who un-self-reflectively expressed a compassion which arises from formlessness. As form emerges from and simultaneously returns to formlessness, as all phenomena arise from what is called "Oriental Nothingness," so too, I realized, does Jesus emerge from and simultaneously die into (return to) the Father who is formless.

Ko'an and Parable

In Matthew we read that Jesus "never spoke except in parables" and in Mark, by inference, that to understand one parable, any parable, is to understand all parables. So it was natural that the disciples would ask Jesus why he spoke with a parabolic tongue, and when they did he replied: "It has been granted to you to know the secrets of the kingdom of heaven; but to those others it has not been granted."[13] Why? Because of the difference between those to whom the secret of the kingdom has been granted, and those to whom it has not? Granted what? Questions such as these and others about the purpose of Jesus' parables continued to haunt me until, through the application of a Zen practice, I discovered a way to allow the parables to reveal themselves—namely, to treat parables as ko'ans.

This particular relation between Zen and Christianity has been enunciated in several recent books. J.K. Kadowaki's *Zen and the Bible* outlines a scriptural hermeneutic in which one is asked to read the parables of Jesus as if they were ko'ans which needed a "single-minded concentration."[14] Dom Aelred Graham, in *Zen Catholicism*, writes that ". . . the purpose of the ko'an is not unlike that of the New Testament parables,"[15] and William Johnston, in *Christian Zen*, writes that ko'ans open a new approach to Christian scripture, and that we might well ". . . use the scriptures as ko'an."[16]

A ko'an is a deliberately nonsensical challenge or question put to human reasonableness which refuses any mind-made solution, a linguistically-congealed, cognition-reversal which demands response from spontaneous mind. Ko'ans cannot be solved; rather they must be lived with, tasted, ruminated upon until the solution announces itself.

Like a Zen ko'an, a parable, too, is a public secret aimed at frustrating our intellectual process by driving it head-on into a truth hidden within the unspeakable nature of language. It cannot be understood by ordinary reasoning but must present its meaning spontaneously in meditative awareness. For example, Jesus compares the kingdom of God to a person who scatters seed on the land: "He goes to bed at night and gets up in the morning, and the seed sprouts and grows—how, he does not know."[17] At the level of surface similitude, the hearer is invited to become the sower who, in time of sowing, just sows, and who, without knowing how growth takes place, in time of harvest, just reaps the full-grown corn.

Beneath this level, however, I am asked to become the parable itself, that is, to so thoroughly enter into the non-dual experience between sowing and harvesting, between knowing and not-knowing, that a radical reversal of consciousness-and-cosmology occurs. I realized that to understand any parable, I must pass through the space which separates myself from the root-source of parabolic meaning, so that the parable, as it were, can understand itself in me.

Reanimating Jesus in these various ways, through the Hindu Aum, the childlike Tao, and the Zen ko'an, not only deepens my understanding of the Christian sacred story, but also re-establishes the relation between the text, the teacher and what is taught.

In the end, by traveling east, I am able to return to the place of my religious origins. Like ancient mythic heroes, I have left my original home, traveled (mentally) through geographical and cultural climates alien to my own, temporally suspended my belief-systems (as much as possible) to enter into the eastern sacred texts, and then returned home. Returning, I re-evaluate my own story in light of the insights discovered and I arrive where I began—knowing the place for the first time.

At the same time I realize that I must set forth again for a further communion with the sacred stories of the world. Like seeing a movie for the second time, when I reread sacred texts, more of their esoteric wisdom is released. I discover an ancient spirit within the script, not discernible at first, against which everything else that I read becomes secondary. The more scriptures I study, the more convincingly I discover humanity's (and therefore my own) wisest voice. The committed traveler cannot cease searching but must be "still and still moving into another intensity for a further union, a deeper communion."[18]

NOTES

1. For instance, the ecumenical and inter-faith focus in the documents of the Second Vatican Council (1962–65) and in pronouncements made at the World Council of Churches expresses this new globalized religious consciousness. With an ever-increasing, ever-expanding regularity, inter-faith conferences and symposia are held to promote dialogues

among members of the various religions (e.g., Christian-Buddhist, Hindu-Muslim, and Jewish-Christian).

2. Hui Neng's discussion of one's relation to the sutras is found in Chapter VII, "Temperament and Circumstances," in the Platform Sutra.

3. Swami Prabhavanada, *The Sermon on the Mount According to Vedanta* (Hollywood: Vedanta Press, 1964), p. 15.

4. John 1:1–2.

5. *Mandukya Upanishad*, 1.

6. *Tao Te Ching*, #62.

7. *Tao Te Ching*, XX.

8. Matthew 18:1–4.

9. Matthew 6:26–29.

10. 1 Corinthians 2:9–11.

11. Chang Chung-Yuan, *Original Teachings of Ch'an Buddhism* (New York: Vintage Press, 1971), p. 49.

12. Philippians 2:6–8.

13. Matthew 13:11.

14. J.K. Kadowaki, *Zen and the Bible* (London: Routledge & Kegan Paul, 1977), p. 121.

15. Dom Aelred Graham, *Zen Catholicism* (New York: Harcourt Brace, 1967), p. 133.

16. William Johnston, *Christian Zen* (New York: Harper & Row, 1974), p. 64.

17. Mark 4:26–27.

18. T.S. Eliot, *Four Quartets* (New York: Harcourt, Brace & World, Inc., 1943), 32.

ANNOTATED BIBLIOGRAPHY

INTRODUCTORY TEXTBOOKS

The following books offer basic introductions to the major sacred traditions and texts of the world. Students may wish to consult one or more of these surveys to provide a more inclusive context for their study of the sacred texts.

Bush, Richard C. et. al., *The Religious World: Communities of Faith*. New York: Macmillan Publishing Co., Inc., 1982. The authors of this hardbound book address the actual interests and questions which students bring to the study of religions, and include many aids for learning such as: definitions, time lines, numerous pictures, maps and illustrations, glossaries, pronunciation guides and suggested readings.

Carmody, Denise L. and John T. *Ways to the Center: An Introduction to World Religions*. Belmont, California: Wadsworth Publishing Co., 1981. This hardbound edition emphasizes a historical and structural (philosophical and comparative) analysis of the data. The text explicitly discusses women's experiences in the various religions. The text is published in separate paperbound versions titled *Eastern Ways to the Center* and *Western Ways to the Center*.

Carmody, Denise L. and John T. *Shamans, Prophets and Sages*. Belmont, California: Wadsworth Publishing Company, 1985. This is a core textbook which organizes its material around various personality types who stand at the center of their tradition. This paperbound edition covers three strands—non-literate, eastern and western—and shows how the personality types within the traditions overlap.

Denny, Fredrick and Rodney Taylor, editors. *The Holy Book in Comparative Perspective*. Columbia, South Carolina: U. of South Carolina Press, 1985. This volume offers a scholarly introduction to western and eastern scriptures as well as to nonliterate holy books.

Eastman, Roger, ed. *The Ways of Religion*. San Francisco: Canfield Press, 1975. This paperbound text is a collection of writings by dedicated spokespersons, believers and those with first hand experience, along with brief selections from selected sacred texts. Of the sixty-three selections, forty-one were written in this century. This is more valuable as a resource book after the student has become acquainted with each sacred tradition.

Ellwood, Robert S. *Many Peoples, Many Faiths*. Englewood Cliffs, N.J.: Prentice-Hall, Inc., 1976. This hardbound edition attempts to encapsulate in non-technical language the combination of conceptual, practical and social factors of religious life, past and present. It would be helpful to read this alongside Ellwood's parallel text, *Words of the World's Religions*, Englewood Cliffs, N.J.: Prentice-Hall, Inc., 1977. In this paperbound edition he quotes brief sections from faith statements, descriptions of religious events and themes, interpretations and scriptures.

Hopfe, Lewis M. *Religions of the World*. Encino, CA: Glencoe Publishing Co., Inc., 1976. Written for the student who wants a concise picture of the historical and philosophical foundations of the world's religions, its style is engaging and easy to follow. This 360 page paperback is not encumbered with scholarly notes and this makes a good first book for the uninitiated reader.

Hutchison, John A. *Paths of Faith*. New York: McGraw-Hill Book Company, 1981. This hard-bound edition was written to place the beginning student with contemporary scholarly research. Hutchison understands "paths" to mean clusters of life values which answer the fundamental human question: Why live?

Lanczkowski, Günter. *Sacred Writings*. New York: Harper & Row, 1956. The purpose of this thin paperback is to provide a useful guide to major sacred books of the world. It is both scholarly and popular in its orientation.

Nielsen, Niels C. et. al., *Religions of the World*. New York: St. Martin's Press, 1983. Written by a collection of scholars, this substantial hardbound edition aims at being as authoritative as current scholarship allows. Each chapter examines the historical, geographical, social and political settings of each religion's basic teachings and rites. If only one text can be read by the serious student, it should be this one. The eastern material from this book has been published in a paperbound edition called *Religions of Asia*.

Noss, John B., *Man's Religions*. New York: Collier Macmillan Publisher, 1949. One of the early introductions to the world's religions, this hardbound edition is comprehensive and informative. Now in its seventh edition, it is structured in four sections: Primitive, Indian, East Asian, and Middle Eastern. It is an excellent first book for the more serious student.

Parrinder, Geoffrey, *World Religions: From Ancient History to the Present*. New York: Facts on File Publications, 1971. A comprehensive survey of twenty-one religious cultures placed in the context of the world that formed them. This paperbound edition includes more pre-historic, tribal, Egyptian and Greco-Roman material than most other introductions do.

Schmidt, Roger, *Exploring Religion*. Belmont, Cal.: Wadsworth, Inc., 1980. This book is designed primarily to introduce students to the principal dimensions of religious expressions (such as symbols, story, rites, myth and parable) and themes (such as belief, suffering and death). Though not an introduction to religious traditions as such, this is an interestingly written guide to how religions are studied.

Smart, Ninian, *The Religious Experience of Mankind*. New York: Charles Scribner's Sons, 1969. A substantial and comprehensive historically-oriented approach to human religious experience. This paperbound edition is the perfect introduction for students who are more interested in the historic flow of events than in a thematic or topical approach to the field

Smith, Huston, *The Religions of Man*. New York: Harper & Row, 1958. This small paperback version remains one of the easiest to understand introductions to the field. Concerned less with historical developments, Smith focuses upon the meaning that religions carry for their practitioners. This is both an informative and stimulating presentation, and is often recommended as the best introduction for the novice reader.

Smith, Wilfred Cantwell, *The Faith of Other Men*. New York: Harper & Row, 1963. In this now classic, paperbound edition, Smith chooses one characteristic symbol from each major faith tradition which serves as a way of introducing the meaning of each system. Smith's contention is that we must study the way people of faith act first, before we can understand the meaning of their sacred traditions.

Zaehner, R.C., ed., *The Concise Encyclopedia of Living Faiths*. Boston: Beacon Press, 1959. An informative, thoughtful compendium of scholarly articles on the major historical and living faiths of the world. Each chapter provides such a thorough introduction that a novice in the field might want to defer this text until a simpler one had been read.

SCRIPTURAL ANTHOLOGIES

Ballou, Robert O., ed., *The Portable World Bible*. New York: Penguin Books, 1944. A handy paperbound version of the scriptures of the world whose most serious flaw is that it doesn't indicate with sufficient clarity the sources of the anthologized passages.

Bouquet, A.C., *Sacred Books of the World*. Baltimore: Penguin Books, 1954. Originally written as a companion sourcebook to Bouquet's *Comparative Religion,* this paperbound edition provides brief selections from the sacred writings of Sumerian, Egyptian, Indian, Iranian, Buddhist, Chinese, Hellenistic, Mid-Eastern, and Islamic cultures.

Frost, S.E., ed., *The Sacred Writings of the World's Great Religions*. New York: McGraw-Hill Book Company, 1943. Selections of appreciable length are included from thirteen sacred traditions so that readers can appreciate the full teaching. This paperbound book includes a valuable topical index which cross-references scriptures according to topics and themes.

Smart, Ninian and Richard Hecht, eds., *Sacred Texts of the World*. New York: The Crossroad Publishing Company, 1982. An anthology of scriptures arranged according to Ninian Smart's analysis of religion propounded in his *Religious Experience of Mankind* (1969): myth, doctrine, ritual, institutional expression, experience and ethics.

EASTERN SACRED TEXTS

HINDU

Sacred Books of the East, trans. by Max Müller. New Delhi: Motilal Banarsidass, 1881. Including the Vedic Hymns (Volumes 32, 46), the Upanishads (Volumes 1, 15) and the Dhammapada (Volume 10), Müller provides scholarly, enthusiastic translations, if a bit dated and stiff. The debt the western world owes to this 50-volume series is monumental, and a student of sacred texts would want to read Müller's "Preface" in the Upanishads, Volume 1 in the series.

A Sourcebook in Indian Philosophy, ed. by S. Radhakrishnan and C. Moore. Princeton: Princeton University Press, 1957. An excellent anthology of Hindu and Buddhist texts including selections from the Vedas, the Upanishads, the Bhagavad Gita, and the Dhammapada.

Hindu Scriptures, trans. by R.C. Zaehner. New York: E.P. Dutton, 1966. Including translations of the Rig-Veda, the Atharva-Veda, the Upanishads, and the Bhagavad Gita, Zaehner attempts to provide a rendering of the Sanskrit which is more metrical than literalistic.

The Rig Veda, trans. by Wendy O'Flaherty. New York: Penguin, 1981. An anthology of 108 Vedic hymns annotated and arranged according to subject matter. The translation is sound and very readable and O'Flaherty provides useful notes which make the esoteric hymns more accessible.

The Thirteen Principal Upanishads, trans. by Robert Hume. New York: Oxford University Press, 1921. A translation for seriously interested teachers and students which builds upon the eminent foundation of Max Müller and improves upon Müller's interpretation and form.

The Upanishads, trans. by Swami Nikhilanda. New York: Harper Torchbooks, 1963. Along with a comprehensive "Glossary" at the end, and an extensive "General Introduction" to Hindu religion, Swami Nikhilanda provides a graceful, instructive and literary translation with short, potent introductions to each Upanishad.

The Ten Principal Upanishads, put into English by W.B. Yeats. New York: Collier Books, 1937. While not Yeats' own translation, he, along with Shree Purohit Swami, attempts to provide a version "that would read as though the original had been written in common English."

The Upanishads, trans. by Juan Mascaro. New York: Penguin Books, 1965. While not always the best translation, it is the best inexpensive anthology of Upanishads. It along with *The Upanishads* translated by Swami Prabhavananda and Frederick Manchester (New York: Mentor, 1948) offers easily accessible entries into the metaphysical depths of Hindu thought.

The Bhagavadgita, trans. by J.A.B. van Buitenen. Chicago: The University of Chicago Press, 1981. This is a scholarly, bilingual edition which attempts to preserve the epic context in which the story of the Gita occurs. His translation retains a friendly, often intimate tone, and does not force the narrative into verse-paragraphs.

The Bhagavad Gita, trans. by Franklin Edgerton. New York: Harper & Row, 1944. A fairly literal translation into somewhat stiff but nevertheless completely intelligible verse forms, followed by excellent introductory commentary on the Gita's pre-history and its teachings.

The Bhagavadgita, trans. by S. Radhakrishnan. New York: Harper & Row, 1948. A distinguished, stimulating, sympathetic approach blended with apt scholarship without pedantry. Aside from an instructive introductory essay, Radhakrishnan intersperses interpretive comments throughout the body of the text.

INDIAN   BUDDHIST

Aside from the two excellent collections already mentioned—S. Radhakrishnan in *A Source-book in Indian Philosophy* and Max Müller in *Sacred Books of the East*—there are several others readily available in paperback.

Buddhist Scriptures, trans. by Edward Conze. New York: Penguin Books, 1959. Conze has arranged, according to Buddhist schools, selections about Buddha and his teachings, especially morality, meditation and wisdom. This translation preserves both the characteristic diction and original meaning of the texts.

Buddhism in Translations, trans. by Henry Clarke Warren. New York: Atheneum Books, 1969. A topic selection of Buddhist texts from the Pali which include selections on the Buddha, Sentient Existence, Karma and Rebirth, Meditation and Nirvana, and the Order.

The Dhammapada, trans. by P. Lal. New York: Noonday, 1967. Lal intends his translation to be a "transcreation" in which Buddha's words and his silences are recreated and reanimated in a non-literal account of the text.

The Dhammapada, trans. by Irving Babbitt. New York: New Directions, 1936. This is a revision of Max Müller's translation (1870) which attempts to preserve the literal sense even at the expense of elegance. He concludes with an interesting, long essay titled, "Buddha and the Occident."

The Dhammapada, trans. by Juan Mascaro. New York: Penguin, 1973. The least expensive translation with a brief interpolative essay in a non-scholarly vein.

CHINESE

A Sourcebook in Chinese Philosophy, trans. by Wing-Tsit Chan. Princeton: Princeton University Press, 1963. An excellent anthology of Chinese texts which includes selections from the Analects, the Tao Te Ching, Chuang Tzu, and the Platform Sutra.

The Analects of Confucius, trans. by Arthur Waley. New York: Vintage, 1938. An eminently readable text which seeks to preserve the content and character of the original. Waley provides valuable introductory essays and textual notes which, while often needlessly scholarly, are instructive.

The Analects, trans. by D.C. Lau. New York: Penguin, 1979. With an extensive introduction, bibliography and glossary, Lau provides a highly readable translation which is considered on a par with, if not better than, Arthur Waley's. He provides an extremely valuable picture of the historic Confucius in the first Appendix.

Tao Te Ching, trans. by D.C. Lau. New York: Penguin, 1963. One of the finest translations of Lao Tzu's work, this text includes a superior introduction to Taoism.

The Way and Its Power, trans. by Arthur Waley. New York: Evergreen, 1958. While technically not as accurate as Lau's in every detail, this translation is highly readable and comes with excellent introductory essays and notes.

Tao: A New Way of Thinking, trans. by Chang Chung-yuan. New York: Harper & Row, 1975. The value of this edition lies in its instructive introduction and in the commentaries which the translator provides after each verse.

Chuang Tzu: Basic Writings, trans. by Burton Watson. New York: Columbia University Press, 1964. Including the seven inner chapters which are the heart of the book, Watson provides an important introduction which places the philosopher in relation to Chinese history and philosophy.

The Way of Chuang Tzu, ed. by Thomas Merton. New York: New Directions, 1965. This is a delightfully lyrical, interpretive reading of Chuang Tzu based on a meditative reading of several translations. While no attempts are made at faithful reproductions, these spiritual interpretations provide an inspiring complement to Watson's more literal translation.

CHINESE BUDDHIST

Aside from the outstanding collections already mentioned—Wing-Tsit Chan in *A sourcebook in Chinese Philosophy,* and Henry Clark Warren in *Buddhism in Translation*—several others are available.

Buddhist Wisdom Books (The Diamond Sutra and The Heart Sutra), trans. by Edward Conze. New York: Harper & Row, 1958. Unanimously recognized as one of the finest translations of the Heart Sutra and the Diamond Sutra which Conze intersperses with extensive and valuable notes. An extremely thorough and valuable commentary is provided for each text which makes this translation difficult to pass over by a student interested in Buddhist texts.

The Platform Scripture, trans. by Wing-Tsit Chan. New York: St. John's University Press, 1963. A sensitive bilingual edition with a minimum of notes.

The Platform Sutra of the Sixth Patriarch, trans. by Philip Yampolski. New York: Columbia University Press, 1967. This is the most often used translation by scholars and teachers in the field.

The Diamond Sutra and the Sutra of Hui-Neng, trans. by A.F. Price and Wong Mon-Lam. Boulder, Col: Shambala, 1969. The best one volume introduction to these crucial Chinese Zen texts with minimal introductions. The difficulties presented by each text are handled well so that the reader can more easily concentrate on the texts.

WESTERN SACRED TEXTS

HEBRAIC

The Torah, The Prophets, and The Writings, a new translation of the Holy Scriptures according to the Masoretic texts. Philadelphia: The Jewish Publication Society of America, 1962, 1978. The next best thing to reading the Hebrew scriptures in the original Hebrew is to read a recognized quality Jewish translation which these are.

The New American Bible, The Jerusalem Bible, The Oxford Annotated Bible, The New English Bible, and *The Holy Bible* (King James Version) include translations of Hebrew scriptures and are described below.

CHRISTIAN

The Jerusalem Bible, Reader's Edition. New York: Doubleday & Company, Inc., 1966. A new translation from the ancient Greek, Aramaic and Hebrew texts into beautiful English. The single-column pages, the separation of verse and hymns from prose and the use of italics to distinguish quotations renders this edition extremely easy to study. It includes an extended chronological table.

The New American Bible. New York: P.J. Kenedy & Sons, 1968. This is a new translation from the original Hebrew, Aramaic and Greek languages. Compiled by some fifty biblical scholars, mostly though not all Catholic, *The New American Bible* is the official Catholic version, and it includes a Glossary of Biblical Theology Terms, an essay on Biblical Geography and maps.

The Oxford Annotated Bible, the Revised Standard Version. New York: Oxford University Press, 1962. Each chapter is supplied with literary, historic and geographical footnotes and valuable cross-references to other passages of scripture.

The New English Bible. Oxford: Oxford University Press, 1970. This is a sound translation though almost void of any notes or introductory material.

The Holy Bible. King James Version. Philadelphia: A.J. Holman Company, n.d. Originally translated in 1611 at the request of King James, and though not always as accurate as more recent translations, it is still considered the most lyrical and musical version.

The R.S.V. Interlinear Greek-English New Testament trans. by Alfred Marshall. Grand Rapids: Zondevan Publishing House, 1958. A line-by-line literal English translation of the original Greek text along with a marginal Revised Standard Version of the same line(s). Serious students of the New Testament will occasionally want to check the literal translation of a key word which sometimes will vary with the more popularly held translations.

ISLAMIC

The Holy Qur-an, trans. by Abdullah Yusuf Ali. United States: McGregor & Werner, Inc., 1946. This is the most accurate translation of the Qur'an into English. Each page has the English and the Arabic side by side. Ample footnotes make this version a student's delight.

The Koran Interpreted, a translation by A.J. Arberry. New York: The Macmillan Co., 1955. This version includes an excellent preface, and numbers only every fifth verse to make the passages more readable.

The Meaning of the Glorious Koran, trans. by Mohammed Marmaduke Pickthall. New York: Mentor Books, 1953. This version is a good, inexpensive translation which contains a brief, insightful introduction to the life of Muhammad.

The Koran, translated by N.J. Dawood. New York: Penguin Books, 1956. This version contains only the briefest introduction to the text, so it will be less valuable to a first time reader than the others already mentioned.

The Qur'an, translated by T.B. Irving. Brattleboro, Vermont: Amana Books, 1985. This is the first American version which presents the "Noble Reading" in a reverent yet contemporary American English. Helpfully, each chapter begins with a brief introduction and includes margin notes of chapter themes.

General Index

Index of Sacred Texts